WOMEN IN AMERICAN LAW

The Struggle toward Equality from the New Deal to the Present

JUDITH A. BAER

HM
Holmes & Meier
New York / London

Published in the United States of America 1991
by Holmes & Meier Publishers, Inc.
30 Irving Place
New York, NY 10003

The first volume of *Women in American Law*, edited by
Marlene Wortman, was published by Holmes & Meier in 1985.

Book design by Marcia Ciro

This book has been printed on acid-free paper.

Library of Congress Cataloging-in-Publication Data
(Revised for vol. 2)

Women in American law.
     Vol. 2 by Judith A. Baer.
     Includes bibliographical references and indexes.
     Contents: v. 1. From colonial times to the New
Deal—v. 2. From the New Deal to the present.
     1. Women—Legal status, laws, etc.—United
States—History. I. Wortman, Marlene Stein. II. Baer,
Judith A.
KF478.W67   1985, 1991   346.7301   83-22527
[34'347.306134]
ISBN 0-8419-0753-6 (pbk.: v. 1)
ISBN 0-8419-0752-8 (hard: v. 1)
ISBN 0-8419-0920-2 (hard: v. 2) (acid-free paper)
ISBN 0-8419-0921-0 (pbk.: v. 2) (acid-free paper)

Manufactured in the United States of America

To the women in my family:
my mother, Dorothy—
my sisters-in law, Janice and Lisa—
and my niece, Michelle.

C O N T E N T S

Preface

Women in American Law has a dual purpose. It is intended to serve both as a general nonfiction work on women and the law and as an undergraduate textbook. Although this book is the second of two volumes, its content, format, and purpose are significantly different from those of its predecessor. Edited by Marlene Stein Wortman, Volume 1 is a rich, valuable collection of primary sources accompanied by commentary from the editor. The included documents speak for themselves, eloquently, about women's legal status from colonial times to the New Deal. Volume 2 is a secondary source, an interpretative work, analyzing developments from 1933 to the present.

Writing this book was not my idea. Holmes & Meier was the second publisher to approach me about writing a book about women and the law. Despite some trepidation, I was intrigued by the challenge of writing a book which could serve as both a textbook for undergraduates and a work of nonfiction intended for the general public. Most important, I had also become more aware of the need for a book like this.

Several books on women and the law written for a general readership were in print in the late 1980s. However, most of these had been published in the early days of the contemporary feminist movement, from the late 1960s to the mid-1970s. Therefore, they were nearly twenty years out of date—a fact that made them equally unsuitable as textbooks. As a teacher of undergraduates, I had no satisfactory textbook on women and the law available to assign to my students.

I first taught women and the law in 1974. The 1979 publication of Leslie Goldstein's invaluable casebook, *The Constitutional Rights of Women*, simplified the task of getting appropriate readings. But since I teach political science and women's studies, not law, I have never felt that I was doing justice to the subject or my students with a casebook alone. I have also become increasingly aware over the years that Supreme Court cases do not make an adequate curriculum by themselves.

I had never written this kind of a book before. I had, however, assigned many. I anticipated constraints absent in the academic writing with which I was familiar. As a scholar, I have consistently ignored part of the advice routinely given to apprentices: keep yourself out of your work. From my Ph.D. thesis on, I have been one of a growing number of academics who produce passionate, committed scholarship. We do not—by a long shot—all share the same opinions, but we share a rejection of the conventional wisdom that personal opinions have no place in scholarly research. Like others, I had learned that doing this kind of scholarship has its costs. It is sometimes harder to get published if you express opinions; once published, you will face criticism, some of it nasty. But I have also learned that you can express opinions and make value judgments as long as you follow two rules. First, you must document what you say. Second, you must say it with reasonable courtesy.

I did not know to what extent this latitude would extend to a book like *Women in American Law*. Since texts are assigned by professors who do not always share one's own values, I knew that expressing opinions might make the book less attractive. I also knew that opinions, trenchantly expressed, make general nonfiction attractive. So I feared that to write a book designed for both these purposes would be to pursue two incompatible ends. But I could not imagine writing about women and the law—for years my primary research interest, and the subject of at least half my published scholarship—without making value judgments. Careful neutrality seemed to me tantamount to intellectual dishonesty. I am committed to feminism, which I define as a belief in the equality of the sexes. Most experts in women and the law share that commitment, but not all of them draw the same conclusions from their feminism as I do from mine.

Throughout the book, I talk about "patriarchy." Not everyone is comfortable with this word, with its implication that male supremacy is an organizing principle of society rather than a regrettable remnant of an unenlightened past. Portions of this book express my growing distrust of capitalist economic systems, my increasing suspicion that capitalism is incompatible with sexual equality. Many scholars vehemently reject this idea, while others find "suspicion" too mild a stance: doesn't everybody know, they insist, that sexual equality requires, at the very least, socialism? (I don't know that, partly because I have little difficulty finding sexist socialism in the real world). In Chapters 6 and 7, I applaud the steady increase in the numbers of women entering politics and the professions. Not everyone shares this optimism, for reasons which I shall discuss.

A consistent theme throughout the book is the contradiction between the goal of sexual equality and women's family responsibilities, the fact that far more of their time and attention is claimed by household and family than is true for men. I express my belief that this social assignment of responsibilities is a grave injustice, and my frustration at the law's inadequacy as an instrument for change. Again, these are not matters on which everyone agrees with me. Some experts regard the disproportionate duties as a product of individual choice. Others believe that these duties properly belong to women, and that feminists should support policies which accommodate the duties and reward women for assuming them.

You, the reader, may well disagree with any or all of my opinions. I hope you will allow those disagreements to stimulate further thought and research. Holmes & Meier assured me that my fears about content control were unjustified. The project's three successive editors, Kevin Davis, Sheila Friedling, and Katharine Turok, and copy editor Miriam Hurewitz, demonstrated that they meant what they had said. Sheila and Katharine have expertly guided the book from the first draft to the final version, doing the editor's work brilliantly while enabling the author to do hers. Professor Sarah Slavin provided a detailed, thorough, and thoughtful critique of the manuscript for which she could not possibly be fairly compensated. Even where I have not followed her advice, her comments stimulated me to further thought and research. Sarah's work has greatly improved the final product.

The Department of Political Science at Texas A&M University has provided indispensable aid in completing this project. Marcia Bastian has taken charge of the manuscript in all its stages.

My debt to her is enormous. Livija Johnson, Hung-sen Chen, Song Kim, Aaron Knight, and Kimberly McGar have worked as my graduate assistants. Their help in reference checking and bibliography preparation saved me untold hours in the library and at the telephone. In particular, I thank Kimberly for her work on the index and proofreading. My former employer, the California State Polytechnic University at Pomona, facilitated this work through its Dean's Faculty Research Award during the spring 1988 quarter.

This book would not have become what it is without the intellectual stimulation, encouragement, and discourse provided by my colleagues in the political science profession who teach women and the law. I have already mentioned two of them, Leslie Goldstein and Sarah Slavin. Sooner or later, they and I, along with Gayle Binion, Liane Kosaki, Susan Gluck Mezey, Karen O'Connor, and Mary Cornelia Porter, wind up together at conference panels or in less formal settings where we share ideas, argue, challenge, and sometimes even agree. Jo Freeman has been an irritant, goad, and inspiration to me for twenty years, ever since we were graduate students together. Each of these scholars has shaped my perceptions in individual ways; each of them is a valued friend. Academia would be a far lonelier place without them.

WOMEN IN AMERICAN LAW

1

Introduction: Women and the Law

Women in American Law is the title of this book. Perhaps the most significant aspect of this topic is that such a title sounds so plausible. *Men in American Law* sounds absurd. The male is the norm; the female, the deviation. Four decades ago, the great French philosopher Simone de Beauvoir wrote, "Humanity is male and man defines woman not in herself but as relative to him. . . . He is the Subject, he is the Absolute—she is the Other."[1] We speak of women the way scholars once spoke of the "Negro problem," but never of the "white problem." Women, like blacks, become an out-group, a special topic.

One way to begin to understand American society is to imagine how it would look to a visitor from another planet, a planet so different from Earth that it had no sexual or social distinctions. This visitor would see two large groups of people who were different from one another in several ways. They were not enemies; in fact, they lived and worked together. They even reproduced their species by means of a highly valued and apparently pleasurable activity performed by pairs consisting of one member of each group. But even a stranger could tell that one group was in charge. Members of this group made the rules and had most of the money. This fact led the stranger to label the groups the A people and the B people. The B people had to do

1

what the A people told them to do. The B's worked hard, but much of the work they did was not valued or rewarded highly. The stranger, being ignorant about this society, naturally wondered why this state of affairs existed. What explained the dominant position of the A's? Solving the puzzle took a while—doing research in another culture is never easy—but eventually the answer became clear. The A's and B's were different from one another in several ways, and the most important difference between the two groups was something the B's could do which the A's could not.

What is wrong with this scenario? The fact that some people have more privileges than others will not come as news to any reader of this book. But we also know that whenever one group has more privileges than another, that difference in status is defended by arguments that the subordinate group is inferior to the dominant group. For example, the proponents of slavery, from ancient Greece to the American South, alleged that slaves were less intelligent, less virtuous, or less responsible than free people. We justify legal restrictions on children by asserting that they are less wise than adults. It seems bizarre to assign to inferior status a group which has a useful ability that the superior group lacks.

But that is just what male supremacist societies do—and most, if not all, human societies have been male supremacist. There are, as our hypothetical visitor discovered, many differences between men and women. Experts disagree vehemently whether or not real, predictable, and universal psychological differences between the sexes exist, but nobody denies that physical differences exist. By far the most important of these differences is that women bear children. Men cannot do this. Reproduction is an essential function for the survival of any species. But performing this function has not given women privilege—just the opposite. Something seems awry here: physical differences between the sexes do not explain the social differences, and probably did not cause them. Perhaps the real explanation for male supremacy lies in another physical difference: that men, on the average, are stronger than women. Could men have used force to establish control in their own interests? Maybe, but neither we nor our hypothetical visitor can prove that conclusion.

Whatever the reasons for male dominance, it exists or has existed in all known human societies. Male supremacist society has another common name. It is often called "patriarchy." This term combines two Greek words, the first meaning "father" and the second meaning "rule." A patriarchy, then, is a society in which the father's rule in the family provides the model for government and social relations. Anthropologists have debated whether any "matriarchy," or woman-dominated society, has ever existed. The professional consensus now holds that most, if not all, societies which exist now or have existed have been patriarchies. This does not mean that all patriarchal societies do things in the same way. As Adrienne Rich puts it,

> Matrilineal societies—in which kinship is traced and property transmitted through the mother's line—or matrilocal societies—where the husband moves into the house or village of the wife's mother—exist as variations on the more familiar western pattern of the patriarchal family. . . . But these variations merely represent different ways of channeling position and property to the male; they may confer more status and dignity on women and reduce the likelihood of polygamy; but they are not to be confused with "matriarchy."[2]

The fact that male dominance appears to be a nearly universal pattern has led some experts to assert that male dominance is therefore natural and inevitable. This book rejects that premise. My analysis presumes that men and women are inherently equal and that very little in society is natural or inevitable. Women's ability to bear children is natural, but male dominance is not. Male supremacy arises not from nature but from convention. Its defenders use nature to justify it, but patriarchy rests on customs, norms, and law.

Patriarchy is a social system in which one group (men) dominates another (women). Social arrangements by which one group is dominant and another subject are often called "asymmetrical" relationships. They are quite common; sexism is one variation on a familiar theme. People often describe American society as "racist" or "white supremacist." These terms describe an asymmetrical relationship in which white people rule people of other races. American slavery was the most extreme example of white supremacy, which, unfortunately, did not end when slavery did. Slavery itself is, of course, an asymmetrical relationship whether or not it is based on racial differences. In ancient Greece and Rome, for example, masters and slaves usually were members of the same racial groups. Colonization or imperialism, the domination of a people by foreign conquerors, is another such relationship, known well in America, Asia, and Africa. Terms like "racist" and "imperialist" have negative connotations now, but to label a relationship asymmetrical is not necessarily to condemn it. Patriarchy itself includes an asymmetry—that between parents and children—which is usually seen as beneficial and necessary.

Not all asymmetrical social relationships are grounded in patriarchy. One influential group of social philosophers, Marxists, holds that subjection and domination are at the core of modern society. Karl Marx asserted that capitalism, the economic system in which production is privately rather than publicly controlled, is based on class oppression. A person's class is his or her relationship to a society's means of production. To Marxists, capitalism is a system in which the ruling class, the owners of the means of production, exploits the labor of the working class, or proletariat.[3] Marxists believe that capitalism is the basic form of social domination. Thus, all other asymmetrical relationships, like racism, sexism, and imperialism, are derived from capitalism, depend on it, and will end if revolution destroys the capitalist system.

Marxist theory can best help us understand patriarchy if we use it less as a basis for comparison than as a basis for analogy. Patriarchy may not be a class system in strict economic terms, although Marxists insist that it is. But patriarchy is a class system if we define class as a relationship not to means of production but to means of reproduction. For it is precisely that relationship which determines the positions of men, women, and children in patriarchal systems. While the foregoing analysis is a class analysis, it is not a Marxist analysis per se because its definition of class is divorced from the economic context.

Most scholars in this capitalist society reject Marxist analysis (although they borrow its concepts freely). But no thoughtful observer denies that class is a type of asymmetrical relationship, or that some employers at some times have exploited some workers. Even if it is inaccurate to say that all oppression is based on class, it is clear that economic factors and asymmetrical relationships are inextricably intertwined.

For example, defenders of slavery often made generalizations that strike us as very bigoted indeed, and that have been discredited long since; slavery was justified because blacks were held to be mentally and morally inferior to whites. Some slave owners went so far as to argue, following Aristotle, that slavery was in the best interests of the slave. Rudyard Kipling made a similar assertion when he described colonization as "the white man's burden," assumed for the sake of the "silent sullen peoples." (Kipling was neither the first nor the last observer to misinterpret sullen silence.) But neither slavery nor imperialism came about *because* Europeans thought Africans and Asians were inferior to themselves. These institutions served important economic purposes; the ideologies were rationalizations which made the institutions acceptable to questioners. Slavery provided very cheap labor for the labor-intensive Southern cotton plantations. Slavery died out when the Industrial Revolution made it unprofitable, even in countries which did not go to war over the issue. The imperial ambitions of nations have often been linked to their financial goals. Male supremacy, as Marx and his collaborator Friedrich Engels saw, served the important economic function of keeping women in the home while releasing men for labor.[4]

We cannot understand any of these social arrangements in isolation from one another or from economic forces. A book on women's status must deal with race and class. Patriarchy is not the only existing form of social oppression. It is dangerous to imply that all men oppress all women. Some aspects of the situation of black or working-class men are far more oppressive than some aspects of the lives of white or middle-class women, and there are even situations where class or race gives some women advantages over some men.

We also need to recognize that women's lives are affected at least as much by race or class as by sex. A white woman and a black woman, for example, lead lives very different from each other because of their racial differences, even when the situations of these women are similar in other ways. It is often misleading to talk in general terms about "women" without realizing that not all women lead similar lives. In this book, we will discuss white, black, Asian, and Hispanic women; middle-class and working-class women; old and young; rural and urban; heterosexual and homosexual; able-bodied and disabled. Feminists who ignore these differences, especially race and class, have often been accused, with some justification, of emphasizing the ways in which white middle-class women are oppressed to the exclusion of the ways in which these women oppress others.

But many critics of the feminist movement, by no means all of them Marxists, have taken this criticism to extremes. Women of different races lead lives that are, in some ways, similar, because of their sex. For all the advantages race and class confer upon white middle-class women, they still sustain injuries imposed by patriarchy. When a woman college graduate earns less money than a man who went no further than high school, gender is affecting her more powerfully than class in that area of her life. And men—even those men oppressed by race or class—benefit from patriarchy, as the man who is less well educated but better paid than a woman does. Speaking in general terms of "men" and "women" is not always a mistake.

It is difficult to accept the conclusion that all oppression can be explained in terms of class. And there are some forms of oppression which do not appear to have any consistent link to class. Racism and sexism obviously do, but what about the situation of homosexuals or disabled people? Members of both of these groups suffer from numerous types of discrimination, some of which, such as limited job opportunities or access to income, take economic forms. Class is certainly not irrelevant here. But neither homosexuality nor disability is a basis for assigning people to a discrete, particular relationship to the means of production, as race and gender are or have been.

Comparing different asymmetrical social relationships, in order to learn their similarities, differences, and the presence or absence of connections among them, can be an enlightening exercise. Not surprisingly, one common comparison in the American context is between women and blacks. This comparison can anger people who find in it the exaggerated claim that women are relegated to the status of slaves. But suspending indignation in favor of reflection will reveal many striking similarities between the two groups.

Long before the rise of the modern feminist movement, sociologists perceived many ways in which women's status resembles that of a "minority group." *An American Dilemma*, Gunnar Myrdal's classic study of prejudice against black Americans, briefly compared the status of blacks to that of women.[5] Helen Mayer Hacker found important similarities between what she called, in 1951, the "caste status of women and Negroes." Among these were ascribed attributes ("inferior intelligence"), accommodation attitudes (pretenses of ignorance or helplessness), and pervasive discriminations against both groups.[6] Feminist scholarship has uncovered many more similarities between the situations of these two groups. For example, historians have learned that many of the first white women who settled in North America came here against their will, as the first African immigrants did. These historians refer not to obedient wives and daughters whose decisions were made for them, but to women suspected of crimes like prostitution or theft who were thrown into an English jail one day and onto a ship the next. After all, someone had to give birth to the next generation of colonists.[7]

We can even extend the analysis beyond race and gender to include analogies with other types of asymmetrical social relationships. Hacker's analysis in particular provides fruitful soil for this exercise. She identified common racial and sexual stereotypes: assumptions that blacks were unintelligent, women were weak, and so forth. We might also consider the labels which society gives to members of certain groups who, somehow, step out of their assigned role by protesting their status or by taking action to change it. Think, for instance, of the use of the adjective "uppity" to modify the noun "black," "strident" for women, and accusations of "self-pity" for the disabled. Do not all three labels serve a similar function: to discredit the person making claims, and, by implication, the claims themselves?

This book will devote more time to the situation of women than to finding analogies and linkages—or, for that matter, differences—between male supremacy and other forms of asymmetry. This preliminary discussion is important because we cannot understand patriarchy in isolation from the society of which it is a part. This book concentrates on one institutional component of patriarchy: law. Therefore, we will not be treating patriarchy in all its aspects. Law is only part of a society; it does not explain or control everything. We do not look to law books alone to tell us how people live their lives anywhere. Charles Dickens's novel *Oliver Twist* provides a famous illustration of this disjunction. Mr. Bumble, a character in the novel, is told that the common law presumes that husband and wife are one person, and that the wife acts under the husband's direction. This statement is an accurate description of the law in Dickens's England. But Mr. Bumble finds the statement wanting as a description of reality. "If the law supposes that," he replies, "the law is a ass, a idiot." In this country, today, the law says that virtually all jobs are open to anyone, regardless of sex. But labor statistics show that the working world is divided into jobs where men predominate and jobs where women predominate.[8] Something is going on, both in family life and in work, which the law does not control.

What is that "something"? Many factors other than law affect people's lives. Income, education, "socialization" (a fancy word for the process by which you learn what's expected of you), societal "norms" (that which is expected of you), technology, and physiology are only a few forces independent of law. Many of the changes which had the greatest effects on women's status resulted from phenomena other than changes in the law. For example, World War II brought women into the labor force in unprecedented numbers. Most of these women lost their jobs when the men came back from military service to reclaim them, but the numbers of employed women never dropped to their prewar levels, and have risen steadily since 1947.[9] The war, not civil rights law, stimulated a change in women's status from full-time unpaid homemaker to salaried worker. Other radical changes in women's lives resulted from two sets of technological advances which have reduced the burdens of motherhood and domestic work: contraceptives, which increase women's control over family size, and the invention of labor-saving devices like washing machines and dishwashers, which make housework easier. Women in the 1990s live lives very different from the lives of women in the 1930s, and more different still from women of the nineteenth century. But law has hardly been the most powerful force in bringing about these changes.

Some scholars have argued that law cannot change society. In the late nineteenth century, sociologists like William Graham Sumner insisted that "folkways" were impervious to law. These ideas were so widely accepted that the Supreme Court even wrote them into the Constitution. "Legislation is powerless to eradicate racial instincts," intoned the justices in a decision upholding racial segregation in the post–Civil War South.[10] The Court saw matters differently in 1954, when it unanimously ruled that legally mandated school segregation violated the Constitution.[11] But it took a long time to enforce this ruling, partly because the president had reservations. "You can't legislate morality," Dwight Eisenhower said as he posed with a Southern governor bent on defying the decision.[12]

Sometimes you can't. The Eighteenth Amendment enacted into the Constitution the "Noble Experiment" of Prohibition, the effort to use law to end the consumption of alcoholic beverages in this country. The ignominious failure of this experiment (repealed by the Twenty-first Amendment) stands as a caution to all who would rely too much on law to change behavior. But Prohibition also shows that Americans have not all believed that law is powerless to change society. The law would never have passed if all Americans had agreed with Sumner.

The "separate but equal" doctrine and Prohibition represent opposite extremes. Law cannot do everything, but it does not therefore follow, that law can do nothing. The 1896 opinion from which I quoted also says: "If the two races are to meet on terms of social equality, it must be as a result of natural affinities, a mutual appreciation of each other's merits and a voluntary consent of individuals."[13] But how is such appreciation to develop if the races are separated? A decision that the railroad cars must be integrated might have brought about the association which could change attitudes. The school integration decision of 1954 resulted in a dramatic increase over a twenty-year period in the percentage of black public school students going to school with any whites in the South. The figure jumped from .001 percent in 1954–55 to 91.3 percent in 1972–73.[14] The Voting Rights Act of 1965 led to the election of many black officials in the South. Law is not, after all, separate from social forces; it is one kind of social force.

What is "legal status?" This term, applied to a group, can have several different meanings. Group members may have a generalized inferior status, as slaves did, as children do now, and as women did before the 1920s. (Of course, if one group is assigned inferior status, some group—free people, adults, men—has a generalized superior status.) "Legal status" may mean the existence of certain specific, limited burdens or restrictions which do not add up to a general inferiority: for instance, laws which limited the hours women could work. Restrictions may only affect women in certain roles. A married woman, for example, has several legal obligations which neither men nor single women have.

The legal status of some women is affected by their membership in other groups. Laws aimed at blacks, homosexuals, or disabled people, for example, affect any women in these groups. Laws which do not mention gender at all may have a disproportionate impact on women. Veterans' preferences, for example (such as laws which favor veterans over other job applicants) apply equally to both male and female veterans. Since well over 90 percent of veterans are men, however, these laws actually favor men over women. A person's legal status may be affected by laws which confer special benefits or which forbid certain kinds of unequal treatment. Civil rights laws have the latter effect.

This book does not deal with women's status throughout American history. It concentrates on a period of about sixty years, from the beginning of the New Deal to the present. The "New Deal" began in 1933, when Franklin D. Roosevelt became president. The country was then in the Great Depression, which had left millions of people desperately poor. Roosevelt and a new Congress controlled by his Democratic Party pledged to commit the national government to the ending of the Depression and the bettering of the lives of Americans.

The New Deal did not, however, effect or cause a direct change in women's legal status. It is by no means the *only* logical starting point for such an analysis. Probably one could start at any time after 1920, the year the Nineteenth Amendment gave women the vote. By then, women also had the other legal rights which might be termed the attributes of full adult citizenship: they could own property, make contracts, sue, and be sued. But 1933 is a good starting point because the New Deal represented a fundamental change in the role of the national government, a change which was a necessary precondition for many of the most dramatic changes in women's status. The Roosevelt administration and the Seventy-third Congress rejected the Jeffersonian principle, "that government is best which governs least." Since 1933, government has been active in providing social services and human opportunities. (The anticipated "Reagan revolution" of the 1980s has not significantly altered this orientation.) The civil rights laws of the 1960s and 1970s which have changed women's status would have been impossible without the New Deal. So, probably, would have been the movement for the civil rights of blacks which inspired the twentieth-century feminist movement.

What has happened to women's legal status during this period? By 1933, it was incorrect to describe women as having a kind of generalized inferiority under law. They had all the legal rights that men enjoyed. But there were still many laws which singled women out for different treatment. Not only were there no laws prohibiting job discrimination, there were laws requiring it. All the states had special labor laws applying only to women. Although this type of policy was termed "protective" legislation, it in fact restricted the jobs women could take and the hours they could work. The marriage and family laws of all states also put many restrictions on married women; for example, a wife had the legal duty to reside where her husband chose. Indirect discrimination was common. Reproductive choice was far from being a legal right in the 1930s. Not only did all states forbid abortions, but even using birth control was not a guaranteed right.

By the late 1980s, all of these policies had changed. The Civil Rights Act of 1964 forbade sex discrimination in employment. Within ten years, federal courts had used this law to invalidate virtually all special labor laws. Other laws and executive orders have prohibited wage discrimination and gender differences in educational benefits. Courts have also struck down many discriminatory civil laws by ruling them unconstitutional. One of the most dramatic, far-reaching changes has been the establishment of limited reproductive choice. The Supreme Court invalidated all existing abortion laws in 1973, in the landmark case of *Roe v. Wade*.[15]

But full equality remains a goal, not a fact. Women do not enjoy constitutional equality with men. The Equal Rights Amendment, which would have forbidden the denial of "equality of rights" on the basis of sex, was not ratified. Nor have courts interpreted the Constitution to extend the same protection to women that the Equal Protection Clause of the Fourteenth Amendment gives to racial minorities. The civil rights laws have not ended sex stereotyping and segregation in the job market. Although the Equal Pay Act of 1963 forbade wage discrimination where men and women hold the same jobs, this law's effect was limited by the fact that men and women usually hold different jobs. Comparable worth—a policy where women's jobs would pay as well as men's jobs that are equally complex and difficult—has not been established in this country. Reproductive choice has been severely limited. Laws prohibiting the use of public funds for abortions have put the procedure beyond the reach of many poor women; many states have passed laws requiring parental intervention before minors may get abortions; and *Roe v. Wade* itself is in grave danger of being overruled.

So, some old laws have not changed, or changed enough. Worse still, some *new* policies threaten women. Changes in divorce laws have left many ex-wives in poverty or threatened mothers with loss of child custody. The discovery that many substances used in the workplace can harm unborn infants has led to rules which exclude all women of childbearing age, pregnant or not, from certain jobs. A new age of protective legislation looms.

Although the relationship between legal status and socioeconomic conditions is complex, the situation of women shows that actual equality lags even behind legal equality. Women earn approximately seventy cents for every dollar that men earn. Men have a virtual monopoly on the best-paying and most influential jobs, while women workers are concentrated in the low-paying job "ghettos," like clerical and domestic work.[16] In public office, women account for only 5 percent of the members of Congress, three of the nation's fifty state governors, and one of the nine justices of the Supreme Court. No woman has ever been president of the United States. These figures lag far behind those for comparable governments.

The United States is still a patriarchy. Men hold power. Though not all men have equal amounts of power, virtually all men have some power over at least some women. Maleness still confers power and privilege. But it would be incorrect to say that men *monopolize* power. Women have some of it; they can exercise the privileges of adult citizens. Women did not always have these privileges. Such changes are fundamental, and they continue to take place.

Fifty-eight years is a long time. The particular decades with which we are concerned brought extraordinary political, socio-economic, and technological changes. World War II, the subsequent Cold War, the development of instantaneous mass communications, the proliferation of nuclear weapons, and the growth of autonomous civil rights movements are only some of the most dramatic of these changes. All these developments influenced one another, and all of them have affected the status of women.

The period might be more manageable if we could divide it into two or more phases. One logical dividing year might be 1963, the year that the President's Commission on the Status of Women made its report and the year that Betty Friedan's *The Feminine Mystique* was published. Until then, except for some short-lived changes during the war, most women were traditional home-makers; their participation in the labor force or public life was minimal. This is certainly the way they were treated in law. Although the President's Commission report was a reactionary document, opposing the ERA and supporting special labor laws, it had the useful result of focusing public attention on women's status (see Chapter 2).[17]

There was nothing reactionary about Friedan's book. She asked, "What force in our culture is strong enough to write 'Occupation: Housewife' so large that all other possibilities for women have been virtually obscured?"[18] (Any reader whom this question now strikes as ludicrous is urged to show this book to a woman of her mother's generation. That woman's reaction will be a measure of the success of modern feminism.) Though book and author met with unprecedented derision, *The Feminine Mystique* became a bestseller. But the social changes that have affected modern women began long before either of these two events in 1963. Women were already moving into the labor force.[19] Women were getting more education than ever before.[20] Even Betty Friedan could not have sparked a social movement with her book had women not been gathered on college campuses in large numbers to read it, and with the money to buy it.

A second reason not to divide the time period into segments stems from the unique nature of legal change. American law comes from several different sources and takes different forms, as we shall see. Thus, laws do not all change at the same time. Furthermore, the relationship between legal change and societal change is too complex to gear one rigidly to the other. It is true that 1963 was a significant year for modern feminism. But except for the Equal Pay Act, it was not a year of great legal activity.

The United States is a federal system. We have a national government and fifty regional governments. Federalism is the principle of dual sovereignty. This principle contains a contradiction in terms: to be sovereign means "to possess entire political power." If some government has entire power, it cannot share power with another government, but that logical impossibility has never bothered the United States much. We continue to insist that our national and state governments are each sovereign in their own sphere. This relationship between nation and states is quite different from the relationship between states and local governments like cities, towns, and counties. The latter are not sovereign at all; they are, constitutionally at least, subordinate to state governments.

The Constitution makes it clear that the federal government is supreme, but the states elect their own officials and make their own laws. The national Congress has the powers listed in Article 1, Section 8 of the Constitution, and all powers which are reasonably related to these enumerated powers.[21] All other legislative powers belong to the states (and may be delegated by those states to their local governments).[22] The implications of federalism for the study of law are that some laws are made by the national government and others—most, in fact—by the individual states. Federal courts may invalidate a state law by declaring it unconstitutional. Congress may pass laws, like the Civil Rights Act of 1964, which preempt any contrary state laws, or laws, like the Uniform Gift to Minors Act, which become binding upon the states if they so choose. Congress may also exercise its power of the purse to withhold federal funds from the states if they refuse to do what Congress wants them to. Although Congress could not force the states to raise the drinking age to twenty-one, it accomplished that goal by making federal highway funds contingent on so doing. All fifty states have complied. But most of the time states pass their laws on their own.

Traditionally, states hold two kinds of power which have significant effects on women. The police power, the power to protect public health, safety, welfare, and morals, includes labor legislation and abortion laws, for instance. The law of domestic relations, of marriage, family, and divorce, is also state law. The presumption that family law is the province of the states is so powerful that the Supreme Court almost never reviews decisions involving divorce and child custody.[23] This book will discuss both state and federal law.

Another important distinction, besides that between state and federal law, is the difference between statutes and common law. "Statute" is another word for what we usually mean when we speak of a law: an act passed by a legislative body. "Common law" is an old term for case law: decisions made by judges, expected to be binding on later judges. Case law existed before there were any legislatures; judges had to decide disputes among citizens and between citizens and the government. Most of the common law of the United States originated in England, where judges were deciding cases before Parliament was established in the thirteenth century. Much of our family law and criminal law began as common law. State legislatures may change this law or adopt it by statute, but they need not. Common law spelled out in detail the reciprocal rights and duties of husband and wife; states have varied in how much of this law they have enacted.

A third important kind of law is, of course, constitutional law. Not all governments have written constitutions, but the federal government and each of the fifty states do. A written constitution is paramount, fundamental law, superior to all existing law where it is binding. If any law—state or federal, case or statute—conflicts with the constitution, the law is void. Judges have the task of deciding these conflicts.

These distinctions are important because they have different degrees of effect on actual practice. Statutes may go unenforced, but usually they describe what public policy is to be. If people disobey them, they may suffer civil or criminal sanctions. Common law, particularly the common law of domestic relations, may bear little resemblance to actual practice. For example, under common law, the husband is obliged to support the family, and the wife to keep the home. But there are many families where both spouses earn money, and there are some where the husband goes to school and the wife is both breadwinner and homemaker. Are these arrangements illegal? Not if both spouses are satisfied with them. Courts become concerned with such arrangements only when the relationship breaks down and one party seeks dissolution through annulment or divorce. Under common law, a divorce was a lawsuit: the "innocent" spouse obtained a settlement from the "guilty" party. In that situation, courts had to determine the legality of private arrangements. But most states now have no-fault divorce laws; either partner may dissolve the marriage without proving the other's "guilt." Thus, it is hard to say whether or not the common law of marriage is binding. However, as Chapters 2 and 4 will show, some Supreme Court decisions have weakened, if not negated, these common law doctrines.

All these kinds of law have changed, but they have changed at different times and at different speeds. These complexities militate against a division of the book into time phases. A division based on topics makes more sense. Chapter 2 will treat constitutional law, an area which has seen dramatic change since 1933. Chapters 3 and 4 will take up, respectively, two crucial aspects of women's lives: paid work and the home. Employment, the focus of Chapter 3, involves two types of changes: the abandonment, for the most part, of laws restricting women and the passage of laws granting them equal opportunity. Chapter 4 will discuss the law of sexuality, marriage, child rearing, divorce, and widowhood. A recurrent theme of these two chapters is the ways in which the law has punished both the women who assume the traditional roles and the women who reject them. Next, the book will deal with the relationship between law and the childbearing function. Chapter 5 will examine the complex issue of reproductive freedom: the right to be a mother and the right not to be one, as well as legal restrictions placed on women for the ostensible purpose of protecting unborn children. Some of the issues examined in Chapter 3 could just as aptly have been included here, such as maternity leaves and other types of policies which indirectly burden or enhance reproductive freedom. Education and barriers, the subjects of Chapter 6, will reveal many ways in which women have been excluded from full, equal participation in American life. Chapter 7 deals with women as actors and subjects in the legal system, as criminals, victims, lawyers, and judges. This chapter has to deal with the unpleasant subjects of rape and domestic violence. It also discusses the relationship between sexism and pornography. Finally, Chapter 8 will attempt to sum up what we have learned and to bring some coherence to this complex subject.

REFERENCES

Beauvoir, Simone de. *The Second Sex*. Translated by H. M. Parshley. New York: Alfred A. Knopf, 1952. A difficult book, but a, if not *the*, classic work of modern feminist thought.

Cherow-O'Leary, Renee. *The State-by-State Guide to Women's Legal Rights*. New York: McGraw-Hill, 1987. A user-friendly guide to the relevant law.

Cook, Beverly B., Leslie F. Goldstein, Karen O'Connor, and **Susette Talarico.** "Women in the Judicial Process." Instructional Unit, *Citizenship and Change: Women and American Politics*. Washington, D.C.: American Political Science Association, 1988. This monograph, like those by Gelb and Klein, Hedblom, Sapiro, and Shanley below, is one of several instructional units prepared for the APSA, the national learned society of political scientists. All these monographs have good bibliographies.

Diamond, Irene, and **Nancy Hartsock.** "Beyond Interests in Politics." *American Political Science Review*, 75 (September 1981): 717–21. A critique of Virginia Sapiro's article, "When Are Interests Interesting?", cited below.

Engels, Friedrich. *Origin of the Family, Private Property, and the State*. Originally published in 1884, this work is available in several English editions. It is the classic Marxist treatment of the position of women.

Flexner, Eleanor. *Century of Struggle*. Rev. ed. New York: Atheneum, 1971. An excellent history of the women's suffrage movement in the United States.

Friedan, Betty. *The Feminine Mystique*. New York: W.W. Norton, 1963. This excellent analysis of now obsolescent, but once influential, scholarship provided a rallying point for the contemporary feminist movement.

———. *The Second Stage*. New York: Summit Books, 1981. Some second thoughts, arguing for a moderate, liberal feminism.

Gelb, Joyce, and **Ethel Klein.** "Women's Movements: Organizing for Change." Washington, D.C.: American Political Science Association, 1988. Another APSA monograph; see Cook, above.

Hedblom, Milda K. "Women and Power in American Politics." Washington, D.C.: American Political Science Association, 1988. See Cook, above.

Hoff, Joan. *Law, Gender and Injustice: A Legal History of U.S. Women.* New York: New York University Press, 1991. The latest work from one of the foremost American scholars.

MacKinnon, Catharine A. *Feminism Unmodified.* Cambridge, Mass.: Harvard University Press, 1987. A collection of provocative, well-reasoned essays by a leading radical feminist legal philosopher.

————. *Toward a Feminist Theory of the State.* Cambridge, Mass.: Harvard University Press, 1989. A scholarly work that discusses such subjects as the relationship between feminism and Marxism; pornography; and reproductive freedom.

McGlen, Nancy E., and **Karen O'Connor.** *Women's Rights: The Struggle for Equality in the Nineteenth and Twentieth Centuries.* New York: Praeger, 1983. Feminist history and contemporary politics.

Millett, Kate. *Sexual Politics.* New York: Doubleday, 1969. This analysis, based on European and American literature, is a classic of the contemporary feminist movement.

Morgan, Robin, ed. *Sisterhood Is Powerful.* New York: Random House, 1970. From the same historical period as Millett, this anthology remains one of the best collections of feminist writings.

Rossi, Alice S., ed. *The Feminist Papers.* New York: Columbia University Press, 1973. A collection of primary U.S. feminist sources from colonial times to the present.

Sapiro, Virginia. "When Are Interests Interesting? The Problem of Political Representation of Women." *American Political Science Review* 75 (September 1981): 701–16. An analysis of the political position of women.

————. "Women, Political Action, and Political Participation." Washington, D.C.: American Political Science Association, 1988. Another APSA monograph; see Cook, above.

Shanley, Mary Lyndon, with introduction and epilogue by **Shelby Lewis.** "Women's Rights, Politics, and Citizenship in the United States." Washington, D.C.: American Political Science Association, 1988. See Cook et al., above.

Wortman, Marlene Stein, ed. *Women in American Law.* Volume 1: *From Colonial Times to the New Deal.* New York: Holmes & Meier, 1985. This book is an excellent collection of documents.

2

Women and the Constitution

A person whose only knowledge of the United States came from reading its Constitution might well be unaware that this is a patriarchal society. The only hints that person would have of this phenomenon come, not from the original document ratified in 1789, but from two subsequent amendments. The first of these, Section 2 of the Fourteenth Amendment, adopted in 1868, appears in many texts between brackets which indicate that it is no longer operative. Section 2 declares that when the right to vote in any general election "is denied to any of the male inhabitants of such State, being twenty-one years of age . . . the basis of representation therein shall be reduced in the proportion which the number of such male citizens shall bear to the whole number of male citizens twenty-one years of age in such State." This section is the only place in which the word "male" appears in the Constitution. The only other hint about sex roles in American society is given by the Nineteenth Amendment, ratified in 1920: "The right of citizens of the United States to vote shall not be denied or abridged by the United States or by any state on account of sex."

Elsewhere, the Constitution always speaks, not of "men," but of "persons" or in the passive voice.[1] For example, no "person" under the age of thirty-five may be elected president; no state may deny equal protection of the laws "to any person within its juris-

18

diction"; and the right of habeas corpus "shall not be suspended."[2] The only information which this document gives us about women's legal status is that they have not always and everywhere been permitted to vote, but they are now. Thus, the constitutional text informs us about one specific guarantee of equality which supersedes the one textual recognition of inequality.

The original Constitution mentioned few rights for anyone. The addition of a "bill of rights"—the first ten amendments—was less a victory for individual rights than for state sovereignty. The Anti-Federalists, who would later form the Republican Party, feared the power of the new central government and refused to vote for ratification unless specific limits on the new nation's powers were added. None of these limits had anything to do with equal rights for anyone. Even though the Declaration of Independence had declared among its "self-evident truths" that "all men are created equal," this commitment to equality is reflected nowhere in the Constitution or its Bill of Rights. There was never any chance that the delegates who met in Independence Hall in Philadelphia during the hot summer of 1787 would give women the vote. The records suggest that the delegates never even considered such a step. Eligibility for voting was considered a matter for the states to decide, not the national government. The Constitution provided that the people eligible to vote for the House of Representatives—the only national officers then chosen by direct popular vote —"shall have the qualifications requisite for electors of the most numerous branch of the state legislature."[3]

Even if the delegates had concerned themselves with voting rights, it is highly unlikely that the idea of woman suffrage would have occurred to them. Some women *could* vote in the eighteenth century; a few communities enfranchised all property owners, of either sex. This right would not disappear until 1806, when New Jersey became the last state to restrict the ballot to males.[4] But no one had ever gone so far as to publicly advocate sexual equality. It was not until 1790 that the first feminist tract in the United States, Judith Sargent Murray's *On the Equality of the Sexes*, would appear in print. There is no evidence that any of the Constitution's framers were familiar with the writings of the English feminist Mary Wollstonecraft, or that they numbered rebellious women among their acquaintances. True, Abigail Adams had admonished her husband, John, to "remember the ladies" while he attended the Second Continental Congress in

1776, but he had brusquely dismissed her concerns: "I cannot but laugh."[5] Feminist ideas were not part of the current political discourse.

And yet, perhaps without meaning to, the authors of the Constitution ensured that women would have access to the political process. The fact that the Constitution consistently uses the word "person" rather than "man" in its common generic sense has made it impossible for anyone to claim that constitutional rights do not apply to women or that women may not run for office. The First Amendment rights of freedom of expression and association, which are essential for any sort of political activity, have been available to women who wished to promote change. And there has never been a question of women's eligibility for the offices that would give them power to pursue their goals. Indeed, the first woman member of the House of Representatives, Jeanette Rankin, was elected in 1916, when most American women still had no right to vote. So, even while the original Constitution was silent on the issue of sexual equality, its gender-neutral provisions did encourage women to try to change the situation.

The recent celebrations of the supposed bicentennial of the Constitution may have obscured the fact that the original Constitution lasted for less than three-quarters of a century. By 1861, the union had dissolved and what had once been the United States was engaged in civil war. The union would be re-formed, but only at the cost of fundamental change. That change was embodied in three constitutional amendments ratified between 1865 and 1870. The Thirteenth Amendment abolished slavery, thus resolving the issue that, unsettled in 1787, had destroyed the union. The Fifteenth Amendment extended the vote to adult male citizens of every race. But it was the Fourteenth Amendment, passed by Congress in 1866 and ratified in 1868, that represented the most significant change. This amendment unambiguously established national supremacy over the states, and it declared for the first time that people had rights against state governments. The states were forbidden to deny "the privileges or immunities of citizens of the United States"; to "deprive any person of life, liberty, or property without due process of law"; and to deny "the equal protection of the laws." This clause contained the first explicit constitutional recognition of equal rights.

By 1865, an American feminist movement did exist. Historians usually date this movement from 1848, when a group of women met at Seneca Falls, New York, and drew up a "Declaration of Sentiments and Resolutions," modeled on Jefferson's Declaration, which had left them out.[6] Many of these early feminists had been active in the movement to abolish slavery; as often happens, organizing for the rights of others had sensitized them to their own unequal status. Getting the vote became their first priority. When the question of voting rights came up before Congress after the war, the suffragists tried hard to get the vote for women, too. They failed. As Frederick Douglass, the great abolitionist leader, put it, "This is the Negro's hour." It was the Negro *man's* hour. It did not seem to dawn on Douglass or anyone else at the time that the failure to enfranchise women deprived black women, too.[7] It is a useful exercise to compare feminist accounts of this episode with the records of the debates in Congress. The *Congressional Globe* leaves the impression that Congress never gave woman's suffrage very serious consideration.[8] It had very little to say about the issue. The women, however, took the issue very seriously indeed, and devoted far more of their energies to their proposal than did the members of the House and Senate.

Although suffragists failed in their effort to get explicit constitutional recognition of women's rights, the provisions of Section 1 of the Fourteenth Amendment were, like much else in the Constitution, gender-neutral. The question of how the rights listed applied to women, or any other group, was one that had to be decided by the courts. Back in 1803, the landmark case of *Marbury v. Madison* had established the judicial branch of government as the arbiter of constitutional issues.[9] It is the Supreme Court which has ultimately decided how the document is to be interpreted. Therefore, this chapter will devote much attention to decisions of the Supreme Court.

Women's rights has never been an area in which court decisions anticipated public opinion. If anything, the courts have tended to lag behind the rest of society. But the constitutional history of women's rights shows the same kinds of complex interplay between social norms and judicial doctrine that typifies the American court system. The second wave of feminism, in particular, has influenced a far from radical Supreme Court to alter fundamentally the constitutional doctrine of sex discrimination.

The Historical Background

Since the Fourteenth Amendment was adopted, the Supreme Court has had the task of deciding exactly what kinds of laws are forbidden by the due process and equal protection clauses. The justices have never adopted either of the two extreme positions that were available. They have not ruled that the amendment prevented government from ever depriving people of rights or treating them differently; nor, on the other hand, have they rendered the clause meaningless by leaving the states free to do as they choose. (The latter position, however, was effectively the constitutional doctrine with respect to women until the 1970s.) The Court has, by a lengthy, complex, tortuous process, carved out a compromise between those extremes.

To make a long story short—a very long story, indeed—the Court has consistently interpreted the due process and equal protection clauses to require that, at the very least, all legislation be reasonable; that is, all laws must bear some rational relationship to a legitimate governmental purpose. Therefore, a law which treats women differently from men cannot survive if it is arbitrary; it must make some sense to at least five of the nine justices. A common hypothetical example of a law which would be struck down under this test is a law discriminating against people with red hair or blue eyes. This "rational basis" test is a pretty lenient standard; most laws survive this scrutiny because judges proceed from the assumption that the legislature has acted constitutionally. In 1933, the beginning of the period with which this book is concerned, the rational basis standard was the prevailing rule. If a law was reasonable, it conformed to the due process and equal protection guarantees. There had been a time—it seemed to be over—when this rule of reason had been interpreted very strictly indeed in certain cases. Usually, these were cases that involved the efforts of state or national governments to deal with some of the abuses that accompanied the Industrial Revolution. In 1905, for example, a bare majority of the Court had invalidated a New York State law limiting the working hours of bakers.[10] The Court had insisted that this law was an arbitrary interference with liberty of contract. The fact that such liberty is mentioned nowhere in the Constitution did not give the justices pause. But in 1917 the Court had upheld a similar law from Oregon, accepting without difficulty the notion of a relationship between working hours and public health and safety.[11]

The New York law had applied only to male workers. Since, then as now, men and women usually worked in different occupations, some states did pass laws regulating the working hours of women only, or of women and children. But the employers' success in getting the New York law invalidated emboldened them to bring a case involving a women's hours law. When Oregon's special hours law was challenged, the state hired Louis Brandeis, a lawyer with experience in these cases, to argue the case before the Supreme Court. Brandeis's sister-in-law, Josephine Goldmark, was a social activist who had worked hard for laws protecting women from corporate exploitation. Goldmark and Brandeis prepared a brief (a written argument) which gathered masses of evidence from Europe, North America, and Australia about the harmful effects of long working hours on women's health. That sort of brief, common now, was unheard of eighty years ago. Such a brief, containing facts rather than just law, became known as a "Brandeis brief."

The strategy worked. *Muller v. Oregon* unanimously upheld the law. In order to do so without violating its three-year-old precedent, the Supreme Court had to emphasize sexual differences. The opinion laid particular emphasis on the physical differences: women's relative lack of muscle strength and their childbearing capacity. *Muller* gave less attention to the very real economic and political differences between men and women at the time, but the Court did mention the fact that women workers in 1908 were subjected to particularly severe exploitation by employers. "Differentiated by these matters from the other sex," the Court wrote, woman "is properly placed in a class by herself, and legislation for her protection may be sustained, even when like legislation is not necessary for men, and could not be sustained."[12]

The *Muller* opinion presumed, of course, that laws restricting the hours women could work were designed for their protection. The nastier possibility that such laws might handicap women in competing with men for good jobs did not seem to occur to anyone at the time—and, in fact, the Oregon law, which applied to the all-female occupation of laundry worker, probably did not present such a danger. Laundresses, like most women workers in 1908, worked longer hours than men did, anyway. But things were less clear in 1924, when the Court upheld a law preventing women from working as waitresses at night—when wages and tips are higher than they are during the day. The aggrieved plaintiffs in this case were women workers, not employers. But the Court relied on *Muller* to find the law reasonable.[13]

By 1933, the Court had found only one instance of sex-based

discrimination invalid. The District of Columbia had passed a minimum wage regulation applying only to women. Then, as now, women's jobs tended to pay less than men's jobs did. In those years, they often paid so poorly that women could not earn a living wage. But *Adkins v. Children's Hospital* found the minimum wage an arbitrary determination that a certain income was necessary for health and safety.[14] The Court did not view *Muller* as binding precedent here, for, reasonably enough, the justices could find no relationship between wages and the physical differences between men and women. It is not clear, however, why the lack of that relationship should have been the decisive point. One newspaper printed a cartoon showing the robed justice who wrote *Adkins* handing the decision to a wraithlike figure labeled "Woman Wage Earner." The caption read, "This decision, madam, represents your constitutional right to starve."[15]

Muller and *Adkins*, taken together, seemed to establish the principle that any sex-based discrimination linked to the physical differences between the sexes was constitutional, while laws which took into account social and economic differences stood on very dubious ground. But *Adkins* was never a very popular decision. At least one state, Washington, enforced its minimum-wage law continuously from its passage in 1913 until the 1930s.[16] So by 1933, while the formal rule was that only laws based on physical differences could survive judicial scrutiny, the informal rule may well have been carte blanche for any and all legal distinctions based on sex, whether they helped or hurt women.

1937: The Battle of the New Deal

By 1933, the Supreme Court had gradually departed from the doctrine of substantive due process. Judges had become more tolerant of state economic regulation. But Franklin Roosevelt's New Deal was too much for the Court. By then, five of the nine justices were over seventy years old. Four of these—James McReynolds, George Sutherland, Willis Van Devanter, and Pierce Butler—usually dissented in cases upholding economic regulation and were known as the "Four Horsemen." As the new laws began reaching the Court, these four were often joined by enough more moderate justices to overturn key elements of FDR's policy program.[17]

Part of Roosevelt's problem was a statistical streak of bad luck. Although on the average a Court vacancy occurs about once every two years, no justice died or retired during Roosevelt's first term.[18] But after his landslide reelection victory, Roosevelt determined to curb the Court. A few weeks after his second inauguration in March 1937, he proposed a statute that would allow the president to appoint a new justice for every incumbent (up to a total of six) who reached the age of seventy and failed to retire. If passed, this law would have given Roosevelt the immediate power to make five new appointments. Although the president called this bill "a plan to reorganize the federal judiciary," it is not hard to see why the bill's opponents called it the "Court-packing plan."[19]

Whatever the bill was called, its fate taught both the president and the judges some valuable lessons on the limits of their powers. Even the Democratic majority in Congress failed to line up solidly behind the bill; it died in committee. But one of the reasons the bill failed is that two justices, Owen Roberts and Chief Justice Charles Evans Hughes, began voting to uphold New Deal laws—thus saving them by a majority of five to four. This "switch in time that saved nine" took most of the fire out of the president's arguments.[20] One case exemplifying that switch was *West Coast Hotel v. Parrish*, which affirmed Washington State's minimum wage for women with only the Four Horsemen voting to uphold *Adkins*.[21]

One Roosevelt biographer concluded that the president "lost the battle, won the campaign, but lost the war."[22] The "campaign" was the dispute over judicial scrutiny of economic regulation, which FDR did indeed win; the Court has never resumed its old activism in this area. The "war" was the controversy over the Court's role in American politics. If FDR wanted that role to be a passive one, he was the loser—but he was never to learn of that defeat. The Court did not reassert itself until several years after Roosevelt's death in 1945. When the justices resumed their old activism, it would be in a new area: protecting the rights of individuals. The developments which have had the strongest impact on the emerging constitutional doctrine of women's rights since the New Deal have been the campaign won by the executive branch and the war won by the judiciary.

The Slough of Patriarchy: 1937–1971

For several years after 1937, the "rational basis" test essentially meant that courts would uphold a law if they could find any minimally adequate justification for it. If the government did not present a plausible rationale, the judges did their best to invent one. Every presumption was entertained in favor of the validity of a statute. The courts' abandonment of independent review in economic cases included cases involving women's employment. With that kind of standard, judges did not have to be male chauvinists (a concept that did not exist at the time, anyway) to uphold laws barring women from certain occupations. Courts did not treat these laws much differently from similar laws that had nothing to do with women. After all, in the 1940s and 1950s the Supreme Court upheld some statutes which greatly restricted workers' rights. *Kotch v. Board of River Pilot Examiners*, for example, allowed Louisiana to require that aspiring licensees serve an apprenticeship with a senior pilot—who had absolute discretion to select his apprentices. The fact that this law effectively restricted eligibility for this occupation to white applicants apparently occurred to none of the justices. The opinion declared, "We can only assume that the Louisiana legislature weighed the obvious possibility of evil against whatever useful function a closely knit pilotage system may serve."[23] *Williamson v. Lee Optical Company* received similar subjunctive judgment several years later. Here, the Court found no fault with an Oklahoma law which made it impossible to get eyeglasses without a prescription from a licensed ophthalmologist or optometrist. The unanimous ruling deferred to the legislature the decision whether this law was a reasonable health measure or a naked power play by professionals against opticians and consumers.[24]

   Goesaert v. Cleary was decided in 1948, chronologically between these two cases. The fact that the Court upheld a Michigan law forbidding most women from working as bartenders comes as no retrospective surprise to the student of constitutional history. What is instructive about this case is the interplay between institutional patriarchy and judicial passivity. As the *Goesaert* opinion would note, bartending has never been an exclusively male occupation. During the early twentieth century, the International Union of Hotel and Restaurant Employees and Bartenders tried to make it one. World War II changed all that, as it temporarily changed much else. The union dropped its prohibition as its members left for military service. Tending bar soon became one of several jobs newly open to women. Bartending is not a bad job. It pays reasonably well, better than waiting tables; the tips are a reliable wage supplement; working conditions are reasonably pleasant; and the threats to health and safety are negligible. When the men came home, they wanted these jobs back. The union adopted a resolution to resume the old ban on women, and lobbied the Michigan legislature to legalize it. The legislature, itself predominantly male, complied. On April 30, 1945, it passed a law forbidding all women from working as bartenders except the wives and daughters of male bar owners. The law ordered the state Liquor Control Commission to begin enforcing the ban on May 1, 1947.[25]

Few people found anything wrong with such policies at the time. Many women had taken jobs outside the home when their labor was needed. Now that the men wanted their jobs back, it was the women's patriotic duty to leave the workplace, go back to full-time homemaking or traditional women's jobs, and even start a family. Some employers just fired women outright.[26] And was it mere coincidence that in the year after the war, the first edition of that now-famous "bible," Dr. Benjamin Spock's *Baby and Child Care*, insisted that motherhood was a full-time job?[27] The departure from the workplace and the resurgence of domesticity seemed very normal indeed.

Four decades later, it is hard to read these accounts without anger. What happened to women is easily explained in Marxist terminology. Women became a "reserve army" of paid workers. When their country needed them, they were encouraged to take good jobs. When their country had a supply of male workers— and when the men wanted their old jobs and their old role as family head and sole wage earner—the women were sent back home. The concept of women which emerges is that of a group peculiarly interest-less. The record is barren of the notion that women might have separate interests, let alone rights in their occupation. Women's duty was to serve others: their families and the state.

There is no evidence that the plaintiffs in the eventual case— Valentine Goesaert, the owner of a bar in Dearborn; her daughter, Margaret; and two other women employees—rejected any of these prevailing social attitudes. But they did bring suit to preserve their livelihood. They argued in federal court that the new law violated their rights under the Fourteenth Amendment. They lost, at every decision point—but not before a few funny (peculiar, not amusing) things happened on the way to the courtroom.

The first peculiar development was the way in which Michigan defended its law. The act metamorphosed from a naked preference for male over female workers into a benevolent effort to protect women from unruly drinkers. The three-judge lower court bought this argument, in an opinion which is its own best refutation:

> It is conceivable that the Legislature was of the opinion that a grave social problem existed because of the presence of female barten-ders. . . . It may have been the Legislature's opinion that this prob-lem would be mitigated . . . where there was a male licensee ultimately responsible for the condition and decorum maintained in his establishment. . . . The Legislature may also have reasoned that a graver responsibility attaches to the bartender who has control of the liquor supply than to the waitress who merely receives prepared orders for liquor. . . .[28]

Clearly, the jurisprudence of the subjunctive mood had spread to the lower courts. The Supreme Court favorably cited this opinion, while adding a second peculiar metamorphosis. The most noticeable aspect of Justice Felix Frankfurter's opinion for the Court in *Goesaert v. Cleary* is its tone. "Beguiling as the subject is," the opinion began, "it need not detain us long." Frankfurter referred to the "historic calling" of "the alewife, sprightly and ribald, [met] in Shakespeare." This language leaves the impres-sion that the Court viewed this controversy as a slightly bawdy joke. The tone is so offensive that it almost obscures the crux of the case: for the Court, *Goesaert* pertained not to women's rights but to economic regulation. The opinion cited, not *Muller* and *West Coast Hotel*, but *Kotch* and similar state cases.[29] The reader has to wonder about the sensitivity of anyone who would join, let alone write, this opinion, but the judicial attitude toward sex discrimination is part and parcel of its post-1937 stance. Judicial passivity thus reinforced patriarchy.

The Warren Court and the Rights Revolution

Goesaert, the signature case of the 1940s, was decided by a distinctly low-profile Court. The tenure of Fred M. Vinson as chief justice was notable more for deference to agencies outside the Court and for divisions within it than for doctrinal innovations from it. All that began to change with Vinson's death in 1953. President Dwight Eisenhower would come to regard his choice for Vinson's successor as "the biggest damned-fool mistake" of his career."[30] But historians rank Earl Warren, the former governor of California and Republican vice-presidential candidate in 1948, among the great chief justices.

The first landmark decision of the Warren Court came on May 17, 1954, when Chief Justice Warren had been in office less than a year. *Brown v. Board of Education* ruled that de jure racial segregation in public schools violated the equal protection clause.[31] This decision was followed by others dismantling racial segregation in the Southern states. Blacks were not the only minority group whose rights were vindicated by the Warren Court. The justices also overturned loyalty-security measures designed to punish left-wing political activists; repressive criminal justice practices; and laws allowing prayer in public schools.[32] By the time Warren retired in 1969, the Supreme Court had established itself in an unprecedented role: the defender of the weak, powerless, and unpopular.

The Warren Court did not include women among the recipients of its special solicitude. To be fair, litigants presented the justices with few opportunities to rethink *Muller* or *Goesaert*. The Court heard only two cases involving women's rights and denied review in about half a dozen others.[33] But the Court did not use even the little encouragement it got. (And, after all, had it been more friendly toward these claims, it might have gotten more petitions for review; litigation does tend to beget litigation.)

The facts of *Hoyt v. Florida* blend tragedy with dark humor. Evangeline Hoyt killed her husband with a baseball bat after he repulsed the advances with which she tried to mend a quarrel. She pleaded temporary insanity, but an all-male jury convicted her of second-degree murder. Most Florida juries were composed exclusively of men, because state law made all male voters eligible for jury duty while summoning only those women who specifically registered their willingness to serve. Ms. Hoyt's appeal alleged that this discrimination denied her equal protection by effectively excluding members of her own sex from her jury.

Whether or not a jury which included women might have been more sympathetic—for all we know, women might have judged Hoyt even more harshly than men did—the claim is far from ludicrous. Even the Hughes Court back in 1935 had held that blacks could not get a fair trial if no blacks were eligible to sit on juries.[34] By 1961, the Warren Court had significantly broadened the rights of suspects under the due process clause. But the justices did not choose to expand Hoyt's rights. They unanimously affirmed her conviction, stating: "This case in no way resembles those involving race or color in which the circumstances . . . compel a conclusion of purposeful discriminatory exclusions from jury service. . . . There is present here neither the unfortunate atmosphere of ethnic or racial prejudice which underlay the situations depicted in those cases, nor the long course of discriminatory administrative practice."[35] Instead, the Court applied the rational basis test, calling Florida's law a reasonable accommodation of women's role as "the center of home and family life."[36] The state could choose to exempt all women from jury duty rather than allow an exemption only for those whose home responsibilities did make jury service a hardship—surely not, by 1961, the entire female population of Florida.

The Warren Court's uncritical acceptance of patriarchal norms contrasts strangely with its receptivity to the claims of racial minorities and individual rights. This approach was never to change while Warren remained chief justice. But the rights revolution would, ultimately, benefit women as women. The task of accommodating doctrine to a changing society fell to judges less amenable than Warren and his colleagues to due process and equal protection claims. These judges would make use of doctrinal developments fostered by, though not original with, the Warren Court.

Tiers and a "Mezzanine": The Burger Court Years

Earl Warren believed that the protection of the disadvantaged was the special responsibility of the Supreme Court. Several of Warren's colleagues shared that conception of their role.[37] His successor, Warren Burger, did not, nor did the other justices appointed by Richard Nixon or Gerald Ford. But the Burger Court did not return to the deference of the Vinson era. The justices evinced a preference for carefully reasoned opinions. The cumulative effects of Burger Court and Warren Court approaches to constitutional doctrine were to have a significant impact upon gender-based discrimination.

If the rulings on individual rights were to make any sense at all, they required departures from the presumption of constitutionality and the rational basis test. The doctrinal seeds for these changes had already been sown, in cases decided while Charles Evans Hughes and Harlan Fiske Stone had been chief justices. The first of these cases was not a case at all but, of all things, a footnote, to an opinion written in 1938 by then Associate Justice Stone, to be precise. Even for a footnote, these paragraphs were remarkably tentative:

> There may be a narrower scope for operation of the presumption of constitutionality when legislation appears on its face to be within a specific prohibition of the Constitution, such as those in the first ten amendments. . . .

> It is unnecessary to consider now whether legislation which restricts those political processes which can ordinarily be expected to bring about repeal of undesirable legislation, is to be subjected to more exacting scrutiny . . . than are most other types of legislation.

> Nor need we inquire . . . whether prejudice against discrete and insular minorities may be a special condition. . . .[38]

Some preliminary discussion of what "a narrower scope for . . . the presumption of constitutionality" might mean came from an even stranger case: one of the most repressive decisions in Supreme Court history. *Korematsu v. United States* sustained a policy now universally regarded as a gratuitous deprivation of the rights of one hundred thousand law-abiding American citizens: the internment of Americans of Japanese descent in camps during World War II. In that time of judicial deference, the fact that the Court upheld the government should not surprise us. After all, even Earl Warren, then attorney general of California, supported internment.

Justice Hugo Black's majority opinion announced a rule which it did not apply. "All legal restrictions which curtail the civil rights of a single racial group are immediately suspect. . . . Courts must subject them to the most rigid scrutiny."[39] This rule, here honored in the breach alone, became part of Fourteenth Amendment constitutional doctrine in the ensuing years. The Warren Court developed and refined a "two-tier" approach to constitutional adjudication. Ordinary laws—that is, those involving neither suspect classifications nor constitutional rights—were assigned to the lower tier. They were upheld if they withstood the minimal scrutiny of the rational basis test—which, since *Goesaert* and its kin, was minimal indeed. The kinds of laws described in the *Carolene Products* footnote were considered in the top tier. In effect, they were presumed invalid; the burden of proof was on the government to show that a compelling, not merely a reasonable, justification existed for the law. Since it did not occur to the

Court that women might be among the targets of hostile legislation, sex discrimination cases received minimal scrutiny.

The tenure of Warren Burger, Earl Warren's successor as chief
justice, brought further complications in the development of
equal protection doctrine. Soon after Burger took office in 1969,
the justices began forging an intermediate level—a "mezzanine,"
perhaps—between the two tiers of strict and minimal scrutiny.
"An emerging model of modest intervention" found courts
"do[ing] more than they would have done in the past to assure
rationality of means, without unduly impinging on legislative
prerogatives regarding ends."[40] This new doctrinal wrinkle had
nothing to do with women's rights or the emerging feminist
movement, but intermediate scrutiny became the foundation of
permanent change in constitutional doctrine regarding sex discrimination.

In 1971, the Court invalidated a gender-based classification
for the first time since *Adkins*, almost half a century earlier. The
law at issue in *Reed v. Reed* seems, by any standard, remarkably
silly. Moreover, the situation presented by the case is one that
seems unlikely to arise very often. Idaho law provided an automatic preference for male over equally qualified female applicants in appointing the administrator of a dead person's estate.
(The basic qualification for this post was relationship by blood or
marriage to the deceased.) Cecil and Sally Reed, who were divorced, each applied to become administrator over the estate of
their dead son. When Cecil won out—as was inevitable, given the
law—Sally sued. The state presented two justifications for the
law: administrative convenience, by removing from no doubt
overtaxed probate court judges the burden of decision, and the
avoidance of conflict among family members.

In the days of *Goesaert* and *Hoyt*, such reasoning would have
sufficed. The Supreme Court's terse unanimous opinion served
clear notice that those old days were over:

> To give a mandatory preference to members of either sex . . . ,
> merely to accomplish the elimination of hearings on the merits, is to
> make the very kind of arbitrary legislative choice forbidden by the
> Equal Protection Clause of the Fourteenth Amendment; and what-
> ever may be said as to the positive values of avoiding intrafamily
> controversy [since the Reeds had already divorced, surely this con-
> cern came too late in this particular case], the choice in this context
> may not lawfully be mandated solely on the basis of sex.[41]

For women's rights, the Burger Court's scrutiny of means had
begun to accomplish change which had been beyond the reach of

the Warren Court's commitment to individual rights. The import of *Reed* as precedent was problematic, because the Court then had only seven justices; President Richard Nixon had not yet filled the vacancies caused by two unexpected retirements.

Two years later, the Court fell one vote short of ranking sex with race as a suspect classification. *Frontiero v. Richardson* held that the federal statute governing dependency benefits in the armed services violated the Fifth Amendment's due process clause. This law provided that the wives of male military personnel automatically qualified as dependents for the purpose of determining medical benefits and the housing allowance. Military husbands, on the other hand, counted as dependents only upon proof that their wives provided more than half their support.

The vote to overturn was eight to one, with only William Rehnquist, a Nixon appointee who would become chief justice in 1986, in dissent. The other three opinions cited *Reed*, indicating agreement that its description of Idaho's intestacy law as an arbitrary legislative choice characterized this regulation as well. But no majority agreed on how that case applied to *Frontiero*. Four justices found sex discrimination inherently suspect, sustainable only upon the showing of a compelling justification. Justice William Brennan's plurality opinion read in part:

> Since sex, like race or national origin, is . . . determined solely by the accident of birth, the imposition of special disabilities upon the members of a particular sex because of their sex would seem to violate the basic concept of our system that legal burdens should bear some relationship to individual responsibility. . . . And what differentiates sex from such nonsuspect statuses as intelligence or physical disability, and aligns it with the recognized suspect criteria, is that the sex characteristic frequently bears no relation to ability to perform or contribute to society.[42]

As egalitarian theory, this statement has its limitations, chiefly its unstated premise that rewards should depend on ability to make contributions and that society may treat the unintelligent or the disabled as it chooses. Nevertheless, this plurality opinion represents the high point in the Court's commitment to gender equality. This was as far as any justice has ever been willing to go, and never since have they been willing to go even this far. After all, the Court had come one vote short of rendering the Equal Rights Amendment, then before the states, superfluous.

Two cases in 1974 and 1975 invoked the due process clause to render decisions favorable to sex equality. *Cleveland Board of Education v. LaFleur* ruled that a mandatory four-month maternity leave was without rational basis; the Court saw no reason to raise the issue of sex discrimination at all. *Taylor v. Louisiana* disposed of *Hoyt*, sustaining a complaint from a *male* defendant that an all-male jury pool deprived him of the chance to have a jury representative of the community.[43]

Up to this point, the Burger Court was still fitting sex discrimination cases into the two-tier model refined by its predecessor. A 1976 case became the basis for a permanent reconstruction of that model. *Craig v. Boren* involved an Oklahoma law which allowed females to buy 3.2 percent beer (but no other alcoholic beverage) at eighteen, while men had to wait to buy it (but not to drink it) until they were twenty-one. The Court was not impressed with the state's assertion that this law was justified as a means of reducing the number of alcohol-related automobile accidents. Brennan's opinion for a seven-justice majority appeared to reach a compromise between *Reed*'s rationality scrutiny and *Frontiero*'s strict scrutiny. In so doing, it added a new level between the two existing tiers. "To withstand constitutional scrutiny, previous cases established that classifications by gender must serve *important* governmental objectives and be *substantially* related to these objectives."[44] This "intermediate scrutiny" standard remains the prevailing test for gender-based discrimination under the due process and equal protection guarantees. Only one other type of discrimination, that between citizens and aliens, has joined gender on the middle tier.[45] *Craig* left due process and equal protection doctrine in a complex state. The new model, two tiers and a middle "mezzanine" level, requires judges to discriminate among the following kinds of laws: innocuous, nonsuspect classifications; semisuspect classifications; and inherently suspect classifications. Once that assignment has been made, the judges then must apply to the law the appropriate level of scrutiny: respectively, minimal ("rational basis"), intermediate ("substantial relationship to important objectives"), and strict ("compelling justification"). These terms may appear to be so much "word salad," incapable of definite application. Indeed, when the decisions made under the *Craig* standard are taken as a whole, it is hard to avoid the conclusion that the Court which wrote the test has had difficulty applying it coherently and consistently.

Craig v. Boren remains binding precedent. But the Court has not decided a sex discrimination case on due process or equal protection grounds since 1984.[46] The Court has been far from idle on women's rights since 1984, but the cases have involved statutes or other parts of the Constitution. Intermediate scrutiny may have suffered the same fate as the famous "clear and present danger" rule in free speech cases: while perfectly valid, it may just not be relevant anymore.[47]

Intermediate Scrutiny, or How to Toss a Word Salad

Between 1976 and 1984, the Supreme Court had to make order out of a collection of cases which fell into no easy pattern. They involved subjects as diverse as government benefits, fathers' rights, and the military draft. Several rulings between 1975 and 1979 dealt with various provisions of the Social Security laws which discriminated between similarly situated recipients of the same sex in determining old age and survivors' benefits. Only one of these provisions survived the elevated scrutiny: a rule, since repealed, which allowed women to calculate retirement benefits by a more favorable formula than that which applied to men. A policy on dependency benefits which similarly compensated women, and was also temporary, was sustained in 1984.[48]

A 1979 ruling, *Orr v. Orr*, invalidated an Alabama statute which restricted eligibility for alimony to women. The Court rejected both "the state's preference for an allocation of family responsibilities in which the wife plays a dependent role" and "a legislative purpose to provide help for a needy spouse" as long as it used "sex as a proxy for need."[49] Two years later, *Kirchberg v. Feenstra* unanimously overturned a Louisiana law giving husbands exclusive control over marital property.[50] (As welcome as this ruling was, it is discouraging news that, first, such a law still existed anywhere in this country, and, second, that it took the Supreme Court to get rid of it.) These rulings indicated that laws justified by traditional assumptions about sex roles would fall, but that legislative efforts to compensate women for tangible disadvantages, like their lower wages, might be sustained, at least until legislatures abandoned them.

The year 1981 was a landmark year for women's rights in the Supreme Court. Not only did this year bring some signs that the limits of doctrinal adaptation were being reached, but the first woman justice in history joined the Court. Sandra Day O'Connor did not take her seat until October, after each of these cases had been decided. Her subsequent performance on the Court does not permit any retroactive guess about how she would have voted in either case. But a reading of the opinions suggests that one of them, at least, might have been written differently had its author known that a woman colleague would read it.[51]

Michael M. v. Superior Court of Sonoma County presented a situation familiar to prosecutors. A violent sex crime had occurred, but with evidence arguably insufficient to convict the defendant; therefore, he was indicted on a lesser charge, involving an illegal but consensual act. The trial transcript established a strong case that seventeen-year-old Michael was a forcible rapist. He and sixteen-year-old Sharon had intercourse only after he had struck her repeatedly. But rape is a crime where defendants and their lawyers often choose a jury trial, on the chance that their story might be believed. Presumably for this reason, Michael was charged not with rape but with "unlawful sexual intercourse," which under California law meant intercourse with any female, not the defendant's wife, under eighteen. This was the sort of statute that used to be called "statutory rape"; it is based on the premise that any female under a certain age is too young to give informed consent to sex. This "age of consent" has varied from as low as seven years to as high as eighteen.

Michael was convicted, but appealed on the grounds that the law violated equal protection by establishing a crime of which only males could be guilty and only females could be the victims. To withstand scrutiny, he insisted, the law would also have to punish females for having sex with young men. The Supreme Court disagreed. A six-member majority insisted that the law bore a substantial relationship to the important state purpose of discouraging teenage pregnancy. "We need not be medical doctors to discern that young men and young women are not similarly situated with respect to the problems and the risks of sexual intercourse. Only women may become pregnant and they suffer disproportionately the profound physical, emotional, and psychological consequences of sexual activity. The statute at issue here protects women from sexual intercourse at an age when these consequences are particularly severe."[52]

This opinion implies that, while sex role stereotypes will not suffice to save legislation, physical differences will—as long as public policies can be linked to them. (That reading of the *Craig* test, of course, might well save *Muller v. Oregon*.) There are, of course, hidden assumptions in the notion that girls must be "protected" from sexual intercourse; and, as Justice Stevens's rhetorical question put it, "Would a rational parent making rules for the conduct of twin children of the opposite sex simultaneously forbid the son and authorize the daughter to engage in conduct that is particularly harmful to the daughter?"[53] The most memorable opinion, however, was written by Justice Harry Blackmun. It was a concurrence that had the flavor of having started out as a dissent. The justice sarcastically questioned the sincerity of the Court's commitment to the prevention of teenage pregnancy by alluding to some recent opinions. Blackmun then went on to cite a long passage from the trial transcript, containing Sharon's description of Michael's actions.

> Sharon testified:
>
> We was laying there and we were kissing each other, and then . . . [he was] kissing me and we were laying on the bench. And he told me to take my pants off.
> **Q:** Did you have sexual intercourse with the defendant?
> **A:** Yeah.
> **Q:** He did put his penis into your vagina?
> **A:** Yes.
> **Q:** You said that he hit you?
> **A:** Yeah. He slugged me in the face. . . .
> **Q:** As a result of that, did you have any bruises or any kind of an injury?
> **A:** Yeah . . . I had bruises.
> **The Court:** Did he hit you one time or did he hit you more than once?
> **The Witness:** He hit me about two or three times.

Blackmun leads into the foregoing quotation with this statement:

> I think, too, that it is only fair, with respect to this particular petitioner, to point out that his partner, Sharon, appears not to have been an unwilling participant in at least the initial stages of the intimacies . . . Petitioner's and Sharon's nonacquaintance with each other before the incident; their drinking, their withdrawal from the others in the group; their foreplay, in which she willingly participated and seems to have encouraged; and the closeness of their ages . . . make this case an unattractive one to prosecute at all.[54]

Stereotypes may no longer suffice as a basis for legislation, but clearly they are alive and well in the Supreme Court. The emphasis on the girl's behavior rather than the boy's, the idea that kissing and drinking are preliminaries to sexual intercourse, and the implication that violence does not coerce women into having sex against their will combines some very old notions that have been discredited long since (see Chapter 7). This concurring opinion provides chilling insight into the views held by privileged, well-educated males—and, furthermore, a group of those elite white men who make policy.

The next case raised one of the most divisive issues of sexual equality: the military draft. Opponents of the Equal Rights Amendment have consistently argued that the ERA would subject women to conscription on the same basis as men. This conclusion is, in fact, difficult to dispute; but since the ERA remains un-ratified, that issue has never been before the Court. What *Rostker v. Goldberg* did force the justices to decide was whether a law requiring only males to register for a possible draft conformed to the due process clause.

Young American males had been subject to the draft from 1940, when the Military Selective Service Act anticipated our entry into World War II, until 1973, when American participation in the Vietnam conflict ended. There has been no draft since, and none exists now. But after Soviet troops invaded Afghanistan late in 1979, President Jimmy Carter asked Congress to reinstate the requirement for draft registration. Carter proposed that both men and women be registered. Congress's eventual law, however, authorized the president to require registration only for men. Since 1980, all American men must register for the draft when they reach the age of eighteen.

Several young men challenged this order, on the grounds that it unfairly discriminated against males. Three days before regis-tration was to begin, a district court granted the injunction. But the Supreme Court majority sided with the government. Justice Rehnquist found it unnecessary to reach any controversial issues of policy. His opinion reasoned as follows: Congress had vast powers over military affairs; Congress and the services barred women troops from combat; the constitutionality of this policy was not presently before the Court; the primary purpose of con-scription was to provide combat-ready troops; therefore, limiting registration to those eligible for combat satisfied the elevated scrutiny test of *Craig v. Boren*.[55]

Anti-ERA spokeswoman Phyllis Schlafly applauded this rul-ing as putting "the nails in the coffin of ERA," while NOW presi-dent Eleanor Smeal feared that *Goldberg* would be used "to perpetuate the myth that women are incapable of doing certain things." (In fact, one will search Rehnquist's opinion in vain for any myths, except perhaps the classic judicial profession of defer-ence to Congress.) A possible third position might be summarized crudely as "No ERA, no draft": as long as patriarchy withholds equal rights from women, perhaps it should hesitate to add to their obligations. This position was absent from public reactions to the decision. But then, none of the justices took this stance, either; it is difficult to imagine their doing so.[56]

The Rights of Unwed Fathers, If They Have Any

Six cases, decided over an eleven-year period, reveal intermediate scrutiny at its murkiest. These cases all involve claims of one kind or another made by fathers who are not married to their children's mothers. Several of these decisions find the Court badly split, and, taken together, they appear mutually contradictory.

The fathers' relationships with their children in all these cases were complex and contradictory. One father had abducted his children; another had lost custody of one child on grounds of neglect; the financial support they provided ranged from total to nil; and several had failed to take available steps, short of marrying the mothers, which would have legally validated their status as natural fathers.[57] Of course, similar contradictions are not unknown among married or divorced fathers. At any rate, the fact that these lawsuits were ever initiated at all shows that these men did depart from the stereotype of the selfish, uninvolved unwed father whose fertility exceeds his responsibility. And the individual cases themselves reveal the existence of bonds of genuine affection and concern. Still, the justices' unease with claims of parental affection outside the bonds of the traditional family has been evident.

A mother's rights, in general, exist whether or not she is married. If her children's father is her husband or ex-husband, she shares those rights with him; if she is single, the parental rights are hers alone. A single mother has custody unless she either relinquishes it or is proved unfit. She may give or withhold consent to adoption. She has the rights and duties that married parents have. A series of cases in the late 1960s and early 1970s removed several legal distinctions between wed and unwed mother–child relations, establishing, for instance, that the surviving children of unwed mothers could bring wrongful death suits and workers' compensation claims.[58] A father's rights, however, depend largely on whether he is or has been married to the child's mother. This generalization is still accurate, but more exceptions exist than was once true.

Stanley v. Illinois was decided four years before *Craig v. Boren*, but it illustrates the development of the Burger Court's "newer equal protection." The Court invalidated a state law which deprived all unwed fathers of any chance to become custodial parents. This decision did not give Peter Stanley custody; it simply meant that he had a right to a hearing. Two dissenters found the law a valid endorsement of traditional marriage and a recognition of real sex differences. "A state is justified in concluding, on the basis of common human experience, that the biological role of the mother in carrying and nursing an infant creates stronger bonds." Furthermore, the clause was not violated "when Illinois gives full recognition only to those father-child relationships that arise in the context of family units bound together by legal obligations."[59] More often than not, these principles have prevailed, and the unwed fathers have lost.

The five subsequent cases defy efforts to reconcile them with one another. The next case after *Stanley* upheld a section of the federal immigration law giving preferred status to prospective immigrants who are the children or parents of citizens or legal permanent residents against a complaint that it included unwed mothers and their children but not unwed fathers. The Court emphasized Congress's plenary power over immigration rather than fathers' rights.[60] A 1979 case found a sharply divided Court sustaining a state law allowing unwed mothers, but not unwed fathers, to sue for the wrongful death of their children.[61] The organizing principle appeared to be that custody was different from immigration, which was similar to wrongful death.

Three cases involved the right of an unwed father to veto the adoption of his children. In all three, the prospective adoptive parent was the children's stepfather. The final score was Stepfathers 2, Natural Fathers 1. All three cases involved some form of discrimination between unwed fathers and unwed mothers, who had an absolute right to veto an adoption. The crucial question appeared to be whether five justices found the natural father a sympathetic figure. And the judges' degree of empathy appeared to depend on how well the father's behavior conformed to patriarchal norms.

Quilloin v. Walcott, in 1978, unanimously upheld a Georgia court order granting custody of Leon Quilloin's son to Randall Walcott. A state law allowed an unwed father to legitimate his child by court petition. Leon Quilloin had never done this, but he had a relationship with his son; he visited, and provided some, admittedly irregular, support. The justices stressed Quilloin's failure to petition rather than the discrimination between unwed fathers and unwed mothers.[62] A majority of six followed this precedent in *Lehr v. Robertson* in 1983. Here, the stepfather won in the court below because the natural father had failed to register himself by postcard as a "putative father" with the New York State registry.[63] In neither case were the justices much disturbed by the possibility that the men had been ignorant of the available options.

Compared to these two rulings, the third case, chronologically in the middle, mystifies. *Caban v. Mohammed*, like *Lehr*, came from New York and involved a state court's application of the same law. Ironically, the victorious natural father emerges from the factual description as the least sympathetic of the three. Maria Mohammed and Abdiel Caban were the parents of two young children. They had lived together for several years, but eventually parted. In November 1975, Caban had gone to Puerto Rico to see the children, then living with their maternal grandmother. She "willingly surrendered the children to Caban with the understanding that they would be returned in a few days. Caban, however, returned to New York with the children. When Mrs. Mohammed learned that the children were in Caban's custody, she attempted to retrieve them with the aid of a police officer." Surely, this excerpt from Justice Lewis Powell's opinion is "Newspeak" worthy of George Orwell. Caban's act was not—in 1975, at least—kidnaping, when a parent did it, but it is usually called abduction. Maria then got custody of the children with her new husband, Kazim Mohammed. Kazim eventually filed for adoption. The Court split, five to four, as it had done on the wrongful death case it decided the same day. Here, however, the majority ruled in Abdiel's favor.

New York's denial of Caban's right to veto an adoption "does not bear a substantial relationship to the State's asserted interests." Justice Powell stressed Abdiel's quasi-marital behavior:

> The present case demonstrates that an unwed father may have a relationship with his children fully comparable to that of the mother. Appellant Caban, appellee Maria Mohammed, and their two children lived together as a family for several years. As members of this family, both mother and father participated in the care and support of their children. There is no reason to believe that the Caban chil-

dren—aged 4 and 6 at the time of the adoption proceedings—had a relationship with their mother unrivaled by the affection and concern of their father. We reject, therefore, the claim that the broad, gender-based distinction . . . is required by any universal difference between maternal and paternal relations at every phase of a child's development.[64]

Even the dissenters ignore the fact that Abdiel had abducted his children, an action which, surely, proves possessiveness rather than unselfish parental love. Justice Stevens's dissent dwells on a possible situation not at issue here: the mother who wishes to give her child up. All of these children, he wrote, " have an interest in acquiring the status of legitimacy; a great many of them have an interest in being adopted by parents who can give them opportunities that would otherwise be denied." Facilitating adoption allowed "the integration of the child into a satisfactory new home [meaning, apparently, a home with two parents married to each other] as soon as possible."[65] This statement fascinates, both for its collection of prejudices and for its irrelevance to the case at hand. The majority did not rule that all unmarried fathers must have an absolute, unconditional veto on all adoptions; it ruled, instead, that they had interests which the state must take into account. Stevens's repetition of the usual bromides about adoption, and his assumption that it serves the interests of the adopted children, also shows a skewed perspective. Whose interests are really being served by easy, unstressful adoption procedures—those of the children, or those of the adoptive parents?

In *Lehr*, three years later, the majority wrote similarly about the virtues of both marriage and adoption:

> The most effective protection of the putative father's opportunity to develop a relationship with his child is provided by the laws that authorize formal marriage and govern its consequences. . . . The legitimate state interests in facilitating the adoption of young children [by their stepfathers, with whom they already live?] and having the adoption proceeding completed expeditiously that underlie the entire statutory scheme also justify a trial judge's determination to require all interested parties to adhere precisely to the procedural requirements of the statute.

The justices also questioned Jonathan Lehr's commitment: "Appellant has never had any significant custodial, personal, or financial relationship with Jessica, and he did not seek to establish a legal tie until after she was two years old." (She was then two and a half.) But, as the dissenters pointed out, Lehr had visited the child and her mother, Lorraine Robertson, in the hospital after Jessica's birth; then, for some time afterward, Lorraine had concealed their whereabouts from him![66] The combined lesson of *Caban* and *Lehr* may be that custody battles are won either by abducting your children or by concealing them from their other parent.

The only consistent link among these three cases is the preference for fathers who act as though they are married to the children's mothers, who conform to patriarchal norms, even when they act them out violently, as Abdiel Caban did. This preference for arrangements that emulate the traditional middle-class family ignores the lives lived by many Americans. Census figures for 1980 estimated that 342,807 unmarried men and women live together with one or more children under age fifteen. This kind of living arrangement is especially common in certain ethnic subcultures; for example, over one third of these Americans are black. The idea that marriage is the ideal family arrangement is a norm associated with the white middle class.[67]

People have children outside marriage, maintain relationships with children with whom they do not live, and frequently separate their relationships with children from their relationships with the co-parents of those children. These life patterns may or may not be ideal, but they are common, and they emerge from court records as genuine, loving relationships. The justices in the majorities in these cases show themselves limited by the assumptions of their own subcultures. Some parents simply never marry each other. Even those who do are increasingly likely to divorce—and postdivorce fatherhood is characterized by behaviors as diverse and ambivalent as those of Quilloin, Caban, and Lehr (see Chapter 4). Yet divorced fathers retain vetoes over adoption, by stepfathers or anyone else.

The opinions echo a popular cliché of the 1960s to the effect that the most important thing a father can do for his children is love their mother. But in the society of the 1970s and 1980s, parent-child relationships became increasingly separate from and independent of relationships between those parents. A child's tie to either parent need not depend on the tie between parents. The Court is, perhaps willfully, out of touch with a large piece of reality. Furthermore, its collective distrust of unwed fathers allows the states to reinforce the kind of behavior the Court dislikes. If a man can lose his child whenever the child's mother decides to remarry, why *not* walk away? The doctrine is questionable both as constitutional interpretation and as public policy. As we shall see, it keeps uneasy peace with emerging doctrines of reproductive rights. But perhaps most strikingly, the cases on unwed fathers' rights show two difficulties with intermediate scrutiny. Not only does it permit results of dubious consistency, but "substantial relationships" and "important purposes" are hard to separate from the assumptions of society's dominant groups. Whose purposes are important, after all?

When Is Discrimination Not Discrimination?

The cases examined so far, from *West Coast Hotel* to *Lehr*, have all dealt with instances of direct gender discrimination. The language of all these laws provided that at least some women would be treated differently from at least some men. But what about a law whose language is gender-neutral and whose impact on one sex is greater than on the other? A regulation providing that all police officers must be at least five feet four inches tall, for example, would exclude more women than men.[68] Cases of indirect discrimination have their counterpart, as the reader might anticipate, in the area of race. The courts, of course, have not treated race and sex classifications alike in general. Race is a suspect category, while gender gets intermediate scrutiny. But courts assess the constitutionality of superficially neutral laws which impact disproportionately on one sex exactly the same as they treat the racial counterparts of these laws—and the doctrine is not friendly to either racial or sexual equality.[69]

Two Burger Court rulings dealt with the racial issue. *Washington v. Davis* upheld regulations requiring police recruits in Washington, D.C., to pass a verbal aptitude test even though four times as many blacks failed the test as did whites.[70] *Arlington Heights v. Metropolitan Housing Development Corporation* rebuffed a claim that the Chicago suburb's zoning policy discouraging multifamily dwellings unconstitutionally kept lower-income black families out.[71] Reversing lower courts, both cases insisted that the equal protection clause forbade intentional discrimination only. Since the Court found that no racial discrimination existed, the policies received only lower-tier scrutiny, which they easily survived.[72] The same nine justices who had heard *Davis* and *Arlington Heights* got *Personnel Administrator v. Feeney* in 1979. The superficially neutral law here challenged was a provision for veterans' preference in civil service jobs. The national government and all but a few states had such a rule. The state of Massachusetts, Helen Feeney's employer for most of her working life, had an "absolute lifetime preference": any veteran who passed the relevant Civil Service test could bump any nonveteran on the eligibility list. This rule applied equally to male and female veterans; however, 98 percent of veterans living in Massachusetts were male. This statistic was almost a mirror image of an Armed Forces rule which remained in effect until 1967: no more than 2 percent of its members could be women. Even with this rule, the state had at least some management-level jobs open to women through the merit system. Feeney, the age of many World War II veterans, held several of these until 1975, when her position was abolished. She took several examinations, placing high on the list each time, but she was consistently bumped by veterans. No nonclerical state job seemed open to her any longer.

Seven justices found no intentional discrimination. Following the line of the two racial cases, Stewart insisted that "the distinction made by [the law] is, as it seems to be, quite simply between veterans and nonveterans, not between men and women."[73] He had no trouble defending the law as a reasonable method of rewarding patriotism and attracting responsible employees to government work. Only Justices Marshall and Brennan dissented. Although they had also been a minority of two in *Davis*, they did not reiterate their attack on indirect discrimination. Instead, they found "purposeful gender based discrimination" because "this consequence [the virtual exclusion of women] followed foreseeably, indeed inexorably, from the long history of policies severely limiting women's participation in the military." They mentioned a fact the majority had ignored: until 1971, the regulations had exempted from veterans' preference any job "especially calling for women," namely, low-ranked clerical jobs.[74] They might also have mentioned—though they did not—the fact that the state's law had last been amended during World War II, soon after which gender discrimination in employment became acceptable social policy. The two sides approached the rule from different angles. The majority scrutinized the preference in isolation from the rest of state civil service law and federal military policy. The dissenters chose to read the statute in a way that might have brought praise from a predecessor, one who had once been Brennan's law professor. However Felix Frankfurter would have voted in *Feeney*, he had once written: "Frequently the sense of a word cannot be got except by fashioning a mosaic of significance out of the innuendos of disjointed bits of statute . . . parts together."[75]

The difficulties with this reliance on the intent of a law are the same as the problems attending the notion that "original intention" should dictate constitutional interpretation.[76] The most troubling problem is that it is impossible to determine, with any degree of certainty, what the intent of a law is. Not all legislators will announce their intent; some may be less than completely candid; and the notion of a collective intent shared by a group or groups of lawmakers raises a host of analytical problems.[77] Any intention that does exist will become increasingly elusive the farther away one gets from the original lawmaking body—and while 1943 is closer than 1789 or 1868, it is at enough remove from 1979 to give the thoughtful jurist pause. In addition, the Fourteenth Amendment does not protect people from the ill will of those who seek to hurt them; it guarantees due process and equal protection, which are rights, not motives. If a law treats women worse than men, or blacks worse than whites, it is not clear why the absence of intention obviates the denial of equality. It is clear, however, that states which have been told that they can do anything as long as they do not *mean* to discriminate will see to it that no discriminatory purpose is ever again expressed in public.[78] There is a more fundamental problem: racism and sexism are so pervasive in American society that it is hardly necessary for anyone to formulate racist or sexist ideas in order to reinforce these social patterns. They reinforce themselves. The crucial norms of a culture are, after all, not those which are discussed: they are those presumptions so entrenched that they need *never* be discussed.

Beyond the issue of indirect discrimination, *Feeney* raises questions which need scrutiny. What is veterans' preference? It is a policy which rewards people who undertake a difficult, uncomfortable, and often unpleasant task which puts them at some physical risk and which is, presumably at least, useful to society. Surely, such public policies have much to recommend them. This particular task, military service, is one performed mostly by men. Is there any risky, somewhat difficult and unpleasant, and socially useful task performed by women? Yes; childbearing. Are women ever rewarded for it by policies like employment preferences? No.

"Mothers' preference" seems, to this author, no more defensible than veterans' preference. Proposing such a policy is not the point of this discussion. What is worthy of notice is that society chooses to reward those who perform tasks associated with conventional male roles, not conventional female roles. That fact, surely, deserves attention when we assess a statute's purpose.

Separate but Equal

"Jim Crow," or de jure racial segregation, was the crucial instrument of white supremacy in the post-Reconstruction South. Separate black and white schools, public accommodations, and transportation marked black citizens as unworthy to associate with whites. It took the Supreme Court until 1954 to recognize, in the landmark case of *Brown v. Board of Education*, that "separate schools are inherently unequal."[79] This decision ending school segregation stimulated the rise of the civil rights movement, which brought about more rulings and federal laws dismantling the whole Jim Crow system. The presence in the Deep South of black mayors, legislators, and other public officials as well as the emergence nationwide of Jesse Jackson as a strong presidential candidate testify to the limited but dramatic changes in American society in less than half a century. "Separate but equal" is no more.

Sexual segregation has existed, too. In public restrooms, of course, it is unexceptionable, but male-only private clubs and sex-segregated public schools raise troubling questions. Sex-segregated education will be treated more fully in Chapter 6, but the Burger Court's one ruling on this issue needs discussion here. In 1884, the Mississippi Industrial Institute and College for the Education of White Girls opened its doors. The oldest all-female public college in the country, its name had been changed to Mississippi University for Women (MUW), reflecting a federally mandated change in its admissions policy. In 1982, by a vote of five to four, the Supreme Court ordered a second policy change. Joe Hogan challenged MUW's refusal to enroll him for credit in its nursing school. The majority, speaking through Justice O'Connor, declared:

> Rather than compensate for discriminatory barriers faced by women [the state's alleged purpose], MUW's policy of excluding males from admission to the School of Nursing tends to perpetuate the stereotyped view of nursing as an exclusively women's job. . . .

> The policy is invalid also because it fails the second part of the equal protection test, for the State has made no showing that the gender-based classification is substantially and directly related to its proposed compensatory objective. To the contrary, MUW's policy of admitting men to attend classes as auditors fatally undermines its claim that women . . . are adversely affected by the presence of men.[80]

Mississippi University for Women v. Hogan was O'Connor's first majority opinion; it represented the one policy area in which she has consistently parted from the justices with whom she usually agrees, the conservative bloc consisting, at that time, of Burger, Rehnquist, and Powell. Both majority and minority stressed the limited application of this holding; it covered only a state-supported nursing school, and did not invalidate all public single-sex education. A school that could make a more convincing case for itself as a bastion of feminism might survive. So far, no apposite case has been decided by the justices.

The Constitutional Mini-Revolution

Neither the history nor the text of the equal protection clause provides judges with any clear clues as to how to apply the guarantee to cases involving women. The paramount concern of the authors of the three Civil War amendments was the status of the former slaves, but recognizing that historical fact does not compel the interpreter to limit the amendments' scope to laws affecting blacks. The legislative history of the Fourteenth Amendment contains neither any suggestion that the framers meant it to apply to sex discrimination, nor any clear statement that sex discrimination lies outside the scope of the guarantee. The language of Section 1 of the amendment is quite broad, if not lavish. There is no mention there of race or any other kind of classification, and only the most general specification of categories of rights. This inclusive language gains significance when we compare it to its two companion amendments. The Thirteenth Amendment mentions only one interest—slavery or involuntary servitude—while the Fifteenth confines itself to one right, voting, and one set of classifications, racial. These differences in wording suggest, though they hardly prove, that the choices of broad or narrow language were deliberate. But assertions that the scope of Section 1 need not be confined to race alone do not settle questions about what specific areas are covered and what standards are appropriate.

The Supreme Court has chosen to fashion a compromise between the minimal scrutiny of cases like *Goesaert* and *Hoyt* and the well-entrenched judicial hostility to racial classifications. The justices have found no mandate in the amendment's text or history to recognize women's rights. Some opinions have indicated a reluctance to accord sexual equality the same status as racial equality in the absence of a clear public preference for such a choice, a preference which might have been indicated by ratification of the Equal Rights Amendment, and the opposite of which may have been evinced by the failure to ratify the ERA.[81]

Although a majority of the Court has refused to conclude that sex discrimination, like its racial counterpart, is inherently suspect, there are two types of cases where the justices have treated gender-based classifications exactly as they have racial classifications. Both of these choices have severely limited the usefulness of constitutional adjudication as a means of improving the status of women. First, as the *Davis* and *Feeney* cases show, the Court has insisted that any discrimination has to be intentional if it is to be unconstitutional. This choice implies that the Fourteenth Amendment does not basically prevent people from being treated in certain ways; it prevents government from acting with certain purposes. As a result, laws which adversely affect either blacks or women will stand unless someone can prove that the state meant to discriminate in this fashion.

Secondly, the Court has chosen to speak in curiously circumscribed terms. Decisions refer not to "white supremacy," "racism," "patriarchy," or "sexism" but to the more neutral concepts of "classification" and "discrimination." Embodied in these choices of words is an assumption (sometimes made explicit) that policies which impose inferior treatment on a dominant group, whites or males, are "just as bad as" policies which disadvantage the out-group—even though the test used for sex discrimination is different from that used for race discrimination. This evenhandedness does not appear to have been the assumption of the legislators who enacted the Freedman's Bureau Bill for the stated purpose of benefiting blacks, an obviously discriminatory purpose. Nor is such neutrality dictated by the constitutional language. And yet the justices have adopted the premise that the amendment is aimed, not at laws which oppress, but at laws which make certain classifications.[82]

This premise is embodied in decisions which assess instances
of "reverse discrimination," policies that discriminate in favor of
disadvantaged groups. Cases like *Hogan* and *Orr* show a growing
mistrust of this sort of rationale. The last sex discrimination cases
to uphold such policies involved Social Security regulations
which are no longer in effect.[83] "Reverse discrimination" for
women seems no more acceptable to the Court than its counterpart for racial minorities in the absence of demonstrated past
discrimination against them. One possible reason for this hesitation, of course, is the fact that the cases brought to the Court are
those, like *Orr* and *Hogan*, where the supposedly compensatory
discrimination seems inextricably linked with presumptions of
women's dependency or inferiority. But there is one famous case
involving reverse racial discrimination which suggests a deeper
reason: the justices' unease with the kinds of distinctions such
cases force them to make.

University of California v. Bakke struck down a medical school
admissions quota that reserved a certain number of places in
each entering class for members of racial minorities. In his plurality opinion, Justice Powell rejected the argument that discrimination in favor of a "minority" group ought to be given less rigid
scrutiny than discrimination favoring the "majority." The problem, Powell insisted, was that "the concepts of 'majority' and
'minority' necessarily reflect temporary arrangements and political judgments. . . . There is no principled basis for deciding
which groups would merit heightened judicial solicitude and
which would not."[84] Powell does not search very hard for a principled basis—if we confine the cases to race or sex, he would
hardly have to—nor does he explain why deciding who is a "majority" and who a "minority" is more difficult than, say, deciding
whether a law meets the *Craig* test. But the justices are more
comfortable discussing discrimination and classification than
majority and minority. Powell's opinion deals similarly with concepts like "stigmatization" and "inferiority"; he finds them meaningless, though many jurists and social scientists have not.[85] The
gender cases underscore what *Bakke* made explicit: the courts
will ask not whom a law hurts, but on what basis it classifies. The
justices will not even touch the question of what is an in-group,
and what an out-group.

The import of this judicial choice is thrown into sharp relief
when we notice that *Kirchberg v. Feenstra*, decided in 1981, was
the last constitutional case involving sex discrimination in which

the successful plaintiff was a woman. All the more recent cases have benefited, or failed to benefit, men. Whatever else this fact means, it seems to warn that we must look to sources other than the Constitution for the roots of patriarchal policy. Men, not women, have been the beneficiaries of the new doctrine. Taken as a whole, these cases support Nora Ephron's comment that "the major concrete achievement of the women's movement in the 1970s was the Dutch treat."[86]

If we reexamine the cases, this metaphor emerges as only partly adequate. Who actually benefited, or failed to benefit, from these rulings? Successful plaintiffs include men whose victories seem worth rather less than the Dutch treat, like the Oklahoma teenagers who may drink 3.2 percent beer and the Mississippian who may now train for a notoriously underrewarded and over-stressed profession.[87] But there was also a man who reneged on a court-ordered alimony payment (William Orr), and a man who abducted his children (Abdiel Caban). The most notorious of the unsuccessful plaintiffs is young Michael, the rapist. The polar opposites of Michael are such men as Leon Quilloin and Jonathan Lehr. Responsible fathers within the limitations of milieu and resources, they fell victim to gaps of generation, class, and culture between them and appellate court judges. One case, *Rostker v. Goldberg*, can be interpreted as a refusal to impose upon women one particular variety of Dutch treat, but that ruling was a mixed message indeed. *MUW v. Hogan*, however, may ultimately prove to be a victory for women. The entry of more men into the nursing profession may upgrade its status, as has been true for social workers and librarians.

It is a truism that courts often forge landmarks of liberty in cases involving people who are far from heroic figures. However true that generalization is in other areas of law, it is hard to see how the victories of Orr and Caban, or *any* possible outcome in *Michael M.*, furthers the cause of women's rights. From *Reed v. Reed* to *Kirchberg v. Feenstra*, it took only ten years for women litigants to exhaust the potential constitutional change possible through adjudication. For now, adjudication is a strategy most useful, though hardly a sure bet, for men who object to sex discrimination. The doctrines forged by the Court have become the tools of the favored, not the disfavored, group. But then, as the "Dutch treat" metaphor indicates, so has the social change that the feminist movement has brought about.

Is it really surprising that men were quick to notice that

women's arguments for equality could be used against those customs which, ostensibly at least, favor women? Men, after all, have at least as much initiative as women do. They can stop paying for their companions' meals, and they can file lawsuits as easily as women can (probably more easily, since they tend to have more money). But once men have laid down their special burdens, they have difficulty defending their (far greater and more powerful) special privileges. And let us remember, women's privileges, like being their dates' dinner guests, often did carry the unstated presumption that they imposed various social burdens which might euphemistically be termed reciprocal obligations. A woman who pays for her own meal is free of such burdens. "Dutch treat" may not be a bad metaphor for equal protection doctrine, after all.

This doctrine, as developed by the Burger Court, is a construct of social customs which lend themselves especially well to manipulation by any group, dominant or subject. Decisions that speak in the evenhanded terms of "classification" and "discrimination," rather than "domination," "stigmatization," "superior" or "inferior," encourage people to view themselves not as members of advantaged or disadvantaged groups, but as individuals subject to the effects of neutral policy. Over the years, the Court—probably without meaning to—has developed doctrines which foster litigation, not by targets of legalized oppression, but by victims of classification. This phenomenon has its racial analogy: after all, the successful plaintiff in *Bakke* was white.

The Equal Rights Amendment

Judicial interpretation is not the only means of constitutional change. Article V of the Constitution establishes several amending processes, only one of which has been used with any frequency. An amendment may be proposed by a two-thirds vote of both houses of Congress and ratified by three-fourths of the state legislatures (it takes both houses, except in unicameral Nebraska, to ratify). Congress may or may not, as it chooses, establish a time limit for ratification. The ultimately unsuccessful struggle to amend the Constitution to establish equal rights for women took almost sixty years, and is a classic study of the limits of the amending process and American society's lack of commitment to sexual equality. Several years after the expiration of the ratification deadline, the dust may have cleared. The defeat of the ERA is a subject about which reasoned reflection, rather than emotional counteraccusations, may now be possible.

The fate of the ERA, and of American women, is best explained through an analogy. In 1964, the incumbent president, Lyndon Johnson, was reelected by what then seemed a landslide over his Republican opponent, Barry Goldwater, who then seemed an extreme conservative. Neither of these men had much influence on the ERA. But a venerable political joke concerns a Goldwater supporter reflecting in 1968, in a time of unprecedented political turmoil. "Four years ago, everyone told me that if I voted for Barry, we'd have war, crime, riots, and inflation. Well, they were right! I voted for Barry and, sure enough, for four years we've had nothing *but* war, crime, riots, and inflation." For years, opponents of the ERA based their stance on a commitment to women's traditional role as wife and mother. Activists like Phyllis Schlafly accused ERA supporters of rejecting family, child rearing, and wifehood in favor of lifestyles patterned after those of male professionals. The ERA, opponents warned, would lead to increased hardships for wives and mothers: the breakdown of the family, the failure of husbands to provide financial support, and hostility in the workplace to women's special needs. Well, developments of the last decade have proved Schlafly correct, haven't they? One supported the ERA, and . . . the divorce rate has risen dramatically, poverty has become a condition shared mainly by women and their children, and working mothers are burdened by scarce and inadequate child care. What is missing, in both anecdotes, is that vital causal connection. The ERA was not ratified. And—or perhaps "but?"—many women's lives have worsened.

But we are getting ahead of our story. It did not take long after the Nineteenth Amendment was ratified in 1920 for some feminists to realize that the vote was not enough to make women truly equal with men. Alice Paul, a leader of the National Women's Party, drafted a prospective constitutional amendment. Its final version read:

1. Equality of rights under the law shall not be denied or abridged by the United States or by any state on account of sex.
2. The Congress shall have the power to enforce, by appropriate legislation, the provisions of this article.

3. This amendment shall take effect two years after the date of ratification.

Initially, the proposed amendment attracted little support. It was identified with "extreme" feminist views. The first group to announce its support was the National Women's Party, which had supported suffrage but opposed protective legislation. Most suffragists followed the lead of the National Consumers' League, the most powerful advocate of protective legislation. They opposed the ERA because they correctly assumed that it would endanger these laws—even though it had become clear that the effects of special legislation were as restrictive as they were protective. During the 1930s, the ERA gained the support of groups like the National Federation of Women Lawyers and the National Federation of Business and Professional Women. Whether or not the common identification of feminism with well-educated, middle-class women is accurate, it is true that, in the early years, supporters of the ERA were almost exclusively these women. By 1944, however, the platforms of both major parties supported the amendment.[88]

Although the ERA was first introduced in Congress in 1923, and again at every subsequent session, it got nowhere for almost thirty years. The Senate did pass it in 1950 and 1953, but added a rider which would have effectively nullified it. This "Hayden rider," named for its sponsor, Carl Hayden of Arizona, provided that the ERA "shall not be construed to impair any rights, benefits, or exemptions now or hereafter conferred by law, upon persons of the female sex." Two years after *Goesaert v. Cleary*, people still worried about the loss of special protection. By now, the principal opponent of the ERA was organized labor, a predominantly male interest group.[89]

By the 1960s, protective labor legislation did not seem as important as it once had. Women workers were becoming more aware of the restrictive potential of these laws, and they benefited more from unionization and collective bargaining agreements. At least one eminent former suffragist and longtime opponent of the ERA was still active and able to rethink her views. Shortly before her death in 1962, Eleanor Roosevelt, FDR's widow, said, "Many of us opposed the amendment because we felt it would do away with protection in the labor field. Now with unionization, there is no reason why you shouldn't have it if you want it."[90]

Some historians believe that President John F. Kennedy was

trying to neutralize support for the ERA when he appointed a blue-ribbon Commission on the Status of Women and named Mrs. Roosevelt as its chair.[91] The Commission's report, issued in 1963, is often regarded, along with Betty Friedan's book, as the major impetus for the modern feminist movement. In fact, if Kennedy had been trying to head off the ERA, he succeeded beyond his wildest dreams, at least for his lifetime.

Not only did the Commission's report oppose the amendment, but it produced a document that was profoundly reactionary. Although the Commission supported better education and job opportunities for women, the report gave priority at every point to family obligations, which were taken throughout as "givens." For example, the committee on education declared, "Expanding career opportunities should not displace traditional responsibilities of women in the home and in the local community." And the Commission's core report assured the American woman that "during her intensive homemaking years, she should be encouraged to prepare for at least three decades for life after 40 when she will be relatively free to use her abilities and will wish to use them as constructively and as interestingly as possible."[92] (Did this statement mean that women under forty are *not* free? If not, what are they?) The Commission report never admitted the possibility of a conflict between these intensive duties and sexual equality. But the ERA did not stay derailed for long. Title VII of the Civil Rights Act of 1964 prohibited sex discrimination in employment. In 1969, federal courts began ruling that "protective" policies which kept women out of competition for jobs (for example, a ban on night work when a job required it) violated this law. Within five years, the laws which had for so long been the stumbling block to the ERA had been rendered dead letter.[93] In 1972, both houses of Congress passed the amendment by large majorities.

Thirty-eight states (three-fourths of fifty) are required for ratification. Fifteen states ratified within a month after Congress sent the amendment to the states; fifteen more, within a year. Then things slowed down. By the original seven-year deadline set by Congress—March 22, 1979—only thirty-five states had ratified. In 1978, Congress extended the deadline to June 30, 1982. On that date, however, the time limit expired; the ERA was still three states short.[94]

The decade when the ERA was a national issue, and the eventual outcome, provided ample opportunities for feminist-bashing. Most observers assumed that the ERA's supporters were responsible for its failure. Were they extremist, "anti-male"? Certainly, there are feminists who have taken positions which can accurately be described in these terms, but they were never prominent in the fight for the ERA—though the media gave them lots of coverage. Other critics suggested that the problem was not the substance of the pro-ERA message but its style: the so-called stridency of many supporters. It is true that mistakes were made in the heat of battle, and that the style of some supporters did seem to alienate some people. But when ERA opponents used phrases like "brainless, bra-less broads" to describe proponents, who was going overboard, and why did this behavior not seem to antagonize people as much as did a supporter's raising her voice?[95]

The political scientist Andrew Hacker had a different explanation. In a widely circulated essay, he suggested that the battle over the ERA was a essentially a contest among women: "few men cared much either way." The fatal defect of the pro-ERA movement was, Hacker argued, a "lack of concern for the housewife."[96] According to this explanation, full-time homemakers feared that the ERA would deprive them of benefits like spousal support. (As Chapter 4 will make abundantly clear, housewives enjoy spousal support only as long as their husbands choose to provide it. That reality, however, went largely unremarked during this controversy.)

At first blush, this explanation seems plausible. The controversy *looked* like a battle among women: careerists for the ERA and homemakers against it. Those were the respective public images of the two most prominent spokeswomen, Eleanor Smeal, president of the National Organization for Women, and Phyllis Schlafly of Stop-ERA. In many ways, the two sides were similar to the two sides of the controversy over reproductive choice brilliantly analyzed by the sociologist Kristin Luker. In *Abortion and the Politics of Motherhood*, Luker studied pro-choice and anti-choice activists. The former, she found, were women who had professional careers and few or no children; these women felt that reproductive choice was essential to their continued freedom. The anti-choice activists were women with less education and larger families who tended not to work outside the home and identified themselves as housewives. The abortion controversy was, therefore, essentially a conflict over two contradictory views of women's role, over tradition versus change.[97] Might not this analysis also apply to the ERA?

Not very closely. Whatever is true of the abortion issue—and Luker's analysis does ignore the role of male-dominated institutions like the Roman Catholic hierarchy—the division over the ERA was not as clear as Hacker thought. The deficiencies in Hacker's model are suggested by the fact that Smeal, before assuming the NOW presidency, was a full-time homemaker, while Schlafly, by the time the ERA battle was over, was a lawyer. While it is true that virtually all women professionals supported the ERA, housewives were by no means united in opposition. Several mass-circulation publications targeted primarily at homemakers supported the ERA. The same feminists who were the prime movers of the ERA, or their successors, have been the authors of programs to aid housewives, such as "displaced homemakers'" bills and protection of pension benefits for widows and divorcées. (Schlafly, by the way, has never supported such legislation; her most prominent public statement since 1982 has been to blame sexual harassment on women victims.) The defects in the explanation of the ERA controversy as a conflict among women go deeper still. The observation that "women killed the ERA" became a cliché. It can be accurate only if we adopt a model of how representative government works which no responsible analyst accepts: the notion that legislative bodies mirror the opinions of their constituents, that the people need only ask, and the legislature will grant. In fact, public support for the ERA between 1972 and 1982 never dropped below 50 percent and rose as high as 63 percent.[98] These poll data indicate a certain discontinuity between what people want and what representatives do—but that finding will not surprise anyone who has taken an introductory course in American government. We know that legislative outcomes depend at least as much on compromises within the legislature as on pressures outside it. And in the case of the ERA, in several states it was these internal factors which were decisive.[99]

The proximate cause of the defeat of the ERA was that not enough legislators in enough states voted for it. The majority of state legislators are male, so it is impossible to relieve men of responsibility for the outcome. The question which must be asked is: What feature of the negative input that lawmakers received made it more persuasive than the positive input? (Legislators are well aware that their mail does not necessarily represent their constituents' majority views; they do know about public opinion polls.) Might it be that, for enough male legislators, Stop-ERA's message was reassuring while NOW's was threatening? The opposition was telling the lawmakers, after all, that most women really do not want change; that they are happy doing the home maintenance work without which men could not function; that it is only a few neurotic malcontents who are complaining. Such a message could be just what a man who has succeeded far enough to hold a public office wanted to hear.

All of the foregoing, however interesting or plausible, is pure speculation. The process of amending the Constitution, however, is fact, not theory. It is a fact that an amendment, once proposed by Congress, must be approved by at least thirty-eight state legislatures, all but one of which have two houses. Therefore, it takes at least seventy-five lawmaking bodies to ratify any constitutional amendment. On the other hand, defeating an amendment requires only that one house in any of thirteen states either reject the amendment or just not vote on it at all. It is always easier, therefore, to defeat an amendment than to get one ratified. The process militates against ratification. Presumably, that was what the Constitution's framers, who devoted much attention to thwarting popular majorities, intended.

The ERA was defeated by a minority. Most American state legislators supported it. However appealing the opponents' arguments might be in theory, they can have convinced relatively few lawmakers in practice. That was all the opponents had to do. That is how the amending process works. It is instructive to look at the unratifying states. Fifteen legislatures, all bicameral, failed to ratify the ERA: Alabama, Arizona, Arkansas, Florida, Georgia, Illinois, Louisiana, Mississippi, Missouri, Nevada, North Carolina, Oklahoma, South Carolina, Utah, and Virginia. A map shows that these are *contiguous* states forming an unbroken block. Most are Southern states. Of the exceptions, Utah is dominated by the Mormon church, a patriarchal religious group which spent at least fifty million dollars to defeat the amendment. The two Southwestern states also have a heavy Mormon influence. The last state, Illinois, has a constitutional provision which requires a three-fifths vote of each house to ratify a federal constitutional amendment. The ERA consistently got simple majorities in that state.[100]

The lesson which emerges from these facts is that state legislatures are not microcosms of Congress, and that the United

States remains a diverse, varied society. No nationwide consensus on the role of women in society appears to exist. If the feminists made any fatal error, it was their failure, in 1972, to appreciate the implications of this fact, and, in the ensuing decade, to present the ERA in a way that would play as well in Richmond, Raleigh, and Atlanta as it did in Washington, Albany, and St. Paul. And this achievement may never have been possible.

How significant was the defeat of the ERA? Politically, it never helps a cause to lose a fight. But it was often pointed out that winning this particular fight might not have helped much, either. Ironically, the ERA could not have brought about the radical changes which opponents so feared. The amendment would not have enforced itself. It would have been interpreted by a Supreme Court that was growing more reluctant every year to expand individual rights. But ratification would have been followed by a two-year period in which Congress and the states would have had ample opportunity to examine allegedly sexist laws and to revise them. And whatever appears to be true, constitutional interpretation is not the sole province of the Court. State judges, in particular, also interpret the Constitution, and they have by no means slavishly followed the lead of Warren Burger and William Rehnquist.

Now that the postmortem feminist-bashing appears to have died down, it is clear that the ERA's defeat did not destroy or devastate the feminist movement. In Jane Mansbridge's words, "The political death of the ERA has in fact corresponded with a flowering in feminist thought."[101] Part of that flowering has been a growing controversy over the desirability of gender-neutral policy, as represented in both the language of the ERA and the constitutional doctrine of the Supreme Court. Later chapters will take up this theme in more detail. For now, it is enough to say that some feminists are beginning to question whether this approach might partake of what the anthropologist Jules Henry, in another context, has called "pathological evenhandedness."[102]

Conclusion

There are at least two ways to change the Constitution: through the amending process, and through judicial interpretation. The first method has been tried twice with respect to women's rights: once successfully, with the Nineteenth Amendment, and once unsuccessfully, with the ERA. The second method is an ongoing process that has been occurring at least since the adoption of the Fourteenth Amendment. The time period with which this book is concerned has seen significant developments in both amending and interpreting. In both cases, a long period of stasis was followed by several years of active change. Little happened until about 1970. Then, at about the same time the ERA became a viable issue, the Supreme Court began changing its doctrine.

Each process influenced the other. Participants in the ERA controversy pondered the relationship of the amendment to the new rulings, while at times judges indicated wariness to expand individual rights in the absence of a clear national consensus. The two developments peaked at about the same time. The battle over the ERA ended in 1982; the Court issued its last decision implementing its intermediate standard two years later.

The cumulative effects of the changes, and refusals to change, echo a phrase from an opinion written early in this century by one of America's greatest jurists. Learned Hand, of the United States Court of Appeals, was not writing here about sexual equality; he was writing about censorship. Still, his words resonate for this issue in this time and place. "Shall not the word 'obscene' be allowed to indicate *the present critical point* between candor and shame *at which the community may have arrived at here and now*"?[103] Current Supreme Court doctrine on women's rights often seems to be searching for the critical point between patriarchy and equality at which the community has arrived. And yet that was not the attitude decisions have taken, since 1954, toward racial equality; nor is it the standard which prevails in cases involving protected rights. *Brown* and *Carolene Products* have set the guidelines. But in women's rights, judges seem to find it necessary not to be too far ahead of society.

Yet social norms have changed since the 1930s, and so has doctrine. *Goesaert* and *Hoyt* no longer stand as binding precedent. The Court will not base a ruling on traditional views about gender roles, even though cases like *Michael M.* and *Lehr v. Robertson* suggest a judicial weakness for generalizations related to differences in reproductive function, and certain views about social roles derivable from those functions. It is all right to punish only men for sex with juveniles because only girls get pregnant, and it is all right to sever relations between children and their fathers because the mother-child bond is greater. The stumbling block seems to be women's traditional family role. The cases, like the history of the ERA, hint at a question which will recur throughout this book: To what extent is that role compatible with "equality of rights"?

REFERENCES

Babcock, Barbara et al., eds. *Sex Discrimination and the Law: Cases and Remedies*. New York: Little, Brown, 1975. The most comprehensive casebook on women and the law.

Baer, Judith A. *Equality Under the Constitution: Reclaiming the Fourteenth Amendment*. Ithaca, N.Y.: Cornell University Press, 1983. Chapters 1 and 5 analyze the present state of equal protection doctrine.

Berry, Mary F. *Why ERA Failed*. Bloomington: Indiana University Press, 1986. One of three indispensable analyses of the fate of the ERA.

Boles, Janet K. *The Politics of the Equal Rights Amendment*. New York: Longman, 1979. With Berry (see above) and Mansbridge (see below), one of the best books on the ERA. The author, a political scientist, describes her purpose in her title. An early but still valuable work.

Goldstein, Leslie Friedman, ed. *The Constitutional Rights of Women*. 2d rev. ed. Madison: University of Wisconsin Press, 1988. A casebook designed for undergraduates.

Harrison, Cynthia E. *On Account of Sex: The Politics of Women's Issues, 1945–1968*. Berkeley: University of California Press, 1988. A thorough treatment of the years between World War II and the rise of contemporary feminism. This book's treatment of the 1963 Commission on the Status of Women is particularly helpful.

Mansbridge, Jane J. *Why We Lost the ERA*. Chicago: University of Chicago Press, 1986. The third important work on the ERA, a later analysis than Boles's by another political scientist. Makes good use of polling data.

Rupp, Leila J., and **Verta Taylor.** *Survival in the Doldrums: The American Women's Rights Movement, 1945 to the 1960s*. New York: Oxford University Press, 1987. An informative history of what feminists were doing at the height of the feminine mystique.

3

Women and Employment

The fact that this book has separate chapters on employment and family life is itself a sign of the drastic changes in American society in modern times. In the eighteenth century, and well into the nineteenth, separating work and family would not have been necessary in discussing either men or women. For much of its history, the United States was an agrarian society, one in which most people engaged in agriculture. For farmers, work and home are joined. Even those who did not grow crops or raise livestock themselves, but were engaged in occupations supportive to farming—the blacksmith, for example—worked in small shops, frequently with family members. The Industrial Revolution of the nineteenth century changed all that, first for men, but ultimately for women, too. Domestic work and gainful employment became separate; the former remained located within the home (which is what "domestic" means) while the latter was relocated outside it. One result of this powerful social change was that the great majority of middle-class women were excluded from gainful employment. Men earned money; women stayed home.

It is only since 1978 that as many American women have been in the labor force as were not employed outside the home.[1] An interesting semantic change, sometime during the years since the Industrial Revolution, applied the term "working women" to women in the labor force. By implication, full-time homemakers did not work, and, in fact, statistics still label them as unemployed. Such labeling would seem to do violence to reality, especially in terms of the dictionary definition of work: "activity in which one exerts strength or faculties to do or perform." The slogan "Every mother is a working mother" reflects that disjunction. When I use terms like "working women" or "women workers" in this chapter, I mean what the title implies: work for pay. This chapter, however, will not—indeed, could not—ignore women's family responsibilities. A recurrent theme will be the complex and problematic interconnections between paid workplace and unpaid workplace, the influences of each upon the other.

In 1933, the year with which this analysis begins, employment was low for everyone. Even in the 1930 census, only 21.9 percent of women had been in the labor force. Nearly all of those women were in clerical or service jobs. By the late 1980s, 55.3 percent of American women were gainfully employed.[2] But the change in numbers has not been matched by changes in the kinds of jobs women do or by increases in the relative value of their earnings. The working world is sex-segregated; most jobs are held either mostly by men or mostly by women. There is a greater variety of "men's" jobs than of "women's" jobs. In 1981, over half of all working women were either clerical (35 percent) or service (20 percent) workers. An additional 5 percent, the next largest category, were schoolteachers. Women numbered 80 percent of clerical workers, 96 percent of private household workers, and 97 percent of nurses, but only 1.2 percent of engineers, 14 percent of physicians, and 6 percent of craft and kindred workers.[3] And the men's jobs paid better. In 1986, the median annual earnings for women working full-time were $16,843; for men, the figure was $25,894.[4]

It is not the law which says that things have to be this way. Laws like the Michigan statute upheld in *Goesaert v. Cleary* (see Chapter 2) did prevent women from tending bar, but no law has forbidden them to be engineers—or, for that matter, forbidden men to be schoolteachers. Indeed, laws like Michigan's exist now, if at all, only as dead letters. Numerous factors—employer preferences, market considerations, custom, socialization, and educational opportunities—have been and remain far more powerful than legislation in determining who gets what jobs.

In 1933, laws existed which barred women from taking certain jobs. By 1991, laws forbade employers to discriminate on the

basis of sex. That change exemplifies the most important development in the period with which this book is concerned: the change
from a legal system which supported sex discrimination to one
which mandates sexual equality. This change is part of, and could
not have occurred without, the fundamental change in the relationship between government and business that the New Deal
represents. Before 1933, legal regulation of business and the economy bore a presumption of illegitimacy. Though such laws did
exist, they stood a good chance of being overturned by the courts.
It is a commonplace observation that the New Deal saved American capitalism by changing it. Perhaps the most important of
those changes is the acceptance, incomplete and reluctant though
it is, of laws limiting the so-called private sector. Equal employment opportunity laws, including those forbidding sex discrimination, are part of that dramatic change. Such laws would have
been impossible without the New Deal.

Chapter 2 has discussed some of the legal changes since 1933.
Goesaert represented the low point: blanket endorsement of any
and all government restrictions on women's work, for whatever
purpose. *Personnel Administrator v. Feeney*, thirty years later, implied that such laws would survive only if the discrimination was
unintentional. But these decisions are far from being the most
significant changes in the legal status of working women. The
Supreme Court has never overruled the line of decisions from
Muller to *Goesaert*, but none of these laws exists today. Those that
were not repealed have been superseded by federal laws. And
although some of those laws contain clauses that all but beg
judges to nullify them, federal courts have usually interpreted the
statutes in reasonably good faith.

The primary concern of this chapter, unlike that of the last, is
not with constitutional adjudication. Instead, its focus is on lawmaking followed by statutory construction. The lawmaking is
often of a rather frustrating sort, because antidiscrimination law
is an area in which Congress does not always leave a full record of
its intentions. Courts have often had little more than the statutory
language to guide construction. The states, too, have passed laws
affecting employment. The Constitution establishes national supremacy; federal law supersedes any state laws which conflict
with it.[5] But the states are free to legislate where Congress has
not, as long as they do not violate the Constitution. This chapter
emphasizes federal law because of its supremacy and because of
the tedium inherent in describing fifty-one separate systems. But

there have been occasions where the issue of federal preemption has involved a state which appears to be a step or two ahead of Congress, rather than the other way around.

We have now seen a quarter century of antidiscrimination law. The first major laws affecting working women, the Equal Pay Act and Civil Rights Act, were passed, respectively, in 1963 and 1964. Congress strengthened the 1964 law in 1972 with amendments broadening its coverage and extending the right to sue. As late as 1988, Congress reversed a court decision narrowing the law's scope. The executive branch, too, was active in the 1960s and 1970s; executive orders covered federally funded programs. Even the 1980s, which brought Ronald Reagan's administration and a Republican Senate majority, showed similar activity. Laws affecting welfare (in 1982), Social Security and pensions (1983 and 1984), and child support (1986 and 1988) were the result of negotiation between the legislative and executive branches. The Civil Rights Restoration Act of 1988 was passed over the president's veto, after the Democrats regained control of the Senate. The Americans with Disabilities Act of 1990, passed during George Bush's second year in office, indicates that we have not seen the last of civil rights legislation.

The labor statistics already quoted—and there will be more—show that civil rights law has not propelled working women into full equality. This kind of law has severely limited potential as an agent of social change. Enforcement has recently depended, for the most part, on cases instigated by individuals who believe that they have been victims of discrimination. Federal agencies can also bring cases, but they have not always been eager to do so. To some extent, enforcement depends on the views of whoever is in office—the heads of those agencies and the president who chooses them.

Individuals may bring cases no matter who is in office. But a potential grievant confronts several obstacles. He or she must risk the disapproval of employer, co-workers, and possibly family and friends. (Although the laws forbid employers to punish workers for bringing charges, these provisions are also hard to enforce.) For all practical purposes, he or she needs a lawyer. Lawyers cost money; they may take some cases on a contingent fee basis (in other words, you pay if and when you win), but no lawyer earns a living that way. Even with a lawyer, a suit is hard work. Litigants have to provide their attorney with evidence, and usually have to testify on their own behalf, thus facing cross-examination. Not surprisingly, observers of the legal process have found that parties who are regularly involved in litigation—corporations, for example—are more likely to win in court than individual plaintiffs such as tenants, customers, or workers. The employer already has a lawyer on the payroll, and knows the ropes.

But law cannot be dismissed as irrelevant to equal opportunity. Census figures now show that, forty years after *Goesaert*, 47 percent of bartenders are women. And one study has estimated that without the laws, the earnings gap between men and women would have widened by 7 percent between 1967 and 1974 instead of remaining relatively constant.[6]

One feature of the New Deal was the assumption by the national government, for the first time, of responsibility for protecting the interests of workers. This development is exemplified by the two "bills of rights" for workers, the National Labor Relations Act (Wagner Act) of 1935 and the Fair Labor Standards Act of 1938. The Wagner Act is of particular importance, because it protects workers' right to organize into unions. Collective bargaining agreements between labor and management have achieved gains for women workers—even though, as of the 1980s, fewer than 20 percent of women workers are represented by unions. Federal labor law is about fifty years old. Federal anti-discrimination labor law is just about half that old. The national government undertook to protect workers from exploitation sometime before it assumed any responsibility for protecting citizens from arbitrary or invidious discrimination. Logically and chronologically, the latter required and depended on the former.

Equal Pay and Comparable Worth

The first federal law prohibiting sex discrimination in employment concerned equal pay. This was an old issue which evokes themes familiar to students of labor history. Organized labor first supported equal pay in 1868; the issue gained national prominence during World War I, when women temporarily replaced men in the civilian labor market—at lower wages. That development created concern that the wages for these jobs would be depressed permanently, even after the men returned.[7] (The fear that the cheaper women workers would displace the men would have been equally realistic. That kind of consideration helped account for the most complete displacement in American labor history: clerical work, now a woman's job, was a predominantly male occupation at the beginning of this century.) So equal pay, like hours legislation, had at least as much to do with male as with female interests.

Whatever interests equal pay legislation served, it was a long time in coming. The law usually called the Equal Pay Act of 1963 was an amendment to the Fair Labor Standards Act. This amendment forbade an employer to "discriminate on the basis of sex by paying wages . . . to employees at a rate less than that which he pays . . . employees of the opposite sex . . . for equal work on jobs the performance of which requires equal skill, effort, and responsibility, and which are performed under similar working conditions." There were four exceptions: sex differences were allowed as part of a seniority system or training program; if earnings depended on quantity or quality of production; or if "based on any factor other than sex."[8] Both aggrieved workers and the Department of Labor could sue under this law.

This statute has obvious defects as an antidiscrimination law. The language of the act amounts to a statement that you may not pay workers of one sex less than those of the opposite sex for the same job unless you do it for a reason other than the sex of the worker. That contradiction sounds strikingly similar to the Hayden rider attached to the ERA in the 1950s: equality of rights, except for special rights for women. The law's other defect is suggested by labor statistics of the type quoted earlier in the chapter. If men and women rarely do the same jobs, how many workers is this law going to affect? At first sight, the law appears both internally contradictory and limited in application.

In practice, however, the Equal Pay Act has done women workers a great deal of good. The federal agencies which enforce it—first the Wage and Hour Administration, now the Equal Employment Opportunity Commission (EEOC)—have conscientiously tried to be faithful to the law's intent. So have the courts. Agency and courts all agreed that the Department of Labor bore the initial burden of proving that the sex-based wage differential existed, but that the burden of proving that one or more of the four exceptions applied *then* shifted to the employer.[9] The problem of the act's limited applicability will be discussed later, but at this point it is necessary to say that enough instances of different pay for the same work were found in the first ten years of the act to result in back pay awards of over $65 million.[10]

The cases fell into several typical patterns. For example, men and women often held jobs differentiable from each other only by the fact that the men had a few additional duties, usually demanding physical strength, occupying as much as 20 percent of their working day. Judges ruled that the act applied here because the jobs, while not identical, were "substantially the same."[11] The Labor Department even won a more complex case where the men were paid extra for physical labor because the women were not compensated for the fact that their work carried more risk of injury.[12] Another situation, particularly common in banks, had female tellers being paid less than male "management trainees." The courts found no instance of a genuine training program.[13] The women lost, however, in the *Robert Hall* case, where the courts upheld a system which paid salesmen more than saleswomen because the clothes sold by the men were higher priced.[14] (The company has since gone out of business.)

One equal pay case presented a clash between the new equality and the old protection. *Corning Glass Works v. Brennan* confronted the Supreme Court with conflicting rulings from two Courts of Appeals. At Corning's plants in upstate New York (Second Circuit) and Pennsylvania (Third), the company hired both men and women as inspectors. The women worked the day shift; the men (and by this time, the early 1970s, a few women), at night. The pay was better at night. Corning had begun running its night shifts between 1925 and 1930, when both states had had laws prohibiting night work for women (see Chapter 2).[15] The practice survived the laws, which had been repealed by 1953. The Pennsylvania court held that the shift difference constituted a "factor other than sex," ruling for Corning; the New York court disagreed, on the grounds that the shift differential was caused by the sex discrimination of the old laws.[16]

As happens more often than not, the Supreme Court sided with the national government. The justices relied not only on the history emphasized by the Second Circuit but also on the fact that there were no other shift differentials at Corning and that American industry did not usually pay night workers more than day workers.[17] *Corning* was the first equal pay case to reach the Supreme Court, which followed the lead of most of the lower courts in making clear that the existence of any exception was a fact to be proved, not a phrase to be incanted by the employer and an assumption to be accepted by the courts. By now it was 1974, and the courts had already ruled that even extant state "protective" laws would fall under Title VII of the Civil Rights Act of 1964.

One difficulty in interpreting the Equal Pay Act arises from the different meanings that attach to the word "equal" itself. The statute does not help much, for it defines "equal" work as that requiring "equal" skill, effort, and responsibility. This circular reasoning throws the question back upon the interpreter: does "equal" mean "identical," or does it mean "equivalent"? In the early cases, as we have seen, the judges did not limit the act to situations where men and women performed absolutely identical tasks. Judges found violations in some cases where men had some extra tasks, thus finding "equal" to mean "essentially equal."

But even the reasonably broad construction of the early decisions limits the law's application to a minority of women workers. Why? We have already seen that women's wages lag behind men's. Indeed, comparisons in every field show men earning more than women. The median annual wages of male and female clerical workers in 1981 were, respectively, $17,310 and $11,703; for managers and administrators, the figures were $26,856 and $14,979. This difference does not, by itself, prove sex bias; one of the most powerful factors in determining wage differences is differences in what is called "work history." Men are more likely than women to work continuously all their adult lives, without interruption, while women often enter the labor force at later ages than men, or leave it for several years to raise families. Some of the differences between men's and women's salaries in the professions are explained by the fact that the average woman physician or lawyer, for instance, tends to be younger than her male counterpart and, therefore, has not worked as long.[18]

But this kind of sex differential accounts for much less of the income disparity than does the fact we already know: men and women do not usually have the same jobs. And, other things being equal, jobs held by women pay less than jobs held by men. The qualification "other things being equal" is important. Not only are men more likely than women to be employed continuously and to have worked long enough to reach the higher levels of their occupations, but women are also more likely to work part-time or to work only part of the year. In interpreting labor statistics, we need to restrict comparisons to those among workers similarly situated. But men often earn more even when other things are not equal. For instance, in 1981 the median full-time, year-round income for women college graduates was four-fifths that of men whose education had stopped with high school.[19] Since 60 percent of all women workers are clustered in three predominantly female occupations of clerical work, service jobs, and teaching, equalizing wages for similar jobs cannot do much to improve the relative financial situation of women workers.

But suppose we interpret the word "equal" to mean "equivalent," or "comparable," rather than "identical" or "similar." Suppose we examine different occupations, and try to determine how much skill, effort, and responsibility they require, and assess the conditions under which they are performed. Suppose, for example, we compare a secretary's job to a mechanic's, or the work done by a nurse in a hospital intensive care unit to that of an air traffic controller. Here, as it happens, we are not without available guidance. Industry has developed a variety of job evaluation systems for use in determining employee compensation. The most widely used system in this country is the point-comparison or point-factor method, which assigns numerical values to "compensable factors" for each job (like skill, effort, or responsibility) and totals them to set a wage.[20]

One 1970 case, *Hodgson v. Daisy Manufacturing Company*, contained this sort of comparison. The judge compared the extra physical exertion required of the male press operators to the additional risk required of the women, who had to place their hands close to high-speed presses. "The males exert greater physical effort than the females when lifting and turning master cartons. . . . The females, however, in performing a variety of operations requiring comparatively greater mental alertness and concentration, exert greater mental effort and their jobs require greater job responsibility. The court simply cannot say that the greater physical effort expended by the males in a basic and uncomplicated operation results in a substantial overall job inequality justifying a significant wage differential."[21] This effort to compare brains to brawn made *Daisy* a precursor of the equal pay issue of the 1980s: the controversy over comparable worth. A comparable worth approach to wages might lead to equalizing the wages of, say, clerical workers and mechanics.

Although the language of the Equal Pay Act could be read as encouraging such equalization, the authors of that law almost certainly intended nothing of the sort; if they had, why make an exemption of differentials based on "factors other than sex"? Title VII of the 1964 Civil Rights Act does forbid sex-based wage discrimination, but it exempts from its coverage any wage differential authorized by the earlier law.[22] No court has interpreted either law to require comparable pay. However, the Supreme Court ruled in *County of Washington v. Gunther* that women guards in the women's jail had grounds for a Title VII case even though their job had been held not to be substantially equal to that of guard in the men's jail. In 1983, a district judge in Washington State (where the county is located) ordered wage increases and back pay for state employees in several female-dominated jobs. In 1986, the state and the major employee union signed a pay equity pact worth almost half a billion dollars.[23]

But the national government has consistently opposed comparable worth. In 1985, all five EEOC commissioners agreed that "Congress never authorized the Government to take on wholesale restructuring of wages that were set by non-sex-based decisions of employers, by collective bargaining, or by the marketplace." Such a decision is not surprising from a group of presidential appointees in the fourth year of the Reagan presidency. The Justice Department sided with Illinois in a pay equity suit brought by nurses' groups. The federal courts, too, have rejected comparable worth. But several states besides Washington have adopted a comparable worth policy for their employees.[24] States are not likely to impose such a scheme on the private sector, however, since corporations have been known to move from one state to another with policies more favorable to their interests—thus depriving large numbers of workers (and voters) of their jobs. Comparable worth, therefore, is still a new idea. Congress does have the power to amend the law to require a comparable worth system. But this step is not likely in the near future, given the Republican victory in the 1988 presidential election and the lack of a two-thirds Democratic majority, sufficient to override vetoes, in either house of Congress. Comparable worth is a highly controversial proposal. It conflicts with a basic principle of capitalism: the free market economy.

According to capitalist theory, wages and prices are determined by the market: what goods and services can be bought and sold. The market model describes not only the way the system does work, but the way free market adherents believe it should work. This theory is as old as the nation itself. The classic capitalist text, Adam Smith's *Wealth of Nations*, was published in

1776. Smith extolled the virtues of the "invisible hand" which regulated prices, wages, consumption, and production: the metaphor referred to that mysterious force which led each person, pursuing individual and even selfish interests, to act in ways that furthered the common good. Any government interference would do more harm than good, interfering with forces more powerful than law itself.

Market factors include, but are not limited to, the laws of supply and demand. If labor is scarce, workers' pay will increase; if, on the other hand, there are more workers than there are jobs, wages will drop. The same relationship exists between prices and the availability of goods, and between the quality of goods and consumers' willingness to buy them; cheap, flimsy clothing, or cigarettes, for example, will be manufactured as long as they can be sold.

Any reader of this book will be aware that the foregoing paragraph is a crude, simplistic description of how the American economy works. Its application to the market for specific occupations is limited. We know, for example, that the supply of performing artists eager for work always exceeds the demand; any student who has ever had ambitions in this field has already been told so, probably more than once. And, as it happens, wages for performers bear a rough correspondence to this glut—rough, because performers have relatively powerful labor unions that negotiate wages and have been known to call strikes. But it is also common knowledge that stars in the entertainment field earn vast amounts of money. So do star athletes. Everyone has his or her favorite example—Michael Jackson? Madonna? Joe Montana? By the time this book is published, who else?—of a star who seems grossly overpaid. On the other end of the scale, consider nursing. A severe shortage of nurses exists in this country, and is getting worse. But, while nurses' salaries have increased in recent years, the profession remains poorly paid. Something other than supply and demand is influencing wages: in both these examples, that "something" is the value society attaches to those occupations. All these factors, some of them mysterious, are known as "market forces." Mechanics earn more than secretaries do, for example, because the market supposedly sets the relative value of the labor of both occupational groups.

A logical extension of Smith's theory was laissez-faire capitalism: hostility to any governmental economic regulation. An advocate of this position might argue that, if the market value of women's wages is less than men's, so be it; it is all for the best. (A capitalist of this stripe would oppose the Equal Pay Act in even its narrow interpretation, not to mention Title VII, the Fair Labor Standards Act, and the Wagner Act.)

One lesson of the Great Depression pertained to the dangers of unregulated capitalism; the position I have just described is extreme for the 1990s, though not unknown. Modern capitalism does not embody the extreme form of the "invisible hand" theory. We have a market-oriented economy, but we do not in fact have a free market system. We deviate from that model in many important respects. A minimum wage represents a departure from free market principles. So do laws which forbid the sale of alcohol to minors, or regulate the quality of foods that can be sold. People who assert that comparable worth departs from free market principles are quite correct. But so do many other existing laws; and, whereas many citizens believe that government regulation is excessive, very few people would wish to have a pure free market. The opponents of comparable worth assert that deviations from the free market should be the exception, not the rule, and that equalizing wages in this manner is an example of excessive governmental interference with individual freedom. Contemporary capitalist philosophy was well articulated by Senator William Proxmire of Wisconsin in recalling the debate in Congress in 1979 over whether the national government should make a billion-dollar loan to the embattled Chrysler Corporation. Chrysler eventually got the money, over the vehement opposition of Proxmire and many other leaders. The senator said, "We'll have far better business management in the long run if we allow the tough, cold, cruel system of free enterprise to work. It's served us very well."[25]

And so it has, from the perspective of someone who has succeeded well enough to become a United States Senator. But we could question the assumption that free enterprise is healthy, and many have. The workers at Chrysler who would have lost their jobs had Proxmire's view prevailed might not have felt comforted by an assertion that in the long run things would be better that way. One argument against comparable worth is similar to Proxmire's argument against the bailout: if the men's jobs pay better (assuming the absence of employment discrimination), women workers will be attracted to those jobs, and the movement into the better-paying jobs will serve societal interests. The workers whom the "tough, cold, cruel system" leaves in the traditional jobs will either be there by choice or because they cannot compete for better jobs. Perhaps. But the free enterprise model makes assumptions about human behavior that have never been proven true. For example, the model assumes that people will seek the highest-paying jobs they can get, regardless of other factors; it also assumes that individuals have a great deal of control over what happens to them. And as poverty becomes more and more a woman's problem, evidence mounts against the assertion that society may rely on free enterprise to work for the best. As far as the Chrysler bailout goes, the benefit of ten years' hindsight indicates that its effects on the free enterprise system have been positive rather than negative.

The opponents of comparable worth or of any other form of governmental economic intervention can be asked one question which is ultimately unanswerable: what's so great about the free market economy, anyway? The answer is nothing, *unless* one shares the assumptions of this theory. There is no obvious reason why wages should be determined by the market value of jobs. But, unfortunately for advocates of comparable worth, that type of argument is a two-edged sword. Neither is there any obvious reason why wages should depend on the job being done rather than on the worker who performs the job. And if there is no proof that some workers should not be paid more than others for similar jobs, there is no proof that men should not be paid more than women.

This suggestion is not as bizarre as it sounds. Nor would it depend on a presumption that men are superior to women. The slogan "From each according to his ability; to each according to his needs" is a recommendation for worker-linked compensation which few Americans accept, probably because its author is Karl Marx—although it should be noted that Marx restricted this principle to conditions *after* the proletarian revolution had succeeded. However, a version of this argument—and one that sounds very Marxist indeed—entered into the debate over equal pay. Men, so the argument runs, deserve higher wages because they must support families, while women workers either support only themselves or work for extra family income—often described by the inaccurate and trivializing term "pin money."

The coexistence of capitalist and Marxist arguments against equal wages is striking. The reader might begin to suspect that the real organizing principle of defenses of the status quo is not capitalism but patriarchy. However, the main difference between the "free market" argument and the "man as breadwinner" argument is that the latter can be tested empirically. And it fails. The facts disprove it. Many women workers support families, as single heads of households or with unemployed or disabled spouses; married women who work full-time in two-earner families contribute an average of 38.3 percent of the family income; and the lower the family income, the higher the percentage contributed by the wife.[26] The "pin money" hypothesis has been false at least since the 1900 census. Women work because they must.[27]

The facts available for the last eighty years have not made the argument go away. As late as 1986, Carl Icahn, the chief executive officer of Trans World Airlines, declared on national television during a flight attendants' strike that most of this predominantly female group did not have to work. Inaccurate as the assertion was, it had its uses; Icahn succeeded in breaking the strike.

There are, it seems, at least three ways of determining wages: by the market; by evaluation of the job; or by assessment of some attribute, like merit or need, of the worker performing the job. The last method is not consistently used in this country; the assertion that men need more money than women because men support families has been an excuse for the status quo, not a reason. A seniority system is one example of a policy which does tie compensation in part to the worker rather than the job—a policy exempted from the original equal pay provision, and one which people commonly accept and from which most of us hope to benefit. Laws allowing employers to pay young, part-time workers a "training wage," perhaps the converse of a seniority system, are another example.

Generally, the occupation matters more than the individual in determining a worker's pay, and the value of that occupation is determined largely by the market. When we examine wage differentials, we discover that the market does not set wages in any truly predictable, rational way. Many observers have found fault with the market's determinations: witness the frequent complaints of the "Why do football players earn more than schoolteachers?" sort. (The answer is, "Because the market so rules," and that is not a very satisfactory explanation, is it?) It is not generally true that the greater the skill, effort, and responsibility required in a job, the higher the pay will be; and as the athlete versus schoolteacher example shows, neither is it true that compensation is directly related to any reasonable assessment of the social value of a job.

There is one generalization, however, which can be made

about wages: women's jobs pay less than men's jobs. This observation seems to hold, not only in the United States in the 1990s,
but globally, cross-culturally, and over time.[28] The market, therefore, is not neutral in the way it sets wages; it reflects certain
social prejudices, including those associated with patriarchy. The
more we learn about wages, the harder it becomes to argue that
the free market serves society well. Even within the language of
the Equal Pay Act, it is questionable whether the market constitutes a "factor other than sex" when that market is permeated
by sex bias.

But since two branches of the national government refuse to
read existing antidiscrimination laws to mandate comparable
worth, and consider the market a "factor other than sex," adopt-
ing this policy nationwide would require new federal laws.
Whether or not anyone supports such laws depends on the relative importance that person assigns to the values of equality and
of free-market capitalism. Americans in general accept both
values. But our historic commitment to equality has tended to
emphasize equality of opportunity, not equality of reward. So,
while we have departed far enough from free market principles to
forbid de jure employment discrimination, it may be a long
time—if ever—before Congress is willing to mandate equal compensation.

Equal Opportunity and Sex Discrimination

Like the Equal Pay Act, the first federal antidiscrimination
law preceded the contemporary feminist movement by several
years. The origins of this policy were a variation of the familiar
strategy of "divide and conquer." The Civil Rights Act of 1964 was
the first strong civil rights law since Reconstruction; its purpose
was to give legal protection to efforts to achieve racial equality,
particularly for blacks. This statute had its enemies; it was opposed by the coalition of white Southern Democrats and conservative, "states' rights" Republicans that still dominated
Congress in the 1960s. Members of this coalition made several
ingenious attempts to defeat the bill.

As drafted, Title VII of the proposed law prohibited employment discrimination on the basis of race, color, religion, or national origin. The amendment adding "sex" was proposed by
Howard Smith of Virginia, the powerful chair of the House Rules
Committee, and opposed by liberal Democrats in an effort to

expunge it "before it sank the bill under gales of laughter." Smith knew what he was doing. His colleagues roared when he urged Congress "to protect our spinster friends in their 'right' to a husband and family."[29] Smith's strategy failed because a coalition of liberals and conservative women legislators saved the amendment. Title VII forbids employment discrimination on the basis of sex.

The bill's history gave rise to the commonplace observation that the sex discrimination provision of Title VII was a "joke." This belief was shared by the first director of the agency created to enforce Title VII, who described it as a "fluke."[30] Even in the hands of less biased interpreters, the troublesome fact is that the only evidence we have of Congress's intentions is the law's language. And the language of Title VII, like that of the Equal Pay Act, contains an exception broad enough to kill the law. Discrimination is prohibited except where sex, religion, or national origin (but never race) is "a bona fide occupational qualification reasonably necessary to the normal operation of that particular business enterprise."[31]

This "BFOQ" exception contains the kind of infinitely expansive language of the decisions examined in Chapter 2. A news story published the week the provision went into effect illustrates the inherent difficulties. " 'What do we do,' asked an airline official, 'when a girl walks in here with all the right credentials and asks for a pilot's job?' "[32] The fact that women pilots now fly for the major airlines shows that Title VII has been neither a joke nor a fluke.

We must never forget that before 1964 it was *acceptable* to discriminate openly against women. In 1958, two researchers in the field of higher education could write: "Women are outside the prestige system entirely . . . [and] cannot look forward to a normal academic career."[33] The airline official who asked a question whose answer seems so clear now, and the Congress which ridiculed single women, remind us how much things have changed. No one would claim that those opinions have disappeared. But in 1991, employers who wish to discriminate must conceal their intentions—sometimes, one suspects, even from themselves—and the camouflage does not always work. Occasionally, concealment takes so much effort that the employers back down and actually treat women fairly. And anyone who calls adult women "girls" is in for trouble.

Amended in 1972 to cover educational institutions and state and local governments, the Civil Rights Act now applies to all employers except those with fewer than fifteen workers, Indian tribes, and religious bodies. The law also applies to employment agencies and labor unions. The original act gave individuals the power to bring charges of discrimination before the Equal Employment Opportunity Commission and eventually before the federal courts; a 1972 amendment gave the agency itself the power to initiate cases. The EEOC refers all charges to the appropriate state or local agency, where one exists; the case goes back to the EEOC only if the state does not act within sixty days or one party is dissatisfied with the results. The EEOC attempts to reach a conciliation agreement between the charging party and the employer; if this effort fails, the charging party may bring suit. Like similar agencies, the EEOC has a considerable case backlog, and the wait is long—as is true in the courts.

The EEOC's powers are not limited to hearing complaints and instigating lawsuits. Like other federal agencies, it also issues regulations, colloquially known as "regs," implementing and interpreting the laws it enforces. Federal agencies publish proposed "regs" in the Federal Register; for a few months, it is open season while all those potentially affected may protest, criticize, and cavil. Once the rules, revised or not, take effect, they are published in the *Code of Federal Regulations* (CFR). Agency decisions made according to these regulations are subject to challenge in the federal courts, which may reverse the agency. This is an important power; in the absence of these regulations, the law exists only on paper.

The EEOC issued its first regulations implementing Title VII in December 1965, less than six months after the provision went into effect. Agency and courts have been busy ever since, enforcing and interpreting all aspects of this law. In some cases, the courts have ultimately overturned the agency; in at least one instance, Congress restored the status quo, overturning the courts; and one of the first sex discrimination controversies involved a question perceived that the EEOC refused to resolve, passing the buck to the judiciary. Whatever Congress's intent had been, the courts' resolution of this issue showed clearly that the laughter had stopped.

Title VII and Protective Legislation

One curious feature of Title VII, other than its legislative history, was its coexistence with state laws that appeared on their face to contradict it. Laws of the type which long ago had been labeled "protective" still limited the hours women might work, the jobs they might do, or the weights they might lift. The previous year, the Commission on the Status of Women had recommended no changes in these laws, and during the debate on Title VII its chair, Esther Peterson, had opposed the Smith amendment.[34] Nevertheless, once the law passed, a conflict did seem to exist between a prohibition of sex discrimination and, say, a law forbidding night work for women. This was hardly a new conflict; back in 1872, the Illinois legislature had passed both a law providing that no person should be barred from any occupation other than military service because of sex and a law prohibiting women from working in coal mines.[35] On paper, there was no problem with Title VII, because federal laws preempt state laws. But the existence of conflicting law would be troublesome to the employer seeking to avoid both state prosecution and federal litigation.

The first EEOC regulations were hard to reconcile with the statutory language: that the law was not meant to overturn protective legislation, and that state laws provided grounds for the BFOQ exception. The EEOC revised the guideline the next year to state that the agency would make no decisions in conflicts between federal and state law unless the latter's effect was clearly discriminatory rather than protective, but would advise women grievants of their right to sue. A 1968 regulation attempted to be faithful both to the presumed will of Congress and to the EEOC's growing constituency; this rule reaffirmed the judgment that Congress had not meant to disturb state laws, but declared its belief that some such laws "have ceased to be relevant" in modern society.[36] In fact, the EEOC never resolved a case involving a state-federal conflict. But by 1970, fourteen states had repealed their old protective laws, stopped enforcing them, or ruled that Title VII nullified them.[37]

While it is tempting to accuse the EEOC of cowardice, there are other explanations for such consistent vacillation. Congress created the EEOC, gave it powers and a budget, and is free to change either. Members of Congress are nominated and elected by, and responsible to, state constituencies. Therefore, Congress is not fond of conflict between national and state governments. The Civil Rights Act reflected a bitter conflict between the national government and several of the states. The national government won, though the victory was costly, and a similar conflict came along the very next year, in the form of the Voting Rights Act of

1965. We must never forget that even when national and state governments are at odds, they are simultaneously engaged in cooperation, over such matters as highways and block grants, for example. Conflict jeopardizes cooperation. The EEOC may well have believed that in the mid-1960s the balance between federal-state consensus and dissensus was too fragile to be disturbed by an issue which few people then regarded as very important.[38]

Federal district courts reached conflicting decisions on this issue. The appellate courts, however, were unified from circuit to circuit, with the result that the issue never reached the Supreme Court. The cases which exposed protective legislation for what in fact it had been for most of its history—discrimination against women workers—both involved a situation common in Title VII cases: a woman who sought the kind of well-paying blue-collar job heretofore held mostly by men. Both women plaintiffs were in the early stages of their working lives. Nineteen-year-old Lorena Weeks had applied for the job of switchman (*sic*) with the telephone company. It refused to hire her because the job required exceeding Georgia's thirty-pound weight-lifting limit for women. The Fifth Circuit Court of Appeals decided *Weeks v. Southern Bell* in 1969. The opinion faced the issues squarely. It rejected the "romantic paternalism" of Southern Bell's concern about women lifting heavy weights and working late hours. "Men have always had the right to determine whether the incremental increase in remuneration for strenuous, dangerous, obnoxious, boring, or unromantic tasks is worth the candle. The promise of Title VII is that women are now to be on an equal footing." Weeks could not be barred from the job unless Southern Bell could prove that "all or substantially all women would be unable to perform safely or efficiently the duties of the job required."[39]

Meanwhile, in California, Leah Rosenfeld, a twenty-two-year-old employee of the Southern Pacific Railroad, was passed over for a position as agent-telegrapher in favor of a man with less seniority. The company relied on a state law barring women from working more than ten hours a day or lifting more than fifty pounds. The district court went even further than *Weeks*, insisting that the laws were invalid and that Rosenfeld must be given a chance to demonstrate her ability to do the job. Two years after *Weeks*, the appellate court upheld this ruling.[40]

The difference between *Weeks* and *Rosenfeld* is important. *Weeks*, read literally, would allow an employer to refuse to hire a woman even if she were the only woman in the world who could do a specific job. Such a result hardly seems fair. However, almost insuperable difficulties confront the person who would prove that "all or substantially all" women could not do something, with the presumed exception of donating sperm. What, precisely, does "substantially all" mean in a national population of 230 million? Even if 99.9 percent of women could not do something, that would leave more than 100,000 who could.

Weeks and *Rosenfeld* ended the era of protective legislation. Since 1971, no employer covered by Title VII may discriminate directly against women *qua* women. But suppose a company disadvantages all married women, or all mothers, or all women above a certain age? Or suppose an employer has a regulation which is neutral on its face, but discriminatory as applied: for example, a minimum height requirement for police recruits? And what happens if, somehow, the great majority of people hired in certain positions are white males? All of these questions have had to be resolved in Title VII law, and not all of them have been easy cases.

"Sex Plus" Discrimination, Redefined

The first Title VII case that reached the Supreme Court involved yet another young woman trying to better her position in the working world. Ida Phillips, a waitress, supported herself and two small children. She applied for an assembly trainee position with the Martin-Marietta Company in Orlando, Florida. The company said it did not hire women with children below school age, although it did not exclude the fathers of young children. The Fifth Circuit, which had ruled in favor of Lorena Weeks a few months earlier, found no sex discrimination: "Violation of the Act can only be discrimination based solely on one of the categories, i.e., in the case of sex, women vis-à-vis men. When another criterion of employment is added to one of the classifications listed in the Act, there is no longer apparent discrimination based solely on race, color, religion, sex, or national origin." Surely, wrote the judges, Congress had not intended "such an irrational purpose" as to make employers treat the fathers and mothers of young children "exactly alike."[41] The irony of a policy handicapping a parent who was the sole support of her children on the grounds of her greater responsibilities toward them apparently struck neither the company nor the court.

The Supreme Court sided unanimously with Ida Phillips. Its brief opinion hewed to statutory language rather than presumed intention: "The Civil Rights Act of 1964 requires that persons of like qualifications be given employment opportunities regardless of their sex." While family obligations, if "demonstrably more relevant to job performance for a woman than for a man," might allow application of the BFOQ exception, "the record before us, however, is not adequate for resolution of these important issues." Only Thurgood Marshall objected to this hint that "ancient canards about the proper role of women" could be a basis for discrimination.[42]

The careful language of *Phillips* has had no more dampening effect on Title VII doctrine than did that of *Weeks*, and perhaps for a similar reason. Although nobody disputes the fact that women take more responsibility for their children than men do, it is very hard to show that a single mother like Ida Phillips will be a less responsible employee than a similarly situated single father. No employer has met the burden of proving that family obligations justify this kind of "sex plus" discrimination.

Ida Phillips prevailed over a policy which was a "sex plus" rule in a literal sense: it applied to anyone who was a woman *and* the mother of small children. Some forms of "sex plus" discrimination are more subtle. It would be accurate to apply this label to rules discriminating against pregnant workers, since all of them are women *and* pregnant; however, the combination of work and motherhood has given rise to such a host of legal issues that, for clarity's sake, they will receive a whole chapter section. Another form of "sex plus" discrimination is the neutral rule that applies only to a group of workers which is exclusively female. Several landmark "sex plus" cases of this type come from one specific industry: the airlines. This industry has had persistent problems with gender-related issues. In 1965, it worried about the possibility of women pilots. The cases, however, have involved not pilots but flight attendants, who used to be called "stewardesses." That occupational name change is in itself an indication of the effects of Title VII.

Those readers who are frequent fliers may have surmised, from observation, that these employees are glorified waitresses— without the tips. That observation, though shrewd, leads to an incorrect conclusion. The flight attendants' primary task is to protect the passengers in case of trouble. But the airlines have been reluctant to present the job in that way, to either potential employees or passengers. Instead, at least since the end of World War II, young women have been attracted to the job with the implicit promise of meeting eligible men (forget job advancement; there has been virtually none) while customers have been drawn to the airlines with an implicit promise expressed by the famous advertising slogan of the now-defunct National Airlines in the early 1970s, "I'm Cheryl; fly me."

This marketing of an occupation and of those who performed it led to an intriguing set of airline policies. Some airlines restricted the job to women. (One airline, United, even restricted a few flights to male passengers.) The stewardesses' looks were carefully monitored; there were minimum and maximum height and weight requirements, for instance. There was a maximum age, typically thirty-five (the Age Discrimination Act of 1978, also enforced by the EEOC, would have invalidated this rule). And married women were ineligible for the job. A stewardess, upon reaching thirty-five or marrying, could choose between resigning or transferring to a ground position such as ticket agent.

The first of these rules to fall under Title VII was the woman-only policy. *Diaz v. Pan American World Airways* discounted the paid testimony of several psychologists that femaleness was a bona fide occupational qualification because anxious passengers would be better reassured by "feminine" attendants.[43] That ruling, which opened the job to men, pulled the rug out from under two district courts which had held that the airlines' prohibition on married attendants was a discrimination based not on sex but on marital status, since all the workers were the same sex.[44]

Sprogis v. United Air Lines, a few months after *Diaz*, did give the woman-only rule serious consideration—but it overturned the ban on married women flight attendants. Another form of "sex plus" discrimination was dead. "Even assuming that Title VII might justify hiring only females for that position," wrote the Seventh Circuit panel, "that conclusion would not automatically legitimate the no-marriage-rule imposed exclusively upon stewardesses [and upon no other United employees, male or female]." Furthermore, "United has failed to offer any salient rationale in support of its marital status policy. The only reason specifically addressed to that rule is that United was led to impose the requirement after it received complaints from husbands about their wives' working schedules and the irregularity of their working hours. This is clearly insufficient."[45]

Sprogis also invalidated the age limitations. In 1976, Northwest Airlines lost a case involving requirements that female, but not male, attendants wear contact lenses, undergo weight checks, or be subjected to a maximum height regulation.[46] Title VII has curbed the airlines' license to offer their employees as sexual bait to their customers, but flight attendants have not yet gained all the protections afforded other women workers. One common airline policy does not strictly belong to the "sex plus" category, but does represent a partial victory for the airlines. They are the only employers still allowed to impose mandatory maternity leaves. One district court even upheld a rule that the leave must commence as soon as the pregnancy is confirmed.[47]

One of the newest developments in antidiscrimination law involves the type of behavior commonly called sexual harassment. This term did not exist in 1964, when Title VII was passed, but the phenomenon appears to be timeless and universal. A generation ago, it was a joke. A popular version of that joke attributed the sexual aggression to the "one-down" woman rather than the "one-up" man: "Oh, Professor, I'll do *anything* to get a good grade!" "Try studying." Similar stereotypes label nurses—never doctors—as sexually "loose."

If the problem were in fact one of subordinates trying to manipulate superiors, it could be resolved exactly as the hypothetical professor did. But all too often, it is the powerful who have been the aggressors. The student who is promised an A if she sleeps with her professor, the secretary menaced by the real-life version of the character portrayed by Dabney Coleman in the film *Nine to Five*, the female junior executive threatened with dismissal unless she submits to her supervisor, the nurse reported by the physician whose advances she spurns—none of these victims can dismiss aggression with a flip rejoinder. They have been in real trouble. And because women are more likely to be junior rather than senior executives, nurses rather than physicians, secretaries rather than bosses, and college students rather than professors—are likely, in short, to be accountable to men—sexual harassment has been largely a woman's problem.[48]

In the 1970s, feminists began arguing that sexual harassment is a form of sex discrimination.[49] After all, this behavior confronts women with a barrier to success which men rarely experience. However, there have been a few male victims, and a few instances of homosexual harassment—the basic rule is, "everything you can think of has happened." A more subtle point is that sexual harassment happens *because* a victim is male or female; in that sense, it links gender to treatment as surely as Martin-Marietta's "no mothers of small children" rule did. In 1980, the EEOC issued guidelines asserting that sexual harassment was a form of sex discrimination. (These rules were last codified in 1985, in the heyday of a conservative Republican administration. Congress, one house of which was controlled by Republicans from 1981 until 1986, could have altered the EEOC's interpretation, but never did.)

There are, the guidelines stated, two basic kinds of harassment. First is the quid pro quo version, in which employment benefits are conditioned upon sexual favors. A second variety was "harassment that, while not affecting economic benefits, creates a hostile or offensive working environment."[50] Therefore, sexual harassment exists where a worker is subjected to constant unwelcome advances even if his or her career is not harmed by rejecting those advances—or if the employee cannot prove such an effect. Of course, the employee usually has to initiate the lawsuit, an action rather like bringing a civil suit and a rape charge simultaneously—and these litigants have no equivalent of "rape shield" laws which prevent rape victims from being asked questions about their sexual history. Many employers (including most colleges and universities) now have rules and procedures for internal complaints; a 1985 episode of the CBS-TV series *Cagney and Lacey* showed a police department hearing on charges brought by a woman detective against a captain. However, a worker need not exhaust internal remedies (as he or she must exhaust state remedies) before bringing a federal charge.

The EEOC rules raise as many questions as they answer. What happens, for example, in the common situation where it is a case of the harassee's word against the alleged harasser's? (The testimony of fellow victims or witnesses, or the existence of written employee evaluations which discredit a counterclaim that the employee was fired or demoted because of incompetence, may buttress the victim's case. Harassers are often repeat offenders, and formal evaluations are now standard employment practice.) What constitutes a "hostile environment"? If a shy or prudish worker is embarrassed by dirty jokes on the job, does telling them constitute harassment? (It certainly constitutes rudeness and insensitivity.) Since cases move through the charging process with the speed of glaciers, and some are deflected to private or state resolution, none of these questions has yet received a definitive answer. However, the Supreme Court, presented with a chance to gut the guidelines, instead gave them partial affirmation.

The story of Mechelle Vinson, Sidney Taylor, and the Meritor Savings Bank of Washington, D.C., is wearily familiar. Vinson started at Meritor as a teller-trainee (the kind of job that only men had had in some of the early equal pay cases) in 1974; Taylor was her supervisor. Four years later, now an assistant branch manager, she was fired for "excessive use of [sick] leave." All parties agree that these facts are correct. Beyond that, factual accounts conflict. Vinson's story is one of a woman worker who took advantage of new opportunities for women opened up by federal civil rights law, only to be derailed by harassment. She alleged that, during her probationary period at the bank, Taylor made sexual advances to her, and that she submitted because she feared losing her job; the relationship continued until 1977, when she began another relationship. Vinson also claimed that Taylor raped her several times, that he made advances to other women employees, and that she did not use the bank's grievance procedures because she was afraid of him. Taylor denied all Vinson's accusations.

The facts permit—though they hardly demand—at least four inferences: first, that Vinson had been forced to have sex with Taylor to get promoted; second, that she was fired because she ended the relationship; third, that she had been subjected to an offensive or hostile working environment; or fourth, that her illness was related to the job stress that she had experienced. The final claim would be only a tangential Title VII case; of the other three, she made only the first. She brought charges against Taylor for his alleged behavior, and against Meritor under EEOC guidelines which made employers responsible for their employees' violations of Title VII.

The environment that Vinson faced in court was initially quite as hostile as that at Meritor. The federal district court refused to let her present evidence that Taylor was a habitual harasser, and ruled against her in a masterful exercise in doublethink: if Vinson and Taylor "did engage in an intimate or sexual relationship . . . that relationship was a voluntary one."[51] The judge seemed unaware that this conclusion conformed to *neither* factual account. Mechelle Vinson's mettle proved equal to that of the other litigants whose cases we have discussed. The Court of Appeals vindicated her on all counts, holding both Taylor and the bank liable in subjecting her to a hostile working environment.[52]

The Supreme Court unanimously upheld the ruling that the existence of such an environment creates a basis for a Title VII lawsuit. Mechelle Vinson had to start over again, but with some doctrinal support: "The fact that sex-related conduct was 'voluntary,' in the sense that the complainant was not forced to participate against her will, is not a defense to a sexual harassment suit brought under Title VII. The gravamen of any sexual harassment claim is that the alleged sexual advances were 'unwelcome' . . . her conduct indicated that the alleged sexual advances were unwelcome, not whether her actual participation in sexual intercourse was voluntary."

The Court split five to four on the question of the bank's liability. The majority, speaking through Justice Rehnquist (who almost never sides with women plaintiffs in sex discrimination cases), rejected a rule of absolute employer liability in favor of case-by-case adjudication. Justice Marshall presented the opposite view: "It is the authority vested in the supervisor by the employer that enables him to commit the wrong: it is precisely because the supervisor is understood to be clothed with the employer's authority that he is able to impose unwelcome sexual conduct on subordinates."[53] A rule which imposes responsibility for ending harassment from the top down, in the form of regulations and discipline, is likely to be far more effective than one which depends on enforcement from the bottom up, in the form of employee grievances. Despite its defects, however, *Meritor* illustrates judicial willingness, not only to hew to statutory language, but to endorse an agency's power to implement laws far beyond any probable aims of the legislators who enacted them.

Indirect Discrimination and Facially Neutral Rules

The 1979 case of *Personnel Administrator v. Feeney* (see Chapter 2) presented the problem of the rule which, though neutral in its language, is discriminatory in its application. Like the equal protection clause, Title VII has confronted the courts with numerous variations on this theme. But the similarity stops there. Statutory construction is a very different judicial enterprise from constitutional adjudication; the rules of the game change. As

Chapter 2 showed, the courts hesitate, more often than not, to interpret the Constitution to tell other branches of the government what to do. But the same courts are willing, more often than not, to let Congress tell people what to do. While constitutional commands are construed narrowly, statutes are construed broadly. In Title VII cases, the rules work in favor of individual plaintiffs. In constitutional law, the rules work against them. Early Title VII doctrine, therefore, could not have been more different from constitutional doctrine in the area of indirect discrimination. *Feeney* was one of several cases (see Chapter 2) which ruled that the Fourteenth Amendment extends only to *deliberate* discrimination. Conversely, a substantial body of anti-discrimination case law established the principle that illegal discrimination can be unintentional—a principle whose validity as a legal rule rests on considerably shaky ground since a series of decisions in 1989.

Title VII forbids employers, their agents, and labor unions to "discriminate . . . because of . . . sex." The key words here are "because of." Read one way, this language demands conclusions similar to those of *Feeney*: therefore, if I refuse to let you into the police academy not because you are a woman but because you are under five feet six inches tall, you have no Title VII case, because I discriminate against you because of height rather than because of sex. However, a broad reading of the law is as defensible as this narrow one. The language may mean that any discrimination because of a characteristic linked to sex, as height is, is a discrimination because of sex; the statute does not contain words like "directly." (That hypothetical regulation would also discriminate against Hispanic and Vietnamese police applicants of either sex.) Some guidance in reading Title VII is available from the other civil rights laws Congress has passed. Consider, for instance, Section 504 of the Rehabilitation Act of 1973: "No otherwise qualified handicapped individual shall, *solely by reason of* his handicap be subjected ,to discrimination in federally assisted programs."[54] Comparison between Title VII and Section 504 (which has even less legislative history than the Smith amendment to Title VII does) seems to suggest that Congress knows the difference between broad and narrow language.

The "ancestor" case of facially neutral discrimination was *Griggs v. Duke Power Company*, decided in 1971. The company required a high school diploma, and minimum scores on standard aptitude tests close to the national median for high school graduates, for employment, except in jobs requiring unskilled labor. Griggs alleged that the effect of these requirements was to restrict the better-paying jobs to whites. The Supreme Court unanimously ruled in his favor. Chief Justice Burger cited data indicating that blacks received lower average scores on these tests than did whites; that the educational opportunities afforded blacks were inadequate; and that the requirements had not been shown to be relevant to job performance. "The Act proscribes not only overt discrimination but also practices that are fair in form, but discriminatory in operation. . . . If an employment practice which operates to exclude Negroes [*sic*] cannot be shown to be related to job performance, the practice is prohibited."[55] This standard was soon applied to sex discrimination.[56] In 1975, the Court ruled that a plaintiff can establish a prima facie case of discrimination by proving that a rule has a disproportionate impact on any group covered by Title VII. Once such a case is established, the burden shifts to the defendant to prove that the policy is relevant to the job.[57]

Not surprisingly, height and weight requirements were among the first neutral rules to fall under Title VII. Women plaintiffs had little difficulty gathering statistics demonstrating that women are, on the average, shorter and lighter than men.[58] Of equal importance in some cases was the failure of employers either to give women applicants below the minimum an opportunity to demonstrate their fitness for the job or to show that the requirement was relevant.[59] The relevance of these requirements could not be proved even in instances where common sense might suggest that they were sound: height requirements for police officers, for example. The assertion that taller officers are more impressive authority figures than their shorter counterparts may seem plausible, but there is no evidence to support this hypothesis.[60]

An employer—yet another airline—did win one case, in 1977, when it satisfied an appellate panel that a five feet seven inches requirement for pilots was necessary because of the location of instruments in the cockpit.[61] This ruling shows the limits of the apparently favorable doctrine of *Griggs* and its successors. In proving "job relevance," the existing conditions are taken as "givens." No one suggested that the airline redesign the cockpit, even though airplanes, like cars, are redesigned rather often—the Federal Aviation Administration, more aggressive than the EEOC, tends to require such changes.

In the same year, the Supreme Court confronted superficially neutral sex discrimination for the first time. *Dothard v. Rawlinson* killed a rule that all Alabama prison guards must be at least five feet two inches tall and weigh at least 120 pounds. This ruling (six to three, on that point) showed that the Court was willing to go a very long way in demanding proof of business necessity. The decision was small help to Dianne Rawlinson, who had a college degree in Correctional Psychology. While her case was pending, the state had adopted a same-sex rule for prison guards. The Court upheld this rule by a vote of seven to two, thus establishing sex as a BFOQ for this job under Title VII, at least in correctional systems which segregate inmates by sex. The justices were not influenced by the fact that, despite safety considerations, several other states have women guards in all-male prisons, even maximum-security facilities.[62] Rawlinson gained nothing from her court battle, but her suit did benefit other women and racial minorities by establishing an important general principle: when the justices said the employer had to prove relevance, they meant it.

The impression that emerges from these cases is a mixed one. The Courts (and the EEOC) have interpreted Title VII far beyond what a minimalist reading of its language would demand. But progress has been limited by an implicit trust of business, and of employers, which pervades the decisions. If the employer can show that a rule with a disproportionate impact serves his or her business *as it now stands*, there is no obligation to take affirmative steps to lessen the relevance of the requirement: no need to restructure the workplace, or to study what is being done elsewhere. As we shall see, several decisions of the 1988–89 term have removed ambiguity. They displayed marked judicial hostility toward broad antidiscrimination law.

Indirection and Subjectivity

This judicial respect for expertise and authority has an even greater impact in the next group of cases: those involving, not rules whose discriminatory effect can be proved, but standards which are highly subjective and cannot be proved discriminatory. This is a complex point, but some discussion should clarify it. A minimum height requirement is an objective standard; one is either five feet two inches tall or more, or one is smaller. All one needs to do to support or refute a claim that this rule excludes more women than men, or more Hispanics than Anglos, is to collect statistics. Once the plaintiff has proved a discriminatory impact, the next question is whether the standard is relevant to job performance.

But suppose the standard is, not a minimum height or a score on an aptitude test, but "competence" or "excellence" in some skill. Standards like these are virtually always relevant to job performance. While it apparently makes little difference how tall a police officer is, that officer's ability to question suspects effectively and legally is a matter of great importance. But these standards are also subjective rather than objective: work that is "excellent" (or even adequate) to one person may not be so to another. There is room for disagreement among judges.

Consider, by way of illustration, any one of the several weekly film review programs that now appear on television. Each of them (as of 1991) has two resident critics. Most of the time, the two agree on whether or not a particular film is worth seeing, whether the performances are good or bad, whether the plot is plausible, and so forth. The standards which these critics apply are subjective, but they are far from idiosyncratic; we agree, for the most part, on what words like "excellent" mean. Every once in a while, however, the two critics disagree. One of them recommends a film which the other dislikes. Applying the same standards (although not necessarily rank-ordering them in the same way), they reach opposite conclusions. And perhaps this occasional disagreement is one of the features that make these shows entertaining. At any rate, what is true of film critics applying subjective standards is equally true of employers, supervisors, and others whose task it is to evaluate work. Universal agreement is impossible. As necessary as subjective standards are, they contain an inherent danger: they can be applied in a discriminatory fashion.

It is no longer likely that an employer will admit to refusing to hire or promote anyone on the grounds of race or sex; no employer covered by Title VII, at any rate. To do so is to admit to violating the law and, therefore, to invite trouble. But suppose an employer disguises such prejudice under an ostensibly neutral evaluation: asserts, for example, that a woman employee's work is less "excellent" than her male counterpart's? Opinions about the relative capacities of the sexes and of different races have been well known in American society. It used to be widely believed that women were not suited for the professions and that blacks were less intelligent than whites. These ideas were once uttered quite freely; the people who held them before the civil rights laws made expressing them counterproductive have not all vanished from positions of power. A person who holds such stereotypes is likely to interpret data in terms of them; if you don't think women can be good scholars, you are unlikely to think highly of a scholarly article written by a woman.

That this possibility is no imaginary horror is suggested by several studies which present evidence of sex bias in subjective assessments. A classic experiment, dating from 1968, divided subjects into two groups, gave members of each group copies of an essay, and asked the subjects to read and criticize the essay. The only difference between the essays was the name that the experimenter assigned to the author. The copies which he distributed to the first group carried a man's name, whereas the second group believed that the author was female. The evaluations of the "woman's" article were far more critical than those produced by the subjects who thought the author was male. A 1985 study replicated these results. Experiments have found similar male bias in student evaluations.[63]

If it seems unlikely that anyone would deliberately judge women's work more harshly than men's, the reader should consider that such bias need not be deliberate; it may be unconscious. It is hard to know, since an evaluator's denial of bias may or may not be an honest response: is X unaware of bias, or simply lying about it? Still, the possibility of biased evaluations—conscious or unconscious, racist, sexist, or just plain personal—is so universally recognized that many professions have found ways to weaken the effects of bias. For example, scholarly journals employ a practice known as "blind review." Editors send articles submitted to these journals to reviewers anonymously; neither author nor reviewer knows the other's name. This practice is much older than civil rights laws. It grew out of people's awareness of their own and others' weaknesses.[64]

But hiring and promotion decisions are not anonymous. It is difficult to eliminate bias from such decisions. There are two opposite sets of dangers here. First, an allegedly neutral decision may in fact have been an instance of race or sex bias. An applicant ostensibly passed over for promotion because of the quality of her work may in fact have been rejected because of her sex. On the other hand, a rejected applicant who claims sex bias may be wrong; the decision may be justifiable by neutral criteria. Subjective standards permit both kinds of misinterpretations.

Several problems arise here. First, how does the law deal with a situation where an applicant claims bias and an employer defends the decision? The Supreme Court dealt with such a case in 1973. *McDonnell-Douglas v. Green* was a "one on one" case; the issue was not, as it would be in later cases, whether a pattern of discriminatory behavior existed, but whether one applicant had suffered discrimination. The Court ruled that the plaintiff had the burden of establishing a prima facie case of discrimination. Green, a black man, had done so by showing (1) that he was a member of a group protected by Title VII; (2) that he was qualified and had applied for an open position; (3) that he was rejected; and (4) that the employer continued to seek applicants after making this decision.[65] This decision is still binding precedent. It is a victory for plaintiffs because they need not prove that the defendant intended to discriminate—a burden which would have been all but insurmountable, since it is rarely possible to prove what someone else's intentions are. The employer still has the chance to prove that the decision was made on other grounds, but the important point is that he or she now *must* offer proof—and this burden, too, can be a difficult one to meet.

The factual situation in *Green* is similar to one which became all too familiar to advocates of fair housing during the civil rights movement: A dwelling was advertised; a black person inquired about it and was told it had already been rented or sold; the ad then reappeared. (A federal law and a Supreme Court decision in 1968 took care of that particular problem.)[66] Not all Title VII cases are of this type. What happens, for instance, if a job applicant is rejected, not because she is unqualified, but because she is allegedly not the *most* qualified applicant? Or what if the disputed personnel action is not hiring, but promotion (or tenure, in academia; or elevation to partnership, in a law firm)? These cases have been difficult for courts to deal with.

One tactic some plaintiffs have used to establish a prima facie case of sex discrimination is compiling statistics showing the small proportion of women in the disputed job. Courts have been reluctant to rule that a case has been made simply upon a showing that the proportion of women in the job is lower than women's proportion in the population (about 53 percent, at last count). A more sophisticated comparison is to show a discrepancy between the percentage of women workers and the number of women in the applicable labor pool. To sum up the existing case law, some federal courts have held that showing such a discrepancy does establish a case, while other courts have ruled the opposite.[67]

Sears, Roebuck won a major victory in 1986, when a federal judge found that the EEOC had failed to establish a prima facie case that Sears had discriminated against women in hiring its sales personnel. The agency had shown that women made up 75 percent of Sears's noncommissioned sales force, the workers who sell items like clothing or housewares and receive a fixed salary, but only 40 percent of the commissioned salespeople, the sellers of "big ticket" items like computers, televisions, or electrical appliances, who receive commissions and usually earn more than the salaried salespeople. The case turned into a battle of statistical analysis. The judge was persuaded by Sears's argument that the disparity reflected women's own choices: their reluctance to take the risk of forgoing a certain income and their unfamiliarity with many big-ticket items (though not, one assumes, refrigerators and washing machines). The case attracted wide publicity, partly because feminist scholars lined up on both sides of the issue as paid expert witnesses.[68] The long, complex opinion dissatisfies the reader because the different interpretations of the same data are so contradictory that any preference appears to reflect a preconceived bias; agreeing with either Sears or the EEOC is difficult unless you have already made up your mind. The case contains a lesson for ambitious women workers: whether or not Sears's explanations for the disparity are correct, some barriers to advancement may be self-imposed. But the ruling is a clear statement of judicial reluctance to allow the government to use disparity as a basis for imposing sanctions.

Statistics of this sort are not relevant to all Title VII cases. An individual may suffer discrimination even if her women co-workers are being treated fairly. Courts have held that a prima facie case is established by evidence that the only woman candidate for tenure in an academic department was not told what the requirements were, or that a university disparaged women's studies.[69] A 1985 case deserves discussion, both because the situation it presents is a common one and because it provides a perfect illustration of the inherent difficulties in civil rights law enforcement. *Namenwirth v. University of Wisconsin* upheld the university's denial of tenure to a woman zoologist. Tenure cases are difficult ones to adjudicate. The decisions to grant or deny permanent appointment on the faculty of most colleges or universities are made according to three criteria: scholarship, teaching, and service, usually in that order. Quantifiable factors—the number of publications, scores on teaching evaluations, and the like—are important, but few institutions are satisfied just to count. Qualitative judgments virtually always enter into tenure reviews, and these assessments are inevitably subjective—just like film criticism. The people who make these judgments are academics, who—like judges—excel at justifying their actions.

Another factor making it difficult to show discrimination in tenure cases is that a candidate does not always have comparable cases to point to in which others, males or whites, were treated differently. Marion Namenwirth, however, was an exception. She had a male cohort, a zoologist who came up for tenure shortly after she did; he got it, and their records were comparable according to the three criteria. But the all-male faculty insisted that only he had earned their respect and satisfied them that he had promise. In the mountain of verbiage which the case produced, that was all the university said to justify its different rulings.

It was enough. The all-male appellate panel found for the university. "Tenure decisions have always relied primarily on judgments about academic potential, and there is no algorithm for producing these judgments. . . . Winning the esteem of one's colleagues is just an essential part of receiving tenure."[70] This statement is intriguing both for its presumption that esteem is earned rather than granted or denied and for its dismissal of the possibility that the judgments of Namenwirth's colleagues could have been affected by sexism—even though the fact was on record that the university had a history of sex discrimination.

Affirmative Action

If the courts have failed to interpret the laws to protect against covert as well as overt discrimination, the legislative and executive branches of government have taken some steps to alleviate the problem. The 1970s saw the development of a countervailing force known as "affirmative action." Several statutes require that any institution receiving federal funds must provide evidence of efforts to hire and promote women, members of minority groups, disabled people, and Vietnam veterans. These required conscious efforts are supposed to balance any conscious or unconscious prejudice on the part of employers. If they have to show that they are trying to hire women, the argument goes, they will be less likely to act out their sexism.

These regulations have their counterparts in state and local government and in the private sector. By the 1980s, few public or private institutions were without an affirmative action officer, committees, plans, goals, and piles of paperwork which accompanied any personnel decision. Of course, ideas about what constitutes "effort" are as subjective as any value judgment. Sometimes it seemed to many members of committees and those who had to complete the endless official forms that the primary accomplishment of affirmative action was to create more tedious work. Most affirmative action officers are appointed by administrators (such as a university president, provost, or academic vice-president), report to that official, and are accountable to him or her. The powers of affirmative action officers are limited by these superiors, and sometimes suspicions have arisen that affirmative action officers are less than fully committed to enforcing the civil rights laws.

But satisfying an administrator that one is making an effort to hire women and minorities requires, at least, that they be made aware of vacancies, and that their applications be reviewed. Affirmative action ended the days when jobs could be filled by word of mouth, through family or social connections, or through the kinds of relationships usually called "old boy networks"—the way many professional and skilled jobs were often filled. Affirmative action also forces employers to justify their personnel decisions, however perfunctory that justification might be. Employers might be able to persist in their old sexist and racist ways, but they must now work harder to get away with it. Sometimes they succeed; Wisconsin's entrenched affirmative action bureaucracy did not prevent the university from winning in *Namenwirth*. But an employer who must answer a charge of sex discrimination in court has had to work very hard indeed.

All of these effects occur even where an affirmative action plan is weak and poorly enforced. A vigorous affirmative action program, strictly enforced, can put some teeth in the laws. Most plans contain goals and timetables: for instance, to hire a certain number or percentage of minority or women workers by a specified date. One of the strongest kinds of plans is a quota: a rule seeking to implement goals and timetables by reserving a specific percentage of jobs for certain categories of workers. Some quotas, though by no means all, have been sustained by federal courts.[71] Many affirmative action plans, less strict than quotas but often effective, require that some sort of preference, of indefinite weight, be given to women and minority applicants.

Quotas and preferences have been and remain controversial policies. One factor about them to which many people object is that they base personnel decisions partly on factors other than merit. There is no law which requires that all personnel decisions be based on merit; this feature of affirmative action plans does not invalidate them by itself. But one of the oldest principles of justice which our society can be said to hold collectively requires that people get what they deserve. And we tend to believe that what people deserve depends on their merit—their ability, diligence, honesty, wisdom, virtue, and so forth—rather than on ascribed characteristics like race or sex. Furthermore, the merit principle seems not only just for individuals but efficacious for society.

The proponents of reverse discrimination, while accepting the merit principle, see difficulties with its definition and application. There are some problems merit does not solve. For instance, when there are several equally qualified applicants for one position, using sex or race as one criterion for choice does no violence to merit. And as we have already seen, merit is often a subjective criterion; ideas of what constitutes "merit" or being "best qualified" in any given position are vague, and may very well be defined in culturally biased ways. It appears to many advocates of equal opportunity that the concept of "merit" is rather like the limerick:

> The limerick is furtive and mean.
> You must keep her in close quarantine,
> Or she sneaks to the slums
> and promptly becomes
> Disorderly, drunk, and obscene.

The concept of "merit" has a way of sneaking to the slums of prejudice. The studies I mentioned earlier (see under "Indirection and Subjectivity") suggest that people tend to rate work done by men higher than that done by women. One form of "quarantine" which the concept of merit requires may be exposure to the countervailing force of institutionalized preference. But some objections to quotas and preferences go beyond merit, and the resultant policies base decisions in part on race or sex, characteristics which are beyond the control of individuals. These plans reward some people, and punish others, because of things they cannot help and cannot change. To the extent that we believe that benefits should bear some relation to individual responsibility, such policies seem as unfair when the victims are white or male as when they are black or female. True, quotas and preferences constitute "reverse discrimination"; they benefit members of groups whom discrimination formerly harmed, and sometimes even help people who have been victims themselves. But the difficulties inherent in distinguishing between "good" and "bad" discrimination, in identifying the appropriate beneficiaries of these preferences, are as present now as they were to Justice Lewis Powell in *University of California v. Bakke* (see Chapter 2).

That case was one of several in which the Supreme Court ruled that race discrimination may be constitutional, but only when it rectifies past official discrimination or is a necessary means to a crucial governmental end.[72] While *Bakke* invalidated a particular racial quota, the decision did not declare all quotas unconstitutional, and it did allow institutions to consider race in making decisions.[73] But the language of the civil rights laws differs from that of the Constitution. The equal protection clause does not explicitly forbid race or sex discrimination. Title VII does. An affirmative action plan which allows, encourages, or requires employers to consider an applicant's sex in deciding whether to hire that person is a plan which discriminates because of sex. What troubles opponents of reverse discrimination is that it appears to do exactly what Congress forbade.

It is the issue of statutory interpretation, rather than that of merit, which has engaged the federal courts. The Supreme Court remains sharply divided over the legality (and, indeed, the constitutionality, as *Bakke* revealed) of reverse discrimination. These decisions have usually split the justices five to four, and no majority has been greater than six to three. But only Chief Justice Rehnquist has so far endorsed the view that all preferential treatment violates the civil rights laws.[74] The majority, variable as it has been, has accepted the validity of reverse discrimination in principle, and this acceptance has extended to quotas.[75]

The prevailing principles were laid out in three early cases: *Bakke* in 1978; *United Steelworkers v. Weber* in 1979; and *Fullilove v. Klutznick* in 1980. *Bakke*, as we have seen, removed any constitutional barrier from these plans. *Fullilove* upheld a federal public works program that reserved 10 percent of spending for minority-owned businesses, a quota by any definition, as a valid exercise of Congress's power to enforce the Fourteenth Amendment.[76] This case can be seen as merely an example of the deference to a coequal branch which the Court often claims to show. But *Weber* went much further. Here, the Court ruled that Title VII permitted the steelworkers' union and the Kaiser Aluminum Corporation to reserve *half* of the openings in craft-training programs for black workers.

The dispute centered on interpretations of Title VII. Justice Rehnquist insisted that to uphold such a quota under a law forbidding racial discrimination evoked the Orwellian world of "Newspeak" in *1984*; he also cited passages from the *Congressional Record* where supporters of the bill had disavowed any intention to allow discrimination against whites. But Justice Brennan's review of the legislative history quoted the statement of the Senate floor leader, Hubert Humphrey, that Title VII was meant to "open employment opportunities to Negroes." Brennan concluded that a literal reading would "bring about an end completely at variance with the purpose of the statute." The majority found in the 1964 law, not a commitment to color-blind policies, but a dedication to equal opportunity for all races and a particular concern with the plight of black Americans. Therefore, a plan which was temporary, and which neither fired white workers nor denied them any opportunity (after all, if half the jobs go to blacks, the other half go to nonblacks) was valid. Although no one had ruled that Kaiser had, in fact, discriminated against blacks in the past, and the company denied it, the decision ruled that racial disparities in the work force justified self-imposed plans.[77] *Weber*—decided in the same year as *Feeney*—was the clearest statement to date that Title VII was a stronger mandate against discrimination than the equal protection clause was.

In 1987, the Court relied on *Weber* to uphold an affirmative action plan which resulted in the promotion of a woman worker because of her sex, in preference to a male competitor who, on paper, appeared more qualified. The case was *Johnson v. Transportation Agency*. In December 1978, the transportation department of Santa Clara, California, adopted an affirmative action plan which apparently made use of some of the cues dropped in *Bakke*, decided six months earlier. The agency sought to "remedy the effects of past practices and to permit attainment of an equitable representation" of women, minorities, and the disabled. To that end, the agency authorized itself to "consider sex as one factor" in

choosing among qualified applicants for "traditionally segregated jobs in which women have been significantly underrepre-
sented." All of the agency positions classified as "skilled craft
worker" met that definition, since none were filled by women.

The plan's long-term goal was to have the agency's proportion
of women workers in all its jobs approximate that of the women's
proportion in the local labor market: about 36 percent at that
time. The agency knew that this goal was realistic only in the long
run; the male workers were not all going to resign any time soon,
nor were many local women currently seeking the skilled craft
jobs. But it did try for "statistically measurable yearly improvement." Short-term goals were established, and adjusted every
year.

The plan had been in effect for only one year when, in December 1979, the agency had a vacancy for a road dispatcher. This
skilled craft position required at least four years of prior experience as a county road worker. This requirement is exactly the sort
of apparently reasonable rule which often excludes more women
than men, but that question was not raised in the resulting case.
It does show, however, that affirmative action goals can be
thwarted by institutional rules which appear irrelevant to these
goals.

Diane Joyce and Paul Johnson were among the nine applicants judged qualified for the position. As the agency's rules
required, they now faced interviews with a two-person board.
Both Joyce and Johnson were long-term agency employees.
Johnson had worked there since 1967, Joyce since 1970; he was
hired as a road yard clerk, she as an accounts clerk. Both had
applied for a dispatcher's job in 1974 and were rejected as unqualified because they lacked prior road experience. Since then,
both had become road maintenance workers: Joyce, the first
woman so hired, in 1975, Johnson in 1977. Both Joyce and
Johnson had in fact done the job which they now sought; they had
worked "out of class" as dispatchers. So both were obviously
qualified to do the job; they had done it. The question was
whether the agency would judge either "qualified" to receive the
rewards accompanying the official job title.

The interviewers' procedure was similar to that used in figure
skating and gymnastics competitions: they awarded each applicant a point score. In Santa Clara County, however, the applicant
gets one total score, and 70 is the passing grade. Seven of the nine
applicants passed. Johnson and Joyce scored, respectively, 75 and

73, second and third; the top applicant scored 80. A second interview was scheduled for all seven applicants. Before that interview, Joyce sought help from the affirmative action office.[78]

It is hard to imagine a more subjective test than a numerical score assigned on the basis of a personal interview.[79] It is also difficult to believe that a two-point difference indicates anything but randomness—although the male district judge would find that "Paul Johnson was more qualified than Diane Joyce."[80] The considerations which troubled Joyce were more concrete. She had had difficulties with members of the second interview panel before, and she feared bias. One of the three members, a former supervisor, had refused to issue her the coveralls routinely provided male road workers until she complained; another had called her "a rebel-rousing [*sic*], skirt-wearing person." (Joyce faced the woman worker's classic dilemma: she couldn't win, no matter what she wore.) After the second series of interviews, the panel recommended to the agency's director that Paul Johnson get the job, while the affirmative action coordinator recommended Joyce. She got the job, and Paul Johnson filed a complaint.[81]

The EEOC refused to make a decision; the district court ruled for Johnson; the appeals panel reversed; and the Supreme Court took the case, with the Justice Department filing a third-party brief supporting Johnson. By the time the Court made its decision, it was March 1987. The Court upheld the plan. Six justices ruled that *Weber*—in which, of course, the plan was much stronger—had established that Title VII permitted discrimination to end discrimination, even in the absence of past deliberate discrimination. Justice Brennan wrote that the agency had shown a "manifest imbalance" in female representation in its work force, that "petitioner had no absolute entitlement to the road dispatcher position," and, finally, that "the Agency appropriately took into account as one factor the sex of Diane Joyce in determining that she be appointed. . . . The decision to do so was made pursuant to an affirmative action plan that represents a moderate, flexible case-by-case approach to effecting a gradual improvement in the representation of minorities and women in the Agency's labor force. Such a plan is fully consistent with Title VII, for it embodies the contribution that voluntary employer action can make in eliminating the vestiges of discrimination in the workplace."[82] Although *EEOC v. Sears, Roebuck* had limited the government's power to impose corrective plans because of disparities, this decision allowed an employer to decide to do something that the state could not make it do.

The majority was tenuous, however. While Justice Stevens wrote separately that he might be willing to go even further than this case, Justice O'Connor insisted that the majority had gone too far; she concurred only because she was convinced that prior gender discrimination had occurred. One of the three dissenters, Justice White, announced that he would now vote to overrule *Weber*, though he had joined that ruling eight years earlier. The minority rejected the conclusion that race or gender imbalance, in themselves, justified even self-imposed compensatory action which hurt white or male workers. The newest justice, Antonin Scalia, was the most vigorous critic of the majority. "A statute designed to establish a color-blind and gender-blind workplace has thus been converted into a powerful engine of racism and sexism." Scalia had no doubt that a gender-blind decision would have given Paul Johnson the job. "Once the promoting officer assures himself that all candidates before him are 'M.Q.s' (minimally qualifieds)," the plan allows him to "ignore, as the Agency Director did here, how much better than minimally qualified some of the candidates may be, and can then proceed to appoint from the pool solely on the basis of race or sex."[83]

Johnson v. Transportation Agency squarely presents the issues inherent in reverse discrimination. One problem is the fact that people who make personnel decisions interpret and structure reality in different ways. Scalia's model—and not his alone—is the pyramid: some are minimally qualified, but some are superior to others, and, possibly, one applicant is best of all. Faculty recruitment decisions are often made according to this model: look at the applications and find the *best* person. This approach persists even though "it is a standard tenet of personnel administration that there is rarely a single 'best qualified' person for a job."[84] Whether or not there is one best applicant, the pyramid approach virtually guarantees that someone will be ranked first. The transportation agency's practice of assigning numerical scores based on interviewers' assessments, while not as severe as a rank-ordering—a tie is possible—is designed to produce one top candidate. Where such a procedure is employed, it is hard to convince those who accept the pyramid model that any outcome except hiring that "best" person is acceptable—whether sex or race issues are present or not.

The model presupposed by the agency's final hiring procedures is not a pyramid; it might better be envisioned as a horizontal line. The director had to choose among several applicants along that line; they got there by being "M.Q.s." This model assumes that all applicants are so nearly equal that differences among them do not matter. The goal is not to choose the best applicant, but to find several good applicants. With these procedures, any outcome which chooses one of the qualified applicants can be seen as acceptable.

Justice Scalia implied that Paul Johnson ranked near the top of the pyramid, "much better" than Diane Joyce. In fact, he ranked two points above her according to a procedure which almost had to rank one applicant above the other. Two interviewers had decided that Johnson was a "75" and Joyce a "73." There was evidence that bias existed against Joyce, and that this bias might have been due to the fact that she was the first woman in the job. So it is not clear that a decision to hire Johnson would have been "gender-blind." If he had gotten the job, it might have been because a competitor was disadvantaged by sex bias. Johnson would not have been hired because he was a man, in the same sense that Joyce was hired because she was a woman; but his hiring would have been related to the fact of his sex. Even if Diane Joyce had had no previous difficulties, Johnson's very eligibility for the job would have been related to the fact that he was a male applicant for a job held exclusively by males. So, it would appear, the transportation agency had a choice, not between a gender-blind decision and a sexist one, but between two gender-linked decisions: one that would have reinforced the present sex segregation and another that would have, and did, reduce it. Under these circumstances, the latter choice was more consistent with Title VII.

If Johnson had gotten the job and Joyce had brought the case, she would almost certainly have lost. The agency's plan imposed no affirmative duty to hire women. If the plan had not existed, she would have had to make a case that sex discrimination was present. She might have convinced a court that her interview scores were related to her previous difficulties, and that those difficulties were related to her sex, but each of these assertions is highly speculative. The gender disparities in the agency work force were not proof of discrimination, since, as Scalia pointed out, few women had even applied for the skilled craft positions.[85] Not only have the courts failed to read Title VII to require employers to root out discrimination they did not cause, but Congress has not seen fit pass stronger civil rights laws which would require such action. Governmental refusal to work to eliminate discrimination "root and branch" has kept the laws relatively weak.[86] But neither Congress nor the courts have frustrated self-imposed affirmative change. The last fifty years have brought a shift from universal sex segregation, imposed both by the private and public sector, to public and private policies ranging from neutral nondiscrimination to affirmative efforts to establish equal employment opportunity.

The Reagan-Rehnquist Court: Civil Rights in Danger

Ronald Reagan hoped, and promised, to transform the federal judiciary into a protector of his conservative values. During his presidency he appointed three new justices—Sandra Day O'Connor, Antonin Scalia, and Anthony Kennedy—and elevated a Nixon appointee, William Rehnquist, to the chief justiceship. Several decisions of the 1988–89 term indicate that, in the area of civil rights at least, Reagan achieved his purpose. A majority on the Court now evinces open hostility toward federal protection of civil rights.

Richmond v. Croson weakened affirmative action plans by reversing an ordinance setting aside 30 percent of public works spending for minority contractors. Justice O'Connor, writing for the new majority of five, found insufficient evidence of past discrimination to justify such a quota. *Wards Cove v. Atonio* effectively reversed *Griggs v. Duke Power Company. Atonio* shifted the burden of proof from employers to (prospective or actual) employees: they must now show that a requirement which screens out minorities is *not* a business necessity. This ruling will make discrimination much harder to prove. *Martin v. Wilks* gave male and nonminority workers the right to reopen settlements by challenging court-approved affirmative action plans. *Patterson v. McLean Credit Union* limited workers' ability to bring discrimination charges focusing on their treatment on the job.[87]

Since these decisions involved statutory rather than constitutional law, Congress has the power to write new laws which will negate these decisions. But President Bush's veto of such a bill in 1990 frustrated these efforts. It is clear that the Court and the president are on the conservative side. The days of legislative hostility and judicial sympathy to minorities are over. Increasingly, the situation may be the converse.

The Worker as Mother, Actual or Potential

Back in 1908, *Muller v. Oregon* emphasized woman's "maternal functions" while upholding the state's power to limit her working hours "for her protection."[88] This emphasis seemed appropriate to the Court, the state, and most commentators on the decision, even though no more than one-fifth of the female labor force was even married and fewer still had children.[89] Now, over half the mothers of preschool-age children are employed. Contemporary discourse reflects a central fact of contemporary life: while most men have one job, most women have two. Women's steadily increasing share in economic responsibility within the family has not been matched by an increase in men's domestic responsibility. And as we learn more and more about fetal development, the primary physical difference between the sexes re-emerges as a basis for efforts to restrict women's participation in the workplace.

How is law to respond to women's assumed responsibility for childbearing and homemaking? *Muller* represents an early answer: limit women's freedom as workers to accommodate their domestic responsibilities—even if the accommodation was more theoretical than real. As late as the 1970s, the Martin-Marietta Company did the same thing, refusing to hire women with young children. But the Court followed Congress's cues and declared this "sex plus" discrimination illegal. *Phillips* announced that employers no longer had license to limit women workers because of their dual role. The policy was a vestige of much stricter rules which had been common in both public and private employment when the New Deal began. In the 1930s, some institutions had refused even to hire married women, let alone mothers. Those employers who did not restrict their labor force so rigidly often fired pregnant workers, or imposed mandatory maternity leaves. Such leaves were rare by the 1970s, but they did exist. They did not survive judicial review, either, but the details of their downfall were somewhat different.

One sort of employer which was slow to abandon mandatory maternity leaves was the public school system, employer of one of the largest categories of women workers. The two cases that reached the Supreme Court both involved pregnant school-teachers, Jo Carol LaFleur of Cleveland, Ohio, and Susan Cohen of Chesterfield County, Virginia. Cleveland's rule forced the teacher to begin her leave no later than the start of her fifth month, and to return no sooner than the first semester beginning after the baby was three months old. Chesterfield County allowed teachers to work a month longer; they could return at the beginning of the first semester following the birth if they had a physician's certificate. The rationales offered for these rules included health (hence the certificate), continuity of education (hence the requirement that the teacher's return to work coincide with a new semester), and social propriety (a Cleveland official testified that the fifth month represented the point when a pregnant woman began to "show," while in Virginia they were worried that children might point and giggle).

None of this reasoning impressed the Supreme Court. Surprisingly, its ruling rested neither on any perceived sex discrimination nor on the fact that a worker might be forced to lose as much as eight months' income. Instead, the Court found all justifications deficient under the rational basis standard. The laws violated the due process clause. Such long leaves were not necessary to protect the mother's or baby's health; continuity was not served by requiring the leave to start anywhere in the semester; and as for showing, pointing, and giggling, the Court found these considerations beneath its collective contempt.[90]

After *LaFleur*, forced maternity leaves were dead letter. Within a few years, however, many employers were considering policies that might be labeled a sort of super-maternity leave. While no one seriously argued that the health of the unborn child required its mother to leave work in her fifth month, new knowledge about real, and serious, hazards to the fetus led to new rules. Protective legislation, presumably negated by Title VII, has again become a live issue. Medical science knows far more about reproductive hazards than it did in 1908, when *Muller* was decided, or even in 1969, when *Weeks* preempted that ruling. Pregnant women are warned about drugs, alcohol, tobacco, and caffeine; as Chapter 5 will show, some states have tried to use criminal sanctions against pregnant women who drink or use drugs. Some harmful substances—gases, chemicals, lead, high levels of radiation—permeate the workplace, the home, and the environment. These substances endanger all living things exposed to them—

men, women, sperm, ova, and fetuses. The incidence of infertility, spontaneous abortions, and birth defects has risen alarmingly in recent years, as exposure to toxic substances increases.[91]

Fetal damage has become a greater social concern than damage to workers. For one thing, we know more about it—although it is quite possible that some damage is not obvious at birth. But many hazards affecting workers, like carcinogenic asbestos, may not make their damage known until long after the exposure occurs. And, of course, the unborn child cannot exercise choice—although the idea that a worker would choose exposure to risk seems bizarre to anyone but the extreme individualist. As medicine learns more about fetal damage, society has sought ways to prevent it. One way is to remove the substance. For example, hospitals have installed waste gas scavenging systems in operating rooms.[92] But even where this action is possible, it may be more expensive and difficult than removing the unborn children—which, of course, requires removing their mothers. This step is not just a matter of letting women transfer out of dangerous jobs, because the fetus is often in the greatest danger before the woman knows she is pregnant. Getting all fertile woman away from the hazards may become an attractive choice for the employer.

This is not a likely outcome if the employer is a hospital. Operating rooms need nurses, 97 percent of whom are women. No wonder hospitals chose to remove the culprit rather than the victim. But many of the jobs that expose workers to toxic substances are not the predominantly female ones; they are the skilled, relatively well-paying blue-collar positions. Before Title VII, men had a virtual monopoly on these jobs. Some women have them now, but these women remain a small minority of the total. In situations like these, industry has adopted an "almost alarmist posture." As one executive declared, companies are "willing to be criticized for not employing some women—but not for causing birth defects."[93]

Some companies fired women of childbearing age outright, or refused to hire them. Others forced them to transfer to other jobs, losing pay and seniority. The American Cyanamid Company at Willow Island, West Virginia, found yet another solution. It forced seven women to either undergo sterilization or take inferior jobs. The five who submitted to this coerced surgery lost their jobs anyway in 1980, when the plant closed. In 1989, a federal appeals court upheld a company's rule barring all fertile women from working in areas with high concentrations of lead. During the 1990–91 term, the Supreme Court will consider *United Auto Workers v. Johnson Controls*, a case involving an employer's refusal to allow *any* women of childbearing age to work in certain jobs.[94]

The apparent sensitivity to the welfare of unborn children becomes suspect when we realize that no woman has been forced to leave a predominantly female job. Nor has much attention focused on the toxic substances that industry provides for housework, such as asbestos in oven mitts and ironing board covers.[95] Public and private concern have seemed to focus on women who are competing for men's jobs. The policies which some commentators have labeled "new" protective legislation appear to have something in common with the old kind: they serve as a way of limiting women's job mobility.

But this problem cannot be dismissed so abruptly. Of course, we should protect fetuses: but why do so in a way that sets the interests of women against those of unborn children? And how is it that employers can get away with measures that restrict the workers the most at the least possible cost to the employers? "The focus on excluding all women from jobs involving harmful exposure evades the reality that no women, and no men, wish to have their offspring or potential offspring exposed to harmful substances; but neither do they wish to lose decent jobs. It is an untenable dilemma."[96] Nor do male or female workers wish to be exposed to toxic substances themselves. Yet, in spite of voluminous evidence of the abundance of workplace hazards, organized labor, industry, and government remain inactive. Millions of workers must risk life and health to earn a living. Concern over fetal protection is both a diversion and a red herring. A social problem is turned into a woman's problem—and restricting women's freedom becomes the solution.

Mandatory leaves and dismissals are not the only policies that make work and motherhood a difficult mix. *LaFleur* was only a few months old when the Court indicated that there were limits to how far it would go to strike down penalties on pregnancy. *Geduldig v. Aiello* sustained a California law (long since revised) which established a medical benefits fund for all workers within the state from contributions from wages, and excluded from coverage care related to a normal pregnancy. The justices found this law a rational way of limiting expenses. It found no sex discrimination: "There is no risk from which men are protected and women are not. Likewise, there is no risk from which women are protected and men are not."[97]

Justice Potter Stewart wrote those two sentences. William Rehnquist, who concurred in *Geduldig*, apparently liked them very much. He quoted them twice in his majority opinion in 1976, when, mystifyingly, the Court ruled that Title VII went no further than the Constitution in forbidding such discrimination—here, a giant corporation's sickness and accident benefits plan. The statement is plain wrong. Under such a plan, women run the risk of having no coverage when they incur a condition requiring medical treatment. Men do not run this risk. But *General Electric v. Gilbert* relied on figures suggesting that "there is no proof that the package is in fact worth more to men than to women," and on an alleged factor other than sex-specificity which differentiated pregnancy from other conditions: it "is not a disease at all, and is often a voluntarily undertaken and desired condition."[98]

Brennan's dissent pointed out that the plan covered other "voluntary" conditions.[99] We could dispute, in fact, whether pregnancy is often or even usually "voluntary." There is a more complex issue lurking here, however, which lies at the heart of social policy toward working mothers. Rehnquist's language suggests that a woman who becomes pregnant puts herself at risk; having conceived willingly, she must then accept the disadvantages attendant on that condition. If her insurance plan will not pay her medical bills, well, that is too bad. She has no grievance, since she has deliberately incurred those bills.

The implication is that work and motherhood are adversarial conditions, and that having children is a private decision to take on a private burden. It is not necessary to believe that whatever is good for General Electric is good for the country to wonder where G.E.'s customers in 2020 will come from, and to suspect that the conflict between individual and corporate interests has been exaggerated. But could not the employer, and the state, assume with equal validity that a woman who bears a child is benefiting society? Might we not, therefore, give the mother all the help we can in return for taking on the double burden of worker and parent? European countries provide a cash allowance to all mothers of young children. Policies like G.E.'s make life harder for working parents; why not make it easier?

The Pregnancy Discrimination Act of 1978 negated *Gilbert*. Employers must now treat pregnancy like any other physical condition.[100] But amending the civil rights law has not settled all the difficulties involved, because pregnancy and childbirth are more than physical conditions. Although some women become indignant at any implication that pregnancy and childbirth are diseases or disabilities, it is true that pregnancy can produce disabling symptoms like nausea and fatigue, and that childbirth requires a short period of recuperation. Congress's action reflected a belief that, to the extent that women's reproductive function is disabling, it is only fair to treat it like any other condition.

But there is a crucial dimension of childbirth which absolutely distinguishes it from other conditions: it produces a baby. The mother experiences physical changes after childbirth which ordinarily foster emotional bonding with the baby. She alone can breast-feed the baby, if she wishes to. By custom, even when not by biological necessity, she is the primary provider of the continuous care that a newborn infant requires. A mother is often physically able to return to work before she has been able to establishing the bonding—or even the feeding schedule—necessary for the baby's welfare and that of the reconstructed family unit. At this point, families may be best served by policies that do *not* treat childbirth like any other condition. Childbirth is a sociopsychological as well as a medical phenomenon.[101]

Some states have been ahead of the national government in this area. California's Fair Employment and Housing Act, passed in 1978, requires employers to grant up to four months' "pregnancy disability leave." But when Lillian Garland tried to return to her receptionist's job with the West Los Angeles branch of the California Federal Savings and Loan Association (Cal Fed) in April 1982, the bank informed her she had no job. Cal Fed maintained that the law on which Garland had relied conflicted with and was preempted by Title VII as amended: it unlawfully discriminated in favor of pregnant workers. The state agency which enforced the law ruled in Garland's favor; the bank then went into federal court.[102]

Like the Sears, Roebuck dispute, this case found feminists on both sides of the issue. The National Organization for Women filed a brief on behalf of the bank. NOW shared the fear of the American Civil Liberties Union that a leave that was, in effect, a parental leave applying only to women would "reinforce stereotypes about women's inclinations and abilities" and "deter employers from hiring women of childbearing age."[103] But other feminists felt that such arguments were a cowardly capitulation to corporate power and a denial of the realities of many women's lives.[104]

Certainly, a woman-only leave of absence presents dangers and problems; whatever its effects on stereotypes, it certainly reinforces women's disproportionate responsibility for child care. The late 1980s saw a growing dispute among feminists over whether this social reality was natural and desirable, or unjust and intolerable.[105] If the current division of domestic labor is unjust, then a sex-neutral parental leave is preferable to California's law. But the current law is all the assistance that Lillian Garland and women like her have. And what is more likely to lead to sex-neutral leaves in the future: a woman-only leave now, or no leave at all? Historians agree that the old special labor laws for women, flawed as they were, helped produce a social consensus in favor of general laws; perhaps laws like California's will do the same.[106]

Another division among feminists which this case exposed concerns economic rather than family philosophies. The fear expressed by NOW that businesses would refuse to hire women of childbearing age if the Court upheld the law might appear misplaced, since Title VII already prevents both sex and "sex plus" discrimination. But the prevalence of this concern revealed not only the well-known fact that enforcement of the civil rights laws is spotty, but also the possibility that feminists might accept American capitalism more or less as they find it, agreeing that business has the right, as a rule, to further its own interests. Some feminists insist that sexual equality requires fundamental changes in this kind of corporate license. The solution to this problem is to limit this license by enforcing existing laws.

The issues which so divided feminists and liberals did not agitate the Supreme Court. *California Federal Savings and Loan Association v. Guerra* found the justices ideologically divided as they had been in *Weber* and would be, two months later, in *Johnson*. Justice Marshall found that the state law was in conformity with the purpose of the 1978 amendment, "to guarantee women the right to participate fully and equally in the workforce, without denying them the fundamental right to full participation in family life." Justice White, joined by Justices Rehnquist and Powell in dissent, reiterated the more literal reading of the *Weber* dissents.[107] The result appears to be a sensible one. To the extent that pregnancy and childbirth are conditions which temporarily disable workers, they must be treated like all such conditions. To the extent that childbirth creates unique social relations and responsibilities, it may be treated differently from physical conditions which do not.

So far, efforts to pass federal laws requiring family parental leaves have failed. In the fall of 1988, the 100th Congress adjourned without acting on a bill which would have guaranteed workers an unpaid parental leave of up to ten weeks. This bill would not only have helped women balance their duties as workers and mothers, but would also have made mothers and fathers freer to divide the family's economic and domestic responsibilities as they chose. Subsidized child care is another area where the United States lags behind; it has gotten on the political agenda only recently. Another bill which the 100th Congress failed to pass was the "ABC"—Act for Better Child Care Services— late in 1988. Opponents charged that ABC, or even a weaker compromise, would spend too much money, inflate the federal bureaucracy, and redistribute income in ways unfair to families with full-time homemakers. When Congress finally passed a family leave bill in 1990, President Bush vetoed it.[108]

As in Chapter 2, a comparison between motherhood and military service is apt. Both activities can conflict with a worker's responsibilities on the job. *Feeney* upheld veterans' preferences, only one of many public and private rules which encourage accommodation between the roles of worker and soldier. But society does not make similar accommodations for the worker who is also a parent. Yet, presumably, both parenthood and military service benefit society. The hypothetical visitor of Chapter 1 might be forgiven for concluding that this society values fighting more than it does child rearing.

Conclusion: One Cheer for a Paycheck

Women have always worked. The fact that most of their work took place within the home did not make their lives less burdensome than men's; it simply meant that women's hard work was unpaid. One aspect of women's lives which has not changed since the 1930s—or, for that matter, since colonial times—is that unpaid domestic labor is still their responsibility. But one of the most profound social changes since the New Deal is the entry of women into the paid labor force. In 1930, only one fifth of American women were gainfully employed; now, more than one half are. Many, perhaps most, of these women will be in the labor force all their adult lives. It is unlikely that women work harder now than they did, say, one hundred or even fifty years ago; homemaking without modern labor-saving devices was grueling labor. Indeed, throughout most of history, women have worked harder than we can easily imagine—a fact that must never be forgotten.[109] But a devotee of conspiracy theories might wonder if, as technological advances made housework less arduous, patriarchy had given women new duties to deprive them of any leisure time. One does not have to go to those extremes to notice that most women now have two full-time jobs.

Most advocates of sexual equality believe that this enormous change is, on balance, a healthy one. Whatever else a wage earner must do when she gets home, her income brings her a measure of independence and security. It is this autonomy which, for all practical purposes, makes a person an adult in modern society. The fact that women have more choices about how to spend their lives than they did in the 1930s brings them nearer to full equality. And the situation of working women is getting better in many respects: pay and opportunities, relative to men's, are better than they were fifty or even ten years ago.[110]

But women still have to work harder than men do, for less reward. Not only do most women have one paid and one unpaid job, but the paying jobs most of them have give them less pay, less prestige, and less opportunity than men's jobs confer. The average salary for women employed full-time and year-round is only 65 percent of the male equivalent. Three fifths of American working women are concentrated in three "pink-collar" ghettos: clerical, service, and teaching jobs. To borrow a phrase from E. M. Forster, the English writer who felt democracy deserved only two cheers, we may give, not even two cheers, but perhaps just one, for women's participation in the labor force.

As society has changed, so has the law. When the New Deal began, deliberate sex discrimination was the official policy of state and national government alike. Now, government forbids sex discrimination. It would be going too far, however, to say that law has moved from an endorsement of sex discrimination to a commitment to full equality. The civil rights cases, agency policies, and legislative inaction which characterized most of the 1970s and 1980s teach the bitter lesson that equality is not simply the absence of discrimination. Affirmative action, comparable worth, parental leave, and an effort to probe the implications of ostensibly neutral personnel decisions are goals whose realization ranges from partial to nil.

The fate of civil rights law has been intimately connected with the fate of the New Deal. Some experts interpret the general election of 1980 as the end of the experiment with a social welfare state which began with the 1932 election. Although it seems unlikely that government will return to the minimalist levels of the years before the Great Depression—and, certainly, the Reagan administration reduced neither the government's size nor its power—it is possible that state intervention in the private sector has gone as far as it will in the foreseeable future. Americans may be more reluctant to use law to limit business than was true before 1980. Whatever views predominate on sexual equality, comparable worth would still interfere with the free market, and quotas and mandatory leaves tell corporations what they must do. Civil rights law can run afoul of capitalism as well as patriarchy.

But even post-Reagan Washington is willing to interfere with individual, corporate, and state freedom when it wants something badly enough. Anti-drug policies and the raising of the drinking age to twenty-one are two examples. In both cases, free market principles and limited government yielded to other values. Sexual equality in the workplace is clearly *not* a value to which the national government assigns a high priority. Society may no longer be so dominated by the principles of patriarchy that it is willing to use law to keep working women in a subordinate place. But patriarchy is still strong enough to limit society's willingness to make other values yield to full equality.

REFERENCES

Baer, Judith A. *The Chains of Protection: The Judicial Response to Women's Labor Legislation.* Westport, Conn.: Greenwood Press, 1978. Historical treatment and case analysis of policies from the Industrial Revolution through Title VII. Published too early to cover the fetal protection debate.

Hewlett, Sylvia Ann. *A Lesser Life: The Myth of Women's Liberation in America.* New York: William Morrow, 1986. A controversial defense of policies based on the assumption that women are primarily mothers and homemakers.

Hochschild, Arlie, with **Anne Machung.** *The Second Shift: Working*

Parents and the Revolution at Home. New York: Viking, 1989. Shows that men have only one job while women have two.

MacKinnon, Catharine A. *Sexual Harassment of Working Women*. New Haven, Conn.: Yale University Press, 1979. The definitive work on its topic.

Myrdal, Alva, and **Viola Klein.** *Women's Two Roles*. 2d ed. London: Routledge & Kegan Paul, 1968. Its title and date provide evidence that the phenomenon Hochschild is discussing is not new.

Rothman, Barbara Katz. *Recreating Motherhood*. New York: W.W. Norton, 1979. A well-researched and provocative discussion of issues of home and work.

4

Women and the Private Sphere: Beyond the Patriarchal Family

Work, the subject of Chapter 3, is an integral part of human life. But it is only part. A striking feature of modern society is our habit of viewing our lives as divided into two separate compartments or spheres. Work belongs to, and often dominates, the public sphere. Contemporary discourse does not delimit this sphere with any precision, but, in general, public activity is that which is centered, physically or emotionally, outside the home. Life's other compartment is, of course, the private sphere, which, again speaking generally, is centered within the home. This sphere includes, and is often dominated by, family life.

The perception of a dichotomy between public and private is conventional rather than natural. People have not always, in every time and place, thought about life this way, let alone lived it this way. As Chapter 3 suggested, before the Industrial Revolution the public-private distinction would have been irrelevant to most Americans. Agrarian societies do not separate work and home into separate compartments, but modern industrial societies do. Here and now, in 1990s America, work and private life are separate spheres.

The distinction between public and private has been a prominent theme in the history of ideas even when it has not been social fact. Aristotle dwelt on it, and so did John Locke and other eminent philosophers in the Western tradition.[1] These themes remain important in contemporary society. Most writers, throughout Western civilization, have identified the private sphere with the conventional "nuclear" family. The basic unit of wife, husband, and their children, sometimes joined by other blood relatives, is the accepted pattern in our society, although it is not the only way in which people organize their private lives. The word "family" has been and remains a powerful symbol in social discourse. Typically, we think of the family as a "haven in a heartless world," an institution based not on power but on love. Husbands and wives, and parents and children, are supposed to love one another; adults are supposed to care for the young, and grown children for their aged parents. Family members subordinate their own desires to the needs of others. The family is the setting where the virtues of unselfish love, nurturance, and mutual responsibility are realized. Popular discourse does not reflect similar presumptions about private relationships which do not conform to this pattern, even though they, too, often embody the virtues of love and caring. Social norms presume that the conventional family is the preferred mode of organization of the private sphere, superior to all other lifestyles.

The decline—or even "death" or "destruction"—of the family is a popular theme in both scholarly journals and the mass media. Candidates for public office proclaim their loyalty to—and, often, their opponents' contempt for—"family values." The family is a good thing to be for, and a bad thing to be against. One sure way to invite accusations of being "antifamily" is to profess a commitment to sexual equality. The feminist movement is prominent among those forces considered hostile to the family. Phyllis Schlafly had considerable success with this theme, and some prominent thinkers have offered their own variations.[2] Feminists have not rushed to fuel this fire by mounting ideological attacks on the family in recent years; anyway, only a minority of feminist thinkers ever did.[3] But, somehow, the idea has arisen that a contradiction exists between family values and sexual equality.

One way to begin to understand this development is to look up the word "family" in the dictionary. Among the word's many meanings is "the basic unit in society having as its nucleus two or more adults living together and cooperating in the care and rearing of their own or adopted children." So far, so good: what is sexist about that? Well, the first definition listed is "a group of individuals living under one group and usually under one head."

The dictionary does not specify who that "head" is supposed to be. But, in all societies, there are some things people just know. In our society, the head of the family is male: the paterfamilias in the patriarchy. The notions of family and patriarchy are hard to separate. There is no reason why a group of adults caring for children has to be dominated by the father. But it is a historical fact that male dominance has been prominent among the "values" intrinsic to the family.

None of the common definitions of "family" mentions the word "love." And, indeed, the idea that husband and wife should love each other is by no means universal in all societies; it is a relatively recent, culture-bound notion. The dictionaries concentrate on kinship, headship, and function. The family is partly an economic unit; its task is to raise children. Another "family value," which dictionary listings do not reveal, is at least as old as Aristotle. Any society or ideology which has compartmentalized public and private life into separate spheres has assigned people to one sphere or the other on the basis of sex. Men have been responsible for the public sphere, while women are responsible for maintaining private life. And these dichotomies have always ranked the private sphere, where women belong, below the public, a ranking which makes devaluing women easy.[4] Power, prestige, male dominance, and social duties are as much a part of family values as love and altruism are. The *traditional* male-headed family is incompatible with feminist principles. But American society, as we will find, has come a long way from the traditional family. So we still do not know whether family life and sexual equality can coexist.

Law enters private life as it enters all of life. American law treats the private sphere in complex and contradictory ways. Cases and statutes reflect the presumption that the conventional family is the best of all possible lives, but do little to enhance the quality of conventional family life. Law no longer embodies the patriarchal values historically associated with the family, but, in its hard-won neutrality, it allows male dominance to continue.

Preserving Family Values

In law, as in society, the conventional family is presumed to be the typical form of private life. Many laws disfavor people who make other choices about their personal lives. But such punishment for those who do not conform is not matched by rewards for those who do. The law does almost nothing to improve the lifestyle it prefers.

All women have private lives. But we do not all choose, as adults, to form families. Census figures reveal that 53.4 percent—just over half—of adult American women live with their husbands. Thirteen percent live alone; 29 percent with other relatives; and 4 percent with nonrelatives. This last group includes almost 2 million women who are part of the couples whom the Census Bureau calls POSSLQ's: persons of the opposite sex (unmarried) sharing living quarters.[5] The Census does not inquire about sexual activity, but it is probable that many of the people who live with nonrelatives are living with their male or female lovers. The lesbian couple, and the woman who does not marry her male lover, are denied privileges which married couples enjoy as a matter of course; so are people in communal living situations, whether or not they are sexually intimate with one another.

A news story published in November 1988 illustrates this kind of discrimination. A public housing project in Chicago had been the scene of several murders. As a result, the city's Housing Authority had sealed off the project to anyone who was not a leaseholder. This decision locked several men out of their homes. These men lived with women renters, many of them on public assistance; in some cases, these unions were of several years' duration and had produced children. Eight of these men, vowing "never to be shut out again," married their lovers in a multiple wedding ceremony. The incomes of some of these couples will now be reduced, since the men have jobs and their new wives' welfare and housing allowances are based on family income.

The reporter apparently considered this event a charming human interest story, but it is a tale with a darker side. The state forced the housing project's residents to conform to middle-class social norms and to choose between their companions and their income. "Once comfortable in their relationships, they were suddenly jarred into the realization that their long-standing unions were recognized by few people other than themselves." Yet these were serious relationships, with commitment and responsibility on both sides; they were the kinds of unions with which these residents were most familiar. Some of the brides and grooms had never attended a wedding before, or known anyone who had been married. The government used its power over the poor to punish them for living outside the traditional family, even though the residents were following the customs of their own subculture. The tenants made the best of a bad situation. But suppose that some of those locked out had been women, living in lesbian relationships. They would have had even less control over their lives. The law forbids marriage between people of the same sex.[6]

Most Americans are not vulnerable to this degree of governmental control. But the law has subtler ways of penalizing unmarried couples, whether they are heterosexual or homosexual. The surviving partner does not inherit when a lover dies intestate. Unmarried couples may remedy this disability by making wills, but lovers cannot get survivors' benefits under Social Security or other pension plans, which cannot be "willed" to another person. A worker cannot get insurance coverage for his or her partner under employee benefit plans. National, state, and local governments have the power to change these policies, but only New York State has done so, by executive order.

Many, perhaps most, heterosexual couples could remove these disabilities by doing as the residents of Rockwell Gardens did: marrying. But why should they have to? The cases involving the rights of unwed fathers showed that this lifestyle is a prevalent one; the fact that many of these relationships are long-standing indicates that they represent responsible choices, not sexual license. The statistics also reveal that this lifestyle is particularly common among black Americans, a fact which brings a racist taint to any efforts to force them to marry (see Chapter 2). Legal preferences for the conventional family sit uneasily with two Supreme Court decisions that will be discussed in Chapter 5, which appear to recognize a right of privacy within heterosexual relationships.[7]

Since homosexual couples cannot legally marry, they lack even the coercively structured choices available to heterosexuals. Homosexuals bear the brunt of pro-family bias. Expert opinion once labeled homosexuals as mentally disturbed. The religious right and the "Moral Majority" now rank them as anti-heroes in their particular demonology. Society has used the AIDS epidemic to reinforce its fear and distrust. Although law does not go to these extremes, it reflects much of the homophobia prevalent in society.

Not only are gay couples powerless to escape the discriminations imposed upon all unmarried couples, but they suffer some additional legal burdens. As we shall see, divorced mothers who are lesbians often risk losing their children to their former husbands. They also may risk criminal penalties. Gay Americans do not enjoy even the limited right of privacy which protects heterosexual activity. Although many states have repealed the laws against homosexual activity, a 1986 decision upheld states' powers to make it a crime, on the grounds that "prescriptions against this conduct have ancient roots."[8] Apparently because of its longevity, homophobia is one prejudice against a "discrete and insular minority" which has become a legitimate basis for law.

There are some signs of gradual, piecemeal change. In July, 1989, the New York Court of Appeals ruled that gay couples who have established a long-term relationship constitute "families" within New York City's rent control regulations (and, therefore, a man whose lover had died had the right to continued tenancy in an apartment). San Francisco's board of supervisors voted to allow heterosexual and homosexual unmarried couples to include each other in health and life insurance plans. However, voters defeated this proposal in a referendum.[9]

The case of Karen Thompson and Sharon Kowalski of Minnesota is a chilling example of legalized homophobia. The two women had been living together for four years when Kowalski was permanently disabled in an automobile accident in 1983. Kowalski's parents went to court to keep Thompson away from her. A judge appointed her father as her guardian; he then put her in a nursing home, where her condition deteriorated, and refused to let Thompson visit her. It took Thompson three and a half years to get court permission to visit Kowalski and to get an expert determination of Kowalski's mental competence. Early in 1989, a judge ruled that Kowalski was competent to make her own decisions. Her father was relieved of his guardianship. But for years, the law intervened to destroy the loving relationship these women had established.[10]

There is no reason to believe that homosexuality would ever have become a social problem by itself, in the absence of prejudice against it. Virtually every society of which we have reliable records has included people whose erotic preference is for members of their own sex. The proportion of homosexuals in any society appears to be relatively constant, approaching 10 percent. Although many societies have labeled homosexuals as sick or evil, there is no objective evidence that they are more likely than heterosexuals to engage in pathological behavior. Nevertheless, society and law continue to stigmatize and oppress this segment of the population.[11]

Not all official distrust of lifestyles other than the conventional family can be linked to feelings about sex. *Village of Belle Terre v. Boraas* had nothing to do with love outside marriage. The village prohibited more than two persons not related by blood, marriage, or adoption from living in the same house. It enforced this ordinance against six students at the State University of New York at Stony Brook, who shared a house in order to cut down on expenses, and their lessor. The Supreme Court upheld the policy, ruling that "the police power . . . is ample to lay out zones where family values, youth values, and the blessings of quiet seclusion and clean air make the area a sanctuary for people." The justices did not explain why and how families were quieter and cleaner than nonfamilies of the same size.[12]

This official hostility to any lifestyle which departs from the conventional family is not accompanied by official efforts to foster the lifestyle that the state claims to prefer. American law does little to help nuclear families. Among the things which our laws do *not* do, which are done in comparable governments, are the following: provide or subsidize child care, provide cash allowances to mothers with young children, grant paid maternity and parental leaves, or make comprehensive health insurance available to all citizens. Surely, such policies do far more to preserve family life than do laws discriminating against unmarried couples. There seems to be a prevalent view that the way to express one's love for the family is to refuse to do anything to make life easier for actual families. President Richard Nixon vetoed a child care bill in 1971 to "cement the family in its rightful position as the keystone of our civilization."[13] In the 1988 presidential campaign, Republican candidate George Bush likened government-provided child care to "licensing grandmothers."

American families must bear alone the responsibilities of work and parenthood, of raising and providing for children and caring for ill or infirm family members. Far too many families must also pay for long-term medical and nursing care for any catastrophic illness or condition. Few resources are available to ease the physical, emotional, and financial burdens of these tragedies. Nor does American society do much to protect families from economic vicissitudes. Although full employment has been the official policy of the national government since the passage of the Employment Act of 1946, the United States tolerates far higher unemployment rates than most European countries do.

The "family farm" has an honored place in American values, but in the last decade the government has stood by while farm after farm failed; often the family has been destroyed along with the farm. Worst of all, the erratic economy of the 1980s has added many families to the growing homeless population. But a society which has shown itself willing to disadvantage, and even punish, people who live outside the conventional family has shown no comparable willingness to lighten the burdens of real families.

Law, Society, and the Family

American law does not do much for families. But law is far from indifferent to this institution. Family law regulates marriage and divorce; it delineates the reciprocal rights and duties of family members; it apportions power and responsibility among husbands and wives, parents and children, the infirm and the able. This law is state law: it has its roots in the old common law. It would be a fair summary of family law history in this country to say that this law has moved through three overlapping, but conceptually distinct, phases: patriarchy; what might be termed asymmetrical reciprocity; and, finally, formal equality. The subfields of family law—marriage, divorce, and child custody—have all progressed through these phases.

The old common law entrenched the situation which the term *paterfamilias* describes. The husband was the master of the household. Even if only "a ass" (as Dickens's Mr. Bumble called the law) could assume that husband and wife were one, the law did make that assumption, as explained by William Blackstone in his *Commentaries on the Law of England*: the doctrine of "coverture" deprived married women of all control over property and earnings. (Single women could make contracts and dispose of property, if they had any; most of them eked out a living at one of the few occupations open to women, or depended on family members for support.) Well into the nineteenth century, the husband could "correct"—that is, hit—his wife as he could his children.[14] The husband did have some duties in return for this dominance; it was his responsibility to support the family. Reciprocal to his family's right to support were his right to their obedience and his wife's domestic duties.

Family law has changed throughout American history as society has changed: slowly and unsystematically. When the Constitution was adopted, American family law was thoroughly patriarchal. By 1933, law had reached a sort of compromise between patriarchy and equality. And by the 1990s, spouses were legally equal. The key word here is "legally." Family law gains its greatest power over relationships when they break down, through death or divorce. Legal relationships are public, and adversary; to speak of "rights" and "duties" is, to an extent, to speak of opposing interests. Any intimate relationship where this terminology is in frequent use is in trouble. There is no police officer in the home—or the television monitor of George Orwell's *1984*—to bring households into line with public policy.

Within an ongoing relationship, the husband might have dominated the wife, but no man ever became master simply because the law made him so. Mr. Bumble's famous line confirms what everybody knows. Women do not lose their identities when they marry, and some wives even rule the domestic roost. The laws which dubbed the husband the breadwinner and the wife the homemaker gibed with several generations of rhetoric and reality, at least in the middle-class family. At that point in history when the home became a discrete sphere of life, woman was virtually restricted to it. So the great books declared, and so public opinion agreed. "Woman's place is in the home" was a common slogan of the opponents of woman suffrage—and an accurate summary of the law.

Today, this sentence is at odds with law, reality, and popular opinion. But while law still parceled these obligations out in the traditional way, common practice had already changed. One family arrangement which has been common since the end of World War II assigned both tasks to the wife. The couple married while the husband was still completing his education; his occupation was that of full-time student, while the wife supported the couple and did the housework. The middle-class wife was thus in a position similar to that which slave, immigrant, and poor women had endured for generations: performer of both the breadwinning and homemaking tasks. Some universities recognized this pattern during the 1950s and 1960s by awarding these women a certificate as a "Ph.T" ("putting hubby through"). Now, in many households both spouses are gainfully employed; the husband could not possibly support the family on his earnings alone. As Chapter 3 showed, more than half of all American women now have jobs outside the home—and no one seriously, realistically suggests sending them back.

Changing the old patriarchal laws had been one goal of the suffrage movement. Here the early feminists had considerable success. Wives gained some control over property long before any women got the vote. This success is particularly noteworthy because family law is state law; thus, every change has to be made, not once, but several times. By the 1930s, wives signed contracts and owned property. All property they owned before marriage remained theirs, under their control. Husbands could no longer legally punish their wives, nor need the wives legally obey—although the abusive husbands were rarely punished, and the marriage services used in many religions still had the wives promise obedience.

But family law remained the exclusive province of the states—and the states differed in their readiness to make spouses equal within marriage. Many states gave husbands primary, or even exclusive, control of jointly owned property. Those states which adhered to the common law system—the majority—made husbands and wives generally equal partners in managing property, but even some of these states gave husbands more control over property than wives. The "community property" states—for whom Mexico, not England, had provided the model—gave husbands primary, though not absolute, control. Although all states had reduced the husband's control over his wife, several still designated him "head of household." Wives still took their husbands' names at marriage. Husbands had sole power to determine the couple's "domicile" or residence. Wives still owed domestic service in return for support. A wife had the legal duty to "submit" to her husband's sexual demands—that was how the law put it—to the extent that no state recognized any such thing as a husband's "rape" of his wife. Husbands were no longer comparable to absolute monarchs, but they remained privileged partners.[15]

That these laws were no mere curiosities is made clear by one case decided in 1961. A couple married in late middle age. They agreed to make wills in each other's favor; the wife agreed to perform "the usual duties of a farm wife" in return for financial support while the husband lived and his estate when he died. But the husband neglected to make his will, something his wife found out only after his death. She sued, arguing that the terms of their contract entitled her to his estate. She lost; the Iowa Supreme Court ruled that the contract was invalid because, as his wife, she was obliged to perform those duties anyway.[16]

Federal courts rarely have to decide issues of family law. But twice in the 1960s the Supreme Court had to resolve federal-state conflicts which hinged on state marital doctrines. *United States v. Dege* reinstated a conspiracy indictment despite the common law doctrine that conspiracy between husband and wife was impossible.[17] But *United States v. Yazell* ruled that Texas's doctrine of coverture prevented the federal government from holding a woman liable for a small business loan she had co-signed with her husband.[18] These two cases indicated that, while the Court was not prepared to enforce common law doctrine as such, it would prefer a state's choice to maintain it over the federal government's presumption of marital equality.

But *Dege* and *Yazell* also reveal another feature of traditional family law: female subordination was not unrelieved oppression. Where the husband was dominant, the wife was dependent; both coverture and the conspiracy law relieved her of responsibility for her own actions. Reciprocal rights and duties are just that. Foremost among the husband's duties has been the obligation to support the family. The traditional wife might have to obey, but at least she did not have to work for a living. Well, no—not if the husband earned an adequate income and was generous with it. Undeniably, the support obligation has given women some protection. But the courts have ruled that the husband need provide only necessities; that he had no obligation to look for employment that would increase his income; and that the wife had virtually no means of getting the obligation enforced. And courts often cited the support obligation as justification for all the laws making the wife subordinate.[19] While the reciprocity of family law kept marriage from being a master-slave relationship, it did not therefore become a relationship between equals.

By the 1990s, patriarchal family law had been quietly invalidated. There was no dramatic event, comparable to a constitutional amendment, federal statute, or landmark court case, which changed the situation. But, while some states retain quasi-patriarchal family laws on the books, no court can enforce them. Four Supreme Court decisions within a ten-year period rendered them dead letter.

The first, *Reed v. Reed*, was discussed in Chapter 2. Decided in 1971, it invalidated laws automatically preferring males over females as "arbitrary" unless some better rationale for them than "administrative convenience" existed.[20] Four years later, *Stanton v. Stanton* overturned a Utah law establishing the age of majority as 18 for women and 21 for men. The justices added "old notions" about sex roles to the list of unacceptable justifications.[21] *Orr v. Orr* ruled that alimony had to be available to ex-wives and ex-husbands on an equal basis; neither the traditional division of labor within marriage nor a presumption that wives depended on their husbands for support could justify sex-specific public policy any longer.[22] Finally, *Kirchberg v. Feenstra* declared that the Constitution prohibited laws based on the notion that the husband was head of the household.[23]

Reed might be dismissed as a special case involving a rare situation. *Orr*, as Chapter 2 showed, is one of many cases which give feminists little to cheer about: after all, the winner was a man who reneged on his alimony. But *Stanton* and *Feenstra* are something else again. Sherry Lynn Stanton's parents divorced when she was seven and her brother, Rick, was five. When she was eighteen, her father stopped paying the support ordered for her, alleging that she was now an adult under Utah law and therefore no longer entitled to support. He continued Rick's payments after the boy reached eighteen. (Interestingly, Utah's differential age-of-majority law did not extend to the voting age. Before the passage of the Twenty-sixth Amendment, it was 21 for both sexes.) The state supreme court upheld the father, ruling that the difference was legitimate because "it is a salutary thing for [a man] to get a good education and/or training before he undertakes [family] responsibilities."[24] In other words, the state sustained a parent's decision to withhold funds that a daughter might use for her education and training. The federal Supreme Court could "perceive nothing rational in the distinction. . . . No longer is the female destined solely for the home and family, and only the male for the marketplace and the world of ideas."[25] *Stanton v. Stanton* was a clear statement that sex role stereotypes were no longer adequate justifications in themselves for public policy.

Reed, *Stanton*, and *Orr* sound exactly like what they were: cases which began in divorce. But the title of *Feenstra* is deceptive, for it, too, began with a marriage at risk, under ugly circumstances. In 1974, Joan Feenstra brought criminal charges against her husband, Harold, for sexually molesting their daughter. Harold sought the help of attorney Karl Kirchberg. To pay the lawyer's retainer, he signed a $3,000 promissory note, executing a second mortgage on the house which the couple owned.

Property cannot ordinarily be mortgaged without the consent of all co-owners, as long as they are legally competent adults. But Louisiana, the community property state where the couple lived, made an exception to this rule. Marital property was under the unilateral control of the husband, as "head and master." The obligation to repay the loan, however, was bilateral. Joan eventually dropped the criminal complaint, but the marriage, not surprisingly, was over. Harold got a legal separation and left the state. But he neglected to pay Kirchberg. Joan continued living in their former home, unaware of the second mortgage. In 1976, the lawyer threatened to foreclose on the home, where Joan still lived, unless she paid. Joan refused; the lawyer sued; and she challenged the constitutionality of the "head and master" statute.

The Supreme Court ruled unanimously in her favor. "By granting the husband exclusive control over the disposition of community property, [the law] clearly embodies the type of gender-based discrimination that we have found unconstitutional absent a showing that the classification is tailored to further an important governmental interest."[26] Kirchberg had not even tried to make such a case; instead, he had insisted that Joan Feenstra was bound by the mortgage because she had failed to use a procedure which would have forbidden her husband to execute it without her consent. That, to the justices, was immaterial. The law fell under the *Craig v. Boren* test.

Craig and *Feenstra* did not automatically expunge all traditional marriage law from the states' codes. Neither the Court nor any other agency of the national government has made authoritative statements about laws which obligate the wife to maintain the home, to adopt her husband's name, or to live where he chooses; or about those laws which impose support obligations on the husband. But it is difficult to see how any of these laws could survive scrutiny now.[27] The Court has categorically stated that laws based on traditional sex role stereotypes do not satisfy the intermediate standard by which sex-based discrimination is judged: such laws lack a substantial relationship to an important objective. The law has moved from reciprocity to equality.

But law corresponds no more closely to reality now than it did in Dickens's day. The law did not make the husband a tyrant then, and it does not make husband and wife equal now. If traditional family law did not make all wives subservient, contemporary law cannot, and has not, removed the asymmetry from marriage. For example, while woman's place is not solely in the home, the home is still woman's place. Study after study has shown that, even in marriages where both partners work full-time, the wife does most of the housework and virtually all the child care. Women also provide most of the home care for old or disabled family members. Men and women share responsibility for the public sphere, but women remain responsible for maintaining the private sphere.[28]

Contemporary family life does not apportion duties equally; women bear extra burdens. What about power? Does the woman's double responsibility increase her share in decision making? Probably not. The knowledge that we have about marriages indicates that the amount of power a spouse has bears a direct relationship to the extent of his or her contribution to the family's income. Wives who work full-time are more nearly equal to their husbands than wives who work part-time, who, in turn, have more power than full-time homemakers. But "the fact is that women simply do not get hold of as much money as they can legally call their own as do the men in their lives."[29] Husbands usually earn more than their wives; but Chapter 3 has shown that this fact does not mean that the husbands must work harder. Husbands also tend to be older and better educated than their wives. The disparities are not as pronounced as those favored by Aristotle, who recommended that men marry at thirty-six and women at seventeen, but it is still true that women "marry up" and men "marry down." To the extent that they are "up," men still benefit from asymmetry. "Underlying all family law principles in the American legal system is the concept of the privatized, closed family system, the belief that intrafamily duties . . . should be left to the private parties for resolution. . . . The 'hands off' principle functions to increase the control of the more powerful party in an institution such as marriage in which one party has the benefit of various forms of social control over the other."[30]

Another inequality between the genders which is important here pertains not to the private sphere, but to the public. Men make the laws. They dominate legislatures, courts, and the legal profession. This state of affairs represents an improvement; men used to *monopolize* these institutions. Some of the most powerful changes in women's lot within the family have been fostered by changes in laws, brought about by men. These changes, which have nothing to do with the constitutional cases already discussed, seemed gender-neutral in purpose and effect. But in fact new laws have often led to gains for men at the expense of women and children.

From Divorce to Dissolution

Throughout most of American history, marriages have been easy to begin and difficult to end. American law presumes what, in fact, has been usual in our society, though it is far from a universal truth: that people marry because both parties want to. A man and woman need only blood tests, a license, and the co-operation of a person with the power to sign the license. (Proof that a marriage was *not* the wish of both parties—that one or both were coerced, by partner or perhaps by parents—is grounds for annulment.) But until recently, law presumed that the end of a marriage was a sad state of affairs indeed; that it happened only when one partner died, or, rarely, when one partner behaved so badly to the other that married life was intolerable. Courts re-fused to take a spouse's word for it that such a situation existed. Divorce was an adversary procedure: the "innocent" party sued the "guilty" party to obtain it, and the court granted it only if the judge was satisfied that the plaintiff was indeed "innocent" and the defendant "guilty." The plaintiff had to have "grounds": he or she had to demonstrate behavior on the part of the defendant which the state considered bad enough to justify ending a mar-riage. The judge might also grant "reparations" to the plaintiff, at least if the plaintiff was the wife, and therefore the dependent party in the marriage. These payments were called "alimony"; although this word comes from the Latin for "food money," a wife got it not only because she was needy, but usually because she was both needy and wronged.

Every divorce was, and remains, individual. State law deter-mines grounds and eligibility for support, but in each separate case, a judge decides whether the grounds exist and how property is to be distributed. For example, although before *Orr v. Orr* an Alabama judge could award alimony only to ex-wives and to any ex-wife, the decision to make an award was individual; not all wives asked for alimony, and not all who did ask for alimony got it. In the eight community property states, all property jointly acquired during marriage was divided equally, even though sev-eral of those states gave the husband sole power to manage it during the marriage. (Property acquired by either spouse before marriage, or by inheritance or gift during marriage, remained his or hers alone.) In common law states, the property belonged to whoever acquired it, usually the husband. Judges might distribute this property *equitably*, not necessarily equally. What was considered "equitable" in a particular situation varied with the couple's resources, relative earning power, marital history, family size, and a host of other factors. Lawyers for each spouse had the duty of convincing the judge to favor his or her client; so it mattered which party had the better lawyer, or, for that matter, any lawyer. It could also matter how sympathetic or unsympathetic each party was; how good a witness each made; or, for all we know, what the judge's disposition was like.

These aspects of divorce law remained relatively constant from the country's founding well into the latter third of the twentieth century. But there were changes in divorce law which paralleled the general developments in family law. In early American divorce law, most of the few divorces granted at all were granted to husbands. By the 1930s, divorce was more common than in the eighteenth and nineteenth centuries, though still relatively rare: 1.6 per thousand people in 1930.[31] A related change was the existence of more grounds for divorce. Only New York restricted the grounds to adultery—always and everywhere reason for divorce where divorce is recognized at all. This state, then the largest in terms of population, would not change its law until 1967. In a large minority of states, "adultery" meant something different for wives than for husbands. A wife often had to prove repeated infidelity, while a husband could get a divorce upon showing only a single act of adultery, or even of unchastity *before* marriage.[32]

Most states also included cruelty (physical or mental), desertion, refusal to have sexual relations, alcoholism, and drug addiction. As late as 1965, only sixteen states granted divorce to men and women on the same grounds. There were states which allowed a wife to divorce her husband for failure to support her, but not vice versa. Often, only women could get alimony. The letter of the law reveals instances of bias toward one sex or another but no consistent pattern of discrimination.[33] Finally, while heretofore men had been the plaintiffs, one common feature of "divorce, American style" since the 1920s was that in a large majority of cases it was instigated by the wife. In order to understand this last change, it is necessary to determine who benefited from mid-

twentieth century divorce law. Ascertaining the facts is enlightening, because these facts discredit the popular mythology that has
grown up around divorce. Myth holds that men are its victims;
reality indicates otherwise.

The most obvious beneficiaries of mid-twentieth century divorce law were those spouses whose partners had given them
grounds for divorce, and who were willing to accept the consequences of ending their marriages. The husband or wife married to an abusive, addicted, unfaithful, or indifferent spouse
could escape. A woman who could support herself (usually a
woman without young children), whose husband had deserted or
failed to support her, or who decided that financial insecurity was
preferable to life with a badly behaved husband, could benefit
from the existing divorce law. Most wives, whether happy, resigned, or wretched, were financially dependent on their husbands. As innocent parties, they might get alimony; however, as
we shall see, this possibility was far from being a certainty.

But marriages do not always end because one partner mis-
treats the other. What happened when neither party was guilty
and both wanted a divorce? Many couples essentially lied in
court. An all-too-common New York scenario became a staple of
nightclub comics. Photographs of a man and woman in bed together were introduced as evidence; the photographer and one of
the "adulterers" were paid. (If you wanted a divorce in New York
before 1967, it helped to be able to afford this sort of charade—or
a trip to a state with more lenient laws.) Usually, the husband
posed and paid for the pictures and the wife got the divorce; but,
the more she wanted to end the marriage, the less likely she was
to demand unreasonable alimony. While this sort of behavior
made a mockery of the law, it is not clear that it worked to
anyone's disadvantage.

There was one common situation, however, which traditional
divorce law was ill-equipped to handle: the divorce sought only
by one spouse and opposed by a partner who had provided no
grounds. One familiar version of this problem was the unfaithful
husband who wanted to marry his new lover. He had given his
wife grounds for divorce; but if she chose not to use them, he was
stuck. (The same was also true when it was the wife who wanted
to change partners.) When the partner who wanted the divorce
had provided no grounds, he or she could not get out if the spouse
refused to cooperate.

The usual way out of this bind was to offer the reluctant partner a financial settlement in return for the divorce. Did wives benefit from this practice? To an extent, yes: they might be able to negotiate a reasonable settlement as a condition of ending the marriage. Many men felt that these settlements were far from reasonable. A popular stereotype saw divorce law as biased in favor of women. This belief, fueled by many prominent American men, persists to the present day, in the face of overwhelming evidence to the contrary. Some wealthy men have been ordered to pay huge sums to one or more ex-wives. It is not clear, however, that such awards are unfair; these wives often gave up their earnings to act as homemakers, hostesses, and showcases of the husband's wealth during the marriage. We also need to remember that multimillionaires are only a tiny segment of the divorcing population. Most divorces have always occurred among the poor and working class.[34]

A wife who was not financially dependent on her husband, but just stubborn and vindictive, might become what disgruntled men called an "alimony drone"—if she and/or her lawyer could convince a judge, usually male, to see things her way. But such women made up a minority of ex-wives. Throughout most of American history, wives did not typically hold paying jobs; they had given up what earning power they had ever possessed to make a home for their husbands and children; and they depended on their husbands for support.[35] Cases like *Adkins v. Children's Hospital* and *West Coast Hotel v. Parrish*, involving minimum wage laws for women, are reminders of the grim fact that in this period, as in the present, many women's jobs did not command a living wage. Unreasonable alimony awards usually occurred not when the wife was punitive but when the husband wanted to get out of the marriage quickly.[36]

Even reasonable alimony, property, and support awards were the exception, not the rule. Wives have typically gotten awards that were quite small, both in real dollars and as a proportion of the husband's income.[37] And there has always been a huge difference between getting an order of support from a court and getting actual support from a former husband. Failure to comply with support agreements is by no means a new phenomenon. One scholar remarked on its prevalence as early as 1921.[38] The sociologist William Goode summed up the situation in 1965: "The divorced wife, then, receives relatively little property from the split of joint possessions, is given very little [alimony or] child support, and in two-fifths of the cases does not receive this support regularly."[39]

Most women did not gain much from the traditional divorce law. But the most vocal victims of the old system were spouses who wanted to get out of their marriages with no fuss, no bother, and as little financial responsibility as possible. The more financial independence women gained, the more likely they were to fall into this category. The changes in many states' laws in the 1960s and 1970s were welcomed by some women as eagerly as by men. By the time the modern feminist movement had sparked the writing of books about women and the law, several states had added "incompatibility" or "irreconcilable differences" to the list of grounds for divorce.[40] Divorce was still an adversary proceeding—one spouse got it from the other—but courts could hardly demand tangible evidence of incompatibility as they could of adultery or cruelty. The divorce rate rose. By 1970, it was 3.5 per thousand, more than twice as high as it had been in 1930.[41]

The 1970s and 1980s brought drastic changes in divorce law. First, in most states it is no longer divorce, but dissolution. Second, it is easier to get; it is now all but impossible to stay married to someone who no longer wants to be married. Third, most states offer, and some require, mediation, whereby a neutral third party, with or without lawyers, helps the couple arrive at an agreement. Fourth, guilt, innocence, and grounds are a thing of the past. No-fault divorce is available in every state. A petition can still be contested, but the law now presumes that marriages end as they begin: because both spouses want them to. Since guilt and innocence are irrelevant, there are no more reparations. And, for many women and children, the results of "divorce reform" have been disastrous.

No-Fault Divorce and the Feminization of Poverty

Legal reformers hailed no-fault divorce as a victory for "honesty over perjury, a concern for the individual over legal fictions, and a commitment to understand and deal fairly with the realities of family interaction, rather than to pursue an artificial search for fault and an unproductive assignment of blame."[42] Although feminists were not the prime movers behind divorce reform, they initially welcomed it. It is easy to see why. The new laws are free of the presumptions which permeated traditional doctrine: that men are dominant and women dependent, or that men's breadwinning confers power, while women's homemaking is only a duty. Nothing in the new laws appears dangerous or inimical to women; nor do the changes provide any basis for accusing feminists of favoring their traditional constituency of professional women over working-class women. Reading the different state laws gives no clue that they should hurt any women. It is true that the people whom no-fault divorce most obviously benefits are those spouses who are financially independent, and that men are more likely than women to be in that position. But the language of the statutes contains no bias, overt or covert, against full-time homemakers or women who earn much less than their husbands.

The Uniform Marriage and Divorce Act of 1974, intended as a model for state laws, speaks in neutral terms of "needs," "resources," and "contributions." Alimony is now "spousal support," and the language of the state laws is gender-blind. But courts which award support and distribute property must consider such factors as financial need and resources; the contribution of each spouse to the other's education or career building, child care, or homemaking; standard of living during the marriage; the behavior of each spouse during the marriage; the age, health, and employability of each spouse; and the number, ages, and needs of children. Wives can even get compensation for financing their husbands' education. About half the states provide "Ph.T" wives a property interest in their ex-husbands' future incomes or allow them to be reimbursed for their contributions.[43] Most judges have discretion to do one or more of the following: order support for a "displaced homemaker" or for young children; order compensation for domestic services; or even compensate a wronged spouse for the other's behavior.[44] Child support is still child support. An ex-wife—or, for that matter, an ex-husband who has custody—may be awarded money for the support of dependent children in any state.

Divorce reform, then, was not overtly sexist either on its face or as applied. The statutes do not scream, "Red Alert!" the way an ostensibly neutral veterans' preference law does. But divorce reform has helped men and hurt women and children. An extensive investigation found that no-fault divorce has been devastating for women and children. This study revealed that a woman's standard of living, with or without children, falls by an average of 73 percent in the year after a divorce; a man, by contrast, enjoys a 42 percent increase. "The net effect of the present rules for property, alimony, and child support is severe financial hardship for most divorced women and their children. They invariably experience a dramatic decline in income and a drastic decline in their standard of living." These findings are confirmed by other studies. Thirty-one percent of all female, divorced family heads are below the poverty line. "The major economic result of the divorce law revolution is the systematic impoverishment of divorced women and their children. They have become the new poor."[45]

Two factors combine to impoverish these women. First, the amount of money which they are awarded—through a combination of property share, spousal support, and child support—is inadequate for their needs. Second, these women may not get even that amount. Dissolution proceedings are as individual as divorce proceedings were; much depends on the quality of the lawyer a party has (which, in turn, depends in large part on the fees he or she can afford), the circumstances of the marriage, and the individual judge; where mediation is used, the relative bargaining power of the parties is crucial. The judges who have discretion to make awards on the basis of need, contributions during the marriage, and potential income also have the discretion to divide property equally between the spouses or to reward financial rather than domestic contributions. (California, now the largest state, requires an equal division of property.)

Cutting the pie in half and giving half to each spouse may appear equal. But most marriages enhance a husband's earning potential at the expense of the wife's; he goes to school while she supports him, or he works while she stays home, or reduces her workload, to care for the children. When young children remain with their mother, as 90 percent of them do, the equal division solution is "an *illusion* of equality."[46] Support orders which reward spouses for making money generally favor the husband as the major breadwinner. Domestic duties often rank in divorce settlements the way they do in the Gross National Product: as nonexistent nonwork, worth nothing.

Whatever the factors which determine support awards, amounts are generally low, regardless of the father's financial circumstances. According to census data, in 1983 only 42 percent of divorced or separated women with children got any support at all from the father, while fewer than 5 percent got alimony. The average amount these women got was $125 per month. An estimated one-half of divorced mothers fail to get the awards their former husbands are ordered to pay. Women generally do not get support; men do not pay it. As a result, divorced women are forced to support themselves and their dependents from their own resources. They are on their own.[47]

Women's economic disadvantages are no longer as pronounced as they were in the first half of this century, when many of the jobs available to women did not pay enough to support them. Most women can now get jobs which provide a living wage for one person. But as Chapter 3 showed, the majority of women workers remain concentrated in jobs that pay less than men's. Husbands are likely to be able to afford better lawyers than their wives can. When children remain with their mother, her earnings have to support more than one person. The secretary, the waitress, the nurse, and the schoolteacher—who, remember, represent the majority of women workers—have to stretch their earnings a long way to support a family.

Women who are marrying today are less likely than they once were to give up their jobs for full-time homemaking. Even mothers of young children must work, because families increasingly need two incomes. It is not always clear that a woman's earning power has been diminished because of her family responsibilities. But women who are now in their forties, fifties, and sixties have often been out of the labor force for many years. If their husbands leave, these women often become "displaced homemakers." With no recent work history and few marketable skills, they are often financially stranded. One study found that these women often had to resort to public assistance. Their destitution was matched by their feelings of powerlessness and low self-esteem.[48]

So, no-fault divorce has made things worse for women. What aspects of women's situation have gotten worse? Divorced women did not fare all that well in the "old days." The number of women who got alimony and child support was never very high; nor did those who got support get very much money. It is not at all clear that reneging on court-ordered payments is any more common than it once was.[49] If the law forces fewer ex-spouses to comply with court orders than it once did—a situation which, by the way, has not been shown to be true—it may be primarily a problem of system overload: there may be more awards to monitor than courts can handle. The new prominence of divorced women and their children in the poverty statistics is probably due to the fact that there are so many more divorces than there were twenty or even ten years ago. In 1970, when the first no-fault law was enacted, the rate was 3.5 per thousand; now, it is 5 per thousand.[50] The primary contribution of divorce reform to the feminization of poverty is to have made divorce easier to get and, therefore, more common.

No-fault divorce may allow people to end their marriages easily, but it does not make the end of a marriage amicable. Most people who dissolve their marriages do not like each other very much. Perhaps it is not surprising that a husband is reluctant to support his former wife, even when she has devoted many years to serving his needs. But children are a different matter. Why do so many fathers neglect to support them?

This question has no easy answers. A man who must support two households rather than one is losing money. The fact that most men earn more than their wives does not mean that most men are rich. Indeed, more wives have paying jobs today precisely because most men cannot support even one household on their earnings alone. The result of divorce is that the income which once supported one household must now support two. Relative financial deprivation for someone is, therefore, an inevitable consequence of divorce. A man may well object to support payments because they make him suffer relative deprivation. However, there is no reason why men should suffer less than women and children do—except for the fact that husbands' (predominantly male) lawyers seem to have better success convincing (predominantly male) judges and mediators.

No one has yet been willing publicly to proclaim his or her nonpayment of support and to defend this behavior. But some men who are not themselves support delinquents have tried to explain and defend other men's refusal to pay. Anthony Astrachan writes, "The system should recognize that some men who don't pay do feel their fatherhood. . . . Individuals and organizations should recognize that a significant minority of nonpaying fathers are not showing indifference to their children but repressing pain over their loss."[51] Still, it is a curious notion of love and caring that gives a parent's feelings priority over a child's needs.

One guess, mine, is this: men are rarely the targets of moral exhortations aimed primarily at them in their private rather than public roles. While many books and mass-circulation magazines marketed for women exhort them to adhere to certain moral and ethical principles—it is hard to think of a magazine marketed to housewives which does not give advice on raising children, for instance—men's magazines do not do this as a rule. The "Ethics" column of *Esquire* is the only exception that comes to mind; and it did not stress family issues. (Similarly, discussions of issues like abortion rarely focus on men's ability to prevent unwanted pregnancies. Although the issue came up in both presidential debates during the 1988 campaign, neither George Bush nor Michael Dukakis even mentioned this aspect of the problem in articulating their different positions.) Women's magazines devote considerable, highly critical attention to men's postdivorce behavior, but few men read these magazines.

One fact is clear, however: men do not pay support because they do not want to. They also get away with not paying support because no one makes them pay. One way to remedy the second part of this equation is for the law to make, and enforce, more equitable support awards. Such a step would not demand abandoning no-fault divorce in favor of the old system of adversary divorce, or abandoning gender-neutral laws in favor of policies premised upon female dependency. Few disinterested Americans want to go back to the old days, when people were stuck in unhappy marriages unless one partner was guilty and the other innocent. The law must respond to the needs of wives who have sacrificed income to maintain their family's home, and the law must also serve those spouses who are not dependent upon one another.

There is no reason why a gender-neutral law cannot fulfill both these aims, as long as it provides for settlements which recognize wives' contributions to their marriages. Laws can, and do, speak in neutral terms of "need," "domestic contributions," "earning potential," and "fairness." Most state laws do allow this kind of award. But, as applied, results favor the former husbands. Justice for divorced wives and their children will not necessarily require changes in the texts of existing laws, but it does require new applications of these laws to individual cases. And that change will require that the legal profession become more sensitive to the needs of families and to the economic realities of marriage. The fact that ever larger numbers of lawyers and judges are women—and some of these are or will be divorced mothers—may help effect urgently needed change (see Chapter 7). But the demasculinization of the bar will not in itself bring about the defeminization of poverty. Women lawyers are no more typical of

American women than male lawyers are of men. Legislatures may need to guide courts more firmly in delineating the permissible and the desirable types of awards.

The Government and the Former Family

Getting fairer support awards is only the first step. These court orders must then be enforced. Now, many men (and some women) are being forced to pay. Since the 1970s, federal statutes have made child support marginally easier to collect and harder to evade. It is still all too easy for parents to renege on support payments. But a 1988 welfare reform law, the national government's third attempt to enforce these awards, has the potential for being truly effective. And these are not the only efforts of the national government to improve the situation of divorced women and their dependents.

Section IV-D of the Social Security Act, which became law in 1975, tried to help the neediest families: those on public assistance. Welfare mothers (and nonwelfare mothers, for a small fee) may use state and federal records such as motor vehicles registrations, driver's licenses, or Internal Revenue Service records to locate delinquent fathers. The states are required to make such a search as a condition of receiving federal funds. The Parent Locator Service was founded to facilitate this process. The law provides for garnishment of the men's wages, that is, deductions from their paychecks. The Office of Child Support Enforcement (OCSE) was set up to facilitate this process.[52]

The Child Support Enforcement Amendments of 1984 amended this provision. These changes require states to adopt procedures to enforce support orders as a condition of receiving federal welfare funds. Among these procedures are garnishment of wages, liens on property, and obtaining information from agencies such as credit bureaus. The law provides that both state and federal income tax refunds can be offset, that is, returned not to the delinquent parent but to the one owed support. These actions do not all have to be initiated by individuals, and they apply to all support orders, not just in cases where families are on public assistance.[53]

Unfortunately, this law did not solve the problem. The states lacked the ability to garnish wages quickly. The Family Support Act of 1988 attempts to remedy this defect. Several provisions, which will go into effect between 1990 and 1994, will allow for automatic garnishment of the wages of parents who do not make payments and will require the states to review all support awards every three years for welfare families and any families which request it. The law addresses the problem of unfair settlements by requiring the states to establish specific formulas (of their own choice) for determining support awards. The states must also establish paternity in cases where the parents are not married. This law represents a rare effort on the part of an administration which has emphasized family values to help actual families. It could help pull families out of welfare and poverty.[54]

To the extent that these laws help female-headed families get off welfare, they would seem to benefit society, and the overburdened public budget, as well as these individuals. Senator Russell Long of Louisiana declared, "Perhaps we cannot stop the father from abandoning his children, but we can certainly improve the system by obtaining child support from him and thereby place the burden of caring for his children on his own shoulders where it belongs." But these laws have their critics, some of whom make legitimate points. The laws are coercive; women must identify their children's father in order to get welfare benefits. The 1975 requirement that all members of welfare families, even children, get Social Security cards will now apply to all parents and children at birth. These rules have aroused fears that the government will build dossiers on individuals. In the light of experience, it is difficult to dismiss these fears.[55] Civil libertarians criticize the 1988 law because automatic garnishment of wages imposes a penalty without due process. The person can, of course, contest the decision, but not until he or she has already suffered financial loss. This is a concern, but the OCSE is not the only agency which duns first and asks questions later. The Internal Revenue Service, for instance, works in the same way.

Some objections seem less substantial. The opposition of fathers' rights groups was predictable, as was the concern of small businesses that they will be burdened with paperwork. One critic, the president of the National Council for Children's Rights, argued that garnishment "drives the parent away." It would appear, however, that a parent who defaults on payments has already gone away. Since only half of the nation's nearly 9 million single mothers get any support award at all, and only about half of these mothers collect the full amount of their awards, ample evidence exists that strong measures are needed.[56]

All of these laws provide important benefits for women impoverished by divorce. But their scope and impact are limited. As Senator Long's speech implies, the government has favored laws which reinforce the notion of the male as provider. We have been even less ready to empower women than to dun former husbands. The decision to let the Comprehensive Employment and Training Act (CETA) expire in 1982 was unfortunate for both mothers and displaced homemakers, since CETA jobs were one route out of destitution that many women took. The Reagan administration tried to abolish the Legal Services Corporation, which provides legal aid to the poor in civil cases, and to adopt new regulations inhibiting potential clients. These steps would have made it harder for poor women (including the "new poor") to get free legal advice which could help them to negotiate a fair settlement. But Congress kept Legal Services alive, though poorer, and a court rejected the new rules. The fact that the support bills were enacted while Legal Services was compromised and CETA killed suggests a lingering official adherence to ideas of female dependency. All three branches of the national government have resisted the idea of comparable worth, which would further increase women's ability to support their families. Nothing forces the government to choose between reinforcing dependence and encouraging independence; it is not *either* collecting child support *or* establishing comparable worth. But so far the government is more willing to force men to support their former families than to enable women to stand alone.[57]

Some laws have helped the older displaced homemaker. Social Security allows a former spouse to receive benefits from the earnings of a working spouse to whom he or she was married for more than ten years. Recent legislation has given divorced military and foreign service wives married for more than ten years a share in their former husbands' benefits. These laws are important, for these women have shared many of the burdens of their husbands' job; they often move their families when he is transferred (or must adjust to his absence, often on dangerous assignments) and act as hostesses on military bases and in foreign posts. The Foreign Services Act of 1980 was sponsored by the senior woman in Congress, Representative Patricia Schroeder of Colorado. The Uniformed Services Former Spouses Protection Act of 1982, which overturned a Supreme Court decision, made retirement pay a potentially divisible asset for property settlement. The Retirement Equity Act of 1984 did the same thing for all pensions. The full impact of these laws will be felt only gradually, as more Americans approach retirement age. They may well improve significantly the situation of older women, who now represent nearly 9 per cent of the nation's poor.[58]

Child Custody

The Seneca Falls Convention of 1848 included this statement in the list of "injuries and usurpations" imposed on women by men: "He has so framed the laws of divorce, . . . and in cases of separation, to whom the children shall be given, as to be wholly regardless of the happiness of women." Although this is no longer an accurate summary of divorce law, it is still true with respect to child custody. The mother has been the forgotten person in American child custody law. Traditional doctrine ranked the father's interest as supreme. This priority gradually gave way to an emphasis on the child's interests. The law has never viewed the mother as having interests which need respect. Once, she lost the children because of the father's economic interest in their labor. For a time, she kept the children because of prevailing notions about their needs. Now, she often risks losing them because of changing perceptions of their needs.

In common law, fathers had an absolute right to the custody of minor children. They were entitled to the fruits of the children's labor, which in agrarian societies was a considerable asset. Well into the nineteenth century, English and American courts entertained a presumption in favor of paternal custody in case of divorce or separation. A father lost custody only in "a clear and strong case of unfitness"; among the situations held *not* to constitute unfitness were living in open adultery and serving a prison sentence.[59]

Suffragists began to effect changes in this patriarchal policy in the same years in which they began to weaken the doctrine of coverture—about the same time that children became less of a benefit and more of an economic burden to their parents. A general shift toward maternal preference was noticeable by the end of the nineteenth century. However, ordering the father to pay child support to the mother did not become common practice until the 1920s (and, as we have seen, these obligations were not always honored). The "tender years doctrine" prevailed in most jurisdictions by the 1930s. Courts presumed, absent a showing of unfitness, that children of "tender years" (which usually meant throughout childhood) were better off with their mothers.

But "unfitness" usually meant something different for women than for men. The case of *Bunim v. Bunim*, decided in New York in 1948, became a famous example of this disparity. All parties agreed that Ethel Bunim was a devoted mother to her two teen-age daughters, who had stated their preference to remain with her after their parents' divorce. But their physician father won custody, even though by some accounts he was "preoccupied with his professional duties." New York's highest court ruled in his favor because Ethel had "admitted numerous deliberate adulteries" (of which the girls were unaware). The divided court insisted that the decision "cannot be one repugnant to all normal concepts of sex, family, and marriage. . . . It cannot be that 'the best interests and welfare' of these impressionable teen-age girls will be 'best served' by awarding their custody to one who proclaims, and lives by, such extraordinary ideas of right conduct."[60] So the double standard reigned.

Buried within the *Bunim* opinion is a phrase which presaged the next development in child custody doctrine. The tender years doctrine was derived from the presumption that the child's "best interests and welfare" demanded maternal custody. The child, not the mother, was paramount. And the doctrine did not prevail for very long. The derivative preference slowly yielded to the fundamental principle; the presumption in favor of the mother was replaced by the "best interests of the child" rule. Standing alone, this rule could be interpreted to demand a custody award to either parent in a given case. By 1983, every state had either explicitly abandoned the "tender years" presumption or subordinated it to the "best interests" standard.[61] This development has led to two important changes in the law. First, the doctrine is gender-neutral on its face; courts make no overt presumption in favor of either parent. (The noncustodial parent almost always gets "visitation rights," which the custodial parent must honor.) Second, most states now allow joint custody, which is the outcome of most mediated divorce settlements. But even with these changes, 90 percent of children remain with their mothers.

Many noncustodial fathers deeply resent this fact. They believe that custody law is unfair to men. They have written books about it, appeared on television, and formed organizations to support fathers' rights.[62] These writings vary in tone, content, and credibility. Some display paternal self-interest with no apparent concern for children. For example, Louis Keifer offers advice on kidnapping, while Michael McFadden states, "It's not that big a deal to take care of your own child. . . . I finally settled on a very pretty 22-year-old and agreed to pay her $200 a month."[63] Indeed, some experts assert that the typical custodial father turns over responsibility for child care to another woman, whether a new wife, a lover, or his mother.[64] Other spokesmen provoke more sympathy, revealing the pain of a parent who must now "visit" his own children.[65] Some people may appear more sympathetic than others simply because they make it easier for the reader or viewer to project his or her feelings onto them. Certainly, these spokesmen have yet to give the impression that they are motivated more by concern for their children than by concern for themselves.[66]

One of the most powerful pleas for fathers' rights was the 1979 film *Kramer v. Kramer*, an impressive commercial and artistic success. It depicts a man whose wife leaves him and their young son. This ambitious young careerist, who has had little responsibility for homemaking or child care and only brief contact with his child, learns, slowly and painfully, to be a parent. Months later, his wife returns—making more money than he does—sues for custody, and wins on the basis of the "tender years" doctrine. It is difficult not to sympathize with this father—although it is significant that the story is told from the father's point of view, not the child's. But fiction does not mirror reality. If a real court had heard such a case in New York, where the Kramers lived, in 1979, the father almost certainly would have won. That state had abandoned the tender years doctrine long since.[67]

Most children stay with their mother not because she "wins" in court, but because the parents agree to this arrangement. Even joint custody is often "joint" in a legal sense only; in most of these arrangements, the mother remains the children's primary caregiver.[68] But a father who seeks custody bears a far lighter burden of proof than he did in the "tender years" days. He need no longer prove the mother unfit in order to get custody. He need only prove—subject to rebuttal by the mother—that the child or children would be better off with him. It is possible that many judges are still biased in favor of mothers, and that men hesitate to seek custody because they anticipate defeat. But the evidence suggests that these fathers have scant cause for pessimism. Studies show that in the last twenty years, between 35 percent and 70 percent of these fathers were awarded custody.[69] A father has no reason to be pessimistic about the outcome of a custody dispute. The notion of automatic maternal preference is twin to the notion of the "alimony drone"; both are nothing more than popular myths which do violence to the facts. Yet these facts, alone, tell us nothing about whether anyone's interests are served by these decisions. A presumption of neutrality might be all to the good. In any given case, the father might be the better custodial parent, or at least the equal of the mother. In order to make judgments, we need both factual and theoretical knowledge.

First, the facts: why, and how, do mothers lose? The 1979 case of *Jarrett v. Jarrett* provides a good illustration of how this process works. Thirty years after *Bunim v. Bunim*, the theory had changed but the outcome was the same. Ethel Bunim lost custody of her children on the grounds that her extramarital sexual activity made her an unfit mother. By the time Jacqueline Jarrett's marriage ended, social attitudes about sex had changed so radically that it would have been highly unlikely for a judge to brand a sexually active divorced woman as an unfit parent. Since the law, too, had changed, Walter Jarrett did not bear so heavy a burden when he sued for custody of his three daughters after Jacqueline's lover moved in with her. The trial judge decided that it was not in the girls' best interests to live in such a household. The Illinois Supreme Court affirmed, stating that "Jacqueline's disregard for existing standards of conduct instructs her children, by example, that they too may ignore them."[70] So Jacqueline Jarrett, like Ethel Bunim thirty years earlier, lost her children because of her chosen lifestyle.

Jarrett v. Jarrett hardly proves that either women or children are worse off under the "best interests" standards than they were under the "tender years" doctrine. After all, the results are the same. And even in the Jarretts's own state, a lower court later affirmed a custody award to a mother living with her male lover.[71] Mothers do not always, or even usually, lose custody because they live with a man to whom they are not married. Are there any circumstances which do favor a custody award to the mother, or to the father? Several recent studies have examined the outcomes of custody disputes. They have found one circumstance common to virtually all cases: whoever wins custody, the mother has nearly always been the primary caregiver, responsible for the child's day-to-day care and spending the most time with the child. Two other patterns also emerge, although neither is by any means a universal truth: fathers often win when they have more money than mothers do, and lesbian mothers are at a high risk of losing custody.

It is impossible to regard these pockets of consistency as "exceptions" to a "general" rule of inconsistency. Recognition of a principle which favors the parent with the better income puts most mothers at risk.[72] When we add lesbian mothers, as lesbians, to that endangered category, the figure of vulnerable mothers in custody disputes could well approach 100 percent. Although that guess may exaggerate matters, it is clear that many, many mothers risk losing their children to their former husbands.

The first widely publicized case in which a father's income, education, and lifestyle got him custody occurred in 1975. This case became notorious because it involved a famous child psychologist, Lee Salk. The doctor won sole custody of his two children even though his former wife had been a full-time homemaker, raising the children from birth, while he admitted that he would hire someone to care for them. Judge Robert Polikoff discounted the care that Kersten Salk had given her children in favor of an "affirmative standard" which judged Lee the better parent because of his "vast interest in the various stages of the children's development," his "high degree of competency," and his "intellectually exciting" lifestyle. (It apparently did not occur to the judge that there might be a relationship between a person's lifestyle and what he can pay for it.)[73] While *Salk v. Salk* may have been the first such case, it was far from the last. Every investigator who has looked at custody cases since 1975 has found similar cases.[74]

As for lesbian mothers, custody disputes expose them to the twin perils of patriarchy and homophobia. This "double whammy" persists, even though American society evinces less prejudice against homosexuals than it did in the 1930s, or even the 1960s. The American Psychiatric Association stopped classifying homosexuality as a mental illness in 1973. Presumably, a homosexual would have been judged an unfit parent in the days of the tender years doctrine. However, the first recorded American custody case involving a lesbian mother was not decided until 1967, in the transition period between tender years and best interests. The mother lost, anyway.[75]

Several more recent decisions have ruled that the child's interests are best served when a heterosexual father rather than a homosexual mother has custody. For example, as recently as 1981 a Tennessee mother lost both custody and visitation rights because, in the judges words, she "flagrantly flaunted" her relationship with her lover.[76] Judges often voice the common fear—supported by no reliable evidence—that a child raised by a homosexual parent will become homosexual. This fear itself is evidence of homophobia; if the prejudice did not exist, why would growing up gay be something to avoid? In one case, even while admitting that there is "insufficient expert testimony" on parents' influence on their children's sexual preference, the judge nevertheless ruled against the mother.[77]

Some mothers retain custody of their children only on the condition that they make drastic modifications in their lifestyles. Often, they must live apart from their lovers, whose presence would presumably influence the children.[78] But some lesbian mothers have won custody outright. One New Jersey judge wrote: "Neither the prejudices of the small community in which they live nor the curiosity of their peers about defendant's sexual nature will be abated by a change of custody. . . . These are matters which courts cannot control, and there is little to gain by creating an artificial world in which the children may dream that life is different than it is."[79]

Beyond those generalizations lies a crazy quilt of rulings. Women have lost because they are lesbians, but also because they live with men. Fathers have won custody because of their greater income, even when the mother's lower income results from the fact that she has been a full-time homemaker. Fathers have won because the mother has a full-time job, and because she is unemployed. Fathers who have remarried have won custody because they can now provide a two-parent family. Violent fathers, addicted fathers, and—in a stunning reversal of *Kramer v. Kramer*, this time for real—fathers who deserted their families have returned to win custody.[80]

To interpret these facts, we need some theory, specifically that of child development. What do children need; what conditions foster their growing up happy and healthy? It seems likely that children awarded to violent parents of either sex, or to parents who have deserted them, are not being served, but most of the cases are nowhere near that simple. Experts agree—and our own common sense confirms—that children need love, emotional security, and intelligent care; they need close relationships with at least one nurturing adult. There is universal agreement among experts that children form powerful emotional ties to a primary caregiver and suffer deep psychic wounds if they are separated from that person.[81] Separation from the caregiver hurts children worse than either relative or absolute poverty; than the absence of a second parent; or than the fact of the caregiver's relationship with another adult of either sex.

If mother and father have been true co-parents, equally involved with, attached to, and loved by the child, there is no reason why either parent should have an advantage in gaining custody. (Even here, however, joint custody would seem a better situation than awarding sole custody to the father.) But this situation remains more hypothetical than real. The mother is nearly always the primary caregiver; the fact that this is also true in custody disputes comes as no surprise. Therefore, children are usually closer to and more dependent on their mothers than on their fathers. When the mother has been the child's primary caregiver, it is in the child's best interests for her to have custody if she is a fit parent. However much the father is hurt by his separation from the child, to award sole custody to the father when the mother has been the primary caregiver is to give the father's interests priority over the child's.

The "best interests of the child" standard, in practice, noticeably serves the interests of fathers. If the father does not want custody, he leaves them with the mother. If he does want custody, he has about an even chance of getting it, for reasons which have little or no bearing on the child's interests. Contemporary custody law, in practice at least, treats the father as a person with interests which merit consideration, interests separate from those of either mother or children. What about the mother? In the few cases where the spouses have shared equally in parenting, her interest in the child's companionship is as strong as the father's. In the vast majority of cases where she has been the primary caregiver, is it not stronger? For all of us, the importance of an intimate relationship tends to be connected to the emotion, time, and energy we have devoted to it. The mother does not need the child as the child needs her, but she has an intense relationship that is an integral part of her emotional well-being. Losing that child's daily companionship is a source of great pain.[82]

If the mothers lose about half the custody cases, then they must win about half of them. But these statistics do not tell the whole story. One researcher, Lenore Weitzman, found that, while about one eighth of the fathers in her sample seriously sought custody, *one third* threatened to seek custody in attempts to "persuade" their wives to accept smaller support awards.[83] The divorcing husband, who usually has more money, education, and access to legal help than his wife, thus has yet another weapon to use to increase the superiority of his bargaining power. A divorced mother often has two possibilities, neither of which is her own choice: either she and her children will be left to manage alone on one woman's salary, or she will lose her children. Two scholars envision parental receptivity to a deal:

> Economic analysis suggests that a parent may, over some range, trade custodial rights for money. Although this notion may offend some, a contrary assumption would mean that a parent with full custody would accept no sum of money in return for slightly less custody, even if the parent were extremely poor. Faced with such alternatives, most parents would prefer to see the child a bit less and be able to give the child better housing, more food, more education, better health care, and some luxuries.[84]

But custody is not apportioned in this manner; a parent gets sole, joint, or no custody. The choice which a mother faces is not that of less custody, but of no custody at all. The fact that most mothers do *not* behave in this way—that they fight for custody and often make concessions to get it—indicates that primary caregivers do indeed have psychological needs for close contact with their children, and recognize their children's need for them. To the extent that children also need what money can buy—and of course they do—it would seem appropriate to make and enforce child support awards from the father. After all, if he is really interested in the children's welfare, wouldn't he pay?

Courts in two states, West Virginia and Pennsylvania, have established a presumption in favor of the primary caregiver. Courts need only determine, first, who that parent is and, second, whether he or she is a *fit*—not the *better*—parent. These determinations have turned out to be relatively easy to make. "The result of our simple, ironclad rule," says a former state chief justice, "is that in West Virginia there is almost no custody litigation."[85] Both state legislatures, which have the power to modify or reject this judicially established rule, have let it stand.

All fifty states award custody according to the best interests of the child. Expert opinion, empirical observation and common sense agree that the child's best interests require placement with the primary caregiver. Why, then, have only two states adopted so sensible a policy? Probably because, given the realities of contemporary family life, such a policy would almost always place the children with the mother. Child custody decisions involve three classes of humankind, if we define "class" not by relationship to the means of production but to the means of reproduction: mothers (women), fathers (men), and children (whose sex, since they are the products of reproduction, is relatively unimportant in this context). The class which is the most powerful of the three is the fathers. It should not surprise us, therefore, that, with one exception, child custody standards have worked to their advantage. The exception is the tender years doctrine, but this standard only prevailed for two or three decades. The common law rule of paternal right recognized no interest but the father's; the "best interests of the child" doctrine, neutral on its face, can be and is interpreted to favor their claims. Once, fathers always got custody. Now, they can either get it if they want it or threaten to seek it to extort financial concessions if they do not want it. Children's interests are easily subsumed into fathers' rights. Mothers' interests have never, in two hundred years of American law, been granted separate standing.

Death, Patriarchy, and the American Family

Here on Earth, at least, all marriages end. One function of case law is to set the conditions under which spouses can dissolve their unions. But the majority of marriages still end when nature, not law, decrees: with the death of one spouse. All spouses whose marriages endure face two possibilities, neither of which is within their control. They will either die first, thus depriving their partner and any children of their love, care, and support, or they will be left to carry on alone. Laws governing estates and the distribution of property after death, and laws regulating survivors' benefits are crucial to both the survivor and to the spouse who anticipates his or her own death. These laws affect men and women differently, both as written and as applied.

The Old Age, Survivors, and Disability Insurance (OASDI) program of the Social Security Administration has a long history of direct sex-based discrimination in survivors' benefits. For nearly forty years, the policy worked as follows: suppose a worker covered by Social Security died. Any minor children who survived that worker got benefits, whether the worker was male or female. The retirement-age widow of a male worker got benefits. (The age of eligibility has varied, but it is now sixty.) A widow with minor children also got a stipend. But widowers got old age benefits only if their wives had been responsible for at least half their support. Widowers with young children got no benefits at all.[86]

These provisions obviously discriminated against men, by denying them benefits to which women similarly situated were entitled. The Supreme Court decisions which invalidated the provisions explained how they discriminated against women as well. Paula Wiesenfeld, a schoolteacher, had been the major family breadwinner throughout her marriage of nearly three years. Her husband, Stephen, was a self-employed consultant who earned only a fraction of Paula's salary. Paula died when their son, Jason, was born. The boy received benefits, but Stephen was not eligible. Justice Brennan wrote, "Social Security taxes were deducted from Paula's salary during the years in which she worked. Thus, she not only failed to receive for her family the same protection which a similarly situated male worker would have received, but she also was deprived of a portion of her own earnings in order to contribute to the fund out of which benefits would be paid to others." This policy "clearly operates . . . to deprive women of protection for their families which men receive as a result of their employment." Two years later, the Court reached the same conclusion about a woman whose 72-year-old widower could not get the benefits a widow would have received.[87]

Even superficially neutral laws do not affect both sexes in the same way. The primary reason for this disparity is the established fact that a woman is more likely to survive her husband than to precede him in death. American women live longer than American men, a generalization that holds among and across all races, regions, and socioeconomic groups. A baby girl born in 1985 can look forward to an average life span of 78.2 years; a boy to only 71.2. Within marriages, the fact that most men are older than their wives exaggerates this disparity. There are about 11 million widows and only 2 million widowers in the United States.[88]

What happens to widows? From Jack and the Beanstalk to *Amahl and the Night Visitors*, folklore and fiction have assumed that widowhood means poverty. This myth conforms to fact. Widows are not much better off than divorcées. One-fifth of all American widows live in poverty.[89]

Widows are poor for the same reason divorcées are: they lose the male earnings that used to provide the bulk of the family income. A young father who dies has usually been the family's highest—and sometimes its only—wage earner. Even if he saved and invested, he was unlikely to have amassed a nest egg sufficient to support his family in perpetuity, since most young workers' earnings are relatively low and most young parents' expenses relatively high. His widow must now manage on the usually lower earnings that she can command. The older widow, who may have been a full-time homemaker all her married life, may well be as displaced a homemaker as her divorced counterpart if her husband did not put money aside. The second reason for the discriminatory effects of gender-neutral policies is the familiar one: men earn more than their wives do.

Widows do qualify for Social Security benefits if they are over 60 or have dependent children. But Social Security benefits do not (and were never intended to) provide an adequate income by themselves (and they are reduced in proportion to a survivor's own earnings or benefits). Most pension plans deny survivors' benefits to any worker whose spouse dies before a specified age, usually 55. These plans used to allow a worker to forgo survivors' coverage in favor of larger retirement payments during his or her lifetime. Since many of us are not very good at facing our own mortality, millions of workers have made that choice. The Retirement Equity Act of 1984 prevents workers from making this decision without their spouses' knowledge or agreement. But this law does not help widows whose husbands died before it went into effect. Neither the national nor the state governments have considered it their duty to mandate, or even encourage, benefits for survivors of younger workers. A woman with no young children whose husband dies before early retirement age is assured only of her share in her husband's estate.[90]

Some widows, of course, are not poor. A rich man who provides for his wife in his will or who dies intestate leaves a rich widow behind. Since the United States has a group of very few, very wealthy people, and since most women outlive their husbands, a large portion of this nation's wealth belongs to widows. They are about as typical as the alimony drone or the evil custodial mother—or, for that matter, the "welfare queen" who collects her many stipends in a chauffeur-driven Cadillac—but they are similarly potent cultural stereotypes. And, if they actually control the money left to them, they can become powerful people indeed—like Joan Kroc, owner of the McDonald's fast food chain and former owner of the San Diego Padres, who has donated millions of dollars to charitable and political causes, or Mary Lasker, who has tirelessly funded, and raised money for, cancer research.

But a rich man—or even a moderately affluent one—can deprive his widow of possession or control of most or all of his property. Common law gave widows "dower rights": they could claim one third of their late husband's estate, even if he disinherited them or made no will. Dower has yielded to gender-neutral statutory provisions. The intestacy laws of all states provide that surviving spouses, children, and sometimes parents or grandchildren inherit. The situation is more complex when the survivor is disinherited, or left only a small sum. Ten states have no laws applying to these situations, thus letting the will stand. Three allot a fixed sum or proportion of the estate to the survivor unless the testator provided for the spouse outside the will, or the survivor waives his or her rights. Eighteen states and the District of Columbia make such an allotment unless there is evidence that the testator's act of omission was deliberate. More than half the states, then, allow a husband to disinherit his widow, no matter how much labor she contributed to the marriage or how dependent she was on him financially. All American jurisdictions permit him to deprive her of a large share of the estate in favor of anyone he chooses. Here, legal changes have operated to deprive many women of rights they once had.[91]

Even widows whose wealthy husbands provide for them generously do not always control the vast sums they have inherited. In the 1970s, magazines marketed to affluent men often contained an advertisement for a firm of investment counselors. The ad showed a sleazy-looking man in a cowboy hat; the caption was, "Ma'am, I'm sure your late husband would have considered this swampland a valuable investment." The ad copy stressed the benefits of putting one's estate in the hands of professionals, presumably less gullible than one's widow, to avoid such a scenario. For years, law has made it possible to provide for one's wife after one's death without actually conferring upon her power to spend money.

Karen DeCrow, a feminist lawyer and former president of NOW, once wrote about her law school class in estates in the 1960s. "The major thrust of the course," she wrote, "seemed to be to teach the class (of a hundred males and a couple of females) how to keep money out of the hands of women, particularly wives." One technique of accomplishing this end is the revocable trust, which places the money in the control of a trustee (often a banker) while the widow gets an allotment; she must obtain the trustee's permission to get access to more than this sum.[92] Testators—will-makers—can leave money in trust to any heir: an adult child, for instance. (Any bequest to a minor will be put into a trust; a court will so order if the will does not so provide.) No law prevents a father from willing money to his son outright while setting up a trust for his daughter. The ancient legal principle that the wishes of the testator are binding overrides the principle that sex discrimination is quasi-suspect. Once again, the "hands off" principle establishes a privatized family system in which the property owner may dispose of his estate as he pleases, without consideration of such societal values as fairness or equality.

Women have gained the ability to provide for their husbands and children after their deaths on an equal basis with men. They do not do the actual providing as well as men can, to the extent that they earn less. A family like the Wiesenfelds, supported mainly by a wife holding a traditionally female job who then dies, is badly off even under the new rules. But it is unlikely that such a family fares worse than many in which the male wage earner dies. His widow and children have no entrenched right to any adequate income based on his earnings after his death. Private benefits plans may give them this interest, but few of them do. Society, and law, leave most widows to fend for themselves. In that small minority of families where there are no financial problems, the law provides ways to deprive women of control of money, and thus of power.

Conclusion

American society has a popular image of what private life should be. The ideal is the conventional nuclear family, in which a man and woman marry and raise children. Marriage is a legal as well as a personal relationship; law establishes, orders, and defines marriage. People who construct their private sphere in other ways may risk criminal penalties for their choices. Even when they do not, law often penalizes them indirectly. Marriage confers a host of benefits which the unmarried simply do not get, however close or committed their relationship. By restricting marriage to heterosexual couples, American law singles out homosexuals for particular disadvantages; some states even make their relationships illegal, thus denying them the freedom of private choice which other citizens have. But society's hostility to those who reject "family values" is not matched by a commitment to make family life less burdensome. Burdening non-families with legal disabilities is far more common than using law to alleviate the burdens borne by the families whose lifestyle we praise.

American law has not restricted itself to establishing a preference for the nuclear family; it has extended to regulation, if not control, of family life. The history of the family is inseparable from the history of patriarchy. Once, family law enshrined patriarchal norms. The father was the head of the family. His wife and children had to obey him. He was entitled to the fruits of their labor. Women were relegated to the domestic sphere of life. The word "relegated" is apt, because society ranked that sphere as inferior to the public sphere reserved for adult males. Those who find a contradiction between family values and sexual equality are at least *historically* correct.

Both family life and family law have changed. Family law has progressed through three recognizable stages. The patriarchy of the founding period yielded to the asymmetry of the mid-nineteenth to mid-twentieth century, which in turn gave way to the ostensible equality of the present. Divorce law and child custody law have gone through the same three stages. None of the statements in the preceding paragraph is accurate now, either as law or as fact. By the beginning of our time period, family law reflected not absolute male dominance but what might be termed an asymmetrical exchange relationship, a compromise between patriarchy and equality. Husbands still had more power than their wives. Laws giving husbands control of the family's domicile and obliging wives to adopt their husbands' last names reflected this fact, as did those states which gave husbands control over community property. But husbands could no longer physically punish their wives or claim their earnings. Marriage had become an institution of largely reciprocal rights and duties. Chief among these were the husband's duty to support the family in return for the wife's duty to maintain the home.

This was the sort of legal relationship that marriage was, until the 1970s. Thus, when many couples who are still married now, or are getting divorced, began their marriages, the relationship into which they entered was an exchange relationship weighted in the husband's favor. Between 1971 and 1981, court rulings changed the law of marriage into one of equality. These decisions have nullified the last vestiges of patriarchy, so that any law based on traditional sex roles is invalid. But the disjunction between law and fact is as great as it ever was, just in another direction. Once, law was more patriarchal than life was; now, law exaggerates the degree of equality within marriage.

Husband and wife are equal before the law, but they are rarely equal in fact. One reason for this enduring male privilege is that, while women are no longer confined to the private sphere, maintaining the home is still almost exclusively their responsibility. One of a man's greatest privileges is his freedom from tasks which women still perform. Another source of marital asymmetry is the situation described in Chapter 3. Men have access to higher-paying jobs than women do. This asymmetry is exaggerated within marriage by the fact that husbands are usually older, better educated, and more affluent than their wives. Married life, as it is actually lived, is more like family law before 1970 than like contemporary law.

Law cannot change this situation by itself. It cannot force men to take equal responsibility for housework or force women to ask them to. It can hardly require that women marry men who earn no more than they do. Therefore, the possibilities of effecting social change through law are limited. Law can stop mirroring the male supremacy and female dependency prevalent in society. But it cannot redistribute benefits and burdens, power and privileges, within the home.

One thing law can do, however, is to take existing asymmetries into account when the state must enter the marriage relationship. This point is usually when the relationship ends, whether by death or dissolution. Divorce law has changed since at least as fundamentally as family law has. Divorce law, too was once patriarchal; in the nineteenth century most divorces were initiated by men. Divorce law had its intermediate phase, as an adversary proceeding in which women were usually the "innocent" and men the "guilty" parties. Divorce law, like family law, has entered a phase of an equality which is more apparent than real.

The movement for divorce reform began at about the same time the courts took a new look at the constitutionality of family law. In two parallel developments, asymmetrical family law gave way to equality, and traditional adversary divorce to no-fault divorce. All of these laws became gender-neutral. Divorce courts, presented with a wide variety of possible choices in individual cases, made decisions whose cumulative result was to disadvantage women and their children. These decisions, permitted but not required by the new law, rewarded breadwinners at the expense of homemakers and presumed an equality between the partners which did not exist. Courts distributed resources as though the spouses actually had equal potential income. Spouses did not, partly because of the inequality prevailing in society, but partly, also, because of the inequality within the marriage. Thus, divorce reform effectively punished women for assuming traditional roles. Not only did law not eliminate asymmetry, which it could not do; as applied, law reinforced and exaggerated it, which it need not have done.

Child custody is a crucial component of divorce law. In the patriarchal eighteenth and nineteenth centuries, the father had the right to custody because he had a property right in his children's labor. The intermediate phase brought a presumption in favor of mothers, in the form of the "tender years" doctrine. This standard did not last very long. It has been replaced by the neutral "best interests of the child rule," with no presumption in favor of either parent. Under this rule, mothers lose as often as they win. One might expect such a result, since a divorcing husband can often command better counsel than his wife. But it is questionable whether neutrality does serve the child's best interests. Expert opinion agrees that children are better off with whichever parent has been the primary caregiver. This parent is nearly always the mother. When she loses custody, both the child's needs and the mother's own interests in maintaining the psychological benefits of her intense relationship with the child yield in favor of the father's preferences.

Those marriages which do not end in divorce end in death. In most marriages, it is the wife who survives; the United States has five times as many widows as widowers. Thus, the spouse who makes the most money is usually the spouse who dies first. Laws governing estates, benefits, and pensions are now gender-neutral. But they have an impact which is far from neutral. There is no law applicable everywhere which guarantees a widow of any age some interest in her husband's assets after his death. In some states, a man can disinherit his wife at will—no pun intended. Widowhood all too often means poverty. Men whose widows will not be poor may, and frequently do, employ legal devices for keeping the bulk of their estates out of the women's' control.

Are divorcées, mothers, and widows worse off now than they were before? Certainly, their situation is no worse than it was when the man was lord and master. At least now women have legal autonomy; they are not routinely deprived of custody; and they may not be legally beaten and raped. The harder questions arise when we compare women's situation under the present laws with the state of affairs before divorce reform and constitutionally mandated neutrality.

The divorce laws before 1970, which permitted innocent parties to collect alimony and presumed that women needed it, appeared, on their face, to have treated women better than the new rules do. But, when we look at the facts about how many women got support and how much they received, we find most women got little or nothing. A maternal preference in child custody cases probably resulted in more decisions that were in the interests of women and children. But a comparison between *Bunim v. Bunim* and *Jarrett v. Jarrett* suggests that the rules may have changed more than the results have. As for widows, law has never done much to remedy their situation; however, some states have deprived them of what was once an absolute right to a portion of the husband's estate, no matter what his wishes were.

There was no "golden age" in which law accommodated women's needs, both on its face and as applied. But it does appear that some women, sometimes, did fare better under rules which presumed their financial dependence and responsibility for home and family. Should we go back to the asymmetrical laws, and enforce them to accommodate the needs of traditional women? To abandon gender-neutral laws would disadvantage many women who have rejected traditional sex roles: the wife who earns more than her husband, the woman eager to get out of an unhappy marriage and willing to take the consequences of divorce, the mother who can support her children handsomely by herself, thank you, with no help from their father. Those who are disenchanted with traditional family life see nothing wrong with this situation. By penalizing these choices, a return to tradition would reinforce the old roles, making it harder for people to change them. But, after all, there are many more women in the traditional roles than outside them, and they need more help.

Fortunately, society does not need to choose between reinforcing patriarchy and hurting women and children. There is no reason why gender-neutral laws cannot be written which will allow for a range of permissible decisions adapted to individual cases. Laws which recognize that there are "financially dependent spouses," "primary caregivers," "differences in potential earnings," and "domestic division of labor" can allow mothers to get generous settlements and custody when they should, and give widows some share in their husbands' income, while they also serve the interests of couples to whom none of these phrases apply. The laws of some states approach this model. The difficult task, of course, is applying these laws to concrete cases in ways which are fair to everyone. And that is a task to which the courts have not, so far, proven equal.

One reason why decisions may so often work to the detriment of women is that family law is an area in which a huge gap exists between myth and reality. It seems that for every fact about women's lot there is an equal and opposite false stereotype. The bitter ex-wife living off an exorbitant alimony award, the mother who snatches the children away from their father, the parasitic rich widow—all of these are stock figures in our cultural repertoire. They mask the facts of struggling divorcées, women who lose the children they have tenderly cared for, and widows living in poverty.

Another stereotype is the selfish feminist, usually an affluent professional, who works to reform law in her own interest. Although this mythic figure claims to speak for all women, she is in fact working for herself; her interests conflict with those of most women, happy homemakers and mothers. According to this myth, these feminists are responsible for changes which have hurt women. Studies of divorce reform, like that of Lenore Weitzman, have shown that this charge is false: that no-fault divorce cannot be attributed to the women's movement. But the charge remains current.

A woman contemplating divorce is unlikely to read this book, or Weitzman's *The Divorce Revolution*. She may, however, buy a "Globe Mini Mag" entitled *Divorced Women's Handbook*. This pamphlet costs seventy-five cents, and is available at many supermarket checkout counters. Its chapter on child custody contains this sentence: "The advent of Women's Liberation, and the desire it stirred up in many for liberation from the stereotypes restricting them, has altered the traditional picture." The reader will not know that this account of legal change is seriously flawed. Interestingly, the chapter on Social Security, which points out that an ex-wife married for at least ten years may be eligible for benefits, does not mention the women's movement, although feminists can claim a large share of the credit for this change.[93] Much of what we think we know about family law is wrong. But legislators and judges, like all of us, are affected by cultural myths. Lawmakers are still more likely to be fathers than mothers, to pay support than to get it, and to predecease their spouses than to be bereaved.

Defenders of the traditional family rarely base their defenses on a premise that women are inferior to men. Instead, they insist that both men and women are best served by an arrangement where the public sphere is man's responsibility and the private sphere, woman's. Patriarchy, at least in its late twentieth-century version, treats men and women as equals because it accommodates their different needs. If men and women actually are equal within the traditional family, we would expect society to reward women who assume the conventional role. In fact, it does not. Law punishes the woman who has sacrificed power in the public sphere in order to devote herself to her family, even when her marriage ends in death rather than divorce. Family law has treated women as though they were inferior to men. Patriarchy does not reward even the women who conform to its norms.

This situation is changing. Merely to talk and write openly about unfair divorce settlements and child custody decisions will help bring about change. Activism of this kind will provide some information on which to base policy besides the cultural stereotypes mentioned earlier. There is action as well as talk. The welfare reform law of 1988, which will make support awards easier to get and the money easier to collect, is the latest in a series of federal laws which have tried to improve the situation of women who are impoverished by the end of a marriage. Still, it is astonishing how little a society which is quick to penalize those who do not conform their lifestyles to the norm of the conventional family is willing to do to benefit those women who maintain families.

REFERENCES

Blumstein, Philip, and **Pepper Schwartz.** *American Couples.* New York: William Morrow, 1983. This title means what it says; the book is a study of married, unmarried, heterosexual, and homosexual couples. A definitive work.

Chesler, Phyllis. *Mothers on Trial: The Battle for Children and Custody.*

New York: McGraw-Hill, 1986. Chesler's self-selected subjects reveal that any situation can result in a mother's loss of custody.

Diamond, Irene, ed. *Families, Politics, and Public Policy*. New York: Longman, 1983. A good collection of articles, with helpful references and bibliography.

Firestone, Shulamith. *The Dialectic of Sex*. New York: William Morrow, 1970. A critique of love, marriage, family, and motherhood.

Goode, William. *Women and Divorce*. New York: Free Press, 1965. An excellent sample survey and analysis of divorce and support in the days before no-fault divorce.

Jacob, Herbert. "Another Look at No-Fault Divorce and the Post-Divorce Finances of Women," *Law and Society Review* 23 (1989): 95–116. An argument against the prevalent assumption that divorce "reform" by itself worsened the situation of women and children.

Piercy, Marge. *Fly Away Home*. New York: Summit Books, 1984. A fictional treatment of divorce and its aftermath, from the wife's viewpoint.

Stern, Richard. *Other Men's Daughters*. New York: E.P. Dutton, 1973. Fictional account of a similar situation, from the husband's viewpoint.

Trebilcot, Joyce, ed. *Mothering: Essays in Feminist Theory*. Totowa, N.J.: Rowman & Allanheld, 1983. Essays from radical feminist perspectives.

Weitzman, Lenore. *The Divorce Revolution*. New York: Free Press, 1986. The landmark study on the effects of contemporary divorce law on women and children.

Wilson, Joan Hoff, and **Albie Sachs.** *Sexism and the Law: A Study of Male Beliefs and Legal Bias in Britain and the United States*. New York: Free Press, 1979. A sound cross-cultural study.

5

Women and Reproduction

The status of women is inseparable from the subject of human reproduction. The most important physiological difference between the sexes is the fact that women bear children and men do not. Society has emphasized this primary sexual difference rather than similarities between men and women which are equally important. Perhaps, if we began not with childbearing but with a recognition that men and women alike have bodies and minds, abilities and limits, needs and desires, we could evolve a society in which the gross disparities of income, opportunity, and status would not exist. But then, if we began at that point, we might have evolved a very different theory of human rights.

American political discourse has been influenced by philosophies which emphasize the individual, a word derived from the Latin for "that which cannot be separated." In the eighteenth century Thomas Jefferson, paraphrasing John Locke, wrote of inalienable rights belonging to each person. Later discourse has borrowed freely from liberal theorists, like the nineteenth-century philosopher John Stuart Mill. The philosophy of "individualism" is still espoused in this century. All of these ideas have met vigorous criticism, but all have deeply affected American political life.[1]

Such emphasis presumes that every person possesses some

core of identity which is distinct from every other person, that more than one person cannot occupy the same space. And herein lies one difficulty for discourse on women's rights. During pregnancy, two individuals *do* occupy the same space: the presumed separateness does not exist. So the limits of social authority proclaimed in liberal theory might not seem to apply to those whose bodies house other individuals.

The fact that women alone can bear children does not mean that all women are permanently engaged in so doing. But the emphasis which society puts on women's reproductive role, combined with a political philosophy which stresses the separateness of individuals, puts women in a difficult position. Liberal theory did not traditionally include those who had babies among those who had rights. "All men are created equal" did not distinguish between the generic and the exclusive meaning of the operative noun. Both *Muller v. Oregon* and *Hoyt v. Florida* (see Chapter 2) were bald statements that women's family responsibilities were incompatible with equal rights. Now that society has recognized, however grudgingly, that women are included among those who have rights, law must deal with the relationship between individual rights and reproductive function.

Where Individualism Fails: Pregnancy and Power

Chapter 3 discussed society's growing awareness of reproductive hazards in the workplace. Not all toxic substances, however, are present in the environment. Some hazards, like drugs, alcohol, tobacco, and caffeine, reach the fetus through the placenta when a pregnant woman ingests them. All of these substances present greater risk to the unborn child than to the mother. Women addicted to heroin or cocaine have borne addicted babies. "Crack babies," in particular, are in danger; they suffer a greater than average risk of premature birth, with all its hazards, and can suffer permanent neurological damage, the symptoms of which include seizures and mental retardation. Fetal exposure to alcohol can also cause mental retardation. Society has begun to deal with this problem in the same way that it is dealing with workplace hazards: by coercing women. As Chapter 3 showed, employers have fired women, refused to hire them, or forced them to undergo sterilization. Society's methods of controlling women who consume harmful chemicals are even more severe. States are making increased efforts to use the criminal sanction against pregnant women who use alcohol and drugs.

There have been about thirty-five cases of this kind. Only one woman, Jennifer Johnson of Florida, has been convicted of such a crime. A judge sentenced Johnson to fifteen years' probation for delivering cocaine to a minor: her own child, through the umbilical cord. She is now appealing the verdict. Two Michigan women are awaiting trial on a similar charge. In February 1990, a Wyoming judge dismissed child abuse charges against Diane Pfannensteil, on the grounds that no evidence existed that the fetus had been harmed. Pfannensteil had told police officers that her husband had beaten her. She went to a hospital emergency room for treatment. When a blood alcohol test showed that she was intoxicated, she was arrested and charged.[2]

The latest medical knowledge suggests that the alcohol that Pfannensteil consumed may indeed have damaged her unborn child if the accounts of her behavior are accurate. Experts have known for some time that children born to alcoholic or heavy-drinking mothers may suffer a form of severe brain damage called "fetal alcohol syndrome," or a less severe condition called "fetal alcohol effect." Symptoms include facial abnormalities, poor memory, and learning disabilities. Even lighter alcohol consumption during pregnancy carries risks. "While a drink each night might never push a mother's blood alcohol level above the danger threshold, a night of drinking . . . might well raise the level enough to endanger the fetus." Consuming enough alcohol to raise one's blood alcohol level over the legal limit does endanger the fetus. But the effects of alcohol are not evident during pregnancy, or even at birth; they may take years to manifest themselves.[3]

Although an estimated 65 percent of children born to alcoholic mothers are free of damage, and occasional, sparing alcohol consumption has not been proved harmful, specialists in fetal alcohol damage advise total abstention for pregnant women. There is even support for using the criminal law to enforce this recommendation. An acclaimed memoir published in 1989 goes so far as to advocate the incarceration of recalcitrant pregnant women. *The Broken Cord* is Michael Dorris's moving account of his alcohol-affected adopted son. Dorris, a professor of Native American Studies at Dartmouth College, adopted Adam, a Sioux, when the boy was three. Dorris knew that Adam's birth mother had died of alcohol poisoning in her thirties, but Adam's seizures, poor coordination, and low intelligence were not traced to fetal alcohol syndrome until he was in his teens. Now in his twenties, Adam will never be able to function normally. In the foreword to the book, writer Louise Erdrich, Dorris' wife, supports her husband's policy recommendations.

> This will outrage some women, and men, good people who believe that it is the right of individuals to put themselves in harm's way, that drinking is a choice we make, that a person's liberty to court either happiness or despair is sacrosanct. I believed this, too, and yet the poignancy and frustration of Adam's life has fed my doubts. . . . After all, where is the measure of responsibility here? Where, exactly, is the demarcation between self-harm and child abuse? Gross negligence is nearly equal to intentional harm, goes a legal maxim. Where do we draw the line?[4]

Erdrich engages the reader's emotions. A better statement of the failure of libertarian individualism is difficult to envision. The principles that support our constitutionally guaranteed rights are not adequate in this situation. But if we subject this moving prose to objective analysis, we perceive that Erdrich and Dorris question only part of the essential presumptions of this philosophy. Libertarian concepts of individual *freedom* fall short; libertarian concepts of individual *responsibility* are accepted without scrutiny. Adam's mother's life was no less wasted than Adam's is. Anyone who dies so young of alcoholism is wretched; more important, so afflicted a person is in the grip of an addiction beyond her control. What claim has she on the state?

The old libertarian principle, "that government governs best which governs least," discourages state intervention to help, but permits state activity to punish. For Michael Dorris, stopping pregnant women from drinking is a higher priority than either curing their alcohol problems or treating the causes of heavy drinking among Native Americans. Diane Pfannensteil sought protection, and got coercion instead. Jennifer Johnson tried to get drug treatment and was turned away. Most alcohol and drug treatment programs exclude pregnant women.[5] No informed person can deny that the effects of drugs and alcohol on unborn children present a grave problem, but it appears that the state's new interest in the fetus does not extend to the rest of the child's life; the government's commitment to poor or addicted women and their children is minimal. Punishing women seems more acceptable than securing a healthy life for women or their children. This same ranking of priorities is present in another type of coercion which government increasingly tries to impose upon women: forced childbearing. It is to this area of public policy that we now turn.

"If We Don't Own the Flesh We Stand in":
Fertility and Freedom

A pro-choice activist interviewed in Kristin Luker's *Abortion and the Politics of Motherhood* gives eloquent expression to this dilemma:

> When we talk about women's rights, we can get all the rights in the world—the right to vote, the right to go to school—and none of them means a doggone thing if we don't own the flesh we stand in, if we can't control what happens to us, if the whole course of our lives can be changed by somebody else that can get us pregnant by accident, or by deceit, or by force. So I consider the right to elective abortion, whether you dream of doing it or not, the cornerstone of the women's movement . . . because without that right, we'd have about as many rights as the cow who is brought to the bull once a year.[6]

To "own the flesh we stand in" is to control our fertility. But for most of human history, in most settings, fertility has controlled women. For most people, most of the time, fertility has been a commodity the supply of which exceeded the demand. Throughout recorded history, women have eloquently recounted the devastating effects of continual pregnancy and childbearing upon their lives. Margaret Sanger, a pioneer in the international birth control movement, provided harrowing descriptions of these effects. In the slums of American cities, she found women whose lives had been ruined through society's denial to them of the power to control their fertility. This institutionally mandated lack of control had ruined these women's physical and mental health and mired their families in ineluctable poverty. Here is Sanger's account of caring for a woman who had nearly died from a self-induced abortion:

> [Sadie Sachs] finally voiced her fears. "Another baby will finish me, I suppose?"
> "It's too early to talk about that," I temporized.
> But when the doctor came to make his last call, I drew him aside. "Mrs. Sachs is terribly worried about having another baby."
> "She may well be," replied the doctor. . . . He laughed good naturedly. "You want to have your cake and eat it too, do you? Well, it can't be done."

Then picking up his hat and bag to depart he said, "Tell Jake to sleep on the roof."

I glanced quickly at Mrs. Sachs. Even through my sudden tears I could see stamped on her face an expression of absolute despair.

. . . The telephone rang one evening three months later, and Jake Sachs' agitated voice begged me to come at once; his wife was sick again and from the same cause. . . . Mrs. Sachs was in a coma and died within ten minutes.[7]

The poor have always suffered most from the effects of uncontrolled fertility, but they are not the only ones at the mercy of their bodies and their men. Middle-class women described their fear of pregnancy and the relief each menstrual period brought. "The old maid came at the appointed time," one American woman wrote euphemistically to her husband in 1849. "I do think you are a very *careful* man." Not all husbands were so sympathetic. In 1867, the wife of a North Carolina legislator wrote to him, "I have not seen anything of my monthlies yet, and you know I hate even to think of such a thing." He responded, "You come of a breed too prolific to stop at your age and if it is the Lord's will why we must submit to it." Not even monarchs were immune from this fear. For Queen Victoria, the English contemporary of these women (and the mother of nine), pregnancy and childbirth were recurrent themes in her letters and diaries. Observers reported that this fear was well grounded. Catharine Beecher, a distinguished nineteenth-century reformer and educator, reported her visits to community after community where most of the married women were in poor health or even invalids.[8]

Nature, technology, and law combined to deny women reproductive freedom. Crude methods of birth control have existed throughout recorded history; coitus interruptus and breast-feeding after childbirth were the most common, but neither method is reliable. The condom has been in use at least since the sixteenth century, but it did not become widely available until the 1870s. Condoms could not be mass-produced until the 1840s, when the technique of vulcanizing rubber was perfected. Since men, not women, use condoms, this device does not enable women to prevent pregnancy. For centuries the only foolproof way for a woman to prevent pregnancy was to abstain from sexual intercourse.[9] Traditional common law took that decision out of women's hands, by requiring them to submit to their husbands' sexual demands. Socioeconomic and political forces coercively structured women's choices still further by making them both financially dependent upon men and subject to them, sexually and otherwise.

Contraception, abortion, and sterilization are the chief artificial means of controlling fertility. By the 1930s, safe and reliable woman-controlled contraceptive devices existed. Indeed, the sharp decline in the birthrate during the Depression was partly due to the use of these devices. Low-risk and effective procedures for abortion and sterilization also existed by 1933. But none of these techniques has consistently been available to women on demand.

Law, custom, and religion deprived women of fertility control for many years. The federal Comstock Act of 1873, and the "little Comstock laws" passed by most states, included contraceptives and abortifacients among the "obscene" materials which could not be sold, mailed, or imported. When Sanger began her efforts, her activities were illegal in most states; she and her associates went to jail more than once. It was not until the 1930s that birth control had become legal in most states. The exceptions play a powerful role in American constitutional history, which will be discussed. But law was not the most formidable barrier to fertility control in our time period. Organized religions, none of which endorsed birth control until the 1930s, used their moral authority to discourage its use. The medical profession also remained hostile for years:

> One has an oppressive sense of *déjà vu* in reading old accounts (written as recently as the early Thirties) of "permissible indications" for doctors to give out contraceptive advice and materials: a huge family; the mother's health at a breaking point; a history of having borne defective children; the threat of her death if childbirth recurs—all very fine reasons, but a *woman's own* simple wish not to bear any more (or even any) children is conspicuously not on those tedious lists.[10]

Women who sought voluntary sterilization had a difficult time getting it. These difficulties were to persist for nearly four decades after birth control became legal in most states. The following information is something I share with my students in my courses in women and the law and constitutional rights every year. They never believe me. Until the late 1960s, the American College of Obstetrics and Gynecology recommended that its members perform sterilizations only if the woman's age, multiplied by the number of living children she had, equaled at least 120. As arbitrary as it was, this "rule of 120" persisted until the

1970s. It did not have the force of law, but hospitals often used it as a guideline to determine whether a given woman could get the operation she sought. Some physicians and hospitals continued to insist that a woman have reached a certain age, or have her husband's written consent if she was married, before they would operate. By the late 1980s, by contrast, medical custom had advanced to the point where the only women who had difficulty getting the surgery were those who had no children, and even this rule was by no means universal.[11]

All the states forbade abortion in the 1930s, except when necessary to save the life of the mother. In 1962, the American Law Institute adopted a Model Penal Code which recommended that abortion be permitted when the mother's physical or mental health was endangered; when the baby was likely to suffer from a grave physical or mental defect (if the mother had had rubella, German measles, during pregnancy, for example); and if the pregnancy resulted from rape, incest, or any other felonious intercourse. Between 1965 and 1970, fourteen states adopted some or all of the ALI recommendations. Three states, New York, Alaska, and Hawaii, repealed their abortion laws outright.[12]

Legal abortions required the approval of at least one physician and, usually, a hospital review committee. Permission was not easy to get. Illegal abortion flourished. Some physicians or other trained professionals did perform the procedure. The price of a safe illegal abortion was too high for many women. Other practitioners provided the service at a lower price, but these "back-alley abortions" often resulted in complications, such as hemorrhaging and infection, which could prove fatal. Many women have given harrowing accounts of their illegal abortions. The following typical experience might well represent all of them.

> After I got home, I developed a high fever. I was so sick I was delirious with the pain and fever. My mother took me to the emergency ward. The doctors asked her who had done the abortion. When she didn't tell them, they refused to treat me. They said that they would let me die if she didn't tell them the name and address of the abortionist. Frightened, she gave them a false name and address and then they started treatment for me. When the police . . . found out that my mother had given false information, they went to my house and arrested my husband.[13]

Two groups of women, the young and the poor, have been at greater than average risk of losing control over their fertility.

Minors have always suffered from a paternalistic assumption that a good way to promote teenage chastity is to deny them access to the means to prevent pregnancy. Whatever one thinks of teenage chastity as a legitimate goal, there is absolutely no evidence to support this assumption, and a great deal that tends to refute it. However, logic has not been a strong motivating force behind these proscriptions for either the parent or the state. Even after the right to use contraceptives was well established for adults, some states had laws forbidding the sale of such devices to minors. *Carey v. Population Services* overturned these laws in 1977.[14] The Reagan administration tried to promote chastity by instituting a regulation which was promptly dubbed the "squeal rule": it required all clinics which received federal funds to notify parents or guardians if they provided birth control to minors. This rule never went into effect; it was allowed to die when a district court granted an injunction against it.[15] As we shall see, however, states and courts have seriously compromised a minor's right to an abortion.

Women's reproductive freedom includes both the right not to become a mother, and the right to be one. All too often, it has seemed as if the law wanted to force us to become mothers, even at the cost of our lives. But that generalization has not been true for all women. Compulsory sterilization—and abortion, for that matter—have often been "dirty little secrets," hidden from view. While some women have not been allowed to avoid motherhood, others have been forbidden to become mothers or to decide how many children they want to have. Patriarchy, with the medical establishment as the father who knows best, appears to be the guiding principle in determining who shall bear children and who must not.

Infertility by Fiat: Compulsory Sterilization

Once humankind learned about genetics, some experts have argued that certain traits ought not to be reproduced. Low intelligence, criminal behavior, and physical disabilities have been among those traits. And at various times, expert opinion—or a large portion of it—has maintained that some or all of these traits are hereditary. The first three decades of the twentieth century were such a period in this country. Theories of "eugenics" dominated informed opinion. The "fit"—the healthy, intelligent, and able—were encouraged to have large families, while the "unfit" were discouraged from having children at all. Since the "unfit" might not read these scholarly tomes, or recognize themselves in this description if they did, some authorities reached the conclusion that coercion might be necessary. The patriarchal state would make the choice.

In *Buck v. Bell*, the "father" who knew best was the superintendent of Virginia's State Colony of Epileptics and Feeble Minded. The irresponsible child was eighteen-year-old Carrie Buck, an inmate of this institution. Bell sought to have Buck sterilized. A state law allowed the superintendents of institutions to compel this procedure for inmates afflicted with "hereditary forms of insanity, imbecility, etc." The terminology itself belongs to an era when medicine's understanding of the brain and how it worked was rudimentary. The specific year was 1924. All we know about Carrie's condition was that experts had labeled her "feeble-minded." They had given the same label to Carrie's mother, also an inmate, and to Carrie's infant daughter. To call a person "feeble-minded" is no more exact a diagnosis than calling her "stupid." Unlike epilepsy or mental retardation, feeble-mindedness is not now, was not then, and has never been a medical term for a condition whose existence is verifiable through testing.

The state law did require notice, hearing, and counsel before the operation could be performed. Carrie Buck's state-appointed guardian and lawyer insisted that the law violated "her constitutional right of bodily integrity." This argument proved unpersuasive, all the way up to the Supreme Court. The judges, who two years earlier had extended substantive due process to forbid the state to establish a minimum wage for women, found no constitutional defect in compulsory surgery. In a short opinion which has since become notorious, Justice Oliver Wendell Holmes wrote:

> We have seen more than once that the public welfare may call upon the best citizens for their lives. It would be strange if it could not call upon those who already sap the strength of the State for lesser sacrifices, often not felt to be such by those concerned [how did the Court know?], in order to prevent our being swamped with incompetence. It is better for all the world, if instead of waiting to execute degenerate offspring for crime [confusing incompetence with criminality], or to let them starve for their imbecility [assuming that society has no obligation to the disabled], society can prevent those who are manifestly unfit from continuing their kind [accepting the state's assumption, verified neither then nor since, that mental dis-

ability and illness are hereditary]. The principle that sustains compulsory vaccination is broad enough to cover cutting the Fallopian tubes. Three generations of imbeciles are enough.[16]

This ruling, over sixty years old and never repudiated, has received extensive criticism from civil libertarians, feminists, scientists, and advocates of the rights of the disabled. Experts no longer believe that mental illness, intellectual incompetence, or brain disorders are hereditary as a general rule, although there is evidence of genetic factors in some conditions. Knowledge available to us now compels the conclusion that the "eugenists" relied upon in Carrie Buck's case did not know what they were talking about.

At present, partly as a result of advances in our knowledge, the sterilization of the mentally incompetent is a controversial issue. Opinion is by no means united against the practice, however. Proponents insist that some developmentally disabled women can become reasonably independent if they are not constantly vulnerable to pregnancy (an argument made with respect to Carrie Buck herself), and that people who cannot make responsible decisions about their fertility should lose it. Opponents challenge the state's power to force any elective surgery on people who cannot make an informed decision, and insist that the developmentally disabled have the same reproductive freedom as other Americans do. But *Buck v. Bell* is vulnerable to criticism even from those who do not expect judges to predict future developments or are not prepared to oppose all compulsory sterilization. The Court assumed that Carrie Buck was mentally incompetent. No reliable evidence supports this finding. The state did not employ even the crude diagnostic techniques available in the 1920s. Carrie Buck was feeble-minded because Superintendent Bell said she was.

One commentator asks, "Is it not probable that any person, regardless of heredity, who was raised from birth in an institution peopled by the feeble-minded and insane, would herself appear to be feeble-minded?" This is a valid point. Contemporary accounts of Carrie Buck's capacity are sketchy. We know that she eventually left the institution, married, and lived independently until she died in 1982. We also know that her daughter impressed several schoolteachers as fairly bright until she died in childhood. Finally, a newspaper series in 1980 reported that Buck was one of over 7,500 inmates in Virginia institutions in a fifty-year period who were sterilized as "social misfits."[17]

Buck v. Bell is striking for its exposure of official arrogance: of a legislature which thought it understood genetics, of bureaucrats who thought they could measure intelligence, and of judges who assumed that citizens who required the state's help had no legitimate claim on it. Securing legal freedom from compulsory sterilization took half a century. The Supreme Court never again upheld such a law. *Skinner v. Oklahoma*, decided in 1942, carefully avoided overruling *Buck*, but it did limit its reach as precedent. The two cases provide an edifying contrast.

An Oklahoma law, enacted in 1935, allowed the court-ordered sterilization (after a jury trial) of any person thrice convicted of "felonies involving moral turpitude." Such a law, which at least punished specific acts rather than a status, might seem less objectionable than Virginia's sterilization law. But the statute's definition of "moral turpitude" was troublesome. Felonies specifically exempted from this definition included "offenses arising out of violation of the prohibitory laws, revenue acts, embezzlement, or political crimes": in other words, white-collar crime. This law would seem to embody the same sort of class bias reflected in Justice Holmes's reference to those who "sap the strength of the state."

In 1942, the justices did not use the dirty word "class"—not, at least, in its economic sense—but a unanimous court overturned the law because of these discriminations. This "legislation which involves one of the basic civil rights of man" violated the equal protection clause because it "lays an unequal hand on those who have committed intrinsically the same kind of offense and punishes one and not the other." The Virginia law, Justice William O. Douglas insisted, had been free of such arbitrary distinctions.[18] The statement that procreation was a "basic civil right" was, in this decision, what is called a "dictum": a statement not central to the case and therefore not binding as precedent. An arbitrary law is unconstitutional whether it involves a basic civil right or not. But the effort to distinguish *Skinner* from *Buck* fails to convince, especially since an accompanying opinion states that "science has been unable to ascertain" that "criminal tendencies of any class of habitual offenders are transmissible."[19] By 1942, scientific opinion no longer agreed that low intelligence was inheritable, either. The Court's careful treatment of the precedent suggests the absence of at least a majority consensus in favor of invalidating compulsory sterilization.

The aftermath of World War II, which included revelation that

forced sterilization had been a common procedure in Nazi concentration camps, considerably dampened the enthusiasm of
those who had approved the practice. But this knowledge did not
end forced sterilization in the United States. The practice went
underground, to affect mainly those who depended on others, the
parents or the state, for their medical care. The focus changed
from a eugenic rationale to a desire to reduce the number of
people who became public dependents.

Squelching and Squealing: The Special Case of the Young

Poor women have not been the only victims of sterilization
abuse. One 1978 case involved, not the state as surrogate parent,
but a real parent successfully controlling her daughter's fertility.
Stump v. Sparkman was a classic Catch-22 case. Several adults
conspired to victimize a teenage girl, and no one was held responsible. The mother of fifteen-year-old Linda Kay Spitler told a
physician that she wanted her daughter to have a tubal ligation.
The mother obtained a court order authorizing the operation
from Judge Harold Stump of the De Kalb County, Indiana, Circuit Court. Her petition alleged that Linda was "somewhat re-
tarded"—although the girl was at the appropriate grade level in
school for her age—and that she had become sexually active. The
mother told Linda that she needed an appendectomy, and the
operation was performed.

Linda married Leo Sparkman two years later. The couple
tried, and failed, to conceive. The doctors whom they consulted
had no difficulty determining the nature of the problem. Linda
learned for the first time that she had been rendered sterile. The
couple sued her mother, the doctor, and the judge. A state court
ruled that the mother and the doctor were immune from suit
because the judge had approved the surgery. It upheld an award
against the judge, who then sought review in the Supreme Court.
The justices ruled that *he* was immune because his order was a
valid exercise of his authority. This was a debatable conclusion.
No statute gave judges the power to order that surgery be performed on minors where parental consent had been given. State
laws did permit court-ordered sterilization, but only of institutionalized people. But, since no one was liable, this act went
unpunished even in civil courts.[20]

While young and poor women lost their right to bear children, until recently adult middle-class women lost their right not to. It would seem as though the organizing principle was distrust of women's ability to govern their own lives: whatever she wants, give her the opposite. In other words, women have no more capacity for self-government than do particularly fractious children. A class bias is also discernible: fewer children for those who drain the state, whether or not they like it, and more for those whose children contribute to the state, whether or not *they* like it. But only the first principle appears to have been continuously in operation. A desire to limit the population among the poor would, applied consistently, lead not only to sterilizing them without their knowledge but also to providing them with contraceptives. However, in at least one major American city, Chicago, public clinics refused for years to give birth control information to their indigent clients.[21] By the mid-twentieth century, however, change was at hand. Much of this change antedated the contemporary feminist movement; it had a civil libertarian orientation. The right not to reproduce now has constitutional recognition, limited at least, precarious though it may be. The right to become a parent has no constitutional protection. But both are on firmer ground than they were when the New Deal began.

The Right to Motherhood

Feminists, civil rights workers, and health activists began exposing sterilization abuse in the 1960s and 1970s. There was no shortage of documented instances. Two groups, the poor and the young, have been prominent among the victims of these policies. Welfare recipients have often been forced to accept sterilization in order to receive benefits. Sometimes, the operation has been performed without the patient's informed consent. The "Mississippi appendectomy" was one popular technique. Many doctors in the Southern states advised welfare recipients to have that operation—and performed a tubal ligation or even a hysterectomy instead, while the women were unconscious. Sterilization abuse was also common on Indian reservations. According to John D'Emilio and Estelle Freedman,

> By the 1960s, with fertility rapidly declining and family planning now universal among the white middle class, medical professionals found ways of sterilizing far larger numbers of women whose fertil-

ity patterns offended their values. In one hospital in the Southwest, a dissident doctor reported, "one staff member would lie to the patient if he felt she had too many kids and tell her her uterus needed to come out when it didn't." In a Texas hospital whose staff pushed tubal ligation, residents wore buttons saying, "Stop at two, damn it." Black, Hispanic, native American, and poor white women were generally the targets of these efforts.

The same study also found that black women were more than twice as likely to be sterilized as whites, that surgical sterilization occurred six times more often among Puerto Rican women in New York City, and that the lower a family's income, the more likely it was for the wife to undergo a tubal ligation than the husband a vasectomy.[22]

The national government finally did respond to the pressure to end sterilization abuse. In 1979, the Department of Health Education and Welfare (now Health and Human Services) issued regulations governing federally funded procedures. These regulations, still in effect, require informed consent in the patient's preferred language, the explanation of alternative methods of birth control, and audits in the states where most federally funded sterilizations are performed. They prohibit any threats to withhold benefits and the use of hysterectomy as a means of sterilization. The government does not monitor compliance with these regulations, making it easy for hospitals to ignore them. Nevertheless, no instances of widespread abuse have been uncovered in this country since they went into effect. But poverty can coercively structure choices without official compulsion. A welfare recipient or an impoverished woman worker may feel that her circumstances force her into sterilization when she does not want it, even without official threats or lies.[23]

Are women ever forced to get abortions? The possibility that some authority—a parent, doctor, or welfare worker—might want a young, poor, or disabled woman (or a woman pregnant with a potentially disabled child) to have an abortion against the woman's own wishes is not beyond the realm of credibility. Incarcerated women, in prisons, mental institutions (remember Carrie Buck), or juvenile centers face increased risk of coercion in all aspects of their lives. Family, lovers, and friends might be able to force young women to have abortions. Parents have power over a minor who lives with them and is dependent on them. The baby's father, and even *his* parents, may exert similar pressure. As we shall see, courts have consistently weakened a minor's right to have an abortion without her parents' consent. *Hodgson v. Minnesota*, the latest Supreme Court ruling on this issue (in June 1990), upheld a law requiring a minor either to notify both parents before the abortion or to get permission from a judge.[24] No state has ever given parents the right to demand that their daughter get an abortion; nor, on the other hand, does any law give a minor any right to refuse such a procedure. The law does require, as a general rule, that minors obey their parents or guardians. As *Stump v. Sparkman* indicates, parents may authorize medical procedures for minor children without the child's consent.

Members of minority groups, in particular, have expressed concern that the medical establishment will pressure them to have abortions or to be sterilized as a form of genocide against them.[25] According to one activist organization,

> The threat of abortion abuse also exists. Women with the AIDS virus may be pressured to abort, although only 30–50 percent of fetuses present become infected. Women of color may feel enormous pressure due to oppressive social conditions. It should be noted that in New York City before 1970, Black and Puerto Rican women accounted for 80 percent of the deaths due to illegal abortion. Currently, women of color are between 2 and 3 times as likely to obtain abortions as are white women. The distinction must be made between choosing an abortion and needing one to avert the effects of a racist society.[26]

Since the national government and most states forbid the use of public funds for elective abortions, it seems unlikely that public agencies which may not even perform abortions on clients who want them are forcing them on clients who do not. In the past, however, some public hospitals which did perform abortions required that their patients be sterilized at the same time. The fact that minority women, who are more likely than white women to be poor, are also more likely to obtain abortions is an indication that women's choices may be coercively structured.[27]

The Surrogate Mother: Technological Oxymoron?

Most people can become parents, whether they want to or not. Fertility is the rule, infertility the exception. But the fact that they are in a minority is no consolation to people who want children and cannot have them. No one knows how many people are in this situation. The *lowest* reliable estimate of the number of

American couples who are clinically infertile—unable to conceive after a full year of unprotected intercourse—is 2.4 million.

Experts agree that about half of all infertile couples are able to conceive after treatment. At least 1.2 million couples who try to conceive will never be able to. When we add to that figure the unknown number of couples who choose not to conceive because pregnancy would endanger the woman's health or because they might pass on a genetic disease, it becomes clear that infertility is a major medical problem. Another point on which experts agree is that infertility is increasing. Causes of this increase include the birth control pill and intrauterine device (IUD), both of which can cause sterility; the increased incidence of sexually transmitted diseases, which have similar effects; environmental and industrial toxic products; and the fact that more people are delaying parenthood past thirty, when fertility declines for both sexes.[28]

What do people who encounter fertility problems do ? Those who are working-class or poor, who do not have access to the latest medical techniques (most of which are expensive and for which medical insurance rarely pays), or whom some gatekeeper (physician, adoption agency, social worker, or "baby broker") deems unsatisfactory candidates for the service being offered, must generally accept life without children. Middle-class, professional, and otherwise privileged people, with access to medical and social services, have sometimes had the means to become parents despite their difficulties. Once, the common middle-class solution to incurable infertility was adoption, through a public or private agency or through an independent arrangement. But adoption has become increasingly difficult over the last few decades. Most prospective adoptive couples want to adopt children who are like them, or, at least, like the children they would have conceived: in other words, healthy, white, able-bodied infants. The supply of such infants has decreased sharply in recent years. Many infertile couples have turned to techniques which permit one of them to beget or bear a child who will be theirs together.

When a man is infertile, a single woman wants to bear a child, or a lesbian couple wishes to become parents, a common method, in use since 1890, is artificial insemination by donor. In this procedure, semen from a sperm donor who has masturbated into a sterile container is injected into a woman's vagina. Usually, artificial insemination occurs in a medical facility, donor and recipient(s) are unknown to one another, the donor is paid for his contribution, and the recipient(s) pay for the semen. However, people often successfully carry out this procedure themselves, with no medical help. Artificial insemination by donor results in about 15,000 pregnancies a year in the United States.[29]

What if the prospective mother cannot or should not conceive? Various medical and surgical techniques, like ways of opening blocked Fallopian tubes, implantation inside a woman's body of ova fertilized outside her body, known as *in vitro* fertilization (the Latin term translates as "in a glass"), and the freezing of fertilized embryos for later implantation, have been developed. These procedures are expensive, often painful, and have high failure rates, but they succeed often enough to have become popular. They are luxuries, requiring money, health, and time for recuperation. They also raise perplexing legal problems. In December 1988, Mary Sue Davis and Junior Davis had nine embryos produced by *in vitro* fertilization, frozen, and stored at the Fertility Center of Eastern Tennessee in Knoxville. Junior Davis sued for divorce the following February. He wanted the embryos destroyed, but Mary Sue Davis wanted custody of the embryos. A Tennessee trial court ruled in her favor; her estranged husband has appealed.[30]

Some couples have sought to have the man artificially inseminate another woman, who will bear the child and give it to the couple. The price for this service is considerably higher than the price of semen: between $10,000 and $20,000, plus expenses. The transaction often takes place with a mediator, usually an agency, lawyer, or physician. It almost always includes a contract among the parties. The media has given women who bear children under these circumstances the bewildering label "surrogate mothers."

The arrangement is fraught with difficulties. Is such a contract invalid, because it is inherently coercive, or against public policy? If the contract is valid, it must carefully spell out such matters as: what restrictions are placed on the pregnant woman? (Typically, she must seek regular medical attention and abstain from drugs, alcohol, and tobacco; but what about sports, or travel?) What compensation is due the birth mother if she suffers a miscarriage, or the child is stillborn? Should the contract obligate the birth mother to breast-feed, or would that increase the possibility of her changing her mind? What rights, if any, does she have to continued contact with the child? What happens if the pregnancy endangers her health? What happens if the child is born disabled? The hardest question of all, of course, is: what if the birth mother changes her mind?

Mary Beth Whitehead Gould of Brick Township, New Jersey, is the most famous mother to have done this. But she is far from being the only one.[31] That mothers should be reluctant to give up the infants who have just emerged from their bodies is hardly surprising. Nature tries to ensure—by producing breast milk, for example—that mothers bond with their infants. The highly publicized story of Whitehead, Baby M, and William and Elizabeth Stern has dramatized the issue of surrogacy and provoked important legal developments.

Dr. Elizabeth Stern, a pediatrician, and her husband, William, a biochemist, wanted children. Dr. Stern has a mild form of multiple sclerosis, which pregnancy might aggravate. The couple approached Noel Keane, a well-known self-styled "baby broker." Whitehead, a homemaker and mother who had not completed high school, had approached Keane's agency seeking a contract as a surrogate mother. Although the agency's psychologist had predicted that Whitehead might have difficulty relinquishing an infant, Keane put the Sterns in touch with her. The three entered into a contract. Whitehead agreed to be inseminated with Stern's sperm and bear a child, which she would turn over to the Sterns for adoption. She would be paid $10,000, out of the $30,000 that the Sterns paid to Keane. Mary Beth Whitehead gave birth to an infant girl in March 1986. The baby was Sara to the Whiteheads, Melissa to the Sterns, and, soon, "Baby M" to the world.

Whitehead found that she could not bear to part with the infant she had carried, borne, and was now nursing. A judge ordered her to give the baby to the Sterns, and the parties went to court. In April 1987, Superior Court Judge Harvey Sorkow awarded custody to the Sterns, allowed Elizabeth to adopt the baby, ordered the couple to pay Whitehead the money, and deprived the natural mother of all parental rights. If that ruling had stood, Whitehead might never have legally seen her child again, until the girl reached adulthood.

Following New Jersey's child custody law, Sorkow insisted that this decision was in Baby M's best interests. The judge devoted much of his opinion to a "stinging attack" on Whitehead. He described her as "manipulative, impulsive, and exploitive." She attached a "reduced level of importance" to education, and her own household was "plagued with separation, domestic violence and severe financial difficulties." Sorkow lavished praise on William and Elizabeth Stern for their "private, quiet and quite unremarkable life. . . . They would be supportive of education and have shown, at least in their own lives, a motivation for learning." Paradoxically, Sorkow ignored the medical title that Elizabeth had earned through her motivation for learning. He referred to her throughout the opinion as "Mrs. Stern."[32]

Although the reporters who covered the trial did not unite in scorning Whitehead, she may well have displayed behaviors which supported Sorkow's character analysis. His characterization of her family life was certainly accurate. But it never occurred to him that class and income might have some effect on her, or that "severe financial difficulties" are not necessarily caused by character deficiencies. She was unemployed; her husband, an alcoholic, worked only irregularly; and she had been on welfare. By all indications, the family badly needed the $10,000 the Sterns agreed to pay her (which she never got). In fact, a bold lawyer might plausibly have argued that her poverty constituted duress: that her entering the contract was not the result of free choice, and that, therefore, the contract was invalid. The possibility that the Sterns's more favorable circumstances might have at least as much to do with class and money as with their own virtue likewise did not occur to Sorkow.

The Baby M case revealed a complex of economic, social, psychological, political, and medical underpinnings of this issue. A woman who agrees to bear, and then relinquish, a child is a woman who needs money; a couple who agrees to pay this much money is a couple who can afford luxuries. As Barbara Katz Rothman has put it, "Thirty-two-year-old attorneys living in wealthy suburbs do not give up their children to nineteen-year-old factory workers living in small towns."[33] Working-class and poor women are bearing children to turn them over to middle-class or rich couples. The lower court decision also indicates that in a conflict, the couples will win because their relatively unstressful lifestyle makes them appear more mentally healthy. The decision is reminiscent of the Salk custody case described in the last chapter.[34]

In February 1988, the state supreme court reversed most of this decision. It upheld the custody award to William Stern but restored Whitehead's parental rights. She is now free to sue for custody, and she may not be denied the right to see her daughter. Elizabeth Stern, though she lives with the baby, may not adopt her; and she has to share the child with another woman, which was not the arrangement that she agreed to back in 1985. The most important part of the court's ruling, however, went beyond this single case. The court ruled that surrogate parenting was illegal in New Jersey because it violated the state's adoption laws by, in effect, selling babies. Several state legislatures have joined New Jersey in banning the practice.[35]

Yet the issue remains a troubling one. It is no defense of the practice to intone, as some commentators, and, in effect, Judge Sorkow, did, that "a contract is a contract." This slogan is not even good law. Our legal system recognizes several situations which make a contract invalid. It is also clear that the arrangement can be economically, physically, and emotionally exploitive for the birth mother. Ten thousand dollars may seem like a lot of money, but over a nine-month pregnancy it averages out to $1.49 an hour. But suppose the fees were higher? Men, after all, can sell their sperm; should women be forbidden to do something similar? Since the United States has a capitalist economy, is it not a capitalist system for everybody?

It is difficult to reach an accommodation between the rights of the natural mother and those of the natural father. To adopt the principle that her interests supersede all others because of the biological facts of reproduction comes dangerously close to embracing the slogan that "anatomy is destiny," and getting back to the philosophy of *Muller v. Oregon*. Perhaps the state supreme court did the best it could, by effecting a compromise between the interests of both natural parents. After the decision, Mary Beth Whitehead said, "I just can't see how four people loving her, five people loving her, can hurt her." Of course it could not—if we could be sure that those people love Baby M at least as much as they love themselves.[36]

Class and gender combine to make surrogacy an issue which defies resolution. We can feel sympathy for William and Elizabeth Stern, who wanted to become parents and could not safely conceive their own child. Many of you who are reading this book may know, or know of, someone who is experiencing the tragedy of infertility and would make great sacrifices for a "Baby M." The pain suffered by people in this situation is real; but we must also recognize that only the privileged can alleviate their pain through surrogate motherhood. The arrangement sought by the Sterns requires class privilege; only the relatively fortunate can become parents in this way. Whatever else happened to Mary Beth White-

head, she was exploited in a manner that Marx and Engels could
have explained. It is a hard lesson to learn, but it is true nevertheless: our own pain does not give us a license to exploit others.

But who exploited Whitehead? Is it fair to scrutinize the
Sterns's behavior while ignoring Keane, who has become rich
from these arrangements? Did the broker not exploit the Sterns's
emotional need as surely as he and the Sterns exploited Whitehead's financial need? Who won this conflict, and who lost? From
one viewpoint, the victors are male; they got what they con-
tracted for. William Stern has his daughter, and Noel Keane his
profit. Yet neither Mary Beth Whitehead nor Elizabeth Stern got
the terms of their contract fulfilled.

The issue of surrogacy encourages us to think about the legal
implications of adoption. William and Elizabeth Stern grew up in
middle-class families in the 1940s and 1950s. Although neither
was an adopted child, they may have been exposed to the justification of conventional adoption as it was presented to children.
"Some couples want a baby very much and can't have one, so they
find a baby whose mommy and daddy can't take care of him.
They bring the baby home, and he becomes theirs, and they are
now his mommy and daddy." In this scenario, the natural parents
relinquish *all* rights to the child, and vice versa. Indeed, until
recent years when pressure from groups of adoptees and birth
parents forced a change in official practices, neither the child nor
the birth parents had any right, ever, to information about one
another.

The Sterns tried to duplicate this situation, with one obvious
difference: the custodial father would be the biological one. But
what they got, courtesy of the courts, was a very different reality.
In effect, they share the child with her natural mother. Mothers
who seek to have their children adopted are increasingly able to
demand concessions similar to those Whitehead had to fight for
in court. If these arrangements become common, both surrogacy
and adoption may become less appealing to couples like the
Sterns. These issues make it clear that safeguarding reproductive
"rights" is scant comfort to people to whom physiology has denied the privilege of safe, healthy parenthood. Surrogacy and
adoption reinforce the lesson that there is only so much that
political freedom, democracy, and legal rights can do to ensure
happiness. Even among affluent Americans, life is not entirely
within our control.[37]

Reproductive Freedom and the Right to Privacy

Throughout most of history, most people have assumed that state concern with private sexual behavior is legitimate. Phrases like "you can't legislate morality" or "in private between consenting adults" belong to the twentieth century. The colonies and the first states all had laws which regulated in varying degrees of detail who could do what and with whom. The common theme of these statutes was a distrust of any sexual act which could not result in a legitimate birth; thus, homosexual activity, extramarital sex, and any marital relations other than genital intercourse were prohibited. In some states, many of these activities still are. Contraception and abortion fell within this category of disapproved activities. The earliest American laws did not forbid them, however. There was little need for prohibition. No effective and easily available contraceptive technique existed, while abortion was so dangerous that few women would risk it. Once this situation changed, federal and state laws classified birth control and abortion among the forbidden activities as either sinful or obscene.

In the first four decades of this century, most state legislatures amended their statutes to remove birth control from the list of forbidden activities. No strong sentiment existed for a general decriminalization of sexual behavior; there would be little such sentiment until the 1950s, when this country was influenced by developments abroad. But the birth control movement had influenced many Americans to support the right of husbands and wives to limit the size of their family. The eugenics movement probably made birth control more acceptable by emphasizing its potential for reducing the "unfit" population. At any rate, "little Comstock laws" were repealed or amended in all but two of the states. The exceptions, Connecticut and Massachusetts, had laws which, enacted by Puritans, were retained by Catholics as the religious composition of the Northeast changed. The statutes banned, respectively, the use and the sale of contraceptive devices. In neither state was the prohibition well enforced. Any woman who had a private physician could get a prescription, first for a diaphragm, by 1960 for a pill. Condoms, too, were widely available. (The fact that Connecticut is a small state, close to the wicked city of New York, made it easier still to evade the law there.) But neither vending machines nor public clinics which prescribed contraceptives were available. While middle-class women could control their fertility, women who depended on publicly funded medical care could not.

The proponents of birth control urged the legislature to amend the law. These efforts failed, mainly because of Catholic opposition. The Birth Control League illegally operated free clinics for four years in the 1930s, but a police raid closed them. The state eventually dropped all charges. Finally, in 1958, a group of Yale University faculty and students, mostly from the medical and law schools, brought several court actions to try to get the law declared unconstitutional. In 1961, the U.S. Supreme Court ruled that no case or controversy existed; the "undeviating policy of nullification" which the state had followed since the law was passed removed any danger of actual or potential harm.[38]

The Planned Parenthood League, as the Birth Control League had renamed itself, opened a clinic in New Haven the following fall. Ten days later, the police arrested its director, Estelle Griswold, and chief physician, Professor C. Lee Buxton of Yale's Department of Obstetrics and Gynecology. They were tried, convicted, and fined; they appealed their case to the Supreme Court, which now could not claim an absence of controversy. In 1965, it declared the state law unconstitutional. The result of *Griswold v. Connecticut* produced little controversy at the time. The state's commitment to its law was so minimal that the state's attorney's office apparently did not even bother to proofread its brief. Even the Roman Catholic hierarchy declared itself untroubled by what was, after all, a secular ruling. The conclusion that a law prohibiting any use of birth control devices violated constitutional rights seemed only to reaffirm what everyone already assumed. But the theory which the Court adopted had far-reaching implications, which have long since come home to roost.

The Court gave constitutional status to a right nowhere mentioned in the Constitution. Earlier rulings had done that, too, in the "substantive due process" cases which had been discredited at least since 1937 (see Chapter 2). *Griswold* did not invoke the due process clause alone. Justice William O. Douglas found a broad right of "privacy" created by "penumbras, emanating" from several guarantees of the Bill of Rights. These were the First Amendment, which protected privacy of association; the Third, which forbade the quartering of soldiers in private homes in peacetime without consent; the Fourth, protecting people against unreasonable invasions of their homes and property; the self-incrimination clause of the Fifth, enabling "the citizen to create a zone of privacy which he may not be forced to surrender to his detriment"; and the Ninth, which admitted the possibility of individual rights not listed in the Constitution.

Having posited a constitutional right of privacy, Douglas then had to show that this right included the right to use birth control. The opinion continued as if the law applied only to married couples (which it did not). Douglas had several good words to say on behalf of marriage, which he called "a coming together for better or worse, hopefully enduring, and intimate to the degree of being sacred." In one of the most blatant non sequiturs in Supreme Court history, he posed a rhetorical question: "Would we allow the police to search the sacred precincts of marital bedrooms for telltale signs of the use of contraceptives? The very idea is repugnant to the notions of privacy surrounding the marriage relationship."[39]

But no bedrooms had been searched. The state had closed a clinic and gotten witnesses to testify that they obtained contraceptives there and later used them. The defendants were not married couples, but outsiders who had provided these couples with birth control. The state may search our sacred bedrooms for telltale signs of any crimes under several legally defined circumstances, the most common being probable cause for believing that a crime has been committed. If searching bedrooms for signs of this particular crime is a repugnant idea, the Court has failed to explain why.

Many commentators were no more satisfied with the Court's mode of constitutional interpretation than with its conclusion. The idea of basing interpretation on several provisions read together rather than one clause at a time was a new approach; this is not the way cases are usually decided. The originality of the approach, however, does not render it illegitimate. On the face of it, there seems nothing wrong with an interpretation derived from more than one provision. However, *Griswold* is a frustrating opinion because it does little more than list apposite rights, throwing them at the reader rather than using them to formulate a theory of privacy.

These weaknesses are unfortunate, because a convincing argument can be made. There emerges from the Bill of Rights the idea that individuals are in some respects immune from governmental control, and retain some autonomy of which the government may not deprive them. Some of this autonomy is recognized through rights which have some relation to privacy. These rights include seclusion within private space (the Third and Fourth Amendments) and the secrecy of private information (the free speech clause of the First, and the self-incrimination clause of the Fifth). There also exist rights of private autonomy, areas of life which the state does not control (the First Amendment, again, in its free exercise of religion clause). The Constitution also permits the recognition of unspecified rights (the Ninth Amendment). Taken together, these provisions imply that some aspect of activity which characteristically goes on within the sphere of private space, and which the individual usually prefers to keep private, makes such activity private rather than public: makes it, in other words, beyond state control. Sexual behavior, including decisions about family size, belongs in this sphere. Therefore, a law forbidding the use of contraceptives violates a constitutional right of privacy.

By accident or design, *Griswold* stayed within the boundaries of mainstream American mores. The right of privacy recognized by this decision resided only within the marriage relationship and belonged not to individuals but to couples. It is doubtful that the Court's ruling in *Eisenstadt v. Baird*, seven years later, was much more controversial. This decision struck down a Massachusetts law allowing only married couples to use birth control. "If the right of privacy means anything, it is the right of the *individual*, whether married or single, to be free from unwarranted governmental intrusion into matters so fundamentally affecting a person as the decision whether to bear or beget a child."[40] *Eisenstadt* was an important ruling because it made clear where the right to privacy resides; it is as personal as the guarantees of the Bill of Rights. And there was no indication that we had heard the last of this individual right.

Abortion and the Constitution

On January 22, 1973, the Supreme Court ruled that the constitutional right of privacy included a limited right to an elective abortion. *Roe v. Wade* may well be the most controversial Supreme Court decision in American history.[41] Every year, its anniversary is celebrated, in both the contemporary and the old-fashioned sense of that word. Pro-choice activists praise the Court's decision, while the self-styled "Right to Life" movement mourns it. Yet the ruling which produced these reactions reads as if it were simply a logical extension of Supreme Court precedents. However aware the justices were of the possible consequences of their ruling, the opinion does not seem to know what the furor is all about.

Not that *Roe* evinced careless or slipshod research. Justice Harry Blackmun, a former trustee of the Mayo Clinic, spent much of the summer of 1972 in the clinic's library. The resulting opinion indicates that his research was not confined to law and medicine alone. "This right of privacy," wrote Blackmun for a seven-judge majority, "is broad enough to encompass a woman's decision whether or not to terminate her pregnancy."[42] The right was not absolute, beyond state regulation. That conclusion was no surprise, since no other constitutional right has ever been ruled absolute—although *Roe* implies that the right to use birth control is. The general rule, however, is that the state may infringe rights when it has a compelling interest in doing so (see Chapter 2).

Blackmun reviewed the common justifications for laws against abortion in search of compelling justifications. He dismissed the notion that "these laws are the product of a Victorian social concern to discourage illicit sexual conduct." Many nineteenth-century laws had been the product of a concern for the health and safety of the mother at a time when abortion was more dangerous than childbirth. "The third reason is the State's interest—some phrase it in terms of duty—in protecting prenatal life."[43]

The Court concluded that the last two justifications had merit, and became compelling at specific stages in pregnancy. "The pregnant woman cannot be isolated in her privacy. . . . It is reasonable and appropriate for a State to decide that at some point another interest, that of health of the mother or that of potential human life, becomes significantly involved." *Roe* followed the lead of expert obstetrical opinion in dividing pregnancy into three "trimesters," or three-month periods. Since early abortion is now much safer than childbirth, maternal health did not justify either banning or regulating abortions in the first trimester. The danger of abortion increases, however, as the pregnancy progresses. Therefore, a state might regulate (but not ban) abortion in the second trimester.[44]

Blackmun then turned to the status of "prenatal life." If human life begins at conception, the state does indeed have a compelling interest in protecting this life. Such a determination

would have rendered the right to terminate pregnancy meaningless. A lengthy discussion of Western intellectual history, delv-
ing into medicine, philosophy, and religion, persuaded the Court
that no authority had convincingly determined when human life
begins. Therefore, the question of the status of fetal life was
unanswerable. But *laws* restricting abortion "are of relatively
recent vintage." The Court's review of legal history "persuades us
that the word 'person,' as used in the Fourteenth Amendment,
does not include the unborn."[45]

While the government had no stake in prenatal life, its interest in what the opinion called "potential human life" did become
compelling at the point in pregnancy when the fetus became
"viable" outside the mother's body. Therefore, the state could
forbid abortion after viability—which in 1973 meant at approximately the beginning of the third trimester. *Roe v. Wade*, then,
ruled: (1) the state must permit unregulated elective abortions in
the first three months of pregnancy; (2) the state may regulate
abortions performed between the third and sixth months; and (3)
the state may prohibit abortions in the last three months except
when necessary to preserve the mother's life or health.[46]

Roe did not rule, however, that a woman has a right to an
abortion in early pregnancy. For what the opinion actually said
was, "For the stage prior to approximately the end of the first
trimester, the abortion decision and its effectuation must be left
to *the medical judgment of the pregnant woman's attending physician.*"[47] The opinion reads as though it were the rights of doctors—who, incidentally, are always "he"—rather than of women
which were being protected. This distinction is far from trivial;
any professional group which denied voluntary sterilization to
women could do the same with abortions. So far, the medical
profession has not done so. Abortion is available on demand to
women in early pregnancy, as long as they are adults and can pay
for the procedure. But suppose physicians change their collective
minds? In such a case, the right to abortion would effectively
disappear—unless women could safely abort themselves or find
professionals other than doctors to abort them. Worse, the language just quoted comes dangerously close to preferring the physician's judgment to the woman's and, therefore, sanctioning
coerced abortion.

Roe v. Wade had all the defects of *Griswold*, plus a few of its
own. And, unlike *Griswold*, *Roe* needed to be well-reasoned and
convincing, because the political issue which it concerned is

explosive. Although public opinion polls over the last twenty years have consistently shown that a majority of Americans support the right to abortion, the minority which opposes it is intense and vociferous, and has become an increasingly powerful single-issue movement. The Court needed all the friends it could get, and its opinion did not earn it many.

Roe failed to answer at least three crucial questions. First, *why* does the constitutional right to privacy include the right to terminate a pregnancy? Second, if the status of the fetus is uncertain, why cannot a state conclude that human life begins at conception? Third, what happens if medical advances extend the point of viability earlier and earlier in pregnancy? A convincing answer to the first question might have defused the second (if not the third). If a woman's right to privacy includes the right to end a pregnancy, the state's decision to impose upon its citizens a highly problematic definition of life does not constitute a compelling interest. Therefore, the state cannot decide that human life begins at conception. But the convincing answer was not forthcoming.

A statement that the right to use birth control is like the right to have an abortion bears a heavy burden of justification. The differences between contraception and abortion are at least as apparent as the similarities. First, abortion is far from private; at least as technology now stands, it demands the cooperation of publicly licensed professionals in a publicly regulated facility. Abortion removes the individual from the precincts of the bedroom. Second, to use birth control is, essentially, to prevent life from beginning. Abortion is ending life (whether "human" or not, the fetus is alive) once it has begun. So why does the right which includes contraception include abortion?

The reason for this conclusion, apparently, was "the detriment that the State would impose upon the pregnant woman by denying this choice altogether." Blackmun went on to list many harmful consequences of unwanted pregnancy: "specific and direct harm medically diagnosable . . . a distressful life and future . . . psychological harm . . . the distress, for all concerned, associated with an unwanted child, and there is the problem of bringing a child into a family already unable, psychologically and otherwise, to care for it."[48] It is impossible to argue with this conclusion; even an unfriendly critic conceded that "having an unwanted pregnancy can go a long way toward ruining a woman's life."[49] But government interferes with our freedom in many ways which have harmful consequences for us. If a right to terminate pregnancy exists, there have to be better reasons than that unwanted pregnancy is rough. There must be something about unwanted pregnancy which makes it a particularly oppressive form of coercion.

More than a few legal scholars who had considered themselves proponents of judicial activism changed their minds when *Roe* was decided.[50] It is noteworthy that—without exception, so far as I know—the constitutionalist critics of the decision were male scholars. That fact does not astound, since virtually all the established legal scholars in the United States in 1973 were men. There were feminist writers and scholars in other fields, however, and nearly all of them welcomed the ruling. Since constitutional doctrine was not their specialty, they focused on result rather than reasoning. A comprehensive feminist defense of the constitutional right to abortion has yet to be made.[51]

A *Feminist* Roe v. Wade: *Remaking Jurisprudence*

Most women who label themselves feminists support legalized abortion. Most women who oppose legalized abortion do not label themselves feminists. Kristin Luker's study, discussed in Chapter 2, illuminated this division. She found that most activists (though not necessarily most, or the largest, financial contributors) on both sides of this issue were women. A further, and significant, finding concerned the nature of the difference of opinion between pro-choice and anti-choice women. Despite the popular anti-choice slogan "Abortion is murder," the conflict between these groups did not center on the status of the fetus. Instead, the crucial disagreement between the two groups concerned the role of women. The pro-choice activists held conventional feminist views, while the anti-choice women accepted the traditional antifeminist view of woman's role.[52] The emergence of the New Right in the 1980s, with its emphasis on "family values," led some feminists to moderate or to apologize for their stance.[53] But there seems to be, in general, an intuitive recognition that a commitment to women's rights entails a commitment to reproductive choice. This basic agreement among feminists has not, however, produced a convincing constitutional argument for such choice.

Perhaps one way to begin to formulate the case is to ask, under what circumstances would a commitment to women's rights be compatible with, or even demand, a *rejection* of the right to abortion? Since this exercise is an intellectual one, the circumstances need not ever be likely to occur. Well, one circumstance which might change feminist positions is if it were men, not women, who became pregnant and had the primary responsibility for child care. This conceptual journey into cloud-cuckooland reinforces the crucial point: the link between sexual equality and abortion has some connection to the fact that only women get pregnant. (Would men be likely to deny themselves reproductive choice? There was a popular feminist slogan of the 1970s which ran, "If men got pregnant, abortion would be a sacrament.") Suppose that both men and women could bear children. Lack of reproductive choice would not then put women at a comparative disadvantage. But it would restrict everyone's freedom by making all sexually active people vulnerable to unwanted pregnancy and parenthood. Women, like men, would thus be less able to fight for their rights. Reproductive choice would be no less necessary for women in this situation than freedom of expression is now.[54]

Knowing that only women get pregnant, when could we adopt an antiabortion stance? Suppose no woman could become pregnant more than once in her lifetime, so that an abortion would mean that she could never bear a child.[55] Feminists do not agree among themselves about the significance of motherhood in a woman's life. Many, perhaps most, feminists believe that, in an ideal world where the choice was absolutely free, some women would have children while some would not. But a few feminists insist that motherhood is so central to a woman's identity that no woman would voluntarily forgo it under ideal circumstances.[56]

Whatever one's views on motherhood, it is difficult to imagine women forcing their views on other women to the extent of denying them the choice to remain child-free. (After all, we do accept women's right to voluntary sterilization.) But a situation where a woman could only get pregnant once in her life would require thinking about abortion in a very different way. Again, fantasy helps clarify reality. One reason the right to abortion seems so crucial to women is the fact that fertility is far from a scarce commodity. Choosing to terminate a pregnancy rarely entails renouncing parenthood.

But suppose we revise this fantasy, too. Suppose that, instead of having to try *not* to conceive, both men and women always had to make an effort to do so. In other words, what if our normal condition was infertility, which both partners must purposefully change, rather than the other way around? A woman who chose to terminate a pregnancy under these circumstances might be seen as trying to renege on an implied contract, to reverse the choice which both she and her partner had freely made. It is still true, of course, that only the woman suffers the physical consequences of pregnancy and childbirth. These can be harsh, even without threatening her life or (long-term) health. And a woman who chose to get pregnant might feel that she had not grasped the physical consequences of this decision, and that, therefore, her decision was not an informed one.

As Blackmun recognized, not all the consequences of pregnancy are physical. *Roe* included "psychological harm," "child care," and "a distressful life and future" among the burdens "that the State would impose *upon the pregnant woman* by denying her this choice altogether."[57] But suppose that these consequences did *not* attend motherhood: that, instead, to be a mother was to be privileged, to have a claim on others for support (of various kinds, presumably including financial and moral) and help, to have family and community share one's responsibilities. The case for abortion becomes less compelling.

Combining some of these fantasies, possible and impossible, makes the hypothetical situation still more difficult. *If* women had to make an effort to conceive, and *if* their partners had to do so as well, and *if* motherhood conferred benefits instead of burdens, could we make a feminist case against abortion? Such a case would still bump against reality to the extent that a woman's situation can change after conception in ways which make motherhood problematical even in these utopian circumstances. It is likely that there would be far fewer abortions if these visions came to pass. Feminists might not have to devote so much energy to defending this right. But reproductive choice would still be essential to self-determination for women. We seem to be left with the conclusion that the only circumstances in which a prohibition of abortion would be compatible with women's rights are those in which men bear and raise children. It would, of course, be selfish to deny men reproductive choice under those circumstances; it would be incompatible with sexual equality. But such a prohibition would not deny *women* freedom.

We must now return to reality. Women get pregnant. It is all too easy to conceive by accident. Women usually bear the responsibility for preventing conception, often at some risk to their health. Men can prevent pregnancy, by using condoms, but are unlikely to take this responsibility.[58] Indeed, for every unwanted pregnancy, there is a man who could have prevented it, and neglected to do so.

Women care for children. Men can care for children, but rarely do. In recent years, men have been free to renege even on the financial responsibility for their children which they have traditionally borne, and many of them have taken full advantage of this freedom. If the pregnant woman can never be isolated in her privacy, physiology and society combine to isolate her in her calamity.[59]

One argument popular among opponents of abortion is that women can relinquish their responsibilities to unwanted infants by giving them up for adoption. This was the position taken by George Bush in the 1988 presidential election debates. However, the argument is not convincing. First, it does not take into account the effects of either the pregnancy itself or of having to make such a decision. Second, not all infants are likely to be adopted; the "market" favors the white and able-bodied. Third, and most compelling, a natural mother who renounces her infant abandons control over the child's future. Late in 1988, the trial of Joel Steinberg for the killing of his illegally adopted daughter, Lisa, drew national attention. Lisa's natural mother, Michelle Launders, trustingly gave up her child—to a man later convicted of beating the child to death.

Justice Blackmun was on the right track when he emphasized the dire effects of unwanted pregnancy. What *Roe v. Wade* failed to do was to link two constitutional concepts, equality and privacy, into a convincing argument. The Court seemed unaware of the fact that reproductive choice involves questions of sexual equality. The reason the right to an abortion is crucial is because of the disproportionate burdens which denial of reproductive choice places on women. The connection with the right of privacy is not the notion that a woman can do as she pleases with her body— that is legally not correct—but the invasion of private autonomy which an unwanted pregnancy is for a woman. A constitutional right to an elective abortion exists. But that right has to be grounded, in part, in a discussion of sexual equality.

Whose Choice? Whose Knowledge? What Conditions? When?

In practice if not in theory, *Roe v. Wade* gave women the right to choose to terminate early pregnancies. It did not take long for some states to try to restrict this choice. The Missouri legislature, for example, quickly passed a law requiring physicians to obtain the consent of the husbands of married women and the parents of unmarried minors. The Supreme Court struck down both provisions in 1976. "We cannot hold that the State has the constitutional authority to give the spouse unilaterally the ability to prohibit the wife from terminating her pregnancy, when the State itself lacks that right." Conceding that "ideally, the decision to terminate a pregnancy should be one concurred in by both wife and husband," the justices nevertheless insisted that "it is difficult to believe that the goal of . . . strengthening the marriage relationship and the marriage institution, will be achieved by giving the husband a veto power exercisable for any reason whatsoever or for no reason at all."[60]

Since *Danforth*, some men have tried to stop their wives or lovers from having abortions by getting restraining orders. A few judges have issued such orders, but so far the women have always gotten the abortions in other jurisdictions. The Supreme Court has not reconsidered the issue of spousal consent. It would be an entirely different matter, however, for a state to require that a husband be notified before his wife had an abortion, or to require prior consultation between the spouses. No state has ever passed such a law. As a result, no constitutional ruling on this subject exists.

This aspect of the *Danforth* ruling was hardly a surprise. As a general principle, the state may not require the consent of one adult before another adult exercises a constitutional right. The status of minors is dramatically different. Although minors are not without all rights, courts have consistently ruled that they do not enjoy the same rights as adults to the same degree.[61] There was no obvious barrier to a decision upholding the state's power to require parental consent. The Court has not done so—not quite, not yet—but its decisions reflect its changing composition and changes in political attitudes.

The landmark 1983 case of *Akron v. Akron Center for Reproductive Health* adhered to the letter of *Danforth* by invalidating a rule demanding parental consent for girls under fifteen. "Under [prior] decisions, it is clear that *Akron* may not make a blanket decision that *all* minors under the age of fifteen are too immature to make this decision or that an abortion may never be in a minor's best interests without parental approval."[62] But state legislatures continue to pass laws imposing similar requirements.

The decisions between 1976 and 1983 indicate why a state might infer that the Court majority is far from stable.

In *Danforth*, Justice Blackmun lost one vote, that of John Paul Stevens, on the parental consent issue. Their opposed positions nicely lay out the issue. Blackmun wrote:

> Just as with the requirement of consent from the spouse, so here, the State does not have the constitutional authority to give a third party an absolute, and possibly arbitrary, veto over the decision of the physician and his patient to terminate the patient's pregnancy, regardless of the reason for withholding the consent.
>
> Constitutional rights do not mature and come into being magically only when one attains the state-defined age of majority. Minors, as well as adults, are protected by the Constitution and possess constitutional rights. The Court indeed, however, long has recognized that the State has somewhat broader authority to regulate the activities of children than of adults. It remains, then, to examine whether there is any significant state interest in conditioning an abortion on the consent of a parent.
>
> One suggested interest is the safeguarding of the family unit and of parental authority. It is difficult, however, to conclude that providing a parent with absolute power to overrule a determination . . . to terminate the patient's pregnancy will strengthen the family unit. Neither is it likely that such veto power will enhance parental authority or control where the minor and the non-consenting parent are so fundamentally in conflict. . . .[63]

Stevens responded to this argument as follows:

> The State's interest in the welfare of its young citizens justifies a variety of protective measures. . . . The State's interest in protecting a young person from harm justifies the imposition of restraints on his or her freedom even though comparable restraints on adults would be constitutionally impermissible . . .
>
> Whatever choice a pregnant young woman makes—to marry, to abort, to bear her child out of wedlock—the consequences of her decision may have a profound impact on her entire future life. A legislative determination that such a choice will be made more wisely in most cases if the advice and moral support of a parent play a part in the decisionmaking process is surely not irrational.[64]

H.L. v. Matheson, five years later, sustained Utah's effort to get parents into the decisional process without giving them a veto. A state law required parental notification, but not consent. This compromise was acceptable to six of the nine justices. Neither the majority nor the dissenters mentioned an important aspect of the law: since minors have a general legal duty to obey their parents, requiring notification may effectively impose a requirement of consent.[65]

Matheson was decided the same day as *Michael M. v. Sonoma County*, the case which upheld California's gender-specific statutory rape law. Justice Blackmun, who dissented in *Matheson*, wrote the concurring opinion in *Michael M.*, which was discussed in Chapter 2. The first few sentences of that opinion are relevant in the present context: "It is gratifying that the plurality recognizes that 'at the risk of stating the obvious, teenage pregnancies . . . have increased dramatically over the last two decades' and 'have significant social, medical, and economic consequences for both the mother and her child, and the State.' There have been times when I have wondered whether the Court was capable of this perception, particularly when it has struggled with the difficult but not unrelated problems that attend abortion issues."[66]

Two marginally consistent decisions have concerned limited, reviewable parental vetoes. *Bellotti v. Baird* invalidated a Massachusetts law requiring written consent from both parents or, if either refused, permission from a judge. (The difference between this ruling and the more recent *Hodgson* case was that the Minnesota law required not parental consent but parental *notification* which could be bypassed with judicial *consent*.) *Planned Parenthood v. Ashcroft*, a companion case to *Akron*, sustained a law which required either parental consent or, in its absence, judicial approval if a girl could convince a judge that she was competent to make the decision (an interesting process, surely).[67]

The emphasis on judgments of the decision-making capacities of minors is not surprising. A similar concern with how "mature" young people are pervades court rulings on other aspects of children's rights.[68] But surely the consequences of the decision to the decision maker are at least as important as the maturity and competence of that individual. However competent the girl is, she, after all, is the one who will bear or abort. Those who question whether minors should be allowed to get abortions without parental consent might well imagine the reverse situation: a young woman, convinced that abortion is a sin, forced by her parents to terminate a pregnancy. Whatever one's opinions, however, it is clear that minors' freedom of choice has been significantly limited by state laws which the Court has upheld.

Several states have passed laws which, while they do not require anyone's consent for an abortion, surround the choice with restrictions and conditions. The Missouri law reviewed in *Danforth*, for instance, also required a woman's written consent; forbade all abortions by saline amniocentesis, the commonest second-trimester technique; required "reasonable care" to keep aborted fetuses alive; and ordered that records of abortions be kept and held for at least seven years. Only the first and last requirements survived judicial scrutiny. The others shared the defect of the ban on saline abortions: it "fails as a reasonable regulation for the protection of maternal health. It comes into focus, instead, as an unreasonable or arbitrary regulation designed to inhibit, and having the effect of inhibiting . . . abortions."[69]

Akron and its two companion cases involved several regulations designed to hamper, or at least discourage, abortions. The Ohio city had required a twenty-four-hour waiting period after a woman's consent; that all late abortions be performed in hospitals; that doctors inform women of all possible negative consequences of, and alternatives to, abortion and tell them that life begins at conception; and that the products of abortion be disposed of in a "humane and sanitary manner." All of these regulations were invalidated, either because they were vague or because they were unreasonable, but the Court upheld laws from Missouri and Virginia requiring pathologist's reports (at the patient's expense), a second physician where abortions produced a viable fetus, and the performance of late abortions only in hospitals or clinics.[70] *Thornburgh v. American College of Obstetrics and Gynecology*, decided in 1986, also reaffirmed *Roe* by invalidating a Pennsylvania law requiring record-keeping, including such information as the age and race of the patient; physicians' informing patients about fetal development and adoption possibilities; and aborting viable fetuses by techniques most likely to keep them alive. "The states are not free," declared Justice Blackmun, "under the guise of protecting maternal health or potential life, to intimidate women into continuing pregnancies."[71]

Why were viable fetuses being aborted, anyway? One reason was that no state was *required* to forbid abortions in the third trimester, and all had to allow them to save the mothers' life. Another reason gets to a persistent difficulty with elective abortion and with *Roe v. Wade*. Justice Sandra Day O'Connor squarely faced this difficulty in her dissent in *Akron*. In 1973, any abortion after the third month carried appreciable risk, and virtually no fetus was viable until the end of the sixth month. But "just as improvements in medical technology will inevitably move *forward* the point at which the State may regulate for reasons of maternal health, different technological improvements will move *backward* the point of viability at which the State may proscribe abortions." Ten years after *Roe*, physicians were using techniques then restricted to first-trimester abortions for much later ones. On the other hand, experts estimated that infants born as prematurely as 22 weeks (a full-term pregnancy is 40) had a good chance of survival. If viability could no longer be set at the beginning of the last trimester, the ruling that the state's interest in preserving potential life did not begin until then could no longer hold. "The *Roe* framework, then, is clearly on a collision course with itself."[72]

O'Connor's dissent provides a valuable lesson in the dangers of basing permanent dogma on time-bound technology. (And, surely, a former trustee of the Mayo Clinic ought to have predicted that medical technology would advance.) As O'Connor herself implies, it is the framework of *Roe*, not its recognition of a right, which the gynecology and neonatology of the 1980s discredit. Subsequent technological advances may well render *Roe* obsolescent rather than obsolete. In 1988, a French pharmaceutical firm developed a drug (RU-486) which allows a woman to abort herself, without risk. This drug is not likely to be made legally available in the United States anytime soon, but market considerations have a way of influencing these decisions in the long run. Abortion may eventually become as simple a matter as taking the Pill.

Abortions and Public Funding

The situation, as of 1991, was this: The state may not forbid abortion. It is not clear whether a state may premise restrictions solely on a desire to discourage abortion. But court decisions have sustained laws which compromise reproductive choice for two groups of women. One group, as we have seen, consists of minors. The other group consists of women who depend on the government for their medical services.

Both state and federal governments subsidize medical care. The two groups in the population most dependent on this funding are the aged, through Medicare, and the poor, through Medicaid. These programs are funded by the national government and administered, within federal guidelines, by the states, which also have programs of their own. Like most medical insurance plans, government-funded programs are selective in deciding what kinds of care they will pay for. Soon after *Roe v. Wade* was decided, some states forbade the use of Medicaid funds for elective abortions. The first "Hyde amendment" to federal appropriations bills—one of a series of such amendments banning the use of any Medicaid funds for abortions—was passed in 1976. These amendments were named after their sponsor, Representative Henry Hyde, Republican of Illinois. The Supreme Court has upheld all of these provisions. As of 1991, the federal government and 41 states had forbidden the use of public funds for abortions unless they are necessary to save the mother's life.

The legislative history of the Hyde amendment provides some valuable knowledge about congressional attitudes and the extent to which they are grounded in accurate information. In 1977, an Arizona representative exhorted "the woman" to "exercise control [over her own body]—before she gets pregnant. But do not ask the taxpayers of America to pay the price when there is a failure to exercise control by forcing taxpayers to subsidize the ending of the lives of unborn children as a convenience to adult women." ("Convenience" was the word Justice White had used in a similar context in his dissent in *Roe*.)[73] This argument ignores the fact that the public price for failure of control is higher when the pregnancy goes to term—not to mention the speaker's unilateral attribution of this laxity to the woman.

Of course, the point may have been that taxpayers who oppose abortion on moral grounds ought not to have to help pay for it. That same argument was decisively rejected in the 1960s when some peace activists refused to pay a proportion of their tax bill equivalent to that part of the federal budget spent on defense. Citizens have never been allowed to refuse to pay for activities of which they disapprove.

Representative Hyde and a colleague opposed the rape exception on the grounds that it was unnecessary: "rape almost never results in pregnancy." In fact, rape results in pregnancy at the same rate of any unprotected intercourse, about 4 percent of the time. Rape is, of course, more likely to occur without contraception than is consensual sex. The exception did demand that the woman report the rape to the police. Even this requirement struck Mr. Hyde as "inducing fraud; we will not stop abortions, because every woman who wants one will doubtless say she was raped by an unknown assailant." Whatever the sincerity of Hyde's concern for infants, his hostility toward women is obvious in these remarks. So is Congress's collective ignorance. Eventually,

Hyde's victory was almost complete; the rape exception was abolished. In 1981, after the Republicans took control of the Senate, the two houses agreed to limit funding to those abortions necessary to save the mother's life. This policy prevails, although in late 1989 Congress voted to restore funding in cases of rape or incest. President Bush vetoed the bill.[74]

By the time the federal law got to the Court, the majority had already tipped its hand. Three cases, decided on the same day in 1977, dealt with state regulations. *Beal v. Doe* and *Maher v. Roe* involved, respectively, the statutory and constitutional permissibility of state Medicaid regulations. *Poelker v. Doe* sustained a St. Louis ordinance banning all "non-therapeutic" abortions in its public hospitals.[75] *Beal* ruled that abortion was not among the "necessary medical services" which Title XIX of the Social Security Act requires the states to fund through Medicaid. The Court upheld Pennsylvania's law allowing payment for abortions only under the following conditions: when necessary to preserve the mother's health; when it was probable that the infant would be born disabled; or when the pregnancy resulted from rape or incest.

Maher upheld Connecticut's similar law against several constitutional challenges. The law was not irrational, insisted Justice Powell, in its refusal to fund abortions while funding childbirth, even though the latter is far more costly. "The subsidizing of cost incident to childbirth is a rational means of encouraging childbirth." Nor was the law invalid as a burden on the exercise of a constitutional right.

> The Texas law in *Roe* was a stark example of impermissible interference with the pregnant woman's decision to terminate her pregnancy. In subsequent cases, we have invalidated other types of restrictions, different in form but similar in effect, on a woman's reproductive choice. Thus, in *Planned Parenthood v. Danforth*, we held that . . . Missouri had interposed an *absolute obstacle* to a woman's decision.
>   . . . . The Connecticut regulation places no obstacle—absolute or otherwise—in the pregnant woman's path to an abortion. An indigent who desires an abortion suffers no disadvantage as a result of Connecticut's decision to fund childbirth; she continues as before to be dependent on private sources for the service she desires. The State may have made childbirth a more attractive alternative, thereby influencing the woman's decision, but it has imposed no restriction on access to abortions that was not already there. The indigency that may make it difficult—and in some cases impossi-

ble—for some women to have abortions is neither created nor in any way affected by the Connecticut regulation.[76]

Justices Brennan, Marshall, and Blackmun dissented in all three cases. Brennan wrote, "The stark reality is that for too many, not just 'some,' indigent pregnant women indigency makes access to competent licensed physicians not merely 'difficult,' but impossible."[77] These decisions seem curiously at odds with prior rulings which have held that the state must provide indigents with certain constitutional rights, such as the right to an appeal or to counsel, at its own expense.[78] But the majority has prevailed.

Harris v. McRae, three years later, upheld the Hyde Amendment. What was true for the states, the Court ruled, was equally true for the federal government. Justice Stewart's opinion did not add much to Justice Powell's doctrine, although it contained an intriguing foray into economics. "Although government may not place obstacles in the path of a woman's exercise of her freedom of choice, it need not remove those not of its own creation. Indigency falls in the latter category."[79] It is hard to dispute Powell's refusal to blame poverty in Connecticut on the state's Medicaid rules, but Stewart's blanket absolution of the government from responsibility for poverty gives the lie to the notion that the Court does not write economic and political theory into law.

Justice Thurgood Marshall dissented in all of these cases. His eloquent, impassioned opinions have a consistent theme.

> The class burdened by the Hyde Amendment consists of indigent women, a substantial proportion of whom are members of minority races. . . . The result will not be to protect what the Court describes as "the legitimate governmental objective of protecting potential life," but to ensure the destruction of both fetal and maternal life. "There is another world 'out there,' the existence of which the Court either chooses to ignore or fears to recognize." In my view, it is only by blinding itself to that other world that the Court can reach the result it announces today.[80]

A federal study published in 1981 claimed that the Hyde Amendment had had little effect on the number of abortions actually performed. It revealed that the vast majority of Medicaid-eligible women who seek abortions live in one of the states which still fund it; half of all Medicaid-funded abortions are performed in two of these states, California and New York. According to this study, the majority of the 15 percent of the women who live in states which do not fund abortions "come up with the money." The researchers estimated that in the first year after the restrictions took effect in August 1977, about 94 percent of the 300,000 women who had Medicaid and wanted abortions got them—which means, of course, that 18,000 women did not.[81]

Many private insurance plans, like the government, refuse to pay for abortions. At present, abortion is available only to adult women who can pay for it themselves. Even they may not have access to it.

> Although legalization has greatly lowered the cost of abortion, millions of women in the United States . . . do not have access to safe, affordable abortions. Difficulties and delays stall many women beyond the first twelve weeks. Southern and rural states and counties have often ignored the Supreme Court decision. State regulations and funding vary widely. It is still hard to get second-trimester abortions. By 1977, when federal funds did pay for abortions, fewer than 20 percent of U.S. (public) county and city hospitals actually provided them. In other words, some 40 percent of American women—perhaps 93 percent of women living in rural areas—never benefited from liberalized abortion laws.[82]

Women still do not own the flesh they stand in.

The Precarious Future of Roe

Remaking the Supreme Court was high on the list of Ronald Reagan's priorities as president. Reversing *Roe v. Wade* was high on the list of decisions which the Reagan administration wanted that Court to make. By the end of the 1988–89 term, it was clear that a consistent, if not rigid, five-to-four conservative majority was in place. On the last day of the term, *Webster v. Reproductive Health Services* made it clear that the goal of recriminalizing abortion was in sight. Almost exactly a year later, *Hodgson v. Minnesota* provided encouragement for parents who wish to force their young daughters to remain pregnant. While parents may not unilaterally veto a minor's decision, the states may put powerful obstacles in front of a minor's exercise of the right.[83]

The Court did not overrule *Roe*, as the Reagan and Bush administrations had asked it to do. But five justices voted to uphold a Missouri law which stated that life began at conception; forbade the use of any public funds and facilities to encourage abortion; and negated the trimester distinction by requiring viability testing at twenty weeks. Chief Justice Rehnquist's plurality opinion and Justice O'Connor's separate opinion contained strong hints that they were looking for persuasive arguments to overturn *Roe*. Justice Scalia lambasted his colleagues for refusing to do so. And the Court's acceptance of three more cases for the 1989–90 term indicated their willingness to consider new limitations.[84]

The states have not jumped on the anti-choice bandwagon. Indeed, just the opposite has happened. Six months after *Webster*, only Pennsylvania had passed new restrictions. The Florida legislature, in a special session, had handed Governor Bob Martinez a stunning defeat by refusing to do so. In Louisiana and Idaho, the situation was the reverse: governors of both states vetoed new restrictions. In the same week that Florida's legislature refused to act, Congress amended Medicaid regulations to allow payment for abortions in cases of rape or incest—a step it had refused to take before *Webster*. President Bush vetoed this provision, but Congress may have enough votes to override him in the future.

This outcome is likely because the abortion issue is already affecting elections. Pro-choice candidates won major victories in 1989, including the governor's races in New Jersey and Virginia. The off-year general election in November 1990 was the first nationwide test of the relative strength of the pro-choice and anti-choice forces. While some anti-choice candidates were elected, the pro-choice movement showed its strength not only in several electoral victories but also in races where both opposing candidates were pro-choice.

Conclusion

> Sexuality must not be described as a stubborn drive, by nature alien and of necessity disobedient to a power which exhausts itself trying to subdue it and often fails to control it entirely. It appears rather as an especially dense transfer point for relations of power: between men and women, young people and old people, parents and offspring, teachers and students, priests and laity, an administration and a population.[85]

Sex and procreation are too important to any society to be left in the private domain. They are matters of vital public concern. American society has rarely been willing to leave reproductive choice in the hands of individuals, whether male or female. Reproductive choice has two aspects: the right to procreate, and

the right not to. Both nature and law have placed powerful restrictions upon both facets of this freedom. Nature makes it
difficult for the vast majority of heterosexually active adults to
avoid conception. At the same time, with cruel irony, nature
denies parenthood to ever larger numbers of people who seek it.

Since it is women who bear children, any regulation of reproduction has a powerful, pervasive impact upon women's lives.
Law, much more than nature, has concentrated on restricting
both facets of women's reproductive freedom. Some women, like
Carrie Buck, Linda Kay Spitler, and untold numbers of poor,
black, Hispanic, and Native American women, have been deprived of the ability to become mothers, against their will and
even, in some cases, without their informed consent. Millions of
other women—Sadie Sachs, Norma McCorvey, the poor women of
New Haven, and the middle-class women whose age multiplied
by the number of their children did not reach 120—have been
denied the right not to become mothers and the right to decide
how many children they will have. Patriarchy has not been consistent in its views about who should bear children and who
should not, but it has imposed those opinions, whatever they
might be at a specific historical moment, upon women.

The last fifty years have seen fundamental changes in the laws
regarding women's reproductive freedom. Slowly and chaot-
ically, control has been wrested from the state and the medical
profession and seized by individuals themselves. Compulsory
sterilization is forbidden, contraception is widely available, and a
right to abortion, limited and precarious though it is, exists. It is
this last right which has been the most controversial. Students of
the dispute over abortion have learned that the controversy is not
primarily about the status of the fetus. Rather, the debate centers
on the role of women. After all, one of the many differences
between abortion and contraception/sterilization is that only
women get abortions. To recognize a right to an abortion is to put
fertility unambiguously and permanently within the control of
each individual woman. Such autonomy is threatening to those,
male and female, who accept the traditional notion of woman as
subject to man and bound to the childbearing role. No matter
how many women accept these views, they are patriarchal ideas,
inseparable from that institution.

Even the Supreme Court, in its landmark decision in *Roe v.
Wade*, seemed unaware of the these ramifications of the abortion
issue. It said little about the fact that it is women who bear
children, care for them, and, most of the time, must take respon-

sibility for preventing conception. Perhaps this neglect of an issue which is, after all, central here is one reason that the Court was so ready to sustain legislative efforts to limit the freedom of the most vulnerable of American women, the poor and the young. The opinion's blinkered vision may also help explain why *Roe* failed to persuade so many people. Whatever the reason, the ruling never gained widespread acceptance (though the result did) and now the right is in peril.

The foes of abortion, who seem so ignorant of and insensitive to the facts of reproductive biology and the needs of many women, will be pleased if the Court reverses *Roe*. So will many others, including some legal scholars, who saw the decision as harmful to the democratic process. But the democratic process does not carry, bear, and raise children. Individual women do. Democracy has never required that all decisions, however intimate and private, be made by the public.

There is a crucial point, however, on which the foes of abortion are correct. Abortion should not have to happen. It represents a failure of technology, a lack of responsibility, or a tragedy such as poverty, maternal illness, or potential disability for the infant. Safe, reliable contraceptive devices for both men and women, available and easy to use, should exist. To the extent that they do, not everyone can use them easily, safely, and reliably. People should take responsibility for preventing conception—especially men, who do not risk pregnancy. People do not take this responsibility—especially men, who mostly leave birth control to their partners. Disease, poverty, and birth defects should not keep people from having children. But they do.

Abortion can also be a response to the fact that pregnancy and motherhood can ruin a woman's life. She bears the lion's share of responsibility for the child, and she is also the one whose life will be limited by parenthood. If these things were not true, abortion would be less attractive. Those who oppose abortion might well turn their attention to changing those factors which make it necessary. To the extent that they do not, they invite the conclusion that their interest is not in preserving the lives of the unborn but in preserving patriarchy.

REFERENCES

Andrews, Lori B. *Between Strangers: Surrogate Mothers, Expectant Fathers, and Brave New Babies.* New York: Harper & Row, 1989. One of several recent studies, this one defends the practice of surrogate motherhood.

Bonnicksen, Andrea. *In Vitro Fertilization: Building Policies from Laboratories to Legislatures*. New York: Columbia University Press, 1989. A discussion of the medical and social problems raised by this procedure for treating infertility.

Boston Women's Health Collective. *The New Our Bodies, Ourselves*. New York: Simon & Schuster, 1984. An indispensable source on any aspect of women's health care.

Eisenstein, Zillah. *The Female Body and the Law*. Berkeley: University of California Press, 1988. Insightful, original treatment of issues relevant to law and procreation.

Field, Martha. *Surrogate Motherhood*. Cambridge, Mass.: Harvard University Press, 1988. An exploration of the legal, political, and social implications of surrogacy.

Luker, Kristin. *Abortion and the Politics of Motherhood*. Berkeley: University of California Press, 1984. A valuable study of pro- and anti-choice activists.

Petchesky, Rosalind P. *Abortion and Woman's Choice*. New York: Longman, 1984. A well-reasoned, thought-provoking analysis of reproductive freedom.

Rich, Adrienne. *Of Woman Born: Motherhood As Experience and Institution*. New York: W.W. Norton, 1976. The author, a famous contemporary feminist poet and scholar, explores the meaning of motherhood beyond the relationship itself.

Rothman, Barbara Katz. *Recreating Motherhood*. New York: W.W. Norton, 1989. An excellent scholarly treatment of medical, family, and employment issues.

Rubin, Eva. *Abortion, Politics, and the Court*. Westport, Conn.: Greenwood Press, 1982. A good analysis of recent history and the judicial process.

Sanger, Margaret. *An Autobiography*. New York: W.W. Norton, 1938. The old days, seen through the eyes of one of the founding mothers of reproductive rights.

Schulder, Diane, and **Florynce Kennedy.** *Abortion Rap*. New York: McGraw-Hill, 1971. Individual accounts of experiences before legalization.

Whitehead, Mary Beth, with **Loretta Schwartz-Nobel.** *A Mother's Story*. New York: St. Martin's Press, 1989. A personal account from the country's most famous surrogate mother.

6

Gateways and Barriers: Education and Participation

Knowledge is power. This statement is a cliché, but, like many clichés, it states a profound truth. Education is, basically, a means of acquiring and transmitting knowledge. The word comes from the Latin *educere*, "to lead out," and education has been the means by which people are "led out" of the ignorance into which all of us are born. At the most rudimentary level, knowing how to read and write—being literate—enables us to cope with the outside world in a modern society. Possession of more complex and specialized knowledge—of law, for example, or of science, or foreign languages—gives people access to even greater power. Education is not limited to formal schooling and training. But society controls access to formal education, and most societies also make earning certain formal credentials qualifications for positions of power, influence, and reward. To the extent that any society controls access to education, it distributes power. Some people get it, and some do not.

Throughout most of Western history, education beyond mere literacy has been a rare privilege. It will not surprise the reader to learn that this privilege has typically been reserved for males, and affluent males at that. At the time that the Constitution was adopted, few people went to school, nearly all of them boys. Girls, to the extent that they were taught at all, learned the "three Rs" at home. Slaves, both male and female, had even less access to schooling than free females did. Several states prohibited teaching slaves to read and write.

Higher education—college or university—was an elite, all-male world. There were only a few private colleges; Harvard, Yale, Princeton, Dartmouth, and William and Mary were among them. No public university would exist until 1795, when the University of North Carolina opened its doors in Chapel Hill. Postgraduate professional education, in law or medicine, for example, took place outside of the universities, as on-the-job training in practitioners' offices. Two hundred years ago, a college education was not a prerequisite for becoming a doctor or lawyer. But women were excluded as effectively as if it had been. Much of the work now done by physicians was done by women—delivering babies, for instance—but these women were labeled nurses or midwives, never doctors.

The nineteenth century brought the development of American education as we know it now. Universal, compulsory schooling; higher education; and postgraduate professional training were firmly in place by the century's end. The Morrill Act of 1862 set aside federal lands in each state for public universities. Legal, medical, and academic training took their present forms; a bachelors' degree became a requirement for entry into one of these schools. And although sexual equality was far from being a reality, the male monopoly on education had been broken.

Once public education was established, it was available for girls as well as for boys. By 1901, girls went to elementary and high school. They got fewer years of schooling than men did, however, and higher education remained a largely male preserve. But it was available for a tiny minority of women, too. The first institution to admit them, Oberlin College in Ohio, graduated its first woman student in 1841. The elite private women's colleges or "Seven Sisters"—Radcliffe, Vassar, Bryn Mawr, Wellesley, Smith, Mount Holyoke, and Barnard—had opened. The black universities founded since the Civil War admitted women, and there were black women's colleges. Many state universities admitted women. A small number of intrepid pioneers had even gone to law or medical school, and an even smaller number were able to practice their professions. But higher education was still closed to all but a tiny minority of women—and to the majority of men.[1]

The trend toward equality was still inching along by the 1930s. The percentage of people who attended college grew, and so did the percentage of women. By 1930, 3.1 percent of American women and 4.6 percent of men over 25 had completed at least four years of college. In 1960, the figures were 5.8 percent of women and 9.7 percent of men.[2] World War II had opened up some opportunities for women by removing the men from campus to the armed services. But after the war, those opportunities dwindled as men, their education funded by the "GI Bill," returned to these institutions. In 1950, women earned only one fourth of all bachelor's degrees, their lowest share since statistics became available in the 1920s.[3]

A recent biography of Bess Myerson, the former cultural affairs commissioner of New York City, makes a revealing point. Myerson first became famous in 1945, when she was chosen Miss America—an achievement which is not honored in the circles to which she aspired and in which she was to excel. But, as one biographer points out, in 1945 beauty contests were virtually the only source of scholarship money available to most women who aspired to higher education. In 1991, the Miss America Pageant remains the largest source of scholarship money for women in the United States.[4]

The GI Bill democratized education for men. Since World War II, it had increasingly been possible for working-class men to go to college. It was not long before women, too, began to benefit from this democratization. The postwar decline in women's college enrollment, like their decline in the labor force, was temporary. Women have gone to college in ever-increasing numbers since the 1950s. In 1979, for the first time, over half (50.9 percent) of all college students were women. But, after all, women are 53 percent of the population. The numbers of women completing college did not reach the wartime levels until 1982, the first year since 1946 that more than half of the recipients of bachelor's degrees were women.[5]

Until very recently, women did not go to college for the same reasons that men did. Students of both sexes sought a liberal education, intellectual stimulation, friends, and, yes, romance. The difference between the male and the female college experience was this: career preparation was an important goal for nearly all male students and for very few women. Most readers of this book have probably heard, at least from their parents' contemporaries, a version of the joke that girls go to college for an "MRS" degree. This gibe is inaccurate, but for many years it was true that women students were far more likely to meet their future husbands in college than they were to be prepared for a career or for further professional education. As late as 1980, women received less than 25 percent of all professional degrees and Ph.Ds awarded in this country.[6]

But even then, dramatic change was at hand. In 1980, 12.8 percent of American lawyers, and 13.4 percent of physicians were women, as compared with 4.9 percent and 9.3 percent in 1970. The figures for 1986 are 18 percent and 15 percent. Today, half of all students entering American law schools and medical schools are women.[7]

Much of this change can probably be attributed to declining fertility rates and the growth and expansion of higher education. But law, too, has been important. Legislatures and courts have played a significant part in advancing women's educational opportunities. This development is particularly impressive when we realize that lawyers provide a disproportionate share of our legislators, and virtually all of our judges. The seeds of change are sown in the increase in educational opportunity.

The Walls Crumble Down: From the Thirties to the Seventies

By the 1930s, women could go to college. They could even go to graduate or professional schools. But it would not be accurate to say that women had a *right* to higher education, or that all qualified women had access to it. These institutions, both public and private, were free to exclude them or to discriminate against them. Harvard, for example, did not admit women to its law school until 1951. Texas A&M University, the public institution where I teach, admitted no women until 1963—several years before it built dormitories for them.

Did these single-sex rules deny women access to education? People are not always free to live anywhere they wish, to pursue a degree or for any other reason. The woman who had to live in Brazos County, Texas, had a hard time getting a college education—as court cases showed. So, of course, did the man tied to an area where the only available college was restricted to women. Since greater Boston is full of law schools, similar difficulties did not frustrate the aspiring lawyer denied entrance to Harvard. But that admissions policy denied women an elite legal education at the school long ranked the nation's best, and the law degree which has often been the ticket to a Supreme Court clerkship, a partnership in a law firm, a Cabinet post, or even a seat on the Court itself. While these policies did not deny women the right to an education, women did not enjoy the right on an equal basis with men.

More equality prevailed between boys and girls than between men and women. Public school systems had to educate children of both sexes, but they could establish single-sex schools. Trade and vocational schools, where boys learned mechanical skills and girls learned cooking and sewing, were common. The elite academic single-sex public school flourished in the East—where the comparable private school was also a tradition. Stuyvesant High School in New York City, Central High in Philadelphia, and Boston Latin were the public equivalent of the boys' "prep" school. Tuition was free, but admission was a highly competitive procedure, often requiring an entrance examination.

Some cities had a comparable school like Girls High in Philadelphia and Girls Latin in Boston. The reader is invited to compare the schools' names in the two cities; does it not become clear which gender is the norm, and which the deviation? The girls' schools were often smaller, and thus harder to get into, than the boys'. New York had no elite girls' school at all. The nearest counterpart to Stuyvesant was the coeducational Bronx High School of Science, which admitted one girl for every two boys.[8]

Racial segregation also existed in many places during these years. *Brown v. Board of Education*, in 1954, unequivocally ruled that such segregation violated the equal protection clause. "Separate educational facilities are inherently unequal," declared Chief Justice Warren.[9] That has been the law ever since. Any public school, and any private or parochial school receiving public funds, must be open to members of all races on an equal basis. This principle has never received universal acceptance, however. Many critics have suggested that schools directed by such educators as Marva Collins of Chicago, or Dunbar High School, the formerly all-black academically oriented public school in Washington, D.C., refute the argument that a single-race school can never provide an equal education.[10] There have even been voices which insisted that minority students with educational deficiencies might do better in schools where they need not compete with more advantaged students.

The principle that separate schools are inherently unequal has never been held to apply to separation by sex. The issue of single-sex education remains controversial. There are cogent arguments both for and against single-sex education. The classic defense of the practice goes something like this: "Single-sex education at the college level is more likely to aid a woman in developing her potential for achievement than is co-ed education. . . . Both male and female students at single-sex high schools in a certain environment are more likely to study longer, and value scholarship more highly, than do their co-ed counterparts." There is abundant evidence to support these generalizations.[11]

The negative case is made, with apparent inadvertence, by the South Carolina law which established Winthrop College in 1962. The curriculum, designed for "young ladies," included "stenography, typewriting . . . designing . . . needlework, cooking, housekeeping and such other industrial arts as may be suitable to their sex and conducive to their support and usefulness."[12] Segregated education may help break down barriers, but it can also be used to train members of a group to know their place.

Court decisions, like *Mississippi v. Hogan*, have tried to remove the second possibility while maintaining the first. No one may be denied an education, or access to a particular curriculum, because of sex. But a state may maintain a single-sex institution as long as it provides the other sex with the same educational opportunities elsewhere and has a justification for its policy which meets the *Craig v. Boren* test of intermediate scrutiny. Arriving at this position took roughly twenty-five years.

The first two court cases were decided in the years between *Goesaert* and *Hoyt*, the "blank check" phase of sex discrimination. Both cases involved Texas A&M University. Founded in 1876, this institution had not only been restricted to men, but had originally required military training for all students. By the 1950s, only two years' membership in the corps of cadets was required, but the university remained all-male.

Texas had eighteen state-supported colleges. Only A&M was restricted to men; its all-female counterpart was Texas Women's University, at Denton, and the other sixteen institutions were coeducational. The first two women to challenge the law were both residents of Bryan, near the university; neither was able to move elsewhere to attend college. Lena Bristol was married and the mother of two children; Barbara Tittle, a widow, had one child. The trial judge in Brazos County ordered their admission, but the appellate court reversed. The Court of Civil Appeals had no difficulty, in 1958, finding a long list of precedents upholding sex discrimination, including *Muller v. Oregon* and *West Coast Hotel v. Parrish*. It did not allude to *Brown*, however; nor did it present any evidence that any men might equally be denied opportunities by their exclusion from TWU. "Such a plan exalts neither sex at the expense of the other, but to the contrary recognizes the equal rights of both sexes to the benefits of the best, most varied system of higher education that the State can supply."[13]

Two years later, A&M was back in court, fighting a class action suit filed by three women on behalf of all others similarly situated. Again, the named plaintiffs were women deprived of important opportunities by the all-male rule. The first wanted to pursue a graduate degree in floriculture, in the one public institution in the state which offered this curriculum; the second was married, with two children; the third, a divorcée, had to work to support herself and her child. Once again, the women lost. The opinion did not recognize the very real deprivation they were experiencing. And no one suggested that, since Texas law then determined that a wife's legal residence was where her husband decided to live, it was the state which effectively denied a married woman living in Bryan equal access to an education.[14]

The Supreme Court denied review in both these cases. The next court to consider the issue, ten years later, still operated under the old doctrines. But *Kirstein v. University of Virginia* did not follow the Texas cases as precedent. Four women brought suit in federal district court to gain admission to the University of Virginia at Charlottesville, then an all-male institution. Two of these women were married to graduate students at the university and could not leave the town to attend college. The judge found this consideration less persuasive than what he called the "prestige factor" of UVA, and the fact that this university, like A&M, offered curricula that were available nowhere else in the state. "The Commonwealth of Virginia may not now deny to women, on the basis of sex, educational opportunities at the Charlottesville campus that are not afforded in other institutions operated by the state." UVA had to admit the women, just in advance of a state-approved plan for gradual integration scheduled to begin that year. The judge stopped short of ruling that all single-sex colleges were banned. The Virginia Military Institute (VMI) could remain all-male, and the three state-supported women's colleges could stay that way because these plaintiffs lacked standing to challenge them.[15]

The "prestige factor" is important. The University of Virginia is, after all, Thomas Jefferson's university. Founding it was one of the accomplishments for which he hoped to be remembered; the fact is recorded on his tombstone at Monticello. The Supreme Court had shown its sensitivity to such intangible considerations in the 1951 case of *Sweatt v. Painter*, in which it had ordered Texas to admit blacks to the state university law school in Austin rather than establish a separate school for them. The Court had found the proposed law school inferior to that of the University of Texas in such criteria as faculty, library size, facilities, and "those qualities which are incapable of objective measurement but which make for greatness in a law school."[16] The *Kirstein* judge applied the same consideration to sex segregation.

This same year, 1970, saw the first case brought by men who had been denied admission to all-female state colleges. *Williams v. McNair* protested the single-sex policy of Winthrop College in Rock Hill, South Carolina. Like Virginia and Texas, this state supported several institutions of higher learning; all were coeducational except Winthrop and the Citadel, an all-male military school. Like the plaintiffs in *Kirstein*, these men had their opportunities limited by geography. Winthrop was more convenient for them than other schools. But the district judge rejected their suit, carefully distinguishing this case from *Kirstein*. "It is not intimated that Winthrop offers a wider range of subject matter or enjoys a position of outstanding prestige over the other State-supported institutions in this State whose admissions policies are co-educational."[17]

Williams was the last "separate but equal" case decided under the old rules. *Reed v. Reed*, the following year, brought sex discrimination within the scope of the equal protection clause. While *Reed* was not cited two years later in *Bray v. Lee*, the first case involving a single-sex high school, its presence was felt. Boston had two schools for academically talented youngsters, Boston Latin and Girls Latin. Each school required a competitive entrance examination and had an intensive six-year curriculum rich in classics, science, mathematics, and other academic subjects. Each school accepted most of its entering students in the seventh grade, but also had an examination for students applying to the ninth grade class. By 1970, Boston Latin, a boys' school, had a 3,000-student capacity, while Girls Latin had room for only 1,500 students.

In March 1970, the seventh-grade entrance exam was given to both boys and girls. A perfect score was 200. All boys who got a score of 120 or above were admitted to Boston Latin, while Girls Latin, apparently because of its smaller size, admitted only applicants whose score was at least 133. Ninety-five girls who scored between 120 and 133, and were not admitted, became plaintiffs.

A curious thing happened in the federal district court opinion. Boston Latin's name was changed to Boys Latin. This change may have resulted from a new Massachusetts statute, enacted in 1971, which forbade any sex discrimination in public schools. But the judge did not order relief for all girls in the plaintiff class. Relying on expert testimony that the passing score would have been 127 if the same score had been used for boys and girls, he ordered only that the 47 girls who had scored this high were to be admitted to the ninth grade at "Boston Latin"—wherever that was—in the fall of 1972. "I rule that the use of separate and different standards to evaluate the examination results to determine the admissibility of boys and girls to the Boston Latin schools constitutes a violation of the Equal Protection Clause of the Fourteenth Amendment, the plain effect of which is to prohibit prejudicial disparities before the law. This means prejudicial disparities between all citizens, including women and girls."[18]

Philadelphia also had two single-sex academic secondary schools, Central High and Girls High. These two were the only exclusively college-preparatory public high schools in the city. The situation was not strictly comparable to that in Boston, since the schools were the same size: about 2,000 students each. Central High did have at least one material advantage over Girls, in the form of a large private endowment, mostly from alumni contributions. "However," wrote the first judge to hear the case, "there is no evidence that as a result of this endowment Central's facilities, faculty, or course of instruction is superior to Girls'."[19]

If Central High had advantages over Girls, these advantages were intangible. Two presidents, James K. Polk and Theodore Roosevelt, had visited the boys' school. More recent speakers had included Robert F. Kennedy and Hubert Humphrey. Such visits provide more than an opportunity for promising young people to get acquainted with national leaders. The youngsters also get a kind of "extended job interview" in which they can bring them-

selves to the attention of prominent people and acquire opportunities denied to those students not fortunate enough to attend
schools like Central.

Susan Vorchheimer, a ninth-grade student in an elite public
school, visited several high schools while making her choice
among them. Central High impressed her the most favorably. "I
liked the atmosphere and also what I heard about it, about its
academic excellence." As for Girls High, "I just didn't like the
impression it gave me. I didn't think I would be able to go there
for three years and not be harmed in any way by it."[20] When
Susan was denied admission to Central, she enrolled, not in Girls,
but in the coeducational George Washington High School. She
and her parents also began a lawsuit.

The school system relied on expert testimony. It presented
two studies, one that compared women graduates of coeducational colleges to graduates of women's colleges and another that
compared boys and girls in coed high schools to their cohorts in
single-sex schools. These studies, whose findings have been mentioned, present the classic case for single-sex elite education. The
first showed that graduates of women's colleges were more likely
to be listed in Who's Who of American Women than women
graduates of co-ed institutions, from the 1910s to the 1950s. The
high school study showed that students in single-sex schools
spent more time on homework and valued academic achievement
more highly than did those in co-ed schools.[21]

The district judge found these studies "problematic at best."
The year was now 1975, and he relied on *Reed* and *Stanton* to rule
that "the result of defendants' policy of excluding young women
from Central High School is to deny them the opportunity to
attend a coeducational, academically superior, public high
school. We believe that this denial is significant. . . ."[22] It is not
clear whether Judge Newcomer would have ruled differently if a
co-ed academic high school had been available. And, indeed, we
might question whether it is sound pedagogy—or psychology—to
force a student who wants a rigorous academic curriculum to go
to a single-sex school.

The city appealed, and eventually won. The three-judge appellate court panel had to contend not only with the equal protection clause but also with the Title IX of the Education
Amendments Act of 1972, which forbids sex and race discrimination in federally funded programs, and the Equal Educational
Opportunity Act of 1974, which prohibits "dual school systems"

on the basis of sex, race, or national origin. Two judges pointed out, correctly, that Congress had classified sex segregation as sex discrimination. This majority distinguished Vorchheimer's case from the apposite available precedents on the grounds that each of these cases had deprived a woman of some benefit that she could not get elsewhere. This was not true of Vorchheimer, they ruled, because Girls High was available to her, and she had not offered persuasive evidence that she would be harmed by attendance there. "If she were to prevail," they wrote, "then all public single-sex schools would have to be abolished. The absence of these schools would stifle the ability of the local school board to continue with a respected educational methodology. It follows too that those students and parents who prefer an education in a public, single-sex school would be denied their freedom of choice."[23] Judge Gibson dissented. He was the first judge to explore the implications of the obvious analogy.

> The majority opinion ironically emphasizes that Vorchheimer's choice of an academic high school was "voluntary." It was "voluntary," but only in the same sense that Mr. Plessy voluntarily chose to ride the train in Louisiana. The train Vorchheimer wants to ride is that of a rigorous academic program among her intellectual peers. Philadelphia, like the state of Louisiana in 1896, offers the service but only if Vorchheimer is willing to submit to segregation.[24]

Schools which are segregated by race deny equal protection. So we have been told, again and again. Perhaps a defense of public single-sex education could be mounted, a case sufficiently strong to negate the racial analogy. If a school system provided both coeducational and single-sex schools, such a practice might be acceptable. It would give girls a choice between getting their education with their male and female peers, and an environment which might foster their intellectual growth in the absence of potential boyfriends and junior-grade patriarchs. Similarly, boys could choose between a mixed environment and one which would encourage them to concentrate on studies, free from social pressure. But that hypothetical situation does not conform to the facts as they prevailed in Boston, Philadelphia, or Charlottesville. The real situation was precisely analogous to de jure racial segregation.

Once, Southern cities had two school systems. In the town of, say, Podunk, the white high school was always Podunk High. The black school was called something else. Compare this nomenclature to Boston Latin and Girls Latin, Central High and Girls

High. These arrangements were all part of "a picture of one in-group enjoying full normal communal life and one out-group that is barred from this life and forced into a life of its own."[25] Judicial reasoning in race and sex cases is curiously stereoscopic, as though the judges could look only through one hole of the telescope, with only one eye, at a time.

Central High admits girls now. A district judge ordered their admission in 1982, shortly after *Mississippi v. Hogan* was decided. *Hogan* did not dictate that result, since the Court made it clear that it was not abolishing all public single-sex education. But this voluntary compliance with the decision of a higher court suggests that opinions may have changed. After all, most of the famous Eastern single-sex colleges, male or female, are now coeducational.

Educational Equality and Congressional Initiative

In the 1950s, it was the Supreme Court which took the lead in promoting racial equality in education. The coalition of Southern Democrats and conservative Republicans which dominated Congress chose to preserve the status quo of Jim Crow. Neither branch had any interest in sexual equality; that issue lay dormant. The old congressional coalition began to dissolve in the 1960s, with the disappearance of the Solid (Democratic) South and the weakening of the seniority system and the power of committee chairs. The situation in the 1970s and 1980s was the opposite of what it had been in the 1950s. Now, Congress was leading and the courts were lagging behind, in protecting both racial and sexual equality.

The civil rights laws of the 1960s did not extend to sex discrimination in educational institutions. Even if they had, the fact that the laws exempted state and local governments would have denied protection to students and employees in public schools and colleges. This situation changed in 1972. Congress amended the Civil Rights Act of 1964 to cover states and municipalities. Title IX of the Educational Amendments Act of 1972 forbade sex discrimination in any educational program or activity receiving federal financial assistance; extended both Title VII and the Equal Pay Act to educational workers; and empowered the attorney general to instigate suits against institutions. This law had an impact which, in one area of school and college life, was all but revolutionary. Many commentators missed this impact at the time.

The most controversial aspect of the law was its impact on busing. The original bill contained a clause which would have suspended enforcement of all federal court orders mandating this increasingly unpopular means of implementing de facto racial integration. This antibusing provision was passed by the House, defeated by the Senate, and removed after conferences. An aspect of the law which received less attention was its limited application to single-sex education, more limited in the final version than in the original.

As introduced, the law exempted from its coverage admissions to elementary and secondary schools, private colleges, and religious organizations. Thus, it would not have forced the Boston and Philadelphia school systems to change their ways. Senator Lloyd Bentsen of Texas introduced an amendment extending this exemption to public undergraduate colleges which have "traditionally and continually" been limited to one sex. Speaking of Texas Women's University, the only such institution left in his state, Bentsen said, "The women attending this institution do so voluntarily because they wish to have the experience of attending an all-female institution." As he pointed out, any woman who felt differently could easily attend North Texas State (now the University of North Texas), also in Denton. Texas's other senator, John Tower, agreed. Tower relied on the statistics cited by the act's sponsor, Birch Bayh of Indiana, showing that far fewer women than men entered the professions and that these few came disproportionately from women's colleges. "Coeducational institutions have not provided the right kind of counselling that would prepare women for professions that we usually think of men being engaged in."[26]

What did Title IX do for women? It prevents public institutions which want to continue getting federal money from *becoming* single-sex. It prevents public and private colleges, graduate and professional schools from holding women to higher standards than men, and vice versa. It prevents the sort of "sex plus" discrimination forbidden by Title VII, such as discrimination against married women, pregnant women, or mothers of young children. And—most innovative of all—Title IX mandates equal opportunity for women athletes.

No co-ed university would admit, by 1972, that it discriminated against women with respect to admissions, financial aid, grading, the awarding of degrees, or anything else. But the figures cited by Senator Bayh showed at least a marked inequality of result. Data collected by the American Council on Education and the Carnegie Commission showed that in 1969 women made up 3.5 percent of American lawyers, 7 percent of physicians, and less than 1 percent of engineers. The equivalent figures for 1986 were 18 percent, 15 percent, and 6 percent.[27] The one area in which no one even bothered to deny inequalities in 1972 was college sports. Men got the lion's share of the money, the facilities, the coaching, the publicity, the athletic scholarships, and the money. It had always been that way. Except for a few unpopular feminists, everyone accepted this state of affairs.

No one would claim, in 1991, that sports is an equal opportunity area. The hypothetical interplanetary visitor introduced in Chapter 1 would not get that impression from the February 16, 1989, issue of the Bryan-College Station *Eagle*. The first page of the sports section contains a story with a three-column head: AGGIES WIN THIRD STRAIGHT. This account of the victory of the Texas A&M men's basketball team over Baylor University is accompanied by a photograph two columns wide. Beside it is an unillustrated story with a one-column head—BAYLOR NO MATCH FOR LADY AGS—referring to the fortunes of the women's basketball team. Sports coverage on Channel 3, the only network (CBS) affiliate in Brazos County, still referred, in January 1991, to the "Aggies" and "Lady Aggies" basketball teams. Obviously, this situation is not one of equality. It brings to mind the sort of story that appeared nearly every July in the sports pages, bemoaning the fact that "no Americans are left at Wimbledon"—when Martina Navratilova, Chris Evert, and Pam Shriver remained in the Grand Slam tennis tournament.

Equality, no. Progress toward equality, definitely. A comparison with the *Eagle* of January 1971 illustrates this progress. Day after day, the first page of the sports section proclaims, AGGIES DROP CLOSE GAME, AG CAGERS HOPE SEARCH FOR WINNING COMBO OVER, AGGIE FRONT LINE SHUFFLES CARDS, or TCU HANDS AGGIES 2ND LOSS. No story about any A&M women's team appears in the paper for the entire month. The girls' teams at A&M Consolidated High School fared somewhat better in terms of press coverage. On January 24, CONSOL GIRLS RAP BOBCATS, appeared on page six, while CONSOL NUDGES BRENHAM, 54–44 made the front page.[28]

This change has occurred mainly as a result of Title IX. The law requires that girls and women have access to athletic facilities equal to those of men and boys; that they be eligible for athletic scholarships on an equal basis; and that they have equal opportunities to engage in sports. Title IX does not require that the girls get to play on the boys' team. It does require, however, that the school either have teams for both girls and boys in a given sport or let the girls try out for the boys' team.

Since 1972, many girls have played Little League baseball on mixed teams. (Little League, a corporation chartered by the federal government, is subject to regulation by it.) As early as 1973, high school girls played varsity football on mixed teams. This has not happened very much, or very often. By high school, the best male athletes usually outperform the best females in most sports; few girls will make the football team. But it is far from clear how fixed these differences are.

Boys still tend to get more encouragement, help, and coaching than girls do. These advantages give males an edge; they will perform better under these circumstances even without physical advantages. As girls get better athletic facilities, their performance will improve. Eventually, we can expect that at least some female world-class athletes will consistently do better than at least some male world-class athletes. The gap between men and women is closing all the time. By 1980, women marathon runners were achieving times better than those of the male winners in the 1960s, when marathons were closed to women. If this trend continues in other sports, women may well be playing college and professional baseball, basketball, and even football on formerly all-male teams.

We may safely predict that, initially at least, these women will not be welcome. Professional and collegiate sports have resisted women's equal participation in ancillary activities, whether as sportswriters, managers, coaches, or referees. The struggles of Pam Postema provide one well-publicized instance of this sexism. Postema, an umpire for the AAA minor league baseball organization, was a candidate for a position with the major leagues in 1989; she lost her eligibility when no team offered her a job after several months. The possibility of a woman umpire in the major leagues was greeted with expressions of disapproval which approached the libelous. Now, as every baseball fan knows, no umpire does the job well. They are notorious for serious defects in both judgment and eyesight. It is hard to believe that Postema performs any better than the other members of her profession. But there is no reason why a woman could not make these bad decisions as well as a man could. Postema will not make them in the major leagues. But there are women AAA umpires, and, before long, one of them is likely to make it to the big leagues.

The law's effects are suggested by the title of an editorial column about the 1984 Olympics: THANK TITLE IX FOR SOME OF THAT GOLD. The column pointed out that almost *ten times* as many women participated in intercollegiate athletic programs in 1984 as had done so twelve years earlier. In 1972, 7 percent of high school athletes were girls; in 1984, the figure was 35 percent. Thus, Title IX was providing women with training opportunities which enable them to become world-class athletes.[29]

But the effects of equal athletic opportunity go far beyond the world opportunities of a select few. The vast majority of the 159,000 women who participated in intercollegiate sports in 1984 will never make the Olympic tryouts, much less the Games themselves. The same is true of male athletes. Many educational experts have developed grave doubts about the value of big-time college sports to participants, even to the ostensibly lucky minority who will go on to world competition, professional athletics, or both. Those of us who teach in college and universities have come to suspect that many of these athletes are not the beneficiaries of the system but its victims. Recreational sports, however, have always provided boys with opportunities to develop mental as well as physical skills, and to learn cooperation as well as competition. Sports teaches teamwork; it teaches participants to cooperate with associates whether they like them or not; it teaches them many other equally important interpersonal skills. At the amateur level—though hardly at the quasi-professional level of varsity college athletics at some schools—participants learn standards of fair play. The playing field is a school in which students learn lessons which enhance their personal and professional futures. The promise of Title IX is that girls and women will receive these opportunities on an equal basis.

The Reagan Court, the Democratic Congress, and Civil Rights

The difference between the 1980s and the 1950s came home in brutal fashion in the case of *Grove City College v. Bell*. Far from leading the way in civil rights as it had thirty years earlier, the

Court went out of its way to limit the reach of Title IX. About 140 students at this small liberal arts college in western Pennsylvania were getting Basic Educational Opportunity Grants (BEOGs) from the national government. These grants go directly to the students, who pay them to the college to cover tuition.

Does a BEOG constitute federal financial assistance to an institution? Therein lay the dispute. The Department of Education—the Department of Health, Education, and Welfare (HEW) when the case began—assumed an affirmative answer to the question. HEW, and DOE, required all institutions which enrolled any BEOG recipients to complete an Assurance of Compliance stating that the college did not practice sex discrimination. The college refused to comply, not because it discriminated—both parties stipulated that it did not—but because it believed the BEOG was aid to students, not to itself. The Grove City administration took no federal money as a matter of principle and rejected all bureaucratic interference with its autonomy. In 1977, the department moved to declare the college's students ineligible for BEOGs because of this noncompliance.

Back then the department was HEW, its secretary was Joseph Califano, the president was Jimmy Carter, and the majority of federal judges had been appointed by Democratic presidents. By the time the government had won in the lower courts and the case went to the Supreme Court, all this had changed. Education was the department, Terrell Bell was the secretary, Ronald Reagan was the president, and the Republicans were firmly in control of judicial appointments. The attitude of the college's administration was made to order for the Reagan administration, and, indeed, the government had modified its position. The Department of Education argued in court that Title IX applied only to specific programs within universities, and that, therefore, Grove City need only show that its financial aid program did not discriminate. The department won. That victory was good news for the Reagan administration, bad news for the university, and dire news indeed for women students and civil rights advocates.

Justice Byron White's opinion for a six-member majority relied on the language of Title IX: "No person in the United States shall, on the basis of sex, be excluded from participation in, denied the benefits of, or be subjected to discrimination under *any education program or activity* receiving Federal financial assistance."[30] White followed the department's lead in interpreting "program or activity" to mean "sub-unit of an institution" not "an entire institution." Therefore, Grove City could not discriminate in financial aid, because the BEOGs constituted federal financial assistance to that program within the college. But since the institution accepted no other money from the government, no other program need comply with Title IX.

> To the extent that the Court of Appeals' holding that BEOGs received by Grove City's students constitute aid to the entire institution rests on the possibility that federal funds received by one program or activity free up the College's own resources for use elsewhere, the Court of Appeals' reasoning is doubly flawed. First, there is no evidence that the federal aid received by Grove City's students results in the diversion of funds from the College's own financial aid program to other areas within the institution. Second, and more important, the Court of Appeals' assumption is inconsistent with the program-specific nature of the statute. Most federal educational assistance has economic ripple effects throughout the aided institution, and it would be difficult, if not impossible, to determine which programs or activities derive such indirect benefits. Under the Court of Appeals' theory, an entire school would be subject to Title IX merely because one of its students received a small BEOG or because one of its departments received an earmarked federal grant. This result cannot be squared with Congress' intent.[31]

The difficulty with this conclusion is that there was no clear evidence of Congress's intent to cover only single programs rather than entire institutions. The debates had centered on busing and single-sex schools. Justice William Brennan's thesis that Title IX was patterned after Title VI of the Civil Rights Act of 1964, which used similar language to ban race discrimination in entire institutions, is at least as plausible as White's counterargument.[32]

White's second point could be used as easily to justify a broad reading of Title IX as in support of the narrow one preferred here. No one disputes him on the first point: Grove City did not discriminate. But the decision applied to programs in any other institution which might. The Court had ruled that if a specific program did not get federal aid, it was free—in the absence of applicable state regulation—to discriminate as much as it pleased. As Justice John Stevens's dissent pointed out, this ruling went further than it needed to. Since the assurance that Grove City must now file required only that it comply with Title IX to the extent that the law applies to it, there was no need for a ruling on how far that application extends.[33]

Athletic programs, where the impact of Title IX has been particularly strong, are less likely than many university programs to get federal aid. This money often comes from student fees, alumni groups, ticket sales, and, in the big time, from television contracts. *Grove City*, therefore, effectively conferred on many schools a license to turn back the clock. Within six months after the decision, twenty-three Title IX cases had been dropped. The department's Office of Civil Rights was no longer able to investigate charges of discrimination in women's athletics on college campuses.[34]

Congress began trying to overturn *Grove City* as soon as it was decided. While Republicans controlled the Senate, these efforts were doomed. Despite the overwhelming majority in the House who voted to amend the civil rights law in June 1984, conservative Senators were able to kill the bill. After the Democrats regained control of the Senate, it was a different story. Large majorities in both houses passed the Civil Rights Restoration Act in early 1988. This law amended prohibitions of discrimination on the basis of sex, race, age, and disability to provide that "notwithstanding the decision of the Supreme Court in *Grove City College v. Bell*, the phrase 'program or activity' as used in this title shall, as applied to educational institutions which are extended Federal financial assistance, mean the educational institution." President Reagan vetoed the bill in March, on the grounds that it "would vastly and unjustifiably expand the powers of the Federal Government over the decisions and affairs of private organizations," threaten "such cherished values as religious liberty," and intrude into the "lives and businesses of American citizens." Both House and Senate overrode the veto on March 22.[35]

For feminists, even this victory was mixed. Opponents of reproductive choice, led by Senator John Danforth of Missouri, succeeded in adding an amendment which assured university hospitals that they would not lose funds if they refused to perform abortions. These legislators feared that the courts might declare that such a policy constituted sex discrimination. Molly Yard, the president of the National Organization for Women, criticized the act because it "put abortion language into civil rights law for the first time and, by making a substantive change in law, limits a woman's constitutional right to an abortion."[36]

The Danforth amendment provoked considerable opposition in both houses of Congress. One senator, for example, lamented:

> I remember when Senator [Warren] Magnuson [of Washington] was a member of this body, and he would say, almost with tears in his eyes, "Why is it that every time I have an appropriation bill, whether it has to do with this subject, that subject, or any of a number of

other subjects, I have to get into a battle on the abortion issue?" . . . The question is, can we stay away from that subject and not jeopardize the enactment of a very much needed piece of legislation to correct the civil rights laws of this country?[37]

No, they could not. It is an indication of the political climate of the late Reagan era that no member of Congress argued that a refusal to perform an abortion would, indeed, constitute sex discrimination.

Among the questions to ask about Title IX and the Civil Rights Restoration Act are: Why were they necessary? Why had no one argued that unequal facilities and opportunities for women violated the equal protection clause? For that matter, why did Congress regulate only those institutions receiving federal aid? Why not base its legislation on its enforcement powers in Section 5 of the Fourteenth Amendment, which allow it to regulate public institutions whether or not they get federal aid?

The answers to these questions lie in some venerable Supreme Court precedents which the judges have never repudiated and Congress has partially evaded. The *Civil Rights Cases* of 1883 invalidated part of the last Reconstruction law, the Civil Rights Act of 1875, and declared that Section 5 gave Congress the power to regulate state action only. Private individuals, like innkeepers who refused to serve blacks, were not covered by the Fourteenth Amendment. One result of this decision was that a "restrictive covenant," a private agreement among property owners not to sell to Jews or blacks, was perfectly legal. But in 1948, *Shelley v. Kraemer* ruled that enforcing these covenants in court did constitute "state action." *Shelley* effectively gave parties to such covenants the freedom to violate them, but it also reaffirmed the principle that the Fourteenth Amendment could not be used to regulate private discrimination. The Civil Rights Acts of 1964 and 1968, which forbade discrimination in public accommodations and housing, were based not on the Fourteenth Amendment but on Congress's power to regulate interstate commerce. What applies to public accommodations applies equally well to private educational institutions, unless they receive federal funds.[38]

But even these doctrines would permit courts to rule that *public* institutions must grant women equal opportunities, and Congress to force these institutions to do so. The truth is that since the end of Reconstruction, the Fourteenth Amendment has never been a source of power which Congress is eager to use. Justice Holmes's statement in *Buck v. Bell* that the equal protection clause is "the usual last resort of constitutional arguments" strikes the reader, sixty-odd years later, as an instance of singularly bad prophecy. But Congress's approach to the power evinces the kind of leery distaste the Court once felt, and may again feel. Congress shows no similar hesitation about using its power to control the spending of federal money.[39]

Title IX lives again, although women may have lost as much as they gained. Some members of Congress put the blame for the abortion controversy where it might seem to belong: on those like Danforth who insisted in tying abortion to the civil rights issue. But NOW and other feminist organizations which opposed the bill because of the Danforth amendment received the public criticism which seems to be the fate of women's rights activists. Whatever the merits of NOW's position, it is interesting to note that feminists do not impose upon other groups the standards often imposed upon them. In 1972, feminists did not subject legislators who opposed the Education Amendments Act because of the original antibusing provision to similar criticism—although if feminist groups deserved this kind of criticism in 1988, they would certainly have been justified in dishing it out sixteen years earlier.

American society seems to hold feminists to a set of rules applied to no other groups. Feminists are not supposed to put their own interests first. Perhaps this kind of argument is a legacy from some advocates of woman suffrage, who expected women to elevate the standards of political life. As effective as this argument may have been in promoting the Nineteenth Amendment, it has its dangerous side. This expectation easily transforms itself into a demand all too familiar to women in other contexts: be better, nobler, and purer than men, or shut up. No further proof of continuing male supremacy in American society is necessary when these expectations are present. To the extent that feminists are criticized for the kind of behavior which is taken for granted from other groups, women's struggle for equality will be more difficult.

Women and Community Life: Removing the Barriers

Education provides opportunity; denial of access to education restricts opportunity. But unequal education has not been the only barrier to equal opportunity for women. Patriarchy has other ways of excluding women from full participation in society. Some of these techniques are no more than adult versions of a familiar juvenile institution: the makeshift clubhouse or tree house with a crudely lettered sign that reads, NO GIRLS ALLOWED. This sort of thing may be funny when children do it. It loses its power to amuse when adult males establish organizations with the same rule.

Perhaps men have always wanted to spend some of their time in all-male company. An old sailor's song celebrates the joys of "a ship with men." The benefits include the freedom to "sweat and stink" and the fact that "you never have to lift the seat." Women, too, have been known to seek one another's exclusive company. There are clubs for women, though not as many. Women's lives seem to provide numerous opportunities to be away from men. Rules have rarely been necessary to keep men out of the kitchen, the laundry, the nursery, or the secretarial pool. But men have felt a need for rules which exclude women from their company.

Bars, for instance, have traditionally been male preserves. *Goesaert v. Cleary* was very much a product of this convention. New York City's Biltmore Hotel had a "Men's Bar," nestled beneath Grand Central Station, until 1970. United Air Lines effectively established a mobile variant of this institution in the 1960s in the form of "men only" flights (referring to customers, not flight attendants). Restaurants once excluded blacks, too, but Title II of the Civil Rights Act of 1964 barred race discrimination in public accommodations. No federal law has yet extended the prohibition to sex discrimination, but some states have done so. Even before *Reed v. Reed*, a district court decision challenged the constitutionality of male-only public accommodations. Because of this ruling, the Biltmore bar, the United stag flight, and their counterparts no longer exist.

The most famous men's bar in New York was McSorleys' Old Ale House, founded in 1855. In 1969, feminists employed a protest technique borrowed from the civil rights movement. They staged a sit-in. "Two determined ladies, both board members of the National Organization for Women, . . . unescorted by any male companion, entered McSorleys' and seated themselves at the bar." The bartender repeatedly refused to serve them. They "voluntarily departed, wisely choosing to stage this battle of the sexes in the courthouse rather than resort to militant tactics."[40] Despite this inauspicious first paragraph, reminiscent of Justice Felix Frankfurter's tone in *Goesaert*, the women won their case. They alleged that the club's policy violated a Reconstruction law, the Civil Rights Act of 1866, by depriving women of "rights, privileges, or immunities secured by the Constitution"; namely, of equal protection. But way back in 1883 the Supreme Court had ruled that the Fourteenth Amendment covered only state action. Since McSorleys' was a privately owned business, how could it be acting "under color of" a "State or Territory"? Because, according to the plaintiffs, the bar was licensed and extensively regulated by the State of New York, and the state knew about the policy.[41]

Judge Walter Mansfield agreed. "We are faced with a *pervasive* regulation by the state of the activities of the defendant, a commercial enterprise voluntarily engaged in serving the public except for women. Furthermore, the state has continued annually to renew defendant's license over the years despite its open discrimination against women, without making any effort . . . to remedy the discrimination." No court had ever ruled that sex discrimination in public accommodations, state-sanctioned or not, violated the Fourteenth Amendment. Mansfield became the first judge to do just that.[42] In his decision, he invoked pre-*Reed* doctrine. "Discrimination based on sex will be tolerated under the Equal Protection Clause only if it bears a rational relation to a permissible purpose of the classification. . . . It may be argued that the occasional preference of men for a haven to which they may retreat from the watchful eye of wives or womanhood in general to have a drink or pass a few hours in their own company, is justification enough," but "such preferences, no matter how widely shared by defendant's male clientele, bear no rational relation to the suitability of women as customers of McSorleys'."[43] So the public men's bar was dead.

Some all-male organizations are, or at least once were, beyond the law's reach. The all-male private club has been a feature of American life. Rural and urban, civilian and military, working-class and professional, these organizations have often been the locus of group activity. The Benevolent and Protective Order of Elks and the Loyal Order of Moose have been all-male refuges for the farmer or worker who might drop in at the lodge for a card game after work or some Monday-morning quarterbacking. The Cosmos Club in Washington, D.C., or the Century Club in New York City, provided a quiet, opulent setting for the businessman, lawyer, senator, or judge—including more than one Supreme Court Justice—to have a drink with an associate or take a client to lunch.

Many observers have found nothing blameworthy in this behavior. People who share attributes or interests—occupation, ethnic background, hobby, religion—have always banded together and kept others out. This exclusion might hurt outsiders' feelings, and, in a community where most people share one of these attributes, the odd person out might effectively be ostracized. But that possibility has never been regarded as a reason to forbid this sort of activity. After all, is not the diversity of the American people, the presence of many different groups which build different communities, one of our strengths?

The difficulties lie in two crucial facts. First, gender is not like other attributes. Secondly, the activities carried on in these groups do not fit into the "private" or "social" side of any secure dichotomy between public and private, social and official. All-male organizations have their analogy not in the union hall but in all-white clubs. And, far from being the product of insignificant choices about social activity, these men's clubs have constituted yet another barrier against women. Some of those men's clubs have been white men's clubs, and Christian white men's clubs at that. So blacks and Jews have been excluded along with women. Congress seemed to find this practice distinguishable from establishing an all-white restaurant or hotel. Title II exempts private clubs from its coverage.

In *Seidenberg v. McSorleys'*, Judge Mansfield devoted much attention to distinguishing McSorleys' from "a private men's club." The ale house "is open to the public. Any adult male who is neither drunk nor disorderly may enter and purchase a drink. The success of the business depends, in fact, upon large numbers of individuals doing just that." A club, in contrast, "does not purport, and is not required, to serve the public."[44] Most clubs admit members only through a selective application process which may result in rejection of a would-be member. But these clubs do need licenses from the state if they wish to serve food and liquor. Does this licensing constitute "state action"? Not surprisingly, decisions on race discrimination have supplied the judicial precedents for these kinds of cases. And courts have refused to extend the equal protection clause to these clubs.

Moose Lodge No. 107 v. Irvis seemed to be the product of fraternal and judicial efforts to go out of their way to accommodate race discrimination. In 1968, Leroy Irvis, a black resident of Harrisburg, Pennsylvania, visited the city's Moose Lodge as the guest of a member. Although Moose admitted only whites to membership, its lodges admitted "members and guests." Guests are people whom members invite to the lodge. Therefore, one interpretation of the Moose's rules would have allowed Irvis to be served in the lodge bar and dining room, in the company of a white friend, in the state's capital, at a time of great racial tension. But the lodge chose the other interpretation. It refused to serve Irvis, presumably to the embarrassment of his friend, the lodge member. Irvis sued, alleging that state action had occurred and that he had, therefore, been denied equal protection.

He could have prevailed without the courts going all the way and ruling that private clubs were public institutions. A compromise position was available. Pennsylvania had a "sumptuary law" which limited the number of liquor licenses any city could have to one for every 1,500 inhabitants. Harrisburg's quota had long since been filled. "A group desiring to form a nondiscriminatory club which would serve blacks must purchase a license held by an existing club, which can exact a monopoly price for the transfer. The availability of such a license is speculative at best, however, for, as Moose Lodge itself concedes, without a liquor license a fraternal organization would be hard-pressed to survive."[45]

The Supreme Court did not take this way out. Nor did it rely on *Seidenberg*'s distinction between a private club and a public bar. The majority ruled that state licensing alone was not state action within the scope of the equal protection clause. Justice William H. Rehnquist's opinion suggested that state action was no longer the crucial point. "There is no suggestion in this record that the Pennsylvania [Liquor Control] Act, either as written or as applied, discriminates against minority groups either in their right to apply for club licenses themselves or in their right to purchase and be served liquor. . . . The [quota], when considered together with the availability of liquor from hotel, restaurant and retail licensees falls far short of conferring upon club licensees a monopoly in the dispensing of liquor."[46]

This logic could have produced a different result in *Seidenberg*. One might argue that, since women could easily get service in public accommodations, New York's law did not itself discriminate, either. The Court has shifted from a consideration of whether state involvement exists to the narrower question of whether that involvement in itself constitutes discrimination. At any rate, *Moose Lodge* was a clear statement that the Fourteenth Amendment would not be read to include private discrimination in the near future. The *Civil Rights Cases* and *Shelley v. Kraemer* remain binding precedents. They apply to men-only clubs just as they do to white-only clubs. But no mode of constitutional interpretation—textual language, original intention, logic, letter, or spirit—requires the conclusion that the clause apply to state action only. "No state shall . . . deny to any person within its jurisdiction the equal protection of the laws" can be read with perfect plausibility to assert that a state must protect its citizens from sex or race discrimination by private associations, and therefore that a state denies equal protection when it allows these organizations to discriminate.

Some evidence of original meaning can be found in the Civil Rights Act of 1875, enacted by many of the same senators and representatives who proposed the Fourteenth Amendment. The portion of the law which the Court invalidated read, "all persons within the jurisdiction of the United States shall be entitled to the full and equal enjoyment" of public accommodations like "inns, public conveyances on land or water, theatres, and other places of public amusement" for "citizens of every race and color."[47] Whatever the Court believed, Congress thought it had the power to regulate private behavior. The Court made a choice in 1883, dictated by no authority; a different set of judges reaffirmed that choice in 1948, with *Shelley*; and *Moose Lodge*, in 1972, made the same unnecessary choice, yet another time.

Why should these clubs be a matter of public concern? If people want to associate in private with members of their own race and sex, that choice may be displeasing on moral grounds, but should it really be any of the state's business? The troubling aspect of exclusive private organizations is that they assume a rigid dichotomy between public and private activity that does not exist. The line between recreation and business is tenuous. A black man who cannot join the group at the Moose Lodge after work, or a woman associate in a law firm who cannot invite her client to lunch at the club where her male peers are members, are both at a disadvantage. They are cut out of a network of associations which can be a valuable asset at work. These private organizations deny them equal opportunity.

Some state legislatures and city councils have recognized this problem and have prohibited discrimination in private associations. The affected groups, varying from the U.S. Jaycees to the New York State Club Association, resorted to the courts to resist this interference with their autonomy. So the adversaries were, not the aggrieved outsider versus the club, but the club versus the government. The Court was faced not with an individual relying on Holmes's "traditional last resort" but with a state exercising its police power.

Prioritizing Rights: Private Association and Public Good

The U.S. Junior Chamber of Commerce, long since renamed the Jaycees, was founded in 1920, when the business of America was business. The group's objectives included the growth of young men's civic organizations, the encouragement of educational and charitable work, the inculcation of "genuine Americanism and civic interest," and the promotion of personal development, achievement, and international friendship and understanding. The Jaycees do not have lodges or clubhouses, but they do hold meetings, sponsor speakers and activities, and raise money for various charities. Any man between the ages of eighteen and thirty-five who could afford the dues was eligible for regular membership. The Jaycees have always admitted men of all races, religions, and nationalities. Women and older men could become associate members, but they could not vote or hold office.

The Jaycees thrived through a Depression, a world war, a Cold War, an unpopular war, and several political movements. They made themselves useful in a variety of causes, from charity fund drives to the local preliminaries of the Miss America pageant. No doubt, all this civic activity furthered many a career in business, the professions, and politics. The Jaycees take positions on public issues and encourage their members to participate in politics and run for office.

Women began to push for admission in the 1970s. Some local chapters, including those in Minneapolis and St. Paul, Minnesota, began admitting women in violation of the national bylaws. In 1978, the national organization threatened to revoke their charters. Since the Minnesota Human Rights Act forbade sex discrimination in places of public accommodation, by race, sex, religion, national origin, or disability, the two chapters found themselves in a no-win situation. Women members filed a complaint with the state Human Rights Department. When this agency upheld their claim of sex discrimination, the U.S. Jaycees went to court.

Their claim that the state law violated their rights of association, as established by the First Amendment and by cases like *Griswold v. Connecticut*, convinced only one of the three courts which heard it. But the court of appeals, which reversed the district court, was itself reversed by a unanimous Supreme Court. Only seven justices heard the case, the two Minnesotans, Warren Burger and Harry Blackmun, having disqualified themselves. The Court had little trouble distinguishing the Jaycees, with its "large and basically unselective" membership and its history of participation in public life, from such intimate associations as the family. "The Jaycees have demonstrated no serious burden on their male members' freedom of association." A month later, even though the decision hardly compelled this action, the national organization voted to admit women.[48]

But not all private associations are as easy to join as the Jaycees. What about Rotary International? Each local club determines its own admissions procedures, but the parent organization recommends the use of selection committees. Rotary, unlike the Jaycees, does not take positions on public issues. The Supreme Court upheld the California antidiscrimination law anyway, finding that, selective or not, Rotary described itself as "inclusive, not exclusive." For Justice Lewis Powell, "factors such as size, purpose, selectivity, and whether others are excluded from critical aspects of the relationship" demanded the conclusion that Rotary was more like the Jaycees than it was like marriage. This, too, was a seven-person decision. Blackmun, an honorary member of Rotary, and Sandra Day O'Connor, the wife of a member, were out.[49]

Both the Jaycees and Rotary have stressed their inclusive character throughout their existence. They have always aimed to remove rather than reinforce racial, religious, and cultural barriers—among men. The Jaycees, in particular, have had a commendable record on racial equality; they never practiced racial discrimination, even when it was socially acceptable. The next kind of organization which the Court had to deal with, however, had never made the slightest pretense of being open to all. These were those most exclusive, not to say snobbish, of organizations, the all-male "city clubs," the bastion of America's professional and corporate elite. These are the types of clubs to which senators and judges belong, and they are very selective indeed. Ability to afford these clubs' high fees and prices is no guarantee of acceptability. And these are the places where the powerful conduct business, make contacts, and negotiate deals. These clubs have a history of excluding Jews and blacks as well as women, but the gender barrier was the last to fall.

California and Minnesota, the only states which had extended their public accommodations laws to cover private organizations, had not made definite decisions about these clubs. But several cities, including New York, Los Angeles, and San Francisco, had passed ordinances barring this kind of discrimination. The New York State Club Association had been fighting this ordinance in court since the City Council passed it in 1984. At the same time, California's huge (2,300-member) Bohemian Club, which numbered then President Ronald Reagan among its members, was fighting the San Francisco ordinance. New York got to the Supreme Court first.

Up to this point, the justices had been vulnerable to accusations of class bias. The kind of club that a Supreme Court Justice was likely to frequent had not been the subject of any decisions. So far, the effect of the justices' actions had been to impose upon other men policies which did not affect them personally. But more than one past and present justice had belonged to such establishments as the Cosmos Club. The Supreme Court itself had even been described as having "a men's-club atmosphere."[50] A desire to avoid even the appearance of evil may have motivated Blackmun's resignation from the Cosmos Club. The Court's newest member, Anthony Kennedy, had resigned from San Francisco's Olympic Club when he was nominated to the Court.

In the event, no class bias was visible in *New York State Club Association v. New York.* A unanimous Court, speaking through Justice Byron White, indicated that the clubs' First Amendment claim would have prevailed only if their purpose had been religious or, in some way, nonpolitical. White stressed the business-related activities of the "city clubs."[51] Thus, the Court has consistently upheld state power to regulate such discrimination. For all we know, it might be similarly receptive to any congressional efforts to ban private clubs. But such efforts have not been forthcoming, and the Court has refused to recognize any constitutional right to be free from this type of sex bias. Without leadership from the national government, we can expect the private men's organization to remain as a barrier to equal opportunity for women.

Conclusion

If learning is natural, education is conventional. Society determines how much formal schooling is available, how much people get, and how much they need for particular social roles.

The American system of twelve years' free elementary and secondary education, four years' study for a bachelor's degree, and further study for advanced professional training resulted from a series of social choices made over a period of several hundred years.

Our educational system, like those of all other societies, serves at least two purposes. It provides people with the knowledge they need to perform the functions they have in society. But education also assigns people to those different functions. Put more crudely, education puts people in their place. How much education you get goes a long way toward determining what kind of job you will have, how much money you will make, where you will live, and how you will conduct your private life. Education opens doors, but it also creates barriers. Your access depends on such factors as income, class background, race, and, yes, sex.

Once, women could not become physicians because they could not get into medical school. Even when most schools admitted women, it was harder for women to get in and to pay for it than it was for men. Women could, however, get into nursing school, which was cheaper, of shorter duration, and less selective. So education channeled women onto the lower rung of the class structure of the medical profession in the United States. Similarly, education traditionally let women become legal secretaries, not lawyers; schoolteachers, not college professors; fact checkers, not journalists.

I do not mean to suggest that any of the traditional women's jobs are intrinsically less important or less noble than the men's jobs. The fact that some jobs are assigned higher economic and social value than others may be unfortunate. What women do has always been as important as what men do. But the men have had options; they could choose a less expensive education and a lower-status job. Women were effectively denied this choice. The injustice did not lie in the fact that women became schoolteachers; what was unfair was that they could not become professors, whether they wanted to or not. Men, having the choice, nearly always opted for rigorous training and high reward. Now that more women have the same choices, fewer and fewer are choosing to be nurses, secretaries, and schoolteachers. Shortages in these occupations are reaching crisis proportions, and may eventually lead to a radical restructuring of certain social institutions. If the school is one of these, American education is bound to change in ways we probably cannot anticipate.

Women's struggle for equal educational opportunity has been long and slow. Fifty years ago, they had essentially won the battle for elementary and secondary education. But few women had access to college, and fewer still to postgraduate training. These inequalities were reflected in the very small numbers of women who entered the high-status professions and in the earnings gap between men and women. The number and proportion of women who got to college rose slowly but steadily in the years after World War II. Some of these women became the nucleus of the feminist movement that arose in the late 1960s; *The Feminine Mystique* sold well on many campuses. Equal educational opportunity became a crucial goal of this movement. Using the desegregation cases as a model, many feminists argued that girls of all races were harmed by separate education and limited access to professional training.

These demands have met with a very different fate from that of their racial counterparts. Not that the feminists' efforts have failed: quite the contrary. But while black civil rights activists obtained victories from the Supreme Court in the face of congressional hostility, for women it has been the other way around. The Court consistently refused to apply its decisions on racial segregation to single-sex education. And it weakened one education law so badly that congressional action was needed to undo the damage and to restore to women their full rights under Title IX of the Education Amendments Act of 1972. In the 1950s and 1960s, when the judiciary was the strongest defender of human rights, it had been unreceptive to women's claims. By the 1970s and 1980s, when Congress essentially traded positions with the Court in this area, the women met with a better reception.

And the changes have been nothing short of extraordinary. Enrollment in American universities has reached sexual parity, while graduate and professional schools are approaching it. Partly as a result, the gap in men's and women's earnings has narrowed in recent years. Even athletics, one of the last bastions of male exclusivity, is providing increasing opportunities for girls and women. While single-sex education is still available, the elite institutions once closed to women now admit them on an equal basis.

Some of the ramifications of these changes are yet unknown; they will become clearer as the women who have benefited from them reach professional maturity. We know, for example, that the proportion of members of Congress who are lawyers is much higher than their proportion in the American population. A lawyer is more likely to end up in Congress than anyone else—and a member of Congress, especially a senator, has at least an outside chance at the presidency. As more and more women become lawyers, the pool of potential women legislators and presidents will grow. We can reasonably anticipate an increase in the proportion of women members of Congress over the next fifty or a hundred years. The increase will inevitably be slow, because over 90 percent of incumbents win reelection, and most incumbents are male. But since no incumbent stays in office forever, women's representation will increase as seats become available.

The movement of women into positions of influence and power has already led to some changes in other institutions that have frustrated women's drive for equality. The all-male club, whatever its size, resources, purpose, or emphasis, has been one of the most notorious of these institutions. These groups have frequently been restricted not only to men but to white Christian men. Even the exceptions, like the Jaycees, have made women the last out-group. No branch of the national government has been eager to attack these exclusionary policies, and only a few state and local governments have done so. Those that have, however, have found the courts no barrier to these changes.

One need hardly be a capitalist, a conservative, or an elitist to doubt that the prospects of economic reform were enhanced by the old policies which could force half the population into the working class. Historically, American radicals have been at least as likely to come from the colleges as from the workplace. Better educational and social opportunities do more than increase our access to things that most people have conventionally wanted; these opportunities also increase our freedom to decide what kind of society we want. Removing barriers is a crucial feminist priority which transcends economic and political beliefs.

REFERENCES

Dziech, Billie Wright, and **Linda Weiner.** *The Lecherous Professor: Sexual Harassment on Campus.* Boston: Beacon Press, 1984. A valuable treatment of a problem faced by many women students.

Faragher, John Mack, and **Florence Howe,** eds. *Women and Higher Education in American History.* A volume prepared for the sesquicentennial of Mount Holyoke College, the subject matter focuses on the elite colleges.

French, Marilyn. *Beyond Power: On Women, Men, and Morals.* New York: Summit Books, 1985. Includes a good discussion of academia, not limited to women's issues.

Howe, Florence, ed. *Women and the Power to Change.* New York: McGraw-Hill, 1975. From the Carnegie Commission on Higher Education, one of the best "data banks" for students of American higher education.

Lewis, Lionel S. *Scaling the Ivory Tower: Merit and Its Limits in Academic Careers.* Baltimore: Johns Hopkins University Press, 1975. A challenge to the myth of university as meritocracy.

Minnich, Elizabeth et al., eds. *Reconstructing the Academy: Women's Education and Women's Studies.* Chicago: University of Chicago Press, 1988. A collection of articles from *SIGNS* (see the Research Guide), concentrating on the emerging interdisciplinary field of women's studies.

Pearson, Carol S. et al., ed. *Educating the Majority: Women Challenge Tradition and Higher Education.* New York: Macmillan, 1989. Articles commissioned by the American Council on Education. The subtitle is an accurate description of their content.

7

Practitioners, Actors, Subjects: Women in the Legal System

So far, this book has examined the American legal system as it acts upon women, through the Constitution, state and federal laws, and court decisions. Women themselves have been the objects, not the subjects. But women play active as well as passive parts in the system. Women bring suits, and are sued; women are accused of crimes, and become victims of crimes. In increasing numbers, women are entering the system as lawyers, lawmakers, and judges.

Women criminals, victims, or lawyers need not differ from their male counterparts in any significant way. Indeed, the system's rules ensure that much male and female behavior will be similar. An armed robbery is an armed robbery, regardless of the sex of either perpetrator or victim. A judge presiding over an armed robbery trial must allow evidence, supervise questioning, and impose sentence according to fixed rules, whether the judge is male or female. But gender differences are very much a part of these aspects of the system.

First, all of these roles and statuses are, in a sense, male. Men invented them, men wrote the rules for them, and, most of the time, men performed and occupied them. Even rape, a crime which until recently could be perpetrated only on a woman, was first recognized as a violation of the property rights of fathers and husbands. A person becomes a lawyer by following a career path which was set up by men and is based on a model of a man's life, with its relative freedom from home responsibilities. This book has presented many examples of male bias in the content of law. A similar bias, intentional or not, pervades law's structures and functions.

Second, when we compare male and female litigants, criminals, victims, lawyers, and judges, we find significant differences between them. Men significantly outnumber women in every category. When we think of criminals and victims, this news is welcome; surely this is one area in which women would rather forgo equality. But not all the gender bias is so benign. Rape is only one example of a phenomenon which pervades the system: a subcategory which is virtually always gender-specific. Prostitution—the buying and selling of sexual contact—has similar aspects. Most offenders are female because, in practice, it is the seller and not the buyer or procurer who has been prosecuted. Finally, there are many categories which, while not gender-specific, seem to involve women disproportionately. Women are far more likely to be victims of domestic violence than men are. For example, 35 percent of all women homicide victims are killed by their husbands or boyfriends. And women are more likely to be victims of men whom they already know than to be victims of other kinds of crime. Patriarchy is a constant force in defining these roles and statuses.

Even the most pessimistic of feminists has to agree that one area of social policy which has shown substantial positive change in the last half century is the treatment of domestic violence and sex crimes. You need go no farther than your local telephone directory to appreciate this change. If "Child Abuse Hotline," "Rape Crisis Center," and, usually, "Aid to Battered Women" are not prominently listed in the front of the directory, you will find them listed alphabetically. If you turn to the listing "Social Service Organizations" in the Yellow Pages, you will find these and maybe a few more. None of these organizations existed fifty, or even twenty, years ago. Many are now subsidized by the government. The social changes of which they are signs have influenced, and been affected by, changes in the law. And these changes constitute an accomplishment for which most of the credit belongs to the feminist movement.

Rape: A Crime of Patriarchy

We have all seen the lists. Pamphlets advising women how to guard themselves against crime are often available, free of charge, in the local library, community center, or police station. Police officers may even have visited your high school classroom or college dormitory, talking about this issue and distributing pamphlets. Any woman reading this book has probably been warned more than once against some or all of the following: going out alone after dark, listing one's first name in the telephone directory, picking up hitchhikers, hanging underwear out to dry, dressing provocatively, going to bars alone or with other women, or "teasing," whatever that means. Instead, we are urged to lock our doors and windows, to answer the doorbell only when we expect a visitor, to conceal our gender from strangers, and to secure a male escort before going out at night.

Some of this advice is sound. But none of it is routinely given to men. Although surveys show that women fear crime more than men do, men are more likely to become crime victims than women.[1] The exceptions to this rule are domestic violence and rape. Since the above advice will hardly protect women from members of their families, the apparent purpose of these lists and pamphlets is to protect us from rape.

What is rape, and why is it so important? A definitive answer to the first question is impossible, because the crime is understood differently now from the way it was defined before the advent of the contemporary feminist movement. We can discover this change from reading the state penal codes, and nothing else. But the statute books tell only a small part of the story. Not only has the law's basic approach to the crime of rape changed, but social attitudes could hardly be more different now from what they were fifty years ago. These changes represent a crucial feminist victory.

Much of the credit for this success belongs to one author, Susan Brownmiller, and one book. *Against Our Will: Men, Women and Rape* was published in 1975.[2] This book and its author must rank with Simone de Beauvoir and *The Second Sex* and Betty Friedan and *The Feminine Mystique*. Like her two predecessors, Brownmiller has changed the conscience of an entire society.

There is one constant in the definition of rape: it consists in a man's having sexual intercourse with a woman to whom he has no right of access. Brownmiller's research showed that the oldest concept of rape was intercourse with some other man's wife or daughter. The male "owner," not the woman, was the victim. In Babylonian law, a married woman who was raped was as guilty as her attacker. Both could be executed. So could a man who raped another man's daughter, while a father who had sex with his own daughter was banished. Ancient law treated the question of a woman's consent as rather beside the point. Rape was a crime against patriarchy.

Anglo-American law recognized two categories of rape. The classic common law (and dictionary) definition of rape was "carnal knowledge of a woman, not the defendant's wife, forcibly and without consent." This felony was called *forcible* rape. The concept represents a change from a crime against patriarchy to a violent acting out of male supremacist norms. The marital exemption was derived from the presumption that "by their mutual matrimonial consent and contract the wife has given herself up in this kind to her husband."[3] Thus, a man could get legal sexual access to a woman in two ways: through marriage, or through her willing participation. *Statutory* rape, the other category, was any sexual intercourse with a female below a stipulated "age of consent," which has ranged from seven to eighteen. These laws presumed that females below this age were incapable of giving true consent. These definitions still held in the 1930s, by which time common law had been incorporated into state statutes, and for some years afterward. The penalties for forcible rape were severe; in many states, they included death.[4]

The social attitudes dominant when our historical period begins, in the early 1930s, and for some years afterward, were discordant with the harsh statutes. Actual enforcement and administration was more in tune with custom than with law. Many people believed that women who accused men of rape were lying, alleging coercion when they had actually consented. Experts often quoted an English judge's assertion that "rape is an accusation easily to be made and hard to be proved." Police officers were taught to distrust rape complaints. The popular saying "When rape is inevitable, relax and enjoy it" trivialized the act.[5]

Consent has been the most common defense against an accusation of rape. Unless there are witnesses to the act or evidence of injury, the consent defense amounts to the woman's word against the man's. He, like any other defendant, is presumed innocent. Accused rapists are more likely than other defendants to choose a jury trial rather than a guilty plea; they know that taking their chances with a jury may pay off.[6] The situation is complicated by the subtleties common to sexual communication, and the fact that men are by convention the initiators in heterosexual activity. An accused rapist will defend himself by insisting that the woman consented. What is hard to understand is the way in which American law made this defense so easy. Focus on the woman's consent rather than on the amount of force used by the defendant led to an emphasis, not on the man's behavior, but on the woman's. This approach often led to more critical scrutiny of the victim than of the aggressor.

Some states, like New York, required independent corroboration in order to convict. That state's revised law, passed in the 1960s, was regarded as a reform; no doubt it was. It required the victim to show that she engaged in "earnest resistance." Saying "no" was never enough, even if she screamed the word. The Model Penal Code of 1962 proposed two degrees of rape: first degree rape was the situation where the victim was not a "voluntary social companion" of the accused—despite the fact that most rapes take place between acquaintances. Until the 1970s, the law operated on the assumption that the victim's sexual history was relevant to the issue of consent. A "chaste" (that is, virginal or monogamous) complainant was more credible than a woman who had engaged in extramarital sexual activity. The underlying assumption would appear to be that women can be divided into those who "do" and those who "don't."

A third category also seemed to exist: women who ask for it. The kinds of warnings from which I quoted have been commonplace since large numbers of women began living and working outside the family home. A jury in a rape trial in Fort Lauderdale, Florida, returned a "not guilty" verdict in October 1989 because "she asked for it. We felt she was up to no good the way she was dressed." The victim, who wore a tank top, a short skirt, and no underwear, was abducted at knife point and repeatedly raped. Since she obviously did not consent, the jury must have felt that she deserved punishment. Yet nothing she did was against the law. The punishment she got could not legally have been imposed upon a prisoner convicted of a felony.[7]

Since traditional law makes rape easy to get away with, it will hardly surprise the reader to learn that rape is a frequent occurrence. One study concludes that "nationally, a *conservative* estimate is that, under current conditions, 20–30 percent of American girls now twelve years old will suffer a violent sexual attack during the remainder of their lives." But between 50 percent and 90 percent of rapes are never reported to the police, and seven out of eight rapes go unpunished.[8] What is going on? Folklore suggests that there is no such thing as rape; that rape is the stuff of comedy; that rape is a calamity to be avoided at all costs; and, finally, that rape is the victim's fault. The 1930s brought the most notorious example of the one universally recognized exception to each and every one of these contradictory messages. The specific instance was the case of the "Scottsboro boys," nine young black men accused of raping two white women in that Alabama town in 1931. The exception was any alleged rape of a white woman by a black man. Such accusations rarely needed to be proved, and they were viewed with utmost seriousness.

The Scottsboro defendants got outrageously unfair trials, death sentences, and a lifetime of appeals and reversals—on the uncorroborated testimony of discredited and coerced witnesses. These men were neither the first nor the last blacks to get such treatment, and worse; the last documented lynching was the murder of Emmett Till in Mississippi in 1955, after the fifteen-year-old had whistled at a white woman. Black men convicted of raping white women still get the heaviest sentences of any sexual-assault defendants. Society abandons the customary disbelief and trivialization of rape in favor of racism in these cases—a phenomenon which made it easier for advocates of racial equality to trivialize rape in general.[9]

Brownmiller focused both on the actual prevalence of rape and what might be called its phenomenology: the meanings attached to the concept, and the ways in which these meanings influence behavior. Rape "is nothing more or less than a conscious process of intimidation by which *all men* keep *all women* in a state of fear." Men need not actually rape women to intimidate them in this way. Although Brownmiller has often been accused of calling all men rapists—the book, not surprisingly, was controversial—she has repeatedly denied, in person and in print, that this was her intention. It is the institution of rape, not the act itself, which men use to instill fear. Her discussion of the common warnings illuminates this point.

> The negative value of this sort of advice, I'm afraid, far outweighs the positive. What it tells us, implicitly and explicitly, is:
>
> 1. A woman alone probably won't be able to defend herself. Another woman who might possibly come to her aid will be of no use whatsoever.
> 2. Despite the fact that it is men who are the rapists, a woman's

ultimate security lies in being accompanied by men at all times.
3. A woman who claims to value her sexual integrity cannot expect the same amount of freedom and independence that men routinely enjoy. . . .
4. In the exercise of rational caution, a woman . . . should deny or obscure her personal identity, lifestyle and independence, and function on a sustained level of suspicion that approaches a clinical definition of paranoia.

. . . A woman who follows this sort of special cautionary advice to the letter and thinks she is acting in society's interest—or even in her own personal interest—is deluding herself rather sadly. While the risk to one potential victim might be slightly diminished. . . , not only does the number of potential rapists on the loose remain constant, but the ultimate effect of rape upon the woman's mental and emotional health has been accomplished *even without the act.* For to accept a special burden of self-protection is to reinforce the concept that women must live and move about in fear and can never expect to achieve the personal freedom, independence, and self-assurance of men.[10]

Brownmiller's discussion of rape's ugly racist component suggests that, in certain times and places in American history, rape has also been used by white men to keep black men in a state of fear. Thus, rape becomes a necessary instrument of patriarchal, racist power. This is why rape is so important.

It is easy to exaggerate the amount of social change which has occurred. After all, women are still warned against exercising legally protected freedoms, like going to bars alone. In Fort Lauderdale, Florida, at least, men are free to rape women who dress in a certain way. But the contemporary feminist movement made rape an issue early on, holding "speak-outs" and other public protests in the late 1960s and early 1970s. Every state has revised its rape laws since 1969, and many states have done so more than once. These changes shift emphasis from victims to defendants and make convictions easier to obtain.

In most jurisdictions, "forcible rape" has become "sexual assault"; "statutory rape" is "unlawful sexual intercourse"; and the marital exemption has been abolished. Penalties remain heavy, although the Supreme Court ruled in 1977 that the death penalty for the rape of an adult woman violated the Eighth Amendment's proscription of cruel and unusual punishments.[11] Gender neutrality is the norm, despite *Michael M.* In effect, a man can be a rape victim, although the law does not define such an assault that way. "Resistance" requirements are being dropped, and scrutiny of the victim's behavior is even more rapidly becoming obsolete. All but two states have "rape shield" laws which exclude all evidence about the complainant's sexual history except prior relations with the defendant. Although a defense attorney can sometimes sneak in this kind of questioning under the guise of attacking the complainant's credibility, the rape shield law has protected some victims from public humiliation.

Yet rape remains commonplace. It is still less frequently reported than other crimes, and convictions are harder to get in cases where the victim already knew her rapist—the majority of cases. "Date rape" is one activity which is familiar on the campus. One study of female college students found that 15 percent of respondents had been raped. Colleges and women's organizations are beginning to teach students how to avoid this form of assault, along with telling them to lock their doors and not to hitchhike.[12]

But, as yet, no universal social condemnation attaches to rape. In 1983, a woman was raped by several men in Big Dan's, a bar in New Bedford, Massachusetts, in the presence of cheering onlookers. Media coverage of the event focused on the life and personality of the victim: the fact that she was a welfare mother, her drinking habits, and what right she thought she had to be in that bar, anyway. All four defendants were convicted, and got long prison terms. But when a similar gang rape occurred in San Diego, Texas, in 1988, the defense attorney alleged that the victim knew her attackers "better than she should have."[13]

Women are still cautioned against "teasing," although "sending signals" is the current trendy term. You may recall that Justice Harry Blackmun's concurring opinion in *Michael M.* referred to "their foreplay, in which [Sharon] willingly participated and seems to have encouraged." But how does he know that Sharon thought that kissing Michael was foreplay? She may have viewed kissing as kissing, and have had no intention of going further. Would this behavior be teasing, sending signals, or simply expressing a preference? That seems to depend on who is doing the interpreting.[14]

Even if we suppose that Sharon, or any other woman, began a tryst wanting to have intercourse and changed her mind, she might not have been trying to tease her partner. Such behavior will certainly frustrate him, but for all we know, she might simply have become shy, fearful, or wary of pregnancy. Men have been known to do this sort of thing to women, who rarely resort to violence as a result. But somehow it is men's perceptions of behavior and situations which count, not women's. In the absence of a social taboo against rape, women will have to trust legal reform to deter and punish the crime.

Dirty Little Secrets: Violence within the Family

"Assault" is "an intentional attempt or threat to physically injure another." "Assault and battery" consists of carrying out the attempt or threat. Depending on the degree of injury which the assailant intends to inflict, these acts are either misdemeanors or felonies. "Aggravated assault," a felony, involves an effort to commit rape, robbery, or murder, or to inflict serious bodily harm. "Simple assault," usually a misdemeanor, occurs when no serious harm is committed or intended.[15]

One might suppose that violence between family members constitutes assault just as any other physical attack does. Except in one situation, where parents punish children, law labels domestic violence as such. Society has only recently begun to do so, slowly and reluctantly. One sign of social attitudes is the fact that American vernacular has special terms for certain kinds of family violence: wife beating, spanking, and even "granny bashing" (the abuse of old people, the majority of whom are women). These labels imply that violence within the family is not as serious as violence in general. One of these, spanking, is not necessarily or even usually a crime. Another, wife battering, has become one only fairly recently in human history.

Spanking is ritualized. We not only have a special name for assaults on children by parents and their deputies, but we also have a culturally sanctioned method for it. Adults "correct" children physically by applying blows with one instrument, the human hand, to one part of the anatomy, the buttocks. This ritualization implies that spanking is somehow different from assault.

Is it? Since fatty deposits cushion the impact of blows on the buttocks, the child may not be seriously hurt. But the buttocks are not the only site of corporal punishment, and canes, belts, or paddles can cause serious injury even there. In one case, two pupils were paddled so hard that one missed several days of school and the other could not use his arm for a week. Yet the Supreme Court upheld the regulation allowing corporal punishment. The notion that parents may hit children is so widely accepted that the issue has yet to be disputed in American courts or legislatures. Every day, hospital emergency rooms are filled with children who have not been "spanked"; they have fractures, concussions, permanent scars, serious burns, and a host of other brutal injuries. Children have died from family violence. The trial of Joel Steinberg in 1988–89 in the death of his illegally adopted daughter, Lisa, is one of the latest in a series of notorious tragedies. It is unlikely to be the last.[16]

The law does distinguish between corporal punishment and child abuse. Although it is not always clear which is which, a parent who causes broken bones, burns, or any permanent injury can be prosecuted for aggravated assault. If the child dies, the parent can be charged with homicide. But attacks on children which would constitute simple assault if committed upon adults are not treated as simple assault when committed by parents or, if state law allows corporal punishment, by teachers.

Just as parents have the power to "correct" their children, common law gave the husband the power to "correct" his wife. After all, the husband was accountable for his wife's actions; it seemed only fair (at least to male judges) that he be able to control them. A judge once told an angry wife, "If you will amend your manners, you may expect better treatment." This sanction of wife beating meant that a wife could neither press charges against a violent husband nor divorce him for cruelty, unless a judge agreed that the violence was excessive.

That rarely happened. North Carolina courts in the nineteenth century refused to intervene in cases involving knives, horsewhips, and public floggings. A few court decisions over the years had put limits on the husband's discretion; for example, a man could not use a switch any larger than his thumb. Some lethal weapons are smaller than that, which may be one reason why the "rule of thumb" (this doctrine is the source of the common expression) had been abandoned by the mid-nineteenth century in favor of emphasis on "the *effect produced* and not the manner of producing it, or the instrument used." By the end of that century, husbands no longer had permission to injure their wives. But stopping them, let alone prosecuting them, was not easy.[17]

Most readers of this book will at least have heard of a husband who abused his wife; unfortunately, for many Americans the connection with domestic violence is closer than that. Contrary to popular beliefs, domestic violence is not confined to drunk, poor, or mentally ill men. Instead, "the simple fact is that in America today almost every man is a potential wife beater." Police officers and military men seem to be especially prone to violence, but some famous men and even world leaders have been wife beaters. John Fedders, the former enforcement chief of the Securities and Exchange Commission, regularly beat his wife, Charlotte, during their twenty-year marriage. The wife of former Premier Sato of Japan divorced him because of his violence. Despite the fact that her allegations were made public, Sato received the Nobel Peace Prize in 1974. Late in 1988, the mass media carried stories about the brief marriage of actor Robin Givens and prizefighter Mike Tyson. He admitted striking her—but the media depicted Givens, not Tyson, as the villain.[18]

Why do men abuse their wives? Some commentators have suggested that the women provoke violence by their behavior; others say that the men have poor impulse control, or are reacting to other pressures in their lives. The authors of a landmark study on domestic violence cast considerable doubt on these explanations:

> Imagine that Chet is the manager of a medium-sized office. The office employs a janitor who comes in the evenings to empty ashtrays, dust, vacuum, and clean the office. David runs an automobile agency. One day, Chet comes to work and finds that although the janitor has been in, there is barely a sign that anything has been cleaned. That same day, a three-year-old overturns David's television. What is the outcome? Does Chet, finding his office a mess, pounce on his janitor and begin to pummel him? Unlikely. Does David slap, spank, or even beat the wayward three-year-old? Absurd. How is it that the very same situations at home can produce anger strong enough to lead to abusive violence? Why can Chet and David control their anger outside of the home, yet lose it with family members?[19]

Chet would be unlikely to hit the janitor even if he himself were in dire financial straits; nor would David slap the child even if he himself had just returned from a multimartini lunch. We all know why the men refrain from violence in those situations: they would be punished if they acted out their anger. People abuse family members because they can get away with it.[20]

How, and why, does an abusive man get away with it? Because the woman tolerates it? That was once a popular belief. In fact, many women do not; there are cases of husbands pursuing wives who have left them. Since husbands tend to be larger and stronger than their wives, victims are not always in a position to do much else besides endure the violence. (What do you do when someone who is a foot taller than you and outweighs you by 100 pounds starts beating on you?) Economic dependency or the presence of children may also impede her leaving. But the larger point is that the same social phenomenon has occurred here that occurred with rape; the victim, not the aggressor, gets critical scrutiny. It makes no difference whether the victim endures abuse. There is no general rule that you can hit people because they let you.

People have gotten away with domestic violence because the state has failed to enforce the law. All too often, police called to the scene of a "wife beating" have failed to respond at all or, responding, have chosen to "cool out" the situation and leave without arresting or even warning the batterer. Acting on a common presumption that battered women will not press charges, police often made this notion a self-fulfilling prophecy by neglecting to inform victims of the choices available to them. Even when police made arrests, their superiors, or prosecutors, often dropped charges. A woman who sought treatment in a hospital emergency room would get it, but rarely would anyone deal with her concerns or probe beneath her explanations for her injuries ("I fell," "I was in a car accident," "I walked into a door," etc.). Society has not used the criminal law to stop domestic violence.[21]

Now, the law is being used to do just that. Resurgence of feminism brought new attention to the plight of abused women. "Battered women's shelters" opened at about the same time that "rape crisis centers" did. Like the centers, the shelters were subsidized first by private contributions and later by federal funds; the shelters, too, began as efforts by citizens to do what the state would not. Some victims have sued municipalities whose police did not respond, or responded ineffectively, to calls for help. Tracey Thurman won a $2.3 million award against the police of Torrington, Connecticut, after she suffered permanent partial paralysis as a result of her husband's stabbing. The police had refused to arrest him although she had called several times.[22]

Government has responded to these pressures. In most jurisdictions, now, the police *must* respond to all calls. Recruits are taught to take complaints seriously, and to advise victims of their alternatives. Despite the Reagan administration's diminished generosity to such agencies, shelters and centers do exist where battered women and their children can hide and get help. (You may find the telephone number of a local Aid to Battered Women group in your local telephone directory, but you are unlikely to find the address of a shelter. Most groups keep their locations secret, to prevent batterers from hunting down their victims.)

Domestic violence has not stopped. Like rape, and, indeed, like most crimes short of homicide, it is not always reported to the police. But it is no longer ignored or dismissed when it is reported. Social agencies are available to women who are reluctant to press criminal charges. And as increased work opportunities make women less dependent upon men, they become less likely to endure this treatment.[23]

Dirty Little Secrets: The Sexual Abuse of Children

Both boys and girls are victims of child abuse, outside the family and within it. The one kind of abuse which girls are more apt to suffer is sexual abuse. Estimates of the incidence of sexual abuse of girls under 18 go as high as 45 percent; the comparable figure for boys is 10 percent. This is the kind of abuse which parental warnings against lurking strangers who offer candy to children attempt to forfend—although over half of all cases involve abuse by acquaintances, and a large minority by relatives. Unlawful intercourse, incest, and child molestation are felonies in all states. All three carry less severe penalties than do rape or sexual assault, even when the act committed was the outright forcible rape of a child. The sexual abuse of children, like abuse and neglect in general, has been a "dirty little secret" which society has buried.[24]

Society has never wanted to know much about sexual abuse. When Sigmund Freud began the practice of psychoanalysis in Vienna in the 1880s, he was appalled by the number of women patients who told him that they had been molested by their fathers as children. Freud could not believe that the incidence of incest in middle- and upper-class families was so high. He theorized—without any evidence to support this conclusion—that the women's accounts were fantasies, the results of their subconscious sexual desire for their fathers. Thus he instructed his followers, who passed the word on to their students—and thus the psychotherapeutic establishment held. Psychotherapists treated accusations of incest the same way that police treated accusations of rape.

It is impossible to determine, at this late date, whether or not

Freud was right about his particular patients. As recently as 1984, a book which criticized Freud for his unsupported assumptions created a major controversy among professional psycho-therapists. It has been established beyond dispute that many true accusations of child abuse have not been believed. Yet, well into the 1970s, expert opinion held some or all of the following inaccu-rate opinions: children lied about sexual abuse; the child was often the aggressor in adult-child sexual encounters; gay men were the segment of the population most likely to abuse children; sexual contact didn't really harm children unless their parents overreacted; and parents should instruct small children that a molester was "friend sick" and deserved pity.[25]

The victim of child abuse, like the rape victim, was twice traumatized, both violated and discredited. She could expect to be disbelieved, blamed, or told either that what had happened was no big deal or that her anger against the person who hurt her was inappropriate. I use the past tense because these generaliza-tions are no longer accurate. The changes in legal and social treatment of child sexual abuse have been as dramatic as those with respect to rape. This kind of abuse is indeed dirty, but it has not remained a secret and it is no longer a "little" problem. Fiction, nonfiction, television, and films have drawn attention to the subject. In the last fifteen years, studies of the problem have increased society's knowledge about the sexual abuse of children.

Experts now agree that false accusations are extremely rare. It is true that very young children do not distinguish clearly between reality and fantasy. But they are not usually capable of making up stories about sexual experience, because they know very little about it. It is also true that children often make poor witnesses in court. While defense attorneys are unlikely to bully child witnesses—such conduct is hardly the way to win sympathy for the defendant—discrediting the opposition's witnesses is an integral part of trial strategy. Children are easily confused; there-fore, it is difficult to convict an abuser on the uncorroborated testimony of a child. Two widely publicized recent cases, the McMartin Preschool case in Southern California and a similar case in Chaska County, Minnesota, ended in acquittals or dismis-sal of the charges. Either innocent people were persecuted, or guilty people got away with vicious crimes. These defeats are no reason for prosecutors not to keep on trying. It is possible to introduce evidence of children's general reliability, and to be diligent in the search for physical evidence of abuse.[26]

Conventional wisdom assures us that incest and adult-child sex are taboo in all societies. That truism is in need of serious revision. If even the lowest recent estimate is correct, 11 percent of all children have had some sort of sexual contact with adults before the age of eighteen. A "taboo" which is observed nine times out of ten is a weak taboo indeed. To appreciate the significance of such a finding, compare it with national crime surveys' estimates that 5 percent of all adults will become victims of violent crime sometime in their lives.[27]

There exists in the United States, and apparently worldwide, a kind of sexual "underground" which will provide men with information about any form of sexual outlet they seek, including children. Like pornography—and "kiddie porn" is a popular variation—this kind of material circulates surreptitiously but extensively. For example, *The Discreet Gentleman's Guide to the Pleasures of Europe* tells the traveler where to find child prostitutes. But not all communications which highlight the sexual appeal of children are clandestine. Advertisements and commercials often use provocatively posed child models to sell clothing, cosmetics, and even telephone services. Beauty contests exist in which children as young as three parade down the runway in swimsuits, evening gowns, and high heels. The observer must assume that these children appear in commercials and contests with their parents' consent; children that young cannot be gainfully employed or participate in a contest without it. Our historic toleration of adult-child sex reflects society's profound ambivalence on this issue.[28]

Sex crimes against children include, but are not limited to, rape. Fondling children, photographing them in revealing or provocative poses, and forcing or otherwise inducing children to satisfy adults' sexual needs are among the activities defined as child molestation. While I think we will all agree that the rape of a young child—and it has happened to infants—constitutes sexual abuse, there is widespread disagreement about the gravity of acts which cannot be so classified. The term "jail bait" trivializes statutory rape when the victim has begun to mature sexually—and notice where it puts the responsibility. Some experts have doubted whether children are abused by being fondled, or fondling, if they are not coerced. A recent novel and film raise the question of where the boundary lies between satisfying a child's curiosity about adult bodies and exploiting the child sexually.[29] And some of the terms used in discussing this problem are hard to define. If a mother photographs her two-year-old son splashing naked in the backyard wading pool, for example, is she abusing him?

The last example presents an easy case. It is at the opposite extreme from sodomization of that same child. Attitudes about nudity vary within our society, and protecting children from exploitation does not require that we impose the most repressive standards upon the entire population. But even here we cannot claim that the child's participation is voluntary. Whether or not he was coerced, his consent is not sought and is not necessary. Similarly, children are not free to say "no" to adults' sexual overtures. Adults have power over children. Most of the time, adults are entitled to command obedience from children; parents *always* can. To say that children can choose to engage in this activity makes no more sense than to say that slaves were free to resist their masters' advances. However, if a child initiates the contact, the adult has the power to refuse. Therefore, the law is correct in labeling sexual contact not obviously coerced or harmful as abusive.

But there is another familiar argument which, while it does not discount the inherent coercion and violence of adult-child sex, implies that it is rather a shame that people make so much fuss about it nowadays. After all, the argument runs, adults are no longer free to play with children they do not know, or even to speak to them; and look how hard it is to find an adult willing to serve as a scoutmaster or soccer coach. Parents must hesitate to give their children any physical affection at all, lest the nosy neighbor call the police. We are told that there is an increasing danger of false accusations of sexual abuse.

One of these observations is supported by the facts; it is harder to recruit volunteers to work with children. That development may well be an unfortunate side effect of society's decreasing tolerance of child sexual abuse. Even if it is true that adults will hesitate to approach children, most children have ample opportunity to interact with adults: parents, other relatives, teachers, child-care workers, their parents' friends, their friends' parents, and so on. It is not the child who needs contact with the adult encountered in the park or the playground; the situation would seem to be the reverse. There is no compelling reason why children should be available to serve adult needs, sexual or merely social.

The possibility of false accusations is a troubling one.

Whether or not it has happened yet, it can. Children may not invent lies, but adults can coach them to lie. Several widely publicized divorce cases have involved accusations and counteraccusations of incest. Whatever the difficulties of obtaining criminal convictions on the basis of children's testimony, a false accusation can come close to ruining a person's life even without a conviction. But to ignore child molestation because false accusations are possible is no more defensible than to dismiss accusations of rape or any other crime of violence for the same reason. Society may regret some of the changes which accompany the new, vigorous condemnation of the sexual abuse of children, but a return to the old days would have a disastrous impact on the rights and well-being of girls and women.

Violence without Force: The Case of Pornography

"Pornography" combines two Greek words meaning "writing" and "prostitute." From this beginning, the word has come to refer to explicitly erotic material designed to produce sexual excitement: the sort of thing available in "adult" bookstores or in "porno" films. Much of this material is sadomasochistic as well as erotic; a common pornographic theme is the depiction of women as eager victims of sexual exploitation and torture. Many feminists have come to believe that pornography, through its effects on its predominantly male audience, amounts to the systematic degradation of women and plays a significant role in keeping women from full equality. This concern has led to efforts to use the law to restrict access to this material.

Constitutional doctrine appears to be on the feminists' side, but that appearance is misleading. Some pornography is what the law calls "obscenity," but obscenity is not necessarily identical with pornography. The Supreme Court ruled more than thirty years ago that obscenity was not entitled to First Amendment protection, because it was not part of the "expression of ideas" which the free speech guarantee was designed to protect. Government, therefore, has broad powers to regulate obscenity. The current definition of obscenity, from a case decided in 1973, is material which, by contemporary community standards, "appeals to the prurient [that is, erotic] interest," which "depicts or describes, in a patently offensive way, sexual conduct specifically defined by the applicable state laws," and which "taken as a whole, lacks serious literary, artistic, political, or scientific value."[30]

The primary concern of many proponents of regulation is the effect of obscene material on the young, who are considered particularly vulnerable to bad influences. But court decisions have made it clear that the state's power is not limited to its interest in protecting youth from moral corruption. These decisions state that society's interests in "order and morality" justify regulation, even of material designed for an adult audience. However, there is a wide gap between what the law says and what actually happens. In effect, a tacit agreement gives most adults in this country access to any obscene material, including pornography, as long as a reasonable effort is made to keep sexually explicit material away from children. The rating scheme developed by the Motion Picture Association of America ("G," "PG-13," "R," "NC-17") and the existence of "adult book stores" are part of this implicit compromise. Occasional, isolated prosecutions of mass-circulation magazines threaten the compromise, as does the existence of video stores, not all of which are careful of what they rent to whom. In general, however, law enforcement concentrates on keeping children and adolescents away from pornography.[31]

This compromise does not satisfy feminist critics. Their concern is with the ways in which exposure to pornography affects men's attitudes and behavior toward women. Catharine MacKinnon, a law professor and a leader in the antipornography movement, puts it this way: "Pornography is an eight-billion-dollar-a-year industry of rape and battery and sexual harassment, an industry that both performs these abuses for the production of pornography and targets women for them societywide."[32]

MacKinnon and Andrea Dworkin drafted several antipornography ordinances which a few cities have considered and adopted. One of the first of these was passed by the city council of Indianapolis. This ordinance, enacted in 1984, attempted to describe pornography in the conventional legal language of sexual equality.

> Pornography is a discriminatory practice based on sex because its effect is to deny women equal opportunities in society. Pornography is central in creating and maintaining sex as a basis of discrimination. Pornography is a systematic practice of exploitation and subordination based on sex which differentially harms women. The bigotry and contempt it promotes, with the acts of aggression it

fosters, harm women's opportunities for equality of rights in employment, education, access to and use of public accommodations, and acquisition of real property, and contribute significantly to restricting women in particular from full exercise of citizenship and participation in public life.[33]

Whatever else this ordinance does, it reveals the deficiencies of antidiscrimination language in the task of expressing the feminist grievance. The provision contains assertions which call for proof but are almost impossible to prove. Yet the lack of proof does not render the statements incorrect or unimportant. They get at a very real problem in the only language which law provides for discourse. No one has ever proved that obscenity corrupts morals or leads to crime, either, but the state is still allowed to censor it. If obscenity does not generally get First Amendment protection, there is no reason why feminists' efforts to regulate pornography should be treated as attacks on the First Amendment.

Nevertheless, First Amendment doctrine has proved fatal to feminist antipornography legislation so far. The district court opinion in the Indianapolis case suggests more than a little judicial scorn. "Defendants repeat throughout their briefs the incantation that their ordinance regulates conduct, not speech. They contend (one senses with a certain sleight of hand) that the production, dissemination, and use of sexually explicit words and pictures *is* the actual subordination of women and not an expression of ideas deserving First Amendment protection." Whatever one's opinion on this question—and feminists are divided—this failure to take the issue seriously suggests a general lack of concern with the ways in which women are victimized.[34]

Women and Crime

Criminologists have often found it a useful enterprise to study crime as a career choice, like law or police work. In that sense, crime is not and has never been an equal opportunity employer. Women's share of those arrested, convicted, and incarcerated has never approached their 53 percent representation in the American population. With two exceptions, to be discussed later, female crime rates lag far behind men's. But the female rates are increasing. Until the 1960s, women accounted for fewer than 10 percent of all people arrested. Recent figures show that 13 percent of persons arrested for murder and aggravated assault, 7 percent for robbery, and as high as 29 percent for larceny-theft are women. The criminal justice system can no longer regard the woman offender as a nuisance, an anomaly with whom an institution designed for men must deal.

This huge increase in women's crime became noticeable during the 1970s, at a time when crime rates in general were rising. Female arrest rates actually began their rise during the 1960s, and increased at a much higher rate than those for men. Between 1974 and 1984, the number of women in prison rose 258 percent, as compared with 199 percent for men. But these dramatic increases did not continue throughout the 1980s. In fact, the arrest rates among women for murder and robbery actually declined during the same decade in which the proportion of women prisoners more than tripled. The increase in women's crime was largely an increase in crimes of property, not crimes of violence. (Women who do commit violent crimes most often injure or kill family members. Some women kill or assault their abusive husbands or their children. Except for sexual abuse, mothers are as likely as fathers to hurt their children; not surprisingly, perhaps, as mothers do most of the child care.) Fraud, robbery, and larceny are no longer virtually all-male occupations. While female arrest rates for property crimes, especially larceny, rose faster than male rates, arrest rates for violent crimes increased similarly for both sexes.[35]

Why the increase? One popular explanation indirectly attributes the rise in female criminality to the women's movement. According to this theory, women's new opportunities include more chances to commit crimes. "When we did not permit women to swim at the beaches, the female drowning rate was quite low. When women were not permitted to work as bank tellers or presidents, the female embezzlement rate was low."[36] This "liberation hypothesis" sounds plausible—and it might seem only fair that, if we credit the women's movement for changes in the treatment of women victims, we assign it responsibility for the increase in the number of women criminals. But closer analysis has discredited the liberation hypothesis. What kinds of robbery, larceny-theft, and fraud do women tend to commit? A comprehensive examination of female criminal behavior has found that the increases have occurred, not in the traditionally male offenses against property, such as armed robbery or white-collar crime, but in the traditionally female offenses like shoplifting and check forgery. The widely publicized cases of women accused of corporate crime have been too few in number to make any impression in the statistics, as have several notorious murders committed by women. Outside of property crimes, much of the increase consisted of arrests for vagrancy and prostitution. The criminal labor force, then, appears to be as sex-segregated as its legitimate counterpart; women are committing more of the classic women's crimes.[37]

Why? The best-selling undergraduate criminal justice textbook in the United States contains a revealing description of "Marge, the new female criminal." Now in her forties, "Marge" was deserted by her husband when her children were young. She got her first paying job, as a waitress, and began supplementing her income through shoplifting. Caught only once, she turned to bank robbery after several years. "The other girls I knew were boosting [shoplifting] or [credit] carding. They said I must be crazy when we talked about it one day. . . . I heard on the radio of a lady who hit a bank and got away, and I figured, what the hell, if she can do it, why can't I?" Marge is now serving an indefinite prison term for robbery.[38]

Marge may be the "new" female criminal, but she is far from typical. She did not turn to prostitution, and she eventually made a "career change" from a female to a male "occupation." Her story does illustrate one similarity between male and female criminal careers: although offenders will often get away with single crimes, sooner or later almost all habitual criminals are caught and punished. Marge's story also suggests a possible relationship between the partial feminization of crime and the feminization of poverty discussed in Chapter 4.

By the spring of 1989, the number of women arrested for drug-related offenses had risen so sharply that New York City experienced a 33 percent increase in the number of women held in city jails, and the number of women prison inmates nationwide had risen from 13,000 to over 30,000 in eight years. These women, many of whom were juveniles, pregnant, mothers of young children, or all three, would probably have been released in earlier years and for other offenses. In the current climate of opinion, "getting tough on drugs" means incarceration for drug-related offenses. "Most everybody in here is here for drugs, period," said one seventeen-year-old inhabitant of the women's house on Rikers Island. "All anybody talks about is doing their time, getting out, selling more drugs to take care of their kids."[39]

Women who choose criminal careers may do so for the same reasons many men do. Like Marge, they are among the working poor. They lack enough money to live the American vision of the good life, and are dissatisfied with the lifestyle they can afford by honest means. There are a variety of possible interpretations, kind or harsh, judgmental or sympathetic, of this phenomenon. Some experts insist that both poverty and crime result from individual failings; laziness and depravity are popular explanations. Others, including Marxist criminologists, locate the explanations in socioeconomic forces like the job market, the cost of living, and so forth. But it is an indisputable fact that prostitution and drug dealing pay better than domestic service, waiting tables, and even most clerical work.[40]

There are two offense categories in which females outnumber males. One of these is running away. Only a juvenile can be a runaway. Adults who leave home voluntarily have not "run away." They may be in grave trouble with their families and their employers, but the fact of their departure will not get them in trouble with the law. Running away is, therefore, a "status offense": it is a crime only because of the juvenile status of the person committing it, and would be perfectly legal if committed by an adult. "Truancy," "incorrigibility," and "disobedience" are other examples of status offenses. Yet the runaway's intentions may not be rebellious at all, let alone criminal. "The runaways of today can't or won't return home because they were thrown out, starved, raped, beaten, and the street, miserable as it is, is better than what they left."[41]

One expert writes, "The juvenile justice system's treatment of girls may well constitute one of the clearest examples of institutionalized sexism in contemporary society." Although studies show that girls are no more likely to commit status offenses than boys, girls are more likely to be arrested for these offenses, are more likely to be declared "persons (or minors, juveniles, or children) in need of supervision" than are boys, are more likely to be detained or put in foster homes (where they may be abused), and are often punished for activities for which boys are not punished. Female status offenders are often treated more harshly than either males or females charged with crime.[42]

There is a connection between the runaway and the other category of lawbreaker in which women comprise a majority. As you might expect, this crime is the "oldest profession": prostitution, the provision of sexual services for pay. The connection is that juvenile runaways often become prostitutes, not necessarily through any process that could be regarded as free choice. Leaving intolerable home situations without money or support networks, these girls are vulnerable to a pimp who promises them riches. Young prostitutes may earn a great deal of money, but it goes to the pimp; the girls are often beaten, threatened, and forcibly introduced to addictive drugs. Yet, as prostitutes, they encounter the punitive and not the benevolent face of society.[43]

Not all prostitutes are minors; nor do they all work for abusive pimps. While *Mayflower Madam* and *The Best Little Whorehouse in Texas* may paint an unrealistically rosy picture, there are prostitutes (often "call girls" who work in their own homes, their clients' homes, or hotels) who become wealthy, work in luxury, and avoid drugs and sexually transmitted diseases. Unlike the women who cruise the "red light district" of large cities, these prostitutes are not recognizable as such on sight to the casual observer. They look like college students, socialites, or executives. Some of these entrepreneurs have formed interest groups like COYOTE (Call Off Your Old Tired Ethics) which support the decriminalization of prostitution. In one state, Nevada, prostitution is legal. Feminist groups like NOW oppose legalization, on the ground that providing sexual services for money inherently degrades the provider.

Who is right? It is important to note that, like many other careers, prostitution has its class structure. The employees of the "Mayflower Madam" were at its pinnacle. In a memorable scene, their boss told a new recruit that she was at liberty to reject any client whose personal hygiene she found unacceptable, let alone any demands for sadomasochism or the more bizarre forms of sexual activity. These women, like the employees of the "chicken ranch," were all adults; neither Ms. Barrows nor Miss Mona catered to pedophiles. But men with those desires, and enough money, will find someone to satisfy them. Procurers who exploit youthful runaways often take full advantage of that particular market. Whether or not legalization is a good idea, it will not improve the status of the most downtrodden prostitutes. Still, the state could combat forced prostitution by arresting the pimps, not their victims.

This happens comparatively rarely. Virtually all prostitutes, however well rewarded, have suffered from a persistent inequality in the way the laws are enforced. Prostitution requires both that the sexual act take place and the payment be made. Therefore, there must be two offenders, the provider and the customer, or none at all. Anyone who makes money from prostitution, procures prostitutes for customers, or forces anyone to work as a prostitute is also guilty of a felony. Yet it is very rare for a client to be prosecuted. It has happened—every once in a while a city like New York or Washington arrests "johns" and may even release their names—but in the overwhelming majority of cases it is the prostitute, not the client or the person for whom the prostitute works, who is arrested, charged, and punished. This distribution of blame is mirrored in social attitudes toward prostitution. For instance, who gives venereal disease to whom, prostitute or client? During the Vietnam conflict, one prevalent strain of gonorrhea was dubbed "Vietnam rose"—certainly not "American invader."[44]

Pimps are hard to catch, and are willing to let the girls take the rap. The prostitutes risk violence, even death, if they inform on pimps or testify against them. (There have also been instances where pimps or madams avoided arrest by paying off police.) Female procurers do exist, as do male prostitutes. Very few women have been numbered among the clients. Male prostitutes have usually served other men. The conclusion is inescapable: prostitution laws, as applied, have been used against women to the advantage of men. The providers are punished, but as long as the customers go free, the demand will continue—unless AIDS spreads to the female population in such numbers as to make anonymous sex with women risky for men. In that event, we can predict another dramatic change in patterns of female criminal behavior.

Women in the Hands of an Angry Law

Women criminals, like their male counterparts, are punished. In American law, the trial judge imposes a criminal penalty (subject to appellate review), except in crimes which carry a mandatory sentence. In the overwhelming majority of cases—more than 90 percent—which are resolved by guilty pleas, the judge usually is ratifying an agreement reached between the prosecutor and the defense attorney. When a jury has convicted a person, the judge's sentence typically represents his or her effort to balance the extreme competing claims made by both sides. Unlike the jury, the judge has access to all information about the defendant's prior criminal record, if any.

The sentencing judge acts within boundaries established by the legislature. The criminal laws of each state and the national government set the ranges of allowable penalties for each crime, sometimes making distinctions according to the severity of the act and the defendant's record. These statutes often give the judge wide discretion. For example, burglary—illegal entry with criminal intent—can carry penalties ranging from probation plus "time served" in jail awaiting sentence to twenty-five years to life imprisonment.

Few judges will go so far as to sentence a first offender to the maximum. Questions of justice aside, long prison terms overtax our already crowded correctional institutions and their overburdened staff. But many lawmakers, and a large segment of the public, believe that "getting tough" with offenders is necessary to deter others from crime—and one has to agree that some sentences for vicious crimes have been too lenient by any reasonable standard. Two criminologists have traced a "severity-softening-severity" cycle in which legislatures increase penalties and limit discretion; criminal justice personnel then soften the penalties, often by agreeing to lesser charges; the public protests; legislatures impose harsher penalties; and the process repeats itself.[45]

All these considerations affect the treatment of female offenders. Beyond these issues, do women get lighter sentences than men (other things being equal, of course), stiffer sentences, or about the same? Any of these outcomes might be plausible. On the one hand, judges might be motivated by chivalrous impulses, or perhaps other impulses such as sympathy for the children of an offender, or even by the appeal of a pretty face. On the other hand, it makes just as much sense that judges might regard a female criminal as even more corrupt and immoral than a male, and deserving of worse punishment. Nor can we summarily dismiss the third possibility, the null hypothesis: that sex makes no difference. What are the facts? Three decades ago, laws existed which mandated harsher penalties for women than for men with similar records. But all the studies indicated that women actually got lighter sentences. Those laws are long gone; it did not even take *Reed v. Reed* to nullify them. But the expert findings disagree as to whether chivalry, severity, or neutrality obtains.

Up to the 1960s, the criminal codes of two states, Connecticut and Pennsylvania, treated women offenders much as juvenile codes have treated young people. Both states provided that women convicted of serious felonies be sentenced to the women's prison for an indeterminate sentence, meaning that the amount of time a woman spent in prison, and the conditions of her release, would be determined by such factors as her behavior while in custody and her prospects outside. These indeterminate sentences usually resulted in a longer sentence for a woman than for a similarly situated male offender. In 1968, one state supreme court and one federal court of original jurisdiction reached the same conclusion about each law. A federal district judge wrote in the Connecticut case, "The state has failed to carry its burden in support of the proposition that a greater period of imprisonment is necessary for the deterrence of women than for men. And it is hardly an open question that women, as such, do not deserve greater punishment. . . . Nor is there any support for the claim that women require a longer time to become rehabilitated as useful members of society."[46]

No other state had laws like these. Studies from the 1960s agreed that, in general, women were treated more leniently than men. Later investigators have faulted the methodology of these studies, so our knowledge of earlier results has to be labeled inexact. As far as current practices go, many rigorous studies have come up with contradictory results. There is support for all three hypotheses about sentencing. No researcher has found evidence of consistent leniency toward women in sentencing for the offenses for which the vast majority of female offenders are charged. However, since the crimes usually committed by women carry lighter sentences than those commonly committed by men, women prisoners do tend to serve less time than men do.[47]

Whether or not the criminal justice system is harder on women than on males, the experience of the woman prisoner differs significantly from that of a comparable man. Some of these differences result from the fact that women number only about 5 percent of all inmates in correctional institutions. There are simply far fewer institutions for women than for men. Some states have no women's prisons; they pay to have prisons in other states house their female felons. While sex segregation is the rule, six states and the federal government maintain coeducational facilities. Some women prisoners are housed in a separate wing of the men's prison. But the majority are held in the forty state and two federal all-female prisons in the United States.

How do these numbers affect the female prison experience? Women's prisons do tend to be smaller and better staffed than men's. But they are also more heterogeneous. Since only three states have more than one women's prison, the typical female institution holds all the female inmates in the state. As a result, the prison has to mix different kinds of offenders—the young, the old, the violent, the habitual criminals, the first-timers, the drug dealers, the prostitutes, and the white-collar criminals. Serving the needs of so diverse a population is almost impossible. Another result of the small number of women's prisons is that, for example, a woman from Buffalo, New York, may be housed in the Bedford Hills Correctional Facility at the opposite end of the state. It is difficult for her family and friends to visit her. She may rarely see her children.

Therein lies another source of the unique character of prison for women: their family responsibilities. About 70 percent of women prisoners are mothers; since prisoners tend to be young, so do their children. Imprisoned mothers, like most mothers, have usually been their children's primary caregivers. An estimated 21,000 children in the United States have mothers in custody. That estimate is a cautious one, because a woman may hide the fact that she has children. Not only do mothers in prison risk losing custody, but they fear that the often arbitrary prison discipline system may use their children as a means of controlling them. These mothers confront many barriers in trying to see and maintain contact with their children. States have begun to develop family visitation programs to alleviate these problems. Such innovations make sense from a rehabilitative standpoint; family ties can be a strong incentive to stay out of trouble after release.

Studies of women prisoners have found that, like men, they may assume several different social roles. "Squares," like the "square john" in a men's prison, have often been law-abiding citizens who, perhaps, killed a family member. They conform to the norms of the outside world and try to be model prisoners. "Cool" inmates, often professional criminals, adapt to the system just enough to make their time tolerable. Inmates who are "in the life," often prostitutes or drug offenders, adjust badly, are frequently in trouble, and generally do the hardest time. One major difference between men's and women's prisons is that the women tend to create a subculture which resembles an extended family. This may be one reason why inmate rape, commonplace among male prisoners, is rare in female institutions; inmate liaisons appear to be the result of mutual interest. Another sex-linked disparity gives women prisoners more limited opportunities for rehabilitation than men have. The academic, vocational, and industrial programs available to women tend to stress domestic work and other traditional women's occupations. If rehabilitation works at all, it sends the woman back into society fitted for a low-paying, stressful job—which may not make her much better off than the archetypical "Marge" before her imprisonment.[48]

Women in the Legal Profession

The law, like other professions, was virtually closed to women until the woman suffrage movement broke the barriers. It was 1870 before the Supreme Court admitted a woman, Belva Lockwood, to its bar—about the same time that Illinois began a successful struggle to keep women from practicing law in that state. This action culminated in the first sex discrimination case ever heard by the Supreme Court. Five justices accepted the state's argument that Myra Bradwell's inability, as a married woman, to enter into binding contracts disqualified her from practicing law. Justice Joseph Bradley wrote for three jurists who went even further. His separate opinion has become a feminist museum piece:

> Man is, or should be, woman's protector and defender. The natural and proper timidity and delicacy which belongs to the female sex evidently unfits it for many of the occupations of civil life. . . . The harmony, not to say identity, of interests and views which belongs, or should belong, to the family institution is repugnant to the idea of a woman adopting a distinct and independent career from that of her husband.
> The paramount destiny and mission of woman are to fulfill the noble and benign offices of wife and mother. This is the law of the Creator. And the rules of civil society must be adapted to the general constitution of things, and cannot be based upon exceptional cases.[49]

Such reasoning does more than assign a woman to a limited sphere of human activity. It simultaneously reserves for men a prestigious, stimulating, and well-paid occupation. Of course, the fact that even then women were practicing before the Court itself indicates that society was changing. By the end of the nineteenth century, women lawyers—few of them, to be sure—were practicing in most parts of the country.[50]

The existence of a few women lawyers—who might, in a later day, have been labeled "tokens"—does not indicate that women have entered the legal profession on an equal basis with men. Nothing could be further from the truth. In 1951, Sandra Day O'Connor graduated from Stanford Law School, third in her class. While the top student, William Rehnquist, went to Washington to clerk for Supreme Court Justice Robert Jackson, O'Connor could not even get an interview with a law firm. In 1970, women numbered only 9 percent of law students and 4 percent of lawyers in the United States.[51]

Those are the last figures available before Title IX forbade sex discrimination in law schools receiving federal aid. The changes since then have been extraordinary. Between 1971 and 1974—a period in which there is a complete turnover in a law school's student body—the proportion of women law students *tripled. Roe v. Wade* was argued and won by a woman, 27-year-old Sarah Weddington of Texas. Between 1985 and 1987, women numbered 40 percent of all law students, 17 percent of all lawyers, and 7 percent of all attorney judges. The proportion of women among Supreme Court law clerks has risen from 3 percent in 1970 to 34.4 percent in 1986.

New law school graduates, however gifted, do not immediately assume the top jobs. Law, like all professions, requires a long apprenticeship. At the pinnacle, women are still tokens and will remain so for some time. But even here, important gains have occurred. Women now hold 13.5 percent of all law school professorships. One woman sits on the Supreme Court, forty have served on the highest courts of thirty states and the District of Columbia, and five women have presided over their state courts as chief justice.[52]

Will the law soon become an equal opportunity employer? No thoughtful observer can deny that sexism still influences lawyers' careers. Until the last few years, women found it difficult to get out of the law library and into the courtroom. Those who could make that move often ended up practicing family law, an area which, for women lawyers, is roughly the equivalent of pediatrics for women physicians: 13 percent of all women lawyers, compared to 5 percent of men, specialized in family law. As late as 1983, a U.S. Attorney (the chief prosecutor in a federal district court) was quoted as saying, "When you're fighting a war against crime, you don't send a girl into the front lines." This would be news to Elizabeth Holtzman, who served as district attorney of Brooklyn, New York, during the 1980s, and to the voters who elected and reelected her. But Holtzman had few counterparts— just as she did in the 1970s, when she served in the House of Representatives.

The kinds of treatment women lawyers encounter in court, from judges, opponents, and witnesses, range from the apparently well-meaning to the consciously insulting to the blatantly bigoted. The following stories are all true, authenticated by respected lawyers and scholars. The district judge who complimented a lawyer in open court on her appearance may have meant no harm. After all, haven't men been taught that women appreciate these remarks? Indeed we do, in an appropriate setting—but "how does a lawyer establish her credibility when she has just been defined by the judge as a fashion plate?"

Other comments, such as "I will tell you what, little girl, you lose," have resulted in the public censure of judges by official commissions. But since lawyers have to maintain working relationships with judges and other lawyers, many women are reluctant to bring these charges. A further difficulty is that the adversary system contains some built-in incentives toward this sort of behavior on the part of male court personnel, incentives not often present in other professions. An internist who refers a patient to a surgeon is unlikely to try to undermine the patient's confidence by referring to his colleague as a "little girl." Trial lawyers, on the other hand, actively seek to discomfit their opponents or discredit them in the eyes of judge, jury, and witnesses, and are permitted wide latitude in attempting to do so. Calling attention to an opponent's sex may be regarded as just another type of trial gamesmanship. Like all gamesmanship, it carries risks; it may offend the same people the attorney is trying to impress. Judges, for their part, must exercise some control over lawyers appearing before them; they are entitled to warn, rebuff, squelch, and run a "tight ship" if they choose.

Task forces in New York and New Jersey conducted surveys which showed that a substantial majority of women attorneys (and up to 68 percent of male respondents) had heard judges and lawyers make sexist comments and jokes or use inappropriate forms of address ("honey," "dear," etc.) to and about women lawyers in court. And, certainly, the defense attorney who brushed against the prosecutor, saying, "Okay baby, let's see what you can show the judge," behaved abominably. He later admitted it.[53]

Even without encountering such obstacles, a woman lawyer may find it difficult to do what all trial lawyers must: establish, to the satisfaction of all concerned, that he or she is a professional, is in command, and must be taken seriously. All women who enter traditionally male professions have this difficulty. Most of them surmount it. But the ability of women attorneys to overcome obstacles created by overt sexism is no excuse for the behavior described above. At the very least, these strains impose an unfair burden on women.

Within and outside the courtroom, women lawyers have often perceived job discrimination. As late as the 1970s, some law firms recruiting associates at the University of Chicago Law School discouraged women applicants and expressed overt bias. A suit between an Atlanta law firm and an associate who was denied promotion to partner was settled out of court on the merits, but established the principle that Title VII applies to partnership decisions and is not overridden by First Amendment rights of association. Elizabeth Hishon, an associate at King & Spaulding since 1972, alleged both that the firm had assured her in recruiting her that partnership decisions would be made fairly, and that the eventual negative decision had been the result of sex discrimination. The firm insisted that the selection of partners was not a "term, condition, or privilege of employment" within the meaning of the 1964 law. The former lawyers in the district and appeals courts agreed, but the Supreme Court reversed.[54]

Another factor that may inhibit women from achieving full equality in the legal profession is one which pervades every occupation and, indeed, every aspect of American society. Women still have far greater responsibilities for home, family, and child care than men do. While this skewed distribution of duty should not have much impact on the careers of women who have no families, it still makes women less free than men to combine public and private life. Women are not equal if they must choose between a family and professional parity.

Many women professionals choose not to have families. Every study ever done has found that women in nontraditional careers are less likely than average to marry; they are less likely to have children; and, if they do, they have fewer children than the average woman.[55] But it is not even necessarily true—especially as one moves from the law to public offices frequently held by lawyers—that these women professionals are on a par with their male peers. In these days of emphasis on "family values," people who do not form traditional families are often suspect. In 1986, for example, when Barbara Mikulski of Maryland ran for the Senate, supporters of her female opponent frequently called her a "San Francisco Democrat." Ostensibly, the label referred to the site of the 1984 Democratic Convention, but its hidden implication was that the never-married Mikulski was a lesbian. Despite the slur, Mikulski won the election. But single politicians are often subject to two other derogatory inferences: either that they are sexually indiscriminate (the private lives of former governor Jerry Brown of California and Senator Bob Kerrey of Nebraska have received widespread public attention) or that they are neuter, passionless, asexual (a frequent innuendo about former New York mayor Ed Koch). It is widely presumed that marriage and children are a prerequisite for the presidency and for most other high offices.

One type of woman lawyer most burdened by conflicting responsibilities is the mother of young children. The first obstacle which she confronts is the American Bar Association's rule that no one can take more than five years to finish law school. Since a law degree requires three years of full-time study, this policy makes it almost impossible to pursue a degree as a part-time student. The law student who does not yet have children may therefore decide to postpone motherhood until she has her J.D. Then, if she becomes a law clerk, an assistant district attorney, or an associate in a law firm, she will find that she is expected to work as much as double the standard forty-hour week. The harder she works, the greater her supposed chances of becoming a partner in her firm or making equivalent advances up the ladder in other jobs. Conversely, the greater her personal responsibilities, the more her advancement is compromised.

Why not postpone motherhood until one is established in one's career? Since fertility declines with age, this choice can jeopardize a woman's chances of bearing children. The majority of women who wait until their thirties to become pregnant do succeed in doing so without drastic medical intervention, but the risk is still present. A woman with an established position confronts problems, too; if she is a partner in a law firm, she may well supervise more people and therefore be less able to cut down on her work responsibilities. Representative Pat Schroeder, who has often said that there is *no* good time for a working woman to have a baby, seems to know what she is talking about. Schroeder herself raised some eyebrows when she entered Congress as the mother of two preschool children.

Law firms and giant corporations have begun to make some efforts to cope with these problems. A controversy has erupted over the phenomenon called the "mommy track," which allows women professionals to choose to cut back on their hours (and their rewards) in order to spend time with their families. Felice Schwartz, the president of Catalyst, a group devoted to advancing working women's interests, recently wrote an article in the *Harvard Business Review* in which she recommends that corporations gear their personnel policies to two types of women, the "career primary" employee who should be treated like a male professional, and the "career and family" woman who will accept less pay and advancement in return for flexibility.

The controversy over this proposal stems from the fact that it implies that women must compromise their interests in order to accommodate the interests of families and employers. What appears to be a choice of career patterns is a coercively structured choice. A woman is not free to insist that her husband share in child care, or to demand concessions from her employer. Of the three separate groups involved—institutions, families, and women—only women are expected to make concessions. The "mommy track" solution accepts as "givens" both the failure of husbands and fathers to share family responsibilities and the right of institutions to shape their policies to serve their own needs at the expense of those of all other parties. Indeed, the proposal encourages employers to find ways to exploit female talent on their own terms. Pat Schroeder put it this way: "It's tragic, because it reinforces the idea, which is so strong in our country, that you can either have a family or a career, but not both, if you're a woman. Of course, the business people love it because it's what they don't feel free to say, and here's a woman saying it for them."[56]

Not only do women lawyers, like all working women, suffer pressures which men are spared, but they are told that it is their responsibility, and no one else's, to deal with this problem. Men and institutions get off the hook. Thirty years from now, women may hold 40 percent of the partnerships, judgeships, and law professorships in this country; one quarter, maybe even more, of the members of Congress may be woman lawyers. But as long as present family patterns persist, it is unlikely that women will have the same freedom to combine public and private lives that men do.

Will the entry of large numbers of women change the legal profession? No definite answer to that question is possible. Women lawyers and jurists do not all agree on all issues. For example, the federal district judge who struck down the Indianapolis antipornography ordinance is a woman. "Feminist jurisprudence" is a growing scholarly subfield; the references at the end of Chapter 8 attest to this academic development. A growing number of woman legal scholars argue that our present legal system is sexist in ways that go beyond overtly male supremacist laws; that even if all laws were gender-neutral, the system would still reflect male priorities. But here again (see Chapter 8), no consensus exists. Law may change significantly as women enter the profession, but the nature and extent of those changes are impossible to predict.

Conclusion

Law need not overtly discriminate on the basis of sex in order to affect men and women differently. The legal system, like all social institutions, contains a variety of roles and statuses, some complementary with, and some adverse to, one another: victims, offenders, and practitioners are perhaps the most common and the most important of these. All three are, and always have been, significantly different for women than they are for men in American society.

The woman criminal is perhaps the "outlyer" in this discussion. She is different from male offenders, but these differences are not comparable to those affecting victims and lawyers. The great change in women's crime since the New Deal is that there is a great deal more of it. However, then and now, far fewer women committed far fewer crimes than did men. Then as now, women are far more likely to commit property crimes or prostitution than they are to commit violent crimes, which are still a virtual male preserve. And, then as now, women commit specific kinds of property crimes, notably larceny and check forgery. The "new women's crimes" tend to be offenses like credit card fraud and drug dealing. They result more from changes in society than from changes in women. Credit cards were rare in the 1930s, and illegal drug use less widespread.

Generally, women commit property crimes for the same reasons that men do: they need or want more money than they can earn by legal means. But women are still more law-abiding than men, despite the fact that they often have much less money. If, as Lenore Weitzman says, women have become the "new poor," they have not become the "new criminals" in as large numbers.[57]

As far as victims and lawyers are concerned, the 1930s had already brought welcome moderations of the old sexist rules. Once, for example, rape was a crime committed not against a woman but against the man who had sexual rights to her. By the 1930s, that was no longer true. But a "chaste" victim was still more likely to be believed than a sexually active one, and most victims were not believed at all. Women were expected to protect themselves against violent men; rape prevention became the victim's responsibility. Rape was trivialized; people made jokes about it. Only when black men were accused of raping white women did the criminal justice system bring its full force to bear on the accused. Rape was primarily a means of maintaining male supremacy, and secondarily of reinforcing white supremacy.

In the nineteenth century, when husband and wife were one, men could beat their wives to make them obey. That legal rule did not survive into the present century. But until very recently, the law dismissed and trivialized domestic violence much as it did rape. Battered wives and molested girls were told either that they had made the whole thing up, or that it was all their fault. The "rule of thumb" which dictated the size of the weapon a man could use in disciplining his wife had vanished from the law books. Men hardly needed it; they could get away with much more. They need not realistically fear punishment unless they killed their wives.

The *Bradwell* ruling was a dead letter by the 1930s, without ever having actually been overruled. Women could practice law— although law schools were free to deny them admission. Those few women who gained admission to the bar could not compete for work on an equal basis with men. Often, they could find work only as law librarians or legal secretaries. When they did actually practice, they might be hidden away in the recesses of law firms, where they could not offend customers. Until the 1980s, a woman trial lawyer, actually appearing in court, was a relatively rare phenomenon. A woman judge was even rarer.

It would hardly be accurate to assert that the glory days of equality have arrived in the 1990s. Unfair gender differences persist. But only part of those differences are due, any longer, to the explicit sex, and "sex plus," discrimination which once pervaded the legal system. Rape, for instance, is now called sexual assault, and no longer requires a female victim and a male perpetrator. Husbands may no longer beat their wives to make them obey. States may no longer exclude women from the practice of law.

All of these aspects of law still bear the effects of this past overt sexism and the indirect, thinly disguised present version. Yet they also show the effects of the contemporary feminist movement. In fact, some of feminism's greatest gains have occurred here. The criminal justice system treats crimes against women and girls far more seriously than was once the case. Police recruits are no longer taught to distrust women's complaints of sexual assault and domestic violence. Men who violently act out the norms of patriarchal power now face a strong possibility of punishment. The police respond to women's calls, suspects are often taken into custody, prosecutors persevere, and sentences, including imprisonment, ensue. A network of support services—the rape crisis center, the child abuse hotline, the battered women's shelter—exists to give women the help they need in dealing with and ending violence in their and their children's lives.

Title IX of the Education Amendments Act of 1972, which forbade sex discrimination in educational programs receiving federal funds, probably did not cause the dramatic increase in the number of women law students, lawyers, and judges that occurred in the next fifteen years. Civil rights law rarely works that directly. But the years since Title IX have seen a steady feminization of the legal profession. The increase with the greatest potential impact on American society is the fact that women now represent 40 percent of law students nationwide. Law students become law clerks, assistant district attorneys, and associates in law firms. Clerks become law professors; assistant district attorneys run for their boss's job, or for the legislature; associates become partners. Law partners and law professors often become judges. Prosecutors may run for the House of Representatives, the Senate, or governor. In 1984, former prosecutor Geraldine Ferraro, a member of the House, ran for vice president. Senators and governors have been known to run for president of the United States.

In Chapter 3, I suggested that the movement of women into the paid labor force deserved one cheer. Perhaps it is fair to say that women's gains in the legal profession deserve two. Women will not enjoy equal opportunity with men as long as they carry the grossly disproportionate share of family responsibilities which now burdens them. Women lawyers are no more likely than women in general to have spouses who share household duties, fathers for their children who assume equal responsibility for child care, brothers who assume equal responsibility for aging parents. Neither are women prisoners—a fact that makes their lives as burdensome and difficult as it does those of professionals who choose a more orthodox law-related career. The special problems of women victims seem, historically, to stem from their sexual and family functions; so much crime against women has been either their sexual violation or injury inflicted by family members and sexual partners. In all these roles, patriarchy has put women in their place. But feminism, education, and social change are rapidly allowing women to claim their own places within the legal system.

REFERENCES

Barry, Kathleen. *Female Sexual Slavery*. New York: New York University Press, 1984. A cross-national study.

Brownmiller, Susan. *Against Our Will: Men, Women, and Rape*. New York: Simon & Schuster, 1975. A book whose importance is difficult to overemphasize. Its extensive documentation makes it a useful source of references as well as a landmark theoretical contribution.

Epstein, Cynthia Fuchs. *Women in Law*. New York: Basic Books, 1981. An excellent, though increasingly dated, study of women lawyers in the United States.

Gelles, Richard J., and **Murray A. Straus.** *Intimate Violence*. New York: Simon & Schuster, 1988. This is the most recent of many valuable studies on its topic; a particularly interesting feature is its criticism of early studies and the public reaction to them. May provoke disagreement.

Rush, Florence. *The Best Kept Secret: Sexual Abuse of Children*. New York: McGraw-Hill, 1980. An analysis of this "dirty little secret" in Western culture, as it has surfaced in history and literature.

Russell, Diana E. H. *The Secret Trauma: Incest in the Lives of Girls and Women*. New York: Basic Books, 1986. A study of the incidence of incest in the United States; notable for both its data and its theory.

SchWeber, Claudine, and **Clarice Feinman,** eds. *Criminal Justice Politics and Women: The Aftermath of Legally Mandated Change*. New York: Haworth Press, 1985. Originally a 1984 issue of *Women and Politics*, this volume focuses on rape law, domestic violence, and prostitution.

8

Conclusion: From Patriarchy toward Equality

American society is, and always has been, patriarchal. Men dominate women and children. Legal and social changes in the past 150 years have made society less male supremacist than it once was. Women can now vote and own property. A small proportion of women have access to the kinds of power and resources—education, the professions, even public office—once reserved for a small proportion of men. These changes are important gains. But it is still true that, in Adrienne Rich's words, "I live under the power of the fathers, and I have access only to so much of privilege or influence as the patriarchy is willing to accede to me, and only for so long as I will pay the price for male approval."[1]

It is not true that all men have power over all women, or that no woman has any power over any man. Nor is it true that no women have power over other women, or that patriarchy affects all women's lives in the same ways and to the same degree. Women are not *equally* oppressed. Male supremacy is not the only asymmetrical relationship in this society. Race and class are powerful forces; their effect combines with that of gender to shape society. But Rich's statement is an accurate description of a general reality. Her "I" refers to a lesbian feminist poet and essayist whose freedom to live with her lover depends on the tolerance of the male-dominated state, and whose ability to reach an audience depends on male-controlled corporations. The statement is true as well for the schoolgirl and her teacher, the law student and her professor, the nurse and the physician, the thirty-year-old single mother and her eighty-year-old grandmother, the woman who cleans the suburban mansion and the executive's wife who lives there.

Power and Patriarchy: A Recapitulation

This book has examined various aspects of patriarchy, the ways in which it works in this particular society. One common feature of all societies is the assignment of roles to particular people. Role assignment helps to explain how American patriarchy has maintained itself. Our society has hardly been unique in assigning women the domestic role: wife, mother, caregiver, homemaker. *Bradwell v. Illinois*, *Muller v. Oregon*, and *Hoyt v. Florida* represent almost a century of judicial endorsement of this role as women's universal and primary responsibility, around which all other possible female roles must be fitted.

While these duties have been women's work, they were never, and are not now, women's only duties. The anti-suffrage slogan, "Woman's place is in the home," applied only to rich and middle-class women. It would be more accurate, though, to describe these women as being members of rich or middle-class families; it makes little sense to label as "rich" a married woman who had no control over property. Before World War II, such women did get to concentrate on domestic duties, which were far more burdensome then than they are now (see Chapter 3). But slave women, farm women, immigrant women, and women with no male relatives to support them had to work outside the home as well as within it.

Now, most middle-class women are in the paid labor force, too. None of the laws upheld in *Bradwell*, *Muller*, and *Hoyt* is binding today. Women practice law, work long hours (and get overtime), and get jury duty. Economic responsibility for the family, and political responsibility in the community, is shared by men and women. But the domestic role still belongs to women. In fact, studies cited earlier in the book suggest that it would not be much of an exaggeration to describe domestic responsibilities as being women's alone. What work women do not do, they are usually responsible for getting done.[2]

Society's assignment of women to the domestic sphere has included various forms of punishment for women who reject some of its aspects. Spinsters, lesbians, unmarried women who live with their male lovers, and women who do not become mothers suffer social disapproval for their rejection of the wife-mother role. To some extent, these penalties also affect men who do not conform to convention. As Chapter 7 showed, any political candidate without a nuclear family is vulnerable to personal attack. People whose most intimate ties are outside kinship or marriage are routinely denied sharing privileges, such as insurance benefits and inheritance rights, granted to members of nuclear families.

People who adopt the "unconventional" lifestyles which, together, now involve almost half the population may even face direct or indirect legal coercion. The experiences of Sharon Kowalski and Karen Thompson, and of the residents of Chicago's Rockwell Gardens, provide dramatic examples of these sanctions (see Chapter 4). Divorced women, whether they have rejected marriage or been ejected from it, are vulnerable to severe financial deprivation as well as to intangible penalties.

Society's entrenched disapproval of women who do not form nuclear families is not matched by rewards for women who do. Rhetoric like Justice Bradley's 1872 reference to "the noble and benign offices of wife and mother" has been common, but society has failed to back up that rhetoric with tangible privileges and benefits. Chapters 2 and 4 gave examples of such rewards—some plausible but imaginary, some in force in comparable countries—which do not exist in the United States.

Worse still, American law has actually penalized women for becoming wives and mothers. Wives' loss of property rights in the 1800s, mandatory unpaid maternity leaves until the 1970s, and the exclusion of pregnancy-related conditions from insurance coverage are policies which are thankfully obsolete. But restrictions on the work opportunities of women of childbearing age are part of present reality, while the use of the criminal law to punish pregnant women who incur medical displeasure is an ominous portent.

American law and society have assigned women to a role and proceeded to devalue the role. Women have been denigrated both outside the domestic role and within it. This role assignment does not suffice to explain every aspect of women's legal status, but it goes a long way toward accomplishing that feat. The relegation of women to the domestic sphere is thus a constant of this particular patriarchy, an organizing principle, a central theme. The details of that role assignment, the consequences that follow from it, have changed and continue to change. This society continues to link male supremacy with female domesticity, as it always has. But society is not patriarchal to the same extent, or in the same ways, as it was in 1789, when the federal government began; or in 1865, when the Civil War ended; or in 1920, when the Nineteenth Amendment was ratified; or even ten years ago. An essential task of this last chapter is to assess and analyze those changes.

From Patriarchy toward Equality

That women's legal status has changed for the better in the two centuries that this government has existed is beyond serious dispute. Suppose we look back at the 1930s, the approximate starting point for this book. Six decades ago, sexual discrimination in employment was official governmental policy. Not that much overt discrimination was necessary; few women could obtain education beyond secondary school. Marriage was an asymmetrical relationship favoring the husband. Women had no control over their fertility or protection from male violence.

Civil rights laws, court decisions, and feminist persistence have changed all these situations. Laws now protect women from employment and educational discrimination; the latter are generally enforced, the former at least part of the time. Supreme Court decisions have removed traditional sex-role assumptions as a permissible basis for family law. Contraception is available to most women, and abortion, at least for now, to many. Rape and domestic violence, once dirty little secrets, are matters of serious public concern. Women are becoming lawyers in ever increasing numbers; as potential lawmakers and judges, they will have a shot at real power.

Neither the failure of the Equal Rights Amendment to win ratification nor the "Reagan Revolution" of the 1980s provided an occasion for regression and retreat. But some changes in the law have been retrograde. The real Reagan Revolution may belong to the 1990s, in the form of the entrenched conservative majority which has emerged on the Supreme Court. Its hostility to civil rights law is evident, and its existence imperils the right to reproductive choice. The so-called divorce reforms of the last twenty years, combined with the soaring divorce rate, have worsened the situation of women; parallel developments in child custody have aggravated the coercion and impoverishment that women face as their marriages end. The increasing tendency to use the criminal law to punish pregnant women for alcohol and drug use, and employers' restriction of women's work opportunities to protect real or potential fetuses, also constitute legal threats to women (see Chapters 3 and 5). Still, the record is more positive than negative.

So much for law. What about facts? Some of the positive changes in the law have led to real improvements in women's situation. Recognition of the legal right to control fertility has meant that the exhausted invalids described by Catharine Beecher and Margaret Sanger have been replaced by women who remain healthy and energetic into their old age. Antidiscrimination laws have given more women access to education and good jobs. The benefits of laws banning sex discrimination have by no means been limited to white middle-class women. As Leah Rosenfeld and Lorena Weeks discovered, Title VII opened up the better blue-collar jobs to women. Lillian Garland, who is black, is one of many minority women in traditionally female jobs who benefited from new state laws. Title IX has helped to provide a degree of class mobility for a few women that was once reserved for a few men and these men's families: for example, the route through the public university and the night law school to a job on the lower rungs of the "stratified bar."[3]

But these improvements have not brought about equality with men in either employment or family life. Although the burdens of motherhood have been lightened, women continue to bear far greater burdens of family life, housework, and personal care than men do. Most women who are employed still work in the badly paid, badly rewarded traditional female jobs. Women simply have less money, less leisure, and less power than the men in their lives do. The lawbooks say that men and women are equal. Reality says otherwise.

We cannot even say unambiguously that women's actual lives have *generally* improved in this century. Women are no less likely to be poor—destitute, undernourished, and even homeless—than at any time since the Great Depression ended; and women and their children constitute a larger proportion of the poor than at any other time in our history. Since a greater proportion of Americans are poor in the 1990s than were poor in the 1970s, we know that poverty among women has increased in the last twenty years. Fifty years ago, a large group of white middle-class married women had one primary job: homemaking. These women had no reliable income of their own; their labor was arduous, tedious, and unappreciated; and they were unequal partners in their marriages. But their duties to home and family were the extent of their responsibilities, and they could usually count on their marriages lasting.

Today, the descendants of these women have similar domestic duties. In addition, most of them have paying jobs, usually in the female job ghetto. Middle-class American women typically have two full-time jobs, one of which pays badly and the other not at all. These women are far more likely than their mothers were to be raising their children alone. If their husbands have not already left, taking their greater earnings and sometimes even the children with them, the possibility is always present. Has woman's lot improved, gotten worse, or stayed the same? The observer has a sense of déjà vu, a suspicion that women are still doing what it is in men's interests for them to do.

The Future of Sexual Equality

All of the positive and negative developments described in the foregoing paragraphs may affect the future. The laws already on the books, and a presidential administration apparently less hostile to these laws than its predecessor, will stimulate further improvements for women. The Family Support Act of 1988 promises improvement in an area of law now particularly oppressive to women: divorce settlements. States will soon be required to put some system and regularity into their child support awards. Mothers whose ex-partners renege on payments will soon be able to get the men's wages garnisheed. The passage of this law is welcome, but feminists should not become overoptimistic. Several federal laws enacted in the past fifteen years have not succeeded in making fathers pay. To the extent that states have been able to collect money from delinquent fathers for welfare families, several have paid themselves back first, not the mother. The promise is there, but ensuring that the promise is kept will take hard work and persistent pressure.

Congressional commitment to equality, the strength of the pro-choice movement, and the increase in the number of women who are entering the legal profession are encouraging trends. The last development is particularly auspicious, because it brings the likelihood that, in a generation or two, women will be sharing in the making and enforcing of rules. It is hard to predict, now, what such a change will mean for public policy and private reality. For example, will men and women share domestic responsibilities equally? Or will these duties still belong to women, but bring tangible rewards and helpful concessions? Feminists do not agree on which change would be preferable, but they do agree that the present sexual division of responsibilities and rewards is intolerable.[4] A society in which women and men share power and influence can begin making these choices in the interests of both sexes.

That great day is a long way from realization, and several ominous trends bring the possibility of retreat. Any present or future civil rights laws will be construed by a Supreme Court far from friendly to them. Any new laws overturning court decisions face hard going in the presence of a stalemate between a Republican president and Democratic Congress. The new Court majority may even pose a threat to the quiet revolution which culminated in *Kirchberg v. Feenstra* in 1981; traditional sex roles could reemerge as an acceptable justification for public policy. (One member of the new majority, Justice O'Connor, has not shown much commitment to these traditional roles, but she has shown a commitment to federalism; state sovereignty ranks high among her priorities.)

Women's experience with no-fault divorce provides ample reason to be pessimistic about the effects of any legal change. "Revolution" is no exaggeration in describing the revision which the divorce laws of every state have undergone in the last twenty years, but "counterrevolution" would be more accurate. On the statute books, these laws *look* gender-neutral. They permit courts to consider a long list of factors in making property settlements, including factors which would tend to favor wives: for example, the contributions of each partner to home maintenance, child care, and the other partner's education, advancement, and well-being. But as applied to actual families, no-fault divorce laws have enriched men at the expense of women and children. Something other than the letter of the law determined results, and skewed those results in favor of men.[5]

Another reason for general pessimism is the omnipresent phenomenon of feminist bashing. Whatever feminists do, they can expect public criticism, much of it inaccurate. This kind of criticism is not new. Feminist bashing has become a popular pastime, especially for the mass media. The phenomenon is important enough, and destructive enough, to require lengthy discussion.

Feminist Bashing: Its Causes and Effects

A typical instance of full-scale feminist bashing occurred in the summer of 1989. You may recall reading or hearing about "NOW and the new political party." In July, the National Organization for Women held its annual national conference in Cincinnati, Ohio. As you might expect, the recent Supreme Court decision in *Reproductive Health Services v. Webster* dominated the agenda. But the delegates did not neglect other matters. Among these was a resolution, passed by unanimous vote, directing the organization to investigate the feasibility of forming a new political party which would address the issues of women's rights, racism, homophobia, peace, and the environment.

This resolution garnered immense media coverage, nearly all of it unfavorable. An endless number of newspaper stories, editorials, columns, magazine articles, and television "news bites" characterized this idea as the stupidest one anybody had heard in a long time. Soon the word "strident," a favorite pejorative adjective used to modify "feminist," entered the descriptions. Some journalists even went so far as to suggest that NOW president Molly Yard was a "mole" (undercover agent) for the Republicans.

Most college students learn in courses in American government that the influence of single-issue splinter parties in American national politics has been negligible. Typical explanations of this phenomenon emphasize the structural features of government and elections which reinforce the two-party system, like single-member congressional districts and the "winner-take-all" Electoral College. These explanations are part of the conventional wisdom of American politics. The media repeated these insights, ad nauseam, after the NOW convention. For any interest group to form a third party, while not necessarily "strident," would certainly seem suicidal. Had NOW lost its collective mind?

No. The resolution referred to not one, but five issues. A new political party need not be a splinter party. It could be a third party, based on a broad coalition of different groups, which might eventually displace one of the two present dominant parties, presumably the Democrats. This kind of political realignment has occurred in two-party systems. In Great Britain, for example, the Labour Party displaced the old Liberal Party early in this century; now, the New Democratic Party is trying to do the same to Labour. Some leftist groups here in the United States have formed the Democratic Socialists of America (DSA), which has similar long-range ambitions. For a feminist group to spearhead such efforts is not a foolish idea at all.

Many political scientists would dispute the notion that the current party system is amenable to displacement. After all, the Democrats and Republicans have been the major parties in the United States since the Civil War. Is it realistic to work for realignment? Maybe not. Since all NOW has done is to agree to study the possibility of forming a new party, the group will be able to assess the project's chances of success when this study is complete. What is stupid, strident, or self-destructive about any of that? Nothing. But, once again, the media made feminists look silly. Such a negative portrait shapes popular perceptions. It feeds the backlash that is an inevitable reaction to any movement; and, as the emergence of a an Islamic theocracy in Iran in the late 1970s showed, antifeminist backlash can be potent. It makes it difficult for groups like NOW to attract new members—is it coincidence that all this negative publicity occurred just when large numbers of people were joining NOW in response to *Webster*?— and to get public officials to listen to feminist demands. Perhaps worst of all, this kind of negative publicity threatens to undermine feminists' collective self-confidence and to deflect them from their mission to attack sexist institutions and to fight for essential changes.

Feminist bashing has a long history. Its use during the ERA ratification campaign, discussed in Chapter 2, was by no means its first appearance. Ridicule was a favorite weapon of the opponents of women's suffrage. They applied the epithet "she-males" to feminists of both sexes. A Boston newspaper published a piece of doggerel praising the man who "with a wedding kiss shuts up the mouth of Lucy Stone."[6] The prediction erred; Stone's marriage to Henry Blackwell was a loving, egalitarian relationship. Her refusal to take his last name brought the term "Lucy Stoner" into the vernacular. A "Lucy Stoner" was a wife who retained her last name. The practice so described is now common; the term has long since become obsolete. The second wave of feminists were called such names as "women's libbers," "loud uglies," and "bra burners." That last epithet resulted from a (probably intentional) misinterpretation of a specific event. A feminist counter-demonstration at the 1968 Miss America Pageant featured "freedom trash cans" into which women were encouraged to throw uncomfortable items of clothing like girdles and brassieres. None of these items was burned. This episode led to talk about "bra burning," a term which, unfortunately, entered the national vocabulary. The ridicule and trivialization which this term exemplifies make the "feminist political party" flap appear mild by comparison.

The militant "suffragette," the ill-dressed "women's libber," and the strident NOW member are stock figures in the anti-feminist repertoire of negative stereotypes. They join several similar personifications the reader has already encountered: the vindictive ex-wife living on her former husband's earnings; the rich, stupid widow; the selfish careerist who serves her own interests to the detriment of women leading more traditional lives.

Another aspect of feminist bashing is the application of different standards to women activists than those applied to others. Chapter 6 presented one example of this phenomenon: the criticism levied at NOW, but not at Senator Danforth, for linking reproductive choice to civil rights. This double standard also reveals itself in the commonly voiced expectation that women officeholders should exhibit kinder, gentler behavior than their male counterparts; consider the frequent criticisms of former British prime minister Margaret Thatcher for doing anything but. This phenomenon makes it difficult even for feminists themselves to remember that women's right to vie for positions of power depends, not on any claim that they are different from men, but solely on the principle of sexual equality.

The coverage of the Miss America protest of 1968 and NOW's political party resolution in 1989 illustrate a familiar process through which feminism has been discredited. In each case, the media made errors of fact or interpretation. In Atlantic City, a trash can became a bonfire; in Cincinnati, studying the prospects for third-party success became the founding of a single-issue party. Then, having spotlighted an attention-getting feature of the event, the stories emphasized that part of the activity which seemed flamboyant, eccentric, or strange. Finally, the familiar adjectives used to criticize feminists (and, on occasion, other political movements) were dragged out. We have already encountered the word "strident"; "shrill" and "extreme" are other favorite labels. Readers and viewers could hardly avoid the impression that feminist activists had made major errors.

Had they? After the 1968 protest, a critical article appeared in the feminist press. The author argued that the demonstration had been a "zap action," undisciplined, and unorganized, She described both its rhetoric and tactics as "anti-woman." Maybe they were; twenty years later, it is hard to judge. The action destroyed neither the Miss America Pageant nor the feminist movement. Certainly, the long-run cost of the "freedom trash cans," in popular perceptions of the women's movement, outweighed the gains, although few could have foreseen that result at the time.[7]

Even if this action was a mistake, so what? All activists make mistakes on their way to achieving their goals. All protest movements need some "guerrilla theater" to maintain the participants' energy, enthusiasm, and solidarity. And activists know that negative publicity is better than no publicity. "First you have to get their attention" is an old movement rule. These benefits must be weighed against the damage which may result if the media blows the drama out of proportion. If the calculations were defective at the Miss America protest, the appropriate feminist response was to learn from that mistake and move on. But it is difficult for any movement to do that when the negative publicity continues indefinitely. The media bore at least as much responsibility for that publicity as the demonstrators did. If the media had not seized upon "bra burning," it is likely that they would have found something else to misrepresent and ridicule.

To return to the present instance, investigating the formation of a new political party does not look like a mistake at all. But, because of the way the media presented this resolution to the public, the wisdom of NOW's actions hardly matters. Should the organization have anticipated the derisive reaction to its proposal? Since the DSA had done the same thing without attracting that kind of publicity, it is difficult to see how NOW could have predicted the reaction. Exercising that degree of caution could paralyze any group. Feminists will have to take those actions which seem correct and productive to them, putting up with the negative publicity along the way. Readers of this book should learn to treat media coverage of feminist activities with skepticism.

Why has feminist bashing happened? Feminists are far from being the only group to suffer from media errors or emphasis on the dramatic. The ubiquitous mistakes result not only from carelessness but also from the pressure to meet deadlines and the need to fit information into available air time and print space. To condense is inevitably to distort. Slanted news stories are a near-universal phenomenon, although not all are slanted in the same direction. Coverage of the Vietnam War, for example, shifted from favorable to unfavorable during that long conflict. Not all coverage of the women's movement has, by any means, been negative; indeed, the critique of the Miss America protest referred to several favorable stories in mass-circulation publications. But the themes of factual errors, misleading emphases, trivialization, and ridicule are so consistent and persistent that they demand at least an attempt at explanation.

Here is my attempt, offered in the hope that it will stimulate reaction, thought, and even criticism among the readers of this book. Sexual equality per se is hard to oppose. The speaker who insists that women are inferior to men, or that woman's place is in the home, will not be taken seriously. It is even difficult to oppose some of feminism's concrete goals, like equal pay, divorce equity, and an end to domestic violence. But sexual equality is a threat to the status quo. An equal distribution of burdens and benefits, privileges and responsibilities, may well be to men's ultimate advantage; some feminists have argued that equality would be conducive to men's "happiness" in the classical sense of that word. In the short run, however, sexual equality will deprive men, and some women, of tangible benefits. For example, men would lose their privileged and advantaged access to money, power, education, meaningful work, and leisure; their relative, if not absolute, freedom from domestic duties; and their license to abandon family obligations. The media, the government, and the "private" sector of business are controlled by men; the proportionately few women who exercise power and influence within these institutions work for and are accountable to men. Should the fact that feminism has met with biased treatment surprise us?

Whatever the causes of feminist bashing, negative publicity has unfortunate effects, both on the public and on feminists themselves. Some people, including voters and public officials, believe the bad press. Because the negative images are widely accepted, feminists have been forced to explain that, no, they do not burn lingerie, hate men, reject the family, or embrace the politics of sulky, cut-off-your-nose-to-spite-your-face isolation. Making these explanations deflects time and energy which could be better spent on efforts to realize the goals that gave rise to feminism in the first place. For example, feminists were the targets of common charges of antimale and antifamily sentiment in the early 1970s, about the same time that the new divorce and child custody laws began to have devastating effects on women. Accurately aimed criticisms at specific instances of male behavior would almost certainly have been interpreted as still more examples of shrill, man-hating diatribes. But enough of these feminist criticisms—soon enough, loud enough, and long enough—might have attracted attention. They might have led the media to discover the "feminization of poverty" in much less time than this process of discovery took.

Like all activists, feminists have to grow a thick skin in order to realize that public responses to their actions often have more to do with the audience's perceptions than with any fault of the actions themselves. Nobody likes to be ridiculed; the danger is always present that anticipation of such reactions will stifle the expression of legitimate grievances. The popularity of statements beginning, "I am not a feminist, but . . ." indicates that even people who may endorse feminist goals hesitate to associate themselves with a movement that has been so discredited. Feminist bashing will be with us for the foreseeable future. The phenomenon will continue to retard progress and frustrate the realization of sexual equality. The antifeminist backlash which this treatment encourages will remain a threat to feminist goals. Worse, backlash may lead to a retreat to patriarchal practices.

What does the future hold? One way to assess prospects is to examine visions of the future. Fiction is a valuable source of such visions. Novelists are not bound by the conventions of scholarship; they are freer than social scientists are to publish their fantasies. The contemporary feminist movement has affected novelists as powerfully as it has affected scholars, encouraging the development of a literary genre of woman-centered futuristic fiction. Two recent novels, in particular, have much to teach us.

Utopian and Dystopian Visions

Utopian fiction is a venerable literary tradition. It dates from

Saint Thomas More's *Utopia*, published in 1535, which depicted the author's vision of an ideal society. The opposite possibility is sometimes called a dystopia. George Orwell's *1984* and Aldous Huxley's *Brave New World* are famous English-language examples of this genre. Contemporary feminist novelists have produced both utopian and dystopian works. Two of these present diametrically opposed visions of the future.

Marge Piercy's *Woman on the Edge of Time* appeared in 1976. Piercy's utopia, Mattapoisett, is located on Massachusetts' Cape Cod in 2137. Mattapoisett is an "autonomous region," a small self-governing community. Public officials are chosen by lot for one-year terms. Men and women are equal. Language is gender-neutral. Children select their own names when they become adults, at twelve. No disapproval attaches to any form of consensual sexual activity, or to celibacy, and human reproduction has no connection with sexual activity.[8]

Margaret Atwood creates a harshly different society in *The Handmaid's Tale*. The setting is what used to be Cambridge, Massachusetts, on the former Harvard University campus, probably in the twenty-first century. As the result of a fundamentalist takeover, the United States has become the Republic of Gilead, a theocracy governed by the principles of the Old Testament. The narrator is a woman of the "transitional generation." She once had a family, a career, and a name. Now, her only name is Offred, derived from the name of the official whose "handmaid" she has become; she lives with Fred and his wife and must bear Fred's child, or face exile to carcinogenic toxic waste dumps. If she fails to produce a healthy child, a new Offred will take her place. The state has dissolved Offred's family, probably murdering her husband and allowing a childless family to adopt her daughter. Because infertility is endemic, there are many prospective adoptive families. In Gilead, as in the Bible, women alone are responsible for infertility. Fred's wife has not become pregnant. Therefore, he is assigned a handmaid to impregnate, as Jacob impregnated Bilhah, Rachel's maid.[9]

In Mattapoisett, women no longer bear children. Embryos gestate in a laboratory. Many of you will recognize this technology from Huxley's dystopian vision; the parallel is deliberate. The Mattapoisans chose this method of reproduction. One character explains:

> It was part of women's long revolution. When we were breaking all the old hierarchies. Finally there was that one thing we had to give

up too, the only power we ever had, in return for no more power for anyone. The original production: the power to give birth. Cause as long as we were biologically enchained, we'd never be equal. And males never would be humanized to be loving and tender. So we all became mothers. Every child has three. To break the nuclear bonding.[10]

In Gilead, by contrast, women may no longer live independently, work for money, or even read. A woman's marital history and reproductive potential determine which of several available subordinate social positions she will have. The government declared Offred's marriage invalid because her husband had been married before; since there is no divorce, second marriages are adulterous unions. She becomes a handmaid because she has borne a child, thus demonstrating her fertility. Virgins, once sexually mature, become wives, assigned to husbands of their own social class. Sexually active women without children, postmenopausal women, and women otherwise physically or socially unsuitable for motherhood face several undesirable alternatives: the toxic waste dumps, life as "Marthas" (household servants) or "aunts" (supervisors of younger women), or the "underworld" of prostitution.

Woman on the Edge of Time and *The Handmaid's Tale* combine to teach two valuable lessons for students of women and the law. First, the past and present contain the seeds of both progression and regression. Patriarchy is fragile and tenuous, but so are feminist gains. Second, women's position in society is linked to their reproductive function and domestic role. Both Piercy's dream and Atwood's nightmare disturb and haunt the reader, partly because neither fictional society is beyond the realm of possibility.

Atwood's Gilead seems all too real. Something similar, a popular revolt which destroyed the tentative gains women had made, happened in Iran in 1979. The other change which made Offred into a handmaid was the rising infertility rate. Chapter 5 showed that infertility has been increasing in Western industrial societies over the past few decades. Suppose the incidence of infertility became high enough to endanger the nation's survival? Atwood posits sexually transmitted diseases, toxic chemicals, and nuclear accidents—all present possibilities, if not realities—as the causes of the crisis in Gilead. Chapters 3 and 5 discussed the growing public sentiment in favor of coercing pregnant women, or even any woman of childbearing age, to protect fetuses from exposure to harmful substances. What effects might these policies eventually have on women's status?

Life in Piercy's Mattapoisett in the twenty-second century has many appealing features. However, the connection Piercy makes between sexual equality and methods of reproduction is not necessarily among them. Mattapoisan reproductive biology is no less grounded in reality than is Gileadean reproductive theology. Our society has the technological capacity, at the present time, to fertilize ova and gestate human beings outside of women's bodies. The former process, *in vitro* fertilization, is already used in cases where sexual intercourse and artificial insemination have failed to produce pregnancy. But I think I can safely predict that no culture, anywhere in the world, is likely to substitute this new method of reproduction for the current one on a large scale any time soon. The fact that the common term for a human being conceived by *in vitro* fertilization is "test-tube baby" illustrates the fact that Huxley's vision has shaped our perceptions far more strongly than Piercy's has.[11]

The prospect of a world in which women no longer bear children troubles most people, including most feminists. It certainly troubles me. Anyone who has grown to adulthood in this country is aware of the extent to which childbearing and motherhood are sentimentalized and overpraised. We have all had more than one occasion to observe the negative side: not only the distressing physical aspects of pregnancy and childbirth, but the difficulties of life with small children that nobody tells you about. Some readers, presumably, have experienced them. But we have observed or experienced the positive side, too; the joys and rewards of motherhood are manifest. Few of us, observers or participants, would choose the word "power" to describe what women would lose if they no longer bore children. Would sexual equality demand giving up childbearing? If your reaction is "I hope not," you are not alone.[12]

But the unwelcome thought nags: the Mattapoisans might, just possibly, be right. Does childbirth "biologically enchain" women: not only women like Sadie Sachs, who had no control over her fertility, but all women, everywhere and forever? We know there is a link between childbirth and child care—women are responsible for both—but that link is as much a product of social convention as of biology. Which is more powerful? Could a society like our own so reshape convention that the biology of childbirth would not enchain women? Or would such change require a degree of equality between men and women that is impossible as long as only women bear children? The difficulty is that no one really knows the answers to these questions.

Back here in the late twentieth century, however, we might wonder whether men really think childbearing is quite as marvelous as the mass-communications industries they control keep telling us it is. Institutions controlled by men have not evinced any enthusiasm for the kind of medical research that might enable men to try motherhood themselves; as a male priority, childbirth ranks way behind space travel and germ warfare. Why? Well, one phenomenon the reader has had frequent occasion to observe throughout this book is the use of women's childbearing function as a rationale for denying them other opportunities and subjecting them to restrictions not imposed upon men. Atwood's Gilead is an extreme example of this phenomenon. Whether or not childbearing is ultimately compatible with sexual equality, women's reproductive role has certainly served a useful purpose in defenses of male supremacy. That connection is all too easy to perceive.

The details of that connection, the elements that constitute chains in the link, vary with particular circumstances. It has been a long time since women were told they could not practice law because they bore children. Although new restrictions based on women's childbearing capacity have appeared in recent years, I think it is accurate to say that such restrictions continue with diminishing intensity. But denying women freedom is not the only way in which patriarchy exerts power over them. Women's reproductive function has also served as a rationale for assigning them the domestic duties we have discussed throughout the book. And this situation is not changing. Women's domestic role is not becoming obsolete.

All the sociological studies and media accounts paint the same picture. A typical family has two parents, both holding full-time paying jobs, and one or more children young enough to require care and supervision. The class, race, income, and education of the parents make no difference to the scene. Both parents return home from a full day of work. The husband enjoys a few hours of leisure before bedtime. The wife prepares and serves dinner, cleans up, gets the children to bed, and may do a load of laundry or pack lunches before her workday is over. An alternative script finds the husband doing one or more of these chores—under the wife's direction, and with her prodding.

Women may now become lawyers and road dispatchers, but they still bear disproportionate, if not exclusive, responsibility for the home and the family. How did things get to be this way? The physical differences between the sexes do not explain, let alone justify, this common situation. The division of labor described in the last paragraph has nothing to do with pregnancy, childbirth, breast-feeding, or any other function that is unique to women. Chapter 4 showed that many social and economic forces combine to entrench the present division of labor. We must be careful also not to underestimate the force of something as ordinary as habit; things are this way because they have always been this way, both within each family unit and in the larger society.

Still another common explanation requires some attention. Do women, and men, freely choose this state of affairs? Sex roles are so intrinsic to this society that many women may never have questioned them, but we should not confuse uncritical acceptance with conscious choice. Contemporary women are more free than most women once were to choose not to marry or not to become mothers (although, since daughters usually end up providing more care for aging parents than sons do, not even single women without children are free of domestic duties). But women are still deprived relative to men, because women are forced to choose between intimacy and freedom in ways that men are not. The woman who refuses to assume responsibility for the management of the home she shares with a man may be putting a love relationship at risk—and we know what the termination of these relationships can do to a woman's financial situation. A woman with a husband and young children may well discover that she is stuck with what Arlie Hochschild calls the "second shift." Even in a two-parent family, the alternative to a mother-administered home may be child neglect.

Women who become wives and mothers incur duties that men who become husbands and fathers do not share; virtually all women who reject these duties as intolerable must also reject marriage and parenthood, while men need not. Again and again—in discussions of work, marriage, divorce, the "mommy track," the Equal Rights Amendment, ad infinitum—sexual equality collides with the burdens women bear that men escape. Finally, the question has to be faced: is our present division of labor according to sex compatible with equality for women? In general terms, is it fair or just to assign burdens to, or force choices on, members of one group that members of another group are spared? In particular, is it fair to assign extra burdens that carry no tangible rewards whatsoever?

The Problem That Won't Go Away

When the question is phrased in those gender-neutral terms, the only possible answer is no. But the question rarely is phrased in a way which subsumes questions of sex roles into questions about justice. Things have usually worked the other way around: notions of justice are shaped around sex roles.[13] This conclusion, that contemporary sex role assignments represent a pervasive sociopolitical injustice, is difficult to accept. But it is inescapable.

I know of no feminist writer who defends the status quo. Feminists do not agree, however, on exactly what kinds of changes would be desirable. Many feminists, including those who think that motherhood is a value-neutral choice, prefer social arrangements which assign equal domestic responsibilities to men and women. Some important scholarly works published in the 1970s argued that women's responsibility for child care, in particular, had adverse psychological effects on both males and females; like Piercy, these authors concluded that traditional sex roles both "biologically enchained" women and inhibited men from being "loving and tender."[14]

Other feminist scholars have insisted that these roles develop important capacities in women that men might not necessarily be able to share. Most of these authors give either express or implied endorsement to arrangements which would compensate women for domestic duties by reducing their other duties and by providing some tangible rewards, including, but not limited to, financial payment. These feminists appear to share with those mentioned in the above paragraph a rejection of the convention which assigns unrewarded tasks disproportionately to one sex.[15]

"The problem that has no name" was Betty Friedan's term for the effects of the post–World War II housewife image upon the lives of American women.[16] Her description of that archetype now seems outdated, if not quaint, a reference to the world of certain cable television channels rather than to contemporary life. But women's domestic role, in all its ramifications, remains; women's share of those responsibilities has not altered appreciably since the 1960s. Since the contemporary problem of women's double duty has names—Hochschild's "second shift" is one of them—we might call it "the problem that won't go away."

Sex roles are so basic, so pervasive, so entrenched in our society that they can easily seem natural and inevitable. Most of us take them for granted—if, indeed, we notice them at all—until something or someone forces us to take account of them. Scholars often use metaphors to describe social phenomena; you may have heard any or all of the following: "the fabric of our society," "the ties that hold us together," "the house in which we live." Sex roles often seem to be like those things, to be so obvious that they are part of the scenery. It is hard to envision life without the current sexual division of labor or something like it. To be more accurate, such a situation is something we can *only* envision; we have no concrete model for equality. We have to go to fiction, the realm of imagination, to find such a society.

Traditional sex roles are part of our lives; they will not vanish anytime soon. For the foreseeable future, women will have to live with injustice. Feminists can choose between reluctantly accepting this injustice and ceaselessly fighting it. The former choice has the merits of making daily life easier, but it incurs the costs of reinforcing sex roles. The latter choice is a permanent commitment to public and private battle. For the time being, women must either assume a grossly disproportionate share of unrewarded burdens or work to get rid of them.

Sex roles are patriarchy's most powerful weapon. They represent the greatest source of injustice to women. Yet law can do little to change them. Even if legislation is not as "powerless to eradicate" custom as nineteenth-century jurists assumed, the customs and traditions of individual households are not amenable to immediate universal mandated change.[17]

Equality and the Law

The prospects for equalizing the burdens of men and women through legal change are dim. The principle that public policy may not be based on traditional sex role stereotypes was settled by *Kirchberg v. Feenstra* a decade ago, but the law is indeed an ass if it supposes that sex roles are obsolete in the home. Any effect which law can have on these social norms will be indirect, remote, and gradual.

But the resistance of private arrangements to mandated

change does not make law powerless to affect the home. Changes which increase women's work opportunities also increase their share of power within the family; whatever feelings we may have about this appearance of capitalist principles in the home, the fact is that study after study has shown a direct relationship between equality and income.[18] Maternal subsidies of the sort that are routine in European countries would have similar effects on women's resources. The more nearly equal women are with their male partners, the greater their ability to effect a redistribution of duties.

Changes which increase the availability and affordability of child care are means of lightening women's burdens which do not require state intrusion into the family. Changes which make support payments easier for women to collect help increase the autonomy of single mothers By making women's lives less burdensome, all of these changes have the potential to increase every woman's ability to decide what distributions of responsibilities and rewards *she* prefers and to put that preference into effect. All the policies I have mentioned can be brought about by changes in the laws. This book has shown that similar changes can improve women's lives. Law cannot eradicate patriarchy by a stroke of the pen. But changes in the law can lead, slowly but steadily, to changes which allow us to envision sexual equality.

REFERENCES

Baer, Judith A. "Nasty Law or Nice Ladies? Jurisprudence, Feminism, and Gender Difference." *Women and Politics* 11, no. 1 (1991). A critique of feminist theory that emphasizes sex differences.

Chodorow, Nancy. *The Reproduction of Mothering: Psychoanalysis and the Sociology of Gender.* Berkeley: University of California Press, 1978. A psychoanalytic explanation of gender difference and a critique of woman-only child rearing.

Dinnerstein, Dorothy. *The Mermaid and the Minotaur: Sexual Arrangements and Human Malaise.* New York: Harper & Row, 1977. A thesis similar to Chodorow's.

Elshtain, Jean Bethke. *Public Man, Private Woman.* Princeton, N.J.: Princeton University Press, 1981. This analysis of the inherent male bias of both traditional and feminist theory contains critiques of Chodorow and Dinnerstein.

Finley, Lucinda M. "Transcending Equality Theory: A Way Out of the Maternity and the Workplace Debate." *Columbia Law Review* 86

(October 1986): 1118–82. An effort to argue that pregnancy and maternity leaves are compatible with the principle of sexual equality.

Gilligan, Carol. *In a Different Voice: Psychological Theory and Women's Development.* Cambridge, Mass.: Harvard University Press, 1982. A landmark study of women's moral reasoning. One of the most influential books in feminist philosophy, this book has influenced much feminist jurisprudence.

Minow, Martha. " 'Forming Under Everything That Grows': Toward a History of Family Law." *Wisconsin Law Review* 1985, 4: 819–88. An argument that women developed a unique "jurisprudence" in family governance.

Ruddick, Sara. "Maternal Thinking." In Joyce Trebilcot, ed. *Mothering: Essays in Feminist Theory.* Totowa, N.J.: Rowman & Allanheld, 1983. An exploration of the intellectual component of an activity often thought of as more emotional than rational. Like Gilligan's book, a classic of feminist theory.

Scales, Ann. "The Emergence of Feminist Jurisprudence: An Essay." *Yale Law Journal* 95 (June 1986): 1373–1403. An overview of the possibilities of a woman-centered jurisprudence.

Sherry, Suzanna. "Civic Virtue and the Feminine Voice in Constitutional Adjudication." *Virginia Law Review* 72 (April 1986): 543–616. This article concentrates on the perspective of Justice O'Connor as evinced in her opinions.

West, Robin. "Jurisprudence and Gender." *University of Chicago Law Review* 55 (Winter 1988): 1–72. An argument that the physical differences between the sexes render contemporary legal theory inapplicable to women's experience.

RESEARCH GUIDE

Many student readers will be writing research papers on women and the law. Your own instructor is the best source of information about references, but I have put this guide together to help you get started.

Supreme Court cases are printed by several publishing companies. The editions that you are likely to encounter are *United States Reports*, printed by the federal government, *Supreme Court Reporter*, and *Lawyers' Edition*. These are in bound volumes except for recent cases (meaning the last two or three years), which are in paperback form. Your library may also get "slip opinions," the earliest available copies of decisions, which look like reprinted copies of journal articles. These are unbound, and are rarely in any logical order. The *Supreme Court Reporter* and *Lawyers' Edition* contain the *U.S. Reports* volume numbers on their spines and the page numbers in their text, so that you can use these editions if you have only the U.S. citation. The unbound volumes and slip opinions do not yet have the U.S. page citations.

Decisions of the federal Courts of Appeals are published in the *Federal Reporter*, 1st and 2nd series (cited as F. or F. 2). Federal district court decisions are published in the *Federal Supplement* (FS or F. Supp). So far, these reports are still in the first series. Every state supreme court publishes its opinions, as do some intermediate appellate or trial courts. Usually, these are cited by an abbreviated version of the state name ("Ala" for the Alabama Supreme Court, for example). The West Publishing Company puts out several regional reports, e.g., *Pacific Reporter, Southern, Southwestern,* and so on. These volumes publish the cases issued by several state supreme courts. The spine of each volume lists the states that are included. (There are some surprises, so never assume that a state is in the region that you would put it in.)

Citations to court cases look like this: *Muller v. Oregon,* 208 U.S. 412 (1908). The 208 stands for the volume number, found on the spine. The U.S. stands for *United States Reports.* The year in parentheses shows the year of the decision. The 412 stands for the page number. That's right; the case will be found on page 412 of volume 208 of *U.S. Reports.* The citation for the state decision in *Muller* is *State v. Muller,* 48 Ore. 252 (1906). "Ore." stands for *Oregon Reports.* This case will also have a *Pacific Reporter* citation. A volume called *Shepherd's Citations* will give you the cross-reference if you need it.

Texts of federal laws are found in two places: arranged chronologically in *Statutes at Large,* or by topic in the *United States Code.* A reference in a court case like "89 Stat. 347" means the 347th statute of the 89th Congress. This will be found in Volume 89 of *Statutes at Large,* but not on page 347; you will have to look in the index for the page. Or, you may see a reference like this: "42 U.S.C. Section 249." This law will be found in Volume 42 of the *U.S. Code,* section (not page) 249. Each state also has its multi-volume code. Your library probably has the code for your state. It may have others as well, but you may need to visit a law library.

Most students will need to consult law reviews. These are journals (usually published quarterly) edited by law students. Every ABA-accredited law school in the country has a law review. The *Index to Legal Periodicals,* located in the reference department of most university libraries, is the equivalent to *Readers' Guide* for law reviews. The *Harvard Women's Law Journal* and the *Women's Rights Law Reporter* are especially useful for research papers on women and the law. Several journals concentrating on women's studies are available. *Women and Politics* should be helpful to you. *Signs: A Journal of Women in Culture and Society* is one of the oldest and best. Other valuable sources include *NWSA Journal* (National Association of Women's Studies) and *Feminist Studies.*

I have provided brief annotated bibliographies at the end of each chapter under "References." These are by no means meant to be exhaustive. They contain mostly books; I listed articles only when no satisfactory book-length source existed. The references cited in the Notes for each chapter also include many valuable sources. In addition to specialized materials, students may need to consult newspaper indexes, the *Congressional Record,* and other commonly used sources.

N O T E S

Chapter 1. *Introduction: Women and the Law*

1. Simone de Beauvoir, *The Second Sex*, trans. H. M. Parshley (New York: Alfred A. Knopf, 1952), pp. xv–xvi.
2. Adrienne Rich, *Of Woman Born: Motherhood As Experience and Institution* (New York: W.W. Norton, 1976), pp. 41–42.
3. Karl Marx, *The Communist Manifesto* (1848); *Capital* (1867). See also Lewis S. Feuer, ed., *Marx and Engels: Basic Writings on Political Philosophy* (Garden City, N.Y.: Doubleday, 1959).
4. Friedrich Engels, *Origin of the Family, Private Property, and the State*, 4th ed. (New York: International Publishers, 1942).
5. Gunnar Myrdal, *An American Dilemma* (New York: Harper, 1944).
6. Helen Mayer Hacker, "Women As a Minority Group," (1951), in Jo Freeman, ed., *Women: A Feminist Perspective*, 2d ed. (Palo Alto, Calif.: Mayfield, 1979), pp. 514–15.
7. Ann Jones, *Women Who Kill* (New York: Holt, Rinehart & Winston, 1980), chap. 1.
8. "Employed Persons by Sex, Race, and Occupation, 1985," Table 657, in *1987 Statistical Abstract of the United States*, pp. 385–86 (U.S. Department of Commerce, Bureau of the Census, *Employment and Earnings*, January 1986).
9. Francine D. Blau, "Women in the Labor Force: An Overview," in Freeman, ed., *Women*, 3d ed. (1984), p. 302.
10. *Plessy v. Ferguson*, 163 U.S. 537, 552 (1896).

303

11. *Brown v. Board of Education*, I, 387 U.S. 483 (1954).
12. New York *Times*, September 15, 1957, p. 1.
13. *Plessy*, note 10 above.
14. Lawrence Baum, *The Supreme Court*, 2d ed. (Washington, D.C.: CQ Press, 1985), p. 199.
15. *Roe v. Wade*, 410 U.S. 113 (1973).
16. See "Employed Persons," note 8 above.
17. For a different interpretation, see Cynthia E. Harrison, *On Account of Sex: The Politics of Women's Issues, 1945–68* (Berkeley: University of California Press, 1988).
18. Betty Friedan, *The Feminine Mystique* (New York: W.W. Norton, 1963), p. 205.
19. See Blau, "Women in the Labor Force."
20. David M. O'Neill and Peter Sepielli, *Education in the United States, 1940–1983* (Washington, D.C.: United States Department of Commerce, Bureau of the Census, Special Demographic Analysis, LDS-85-1, 1985), Table A-2, pp. 48–49.
21. See *McCulloch v. Maryland*, 4 Wheaton (17 U.S.) 316 (1819).
22. U.S. Const. Amend. X.
23. See Eva Rubin, *The Supreme Court and the American Family* (Westport, Conn.: Greenwood Press, 1986). *Palmore v. Sidoti*, 446 U.S. 429 (1984), was an important exception to this generalization. Here, a unanimous Court reversed a Florida custody award of a white child to her father after her mother married a black man.

Chapter 2. *Women and the Constitution*

1. In law, the word "man" is interpreted in the generic sense, to refer not merely to adult males but to all human beings. Therefore, even if the Constitution had referred to "men," the words probably would have been interpreted to apply to women as well. However, this probability is far from a certainty. Children are "men" in the generic sense, too, but they do not enjoy the same constitutional rights as adults. Incidentally, one example of restrictive constitutional language came to light as recently as 1988, and under embarrassing circumstances. Evan Mecham, the governor of Arizona, was impeached. During his trial, the secretary of state, Rose Mofford, became acting governor. It was discovered that the state constitution provides that only "a male person" may fill this office. The language was quickly changed.
2. Respectively, U.S. Const. Art. II. Sec. 5; Amend. XIV. Sec. 1; Art. I. Sec. 9(2).
3. U.S. Const. Art. I. Sec. 2(1).
4. Marlene Stein Wortman, ed., *Women in American Law*, vol. 1 (New York: Holmes & Meier, 1985), p. 62.

5. Abigail Adams to John Adams, March 31, 1776; John Adams to Abigail Adams, April 14, 1776; ibid., p. 74.

6. Henry Steele Commager, ed., *Documents in American History*, 7th ed., vol. 1 (New York: Appleton-Century-Crofts, 1963), pp. 315–16.

7. Eleanor Flexner, *Century of Struggle*, rev. ed. (New York: Atheneum, 1971), chap. 10.

8. *Congressional Globe*, May 23, 1866, Senate, pp. 2766–67; June 5 and 8, 1866, Senate, pp. 2961, 3035.

9. *Marbury v. Madison*, 1 Cranch 137 (1803).

10. *Lochner v. New York*, 198 U.S. 45 (1905).

11. *Bunting v. Oregon*, 243 U.S. 426 (1917).

12. *Muller v. Oregon*, 208 U.S. 412, 422 (1908).

13. *Radice v. New York*, 264 U.S. 292 (1924).

14. *Adkins v. Children's Hospital*, 261 U.S. 525 (1923). See Judith A. Baer, *The Chains of Protection: The Judicial Response to Women's Labor Legislation* (Westport, Conn.: Greenwood Press, 1978), chaps. 2, 3.

15. Thomas J. Parkinson, "Minimum Wage and the Constitution," *American Labor Legislation Review* 13 (June 1923): 131–36, 131.

16. C. Herman Pritchett, *Constitutional Civil Liberties* (Englewood Cliffs, N.J.: Prentice-Hall, 1984), pp. 307–08.

17. For example, *Schechter Poultry Corp. v. U.S.*, 295 U.S. 495 (1935); and *U.S. v. Butler*, 297 U.S. 1 (1936).

18. See Robert A. Dahl, "Decision-Making in a Democracy: The Role of the Supreme Court as a National Policy Maker," *Journal of Public Law* 6/2 (1957): 279–85. Arithmetic reveals no significant interval change in the years since this article was published.

19. "Re-organizing the Federal Judiciary," March 9, 1937, Senate Report No. 711, 75th Cong., 1st Sess., pp. 41–44.

20. The best source of information on the Court-packing plan is Joseph Alsop and Turner Catledge, *The 168 Days* (New York: Doubleday Doran, 1938).

21. *West Coast Hotel v. Parrish*, 300 U.S. 379 (1937).

22. James MacGregor Burns, *Roosevelt: The Lion and the Fox* (New York: Harcourt, Brace & World, 1956), p. 315.

23. *Kotch v. Board of River Pilot Examiners*, 330 U.S. 552, 563 (1947).

24. *Williamson v. Lee Optical Company*, 348 U.S. 483 (1955).

25. *Goesaert v. Cleary*, 335 U.S. 464 (1948); Barbara Babcock et al., eds., *Sex Discrimination and the Law: Cases and Remedies* (Boston: Little, Brown, 1975), pp. 277–78; Baer, *Chains of Protection*, pp. 111–21.

26. See, for example, Caroline Bird, *Born Female: The High Cost of Keeping Women Down*, rev. ed. (New York: David McKay, 1971), pp. 32–37.

27. Benjamin Spock, *Baby and Child Care* (New York: E.P. Dutton, 1946). Working mothers are discussed in the section on "Special Problems" like divorce and disability. The latest edition, published in 1985, contains no such recommendations. See Betty

Friedan, *The Feminine Mystique* (New York: W.W. Norton, 1963), chap. 8.

28. *Goesaert v. Cleary,* 74 Supp. 745, 749 (1947).
29. *Goesaert v. Cleary,* 335 U.S. 464, 465–68 (1948).
30. The post-1937 Court is well described by C. Herman Pritchett, *The Roosevelt Court: A Study in Judicial Politics and Values, 1937–1947* (New York: Macmillan, 1948); and *Civil Liberties and the Vinson Court* (Chicago: University of Chicago Press, 1954). Eisenhower's comment on Warren is quoted in David M. O'Brien, *Storm Center: The Supreme Court in American Politics* (New York: W.W. Norton, 1986), p. 81.
31. *Brown v. Board of Education,* 347 U.S. 483 (1954).
32. On First Amendment rights, the most famous cases included *Watkins v. U.S.,* 354 U.S. 178 (1957), and *Pennsylvania v. Nelson,* 350 U.S. 497 (1956); on suspects' rights, *Mapp v. Ohio,* 367 U.S. 643 (1961), *Gideon v. Wainwright,* 372 U.S. 335 (1963), and *Miranda v. Arizona,* 384 U.S. 436 (1966); on school prayer, *Engel v. Vitale,* 370 U.S. 421 (1962), and *Abington School District v. Schempp,* 374 U.S. 203 (1963).
33. See Judith A. Baer, "Sexual Equality and the Burger Court," *Western Political Quarterly* 31 (December 1978): 470–91, n. 28.
34. *Norris v. Alabama,* 294 U.S. 587 (1935).
35. *Hoyt v. Florida,* 368 U.S. 57, 68 (1961).
36. Ibid., p. 62.
37. For Warren's attitude, see Bob Woodward and Scott Armstrong, *The Brethren* (New York: Simon & Schuster, 1979), pp. 33–34. For his colleague Hugo Black's view of the Court's role, see *Chambers v. Florida,* 309 U.S. 227 (1940).
38. *U.S. v. Carolene Products,* 304 U.S. 144, 152, n. 4 (1938).
39. *Korematsu v. United States,* 323 U.S. 214 (1944).
40. Gerald Gunther, "In Search of Evolving Doctrine on a Changing Court: A Model for a Newer Equal Protection," *Harvard Law Review* 86 (November 1972): 1–48, 23.
41. *Reed v. Reed,* 404 U.S. 71, 76 (1971), interpolations supplied. This law applies when a person dies intestate (without having made a will). The maker of a will can decide whom to name as the administrator of his or her estate.
42. *Frontiero v. Richardson,* 411 U.S. 677, 686–87 (1973).
43. *Cleveland Board of Education v. LaFleur,* 414 U.S. 632 (1974); *Taylor v. Louisiana,* 419 U.S. 522 (1975).
44. *Craig v. Boren,* 429 U.S. 190, 197 (1976). Emphasis added.
45. See, for example, *Foley v. Conellie,* 435 U.S. 291 (1978); *Ambach v. Norwick,* 441 U.S. 68 (1979).
46. *Heckler v. Mathews,* 465 U.S. 728 (1984).
47. *Schenck v. United States,* 249 U.S. 47 (1919).
48. The successful cases were *Califano v. Webster,* 430 U.S. 313 (1977), and *Heckler v. Mathews,* 465 U.S. 728 (1984). See also *Weinberger v. Wiesenfeld,* 420 U.S. 636 (1975); *Califano v. Goldfarb,* 430 U.S. 199 (1977); *Califano v. Westcott,* 443 U.S. 76 (1979).

49. *Orr v. Orr*, 440 U.S. 268, 279, 280 (1979).

50. *Kirchberg v. Feenstra*, 450 U.S. 455 (1981).

51. Supreme Court custom provides that drafts of all opinions, whether majority, plurality, concurring, or dissenting, are circulated among the justices before publication. Each justice has a chance to edit and criticize, whether or not he or she signs the opinion. All students of the Court have reported that justices make full use of these opportunities.

52. *Michael M. v. Superior Court of Sonoma County*, 450 U.S. 464, 471–72 (1981).

53. Ibid., p. 494.

54. Ibid., pp. 483–85 and n.

55. *Rostker v. Goldberg*, 453 U.S. 57 (1981).

56. *New York Times*, June 26, 1981, p. A12.

57. Respectively, *Caban v. Mohammed*, 441 U.S. 380 (1979); *Stanley v. Illinois*, 405 U.S. 142 (1972). See also *Quilloin v. Walcott*, 434 U.S. 246 (1978); *Lehr v. Robertson*, 463 U.S. 248 (1983).

58. *Levy v. Louisiana*, 391 U.S. 68 (1968); *Weber v. Aetna Casualty and Surety Company*, 406 U.S. 164 (1972).

59. *Stanley v. Illinois*, 405 U.S. 645, 665, 663 (1972).

60. *Fiallo v. Bell*, 430 U.S. 787 (1977).

61. *Parham v. Hughes*, 441 U.S. 347 (1979).

62. *Quilloin v. Walcott*, 434 U.S. 246 (1978).

63. *Lehr v. Robertson*, 463 U.S. 248 (1983).

64. *Caban v. Mohammed*, 441 U.S. 380, 382–83, 389 (1979).

65. Ibid., pp. 407–08.

66. *Lehr v. Robertson*, 463 U.S. 248, 262, 269 (1983).

67. United States Department of Commerce, Bureau of the Census, *1980 Census of Population, United States Summary*, Section A, Table 267 (Washington, D.C.: U.S. Government Printing Office, 1984). These figures are estimates, based on a sample survey.

68. These no longer exist. See Baer, *Chains*, pp. 158–59; "Height Standards in Police Employment and the Question of Sex Discrimination," *Southern California Law Review* 47 (February 1974): 585.

69. This is true only in constitutional cases. Federal laws prohibiting sex discrimination have been held to reach indirect discrimination, but several decisions in the spring of 1989 weakened that principle. See Chapter 3.

70. *Washington v. Davis*, 426 U.S. 229 (1976).

71. *Arlington Heights v. Metropolitan Housing Development Corporation*, 429 U.S. 252 (1977).

72. The Court affirmed this principle in *McCleskey v. Kemp*, 95 L. Ed. 2d 262 (1987). Here, it rejected claims that the death penalty in several states was unconstitutional as applied because it was used disproportionately against members of minority groups and murderers of white victims. It did not occur to the Court to hesitate to apply to the state's ultimate punishment principles that it found appropriate for zoning and police recruitment.

73. *Personnel Administrator v. Feeney,* 442 U.S. 256, 275 (1979).

74. Ibid., pp. 283–85.

75. "Some Reflections on the Reading of Statutes" (1947), in Walter F. Murphy and C. Herman Pritchett, eds., *Courts, Judges, and Politics,* 4th ed. (New York: Random House, 1986), p. 444.

76. Edwin Meese III, Address to the American Bar Association, July 9, 1985. See also Robert H. Bork, *Tradition and Morality in Constitutional Law* (Washington, D.C.: American Enterprise Institute, 1984).

77. See Judith A. Baer, "The Fruitless Search for Original Intent," in Michael W. McCann and Gerald Houseman, eds., *Judging the Constitution* (Glenview, Ill.: Scott, Foresman, 1989), pp. 49–71.

78. However, the Court will invalidate a law if any evidence of impermissible intent is left lying around, so to speak. *Wallace v. Jaffree,* 472 U.S. 105 (1985), struck down a law establishing a "moment of silence" in school opening exercises because several politicians had stated that this was to be a substitute for prayer. Therefore, the law's purpose was to advance religion—a violation of the establishment clause of the First Amendment.

79. *Brown v. Board of Education,* 347 U.S. 483, 492 (1954).

80. *Mississippi University for Women v. Hogan,* 458 U.S. 718, 729, 730 (1982).

81. See Baum, *Supreme Court,* p. 139. See, for example, *Frontiero v. Richardson,* note 42 above, p. 692 (opinion of Justice Powell).

82. See Timothy J. O'Neill, "The Language of Equality in Constitutional Order," *American Political Science Review* 75 (September 1981): 626–31.

83. See note 46 above.

84. *University of California v. Bakke,* 438 U.S. 265, 295–96 (1978).

85. Ibid., p. 294, n. 34. But see *Strauder v. Virginia,* 100 U.S. 303, 307–08 (1880); *Civil Rights Cases,* 109 U.S. 3, 20 (1883); *Jones v. Alfred H. Mayer Corp.,* 392 U.S. 409, 439, 440 (1968); Erving Goffman, *Stigma* (Englewood Cliffs, N.J.: Prentice-Hall, 1963), p. 3.

86. Nora Ephron, *Heartburn* (New York: Alfred A. Knopf, 1983), p. 81.

87. See *Craig v. Boren* and *MUW v. Hogan,* notes 44 and 80 above.

88. Jane J. Mansbridge, *Why We Lost the ERA* (Chicago: University of Chicago Press, 1986), chap. 2.

89. See Leo Kanowitz, *Women and the Law: The Unfinished Revolution,* 2d ed. (Albuquerque: University of New Mexico Press, 1969), pp. 192–96.

90. Joseph P. Lash, *Eleanor: The Years Alone* (New York: W.W. Norton, 1972), p. 312.

91. See, for example, Cynthia E. Harrison, *On Account of Sex: The Politics of Women's Issues, 1945–68* (Berkeley: University of California Press, 1988); Leila J. Rupp and Verta Taylor, *Survival in the Doldrums: The American Women's Rights Movement, 1945 to the 1960s* (New York: Oxford University Press, 1987).

92. Report of the Committee on Education, President's Commission

on the Status of Women (Washington, D.C.: U.S. Government
Printing Office, 1963), p. 1; *American Women*, Report of the
President's Commission on the Status of Women, same publisher
and date, p. 10.

93. See Baer, *Chains*, chap. 5.
94. Janet K. Boles, *The Politics of the Equal Rights Amendment* (New
York: Longman, 1979), chap. 1. Four state legislatures eventually
rescinded their ratification. The question of whether or not rescis-
sion is binding has never been resolved, however. Another good
study is Mary Frances Berry, *Why ERA Failed* (Bloomington:
Indiana University Press, 1986).
95. Mansbridge, *Why We Lost*, p. 147.
96. "What Killed the ERA? A Lack of Concern for the Housewife,"
Albany (N.Y.) *Times-Union*, October 19, 1980, p. H1ff. (Originally
published as "ERA-RIP," *Harpers*, 1980.)
97. Kristin Luker, *Abortion and the Politics of Motherhood* (Berkeley:
University of California Press, 1984).
98. Mansbridge, *Lost*, Appendix.
99. Boles, *Politics*, chaps. 3–5.
100. Judith A. Baer, "Men Against Women Over Equal Rights?" *Albany
Times-Union*, November 16, 1980, pp. D1ff.
101. Mansbridge, *Lost*, p. 197.
102. Jules Henry, *Culture against Man* (New York: Random House,
1963), chap. 9; *Pathways to Madness* (New York: Random House,
1965), p. 33.
103. *United States v. Kennerly*, 209 F. 119, 121 (1913). Emphasis added.

Chapter 3. *Women and Employment*

1. U.S. Department of Labor, *Time of Change: 1983 Handbook of
Women Workers* (Washington, D.C.: U.S. Government Printing
Office, 1983), Table I-3, p. 11.
2. U.S. Department of Commerce, Bureau of the Census, *Historical
Statistics of the United States, Colonial Times to 1970*, p. 132; U.S.
Department of Commerce, *Statistical Abstract of the United States*,
1988, Table No. 608, p. 366.
3. *Time of Change*, Table II-3, p. 55; Table II-4, p. 58.
4. Economic Report of the President, transmitted to Congress February 1988, Table 3-30, p. 282 (from Department of Commerce,
Bureau of the Census).
5. U.S. Const. Article VI, Section 2. "This Constitution, and the laws
of the United States which shall be made in pursuance thereof . . .
shall be the supreme law of the land; and the judges in every state
shall be bound thereby, any thing in the Constitution or laws of
any state to the contrary notwithstanding."
6. Respectively, *Time of Change*, Table II-3, pp. 55–56; ibid., p. 91;

Cynthia B. Lloyd et al. eds., *Women in the Labor Market* (New York: Columbia University Press, 1979), p. 304.

7. Jo Freeman, "Women, Law, and Public Policy," in Jo Freeman, ed., *Women: A Feminist Perspective*, 3d ed. (Palo Alto, Calif.: Mayfield, 1984), p. 393.

8. 29 U.S.C. Sec. 206(d)(1).

9. 29 C.F.R. Sec. 800.141(b).

10. Barbara Babcock et al., eds., *Sex Discrimination and the Law: Cases and Remedies* (New York: Little, Brown, 1975), p. 440.

11. *Wirtz v. Rainbo Baking Co.*, 303 F. Supp. 1049, 1051–52 (E.D. Ky. 1967). See also *Shultz v. Wheaton Glass Co.*, 421 F. 2d 259 (3rd Circ. 1970); *Shultz v. American Can Co.—Dixie Products*, 424 F. 2d 356 (8th Circ. 1970).

12. *Hodgson v. Daisy Manufacturing Co.*, 317 F. Supp. 538 (W.D. Ark. 1970).

13. See, for example, *Shultz v. First Victoria National Bank*, 420 F. 2d 648 (5th Circ. 1969).

14. *Hodgson v. Robert Hall Clothes, Inc.*, 473 F. 2d 589 (3rd Circ. 1973).

15. *Radice v. New York*, 264 U.S. 292 (1924).

16. Respectively, *Brennan v. Corning Glass Works*, 480 F. 2d 1254 (3rd Circ. 1973); *Hodgson v. Corning Glass Works*, 474 F. 2d 266 (2d Circ. 1973).

17. *Corning Glass Works v. Brennan*, 417 U.S. 188 (1974).

18. *Time of Change*, Table III-12, p. 93; Tables III-8 and III-9, Chart III-1, pp. 87–91.

19. *Time of Change*, Table III-16, p. 98.

20. California Comparable Worth Task Force, *Report to the Legislature*, August 1985, pp. B12–B13.

21. *Hodgson v. Daisy Manufacturing Company*, 317 F. Supp. 538, 550 (W.D. Ark. 1970).

22. The "Bennett Amendment": 42 U.S.C. Sec. 2000e-2(h).

23. See *Washington v. AFSCME*, 33 F.E.P. Cases 808 (D. Wash. 1983), 770 F. 2d 1401 (9th Circ. 1985). *County of Washington v. Gunther* is at 452 U.S. 161 (1981).

24. The EEOC ruling is discussed in Robert Pear, "Equal Pay Is Not Needed for Jobs of Comparable Worth," *New York Times*, June 18, 1985, p. A12. The administration's role in the Illinois comparable worth case was reported by Pear, "Court Cases Reveal New Inequalities in Women's Pay," *New York Times*, August 21, 1985, pp. C1, C6. The court decisions are *Spaulding v. University of Washington*, 740 F. 2d 686 (9th Circ. 1984); *cert. denied* 469 U.S. 1036 (1984); *Lemons v. Denver*, 620 F. 2d 228 (10th Circ. 1980); *Christenson v. Iowa*, 563 F. 2d 353 (8th Circ. 1977). The following states have adopted some kind of gradual comparable worth plan for state and local employees: Connecticut, Iowa, Massachusetts, Minnesota, New York, Ohio, Washington, and Wisconsin. See also Debra Stewart, "State Initiatives in the Federal System: The Politics and Policy of Comparable Worth," *Publius* 15 (Summer 1985): 81–95.

25. James MacGregor Burns, Jack W. Peltason, and Thomas E. Cronin, *Government by the People*, bicentennial edition 1987–89, national, state, and local edition (Englewood Cliffs, N.J.: Prentice-Hall, 1987), p. 540. A federal appeals court ruled that market prices are job-related, gender-neutral factors which justify wage differentials; *Spaulding v. University of Washington*, note 24 above, p. 708.

26. *Time of Change*, Tables I-9 and I-13, pp. 15–19.

27. United States Senate, 61st Cong., 2nd Sess., 62nd Cong., 1st & 2nd Sess., Doc. No. 645, *Report on the Condition of Women and Child Wage-Earners in the United States* (Washington, D.C.: U.S. Government Printing Office, 1910–15), vol. 5, chaps. 1 and 2; U.S. Bureau of the Census, Monograph No. 9, *Women in Gainful Occupations, 1870 to 1920* (Washington, D.C.: U.S. Government Printing Office, 1929), pp. 23–25, 79.

28. *Time of Change*, pp. 91–92; California Task Force, *Report*, pp. 10–11. See also Margaret Mead, *Male and Female* (New York: William Morrow, 1949); Alva Myrdal and Viola Klein, *Women's Two Roles*, 2d ed. (London: Routledge & Kegan Paul, 1968); Michelle Zimbalist Rosaldo and Louise Lamphere, eds., *Women, Culture, and Society* (Stanford, Calif.: Stanford University Press, 1974).

29. Caroline Bird, *Born Female: The High Cost of Keeping Women Down*, rev. ed. (New York: David McKay, 1973), pp. 4–5.

30. Jo Freeman, *The Politics of Women's Liberation* (New York: David McKay, 1975), p. 54.

31. 42 U.S.C. Sec. 2000e 703(e).

32. "Sex and Title VII," *Time*, July 9, 1965, p. 62.

33. Theodore Caplow and Reece McGee, *The Academic Marketplace* (New York: Basic Books, 1958), pp. 226, 111.

34. Bird, *Born Female*, p. 5.

35. U.S. Women's Bureau, Bulletin No. 66-II, *Chronological Development of Labor Legislation for Women in the United States*, rev. ed. (Washington, D.C.: U.S. Government Printing Office, 1935).

36. Respectively, 29 C.F.R. Sec. 1604.1(3)(b) (1965); 30 F.R. 14927 (1966); 33 F.R. 3349 (1968).

37. Bird, *Female*, p. 201.

38. See Cynthia E. Harrison, *On Account of Sex: The Politics of Women's Issues, 1945–1968* (Berkeley: University of California Press, 1988), chap. 9.

39. See for example, *Weeks v. Southern Bell*, 277 F. Supp. 117 (S.D. Ga. 1967), 408 F. 2d 228 (5th Circ. 1969); *Rosenfeld v. Southern Pacific Co.*, 293 F. Supp. 1219 (C.D. Cal. 1968); *Gudbrandson v. Genuine Parts Co.*, 297 F. Supp. 134 (D. Minn. 1968).

40. *Rosenfeld v. Southern Pacific Railroad*, 293 F. Supp. 1219, 1226–27, and 444 F. 2d 1219 (9th Circ. 1971).

41. *Phillips v. Martin-Marietta*, 411 F. 2d 1, 4 (5th Circ. 1969).

42. *Phillips v. Martin-Marietta*, 400 U.S. 542, 544, 545 (1971).

43. *Diaz v. Pan American World Airways*, 442 F. 2d 385 (5th Circ. 1971).

44. *Cooper v. Delta Air Lines*, 274 F. Supp. 781 (E.D. La. 1967); *Lansdale*

v. United Air Lines, 2 F.E.P. Cases 461 (S.D. Fla. 1969), *vacated* 437 F. 2d 454 (5th Circ. 1971).

45. *Sprogis v. United Air Lines*, 444 F. 2d 1194, 1199 (7th Circ. 1971).
46. *Laffey v. Northwest Airlines*, 567 F. 2d 429 (D.C. Circ. 1976).
47. *Condit v. United Air Lines*, 558 F. 2d 1176 (4th Circ. 1977). A mandatory leave beginning at the thirteenth week of pregnancy was upheld in *Burwell v. Eastern Air Lines*, 633 F.2d 361 (4th Circ. 1980).
48. See Lyn Farley, *Sexual Shakedown* (New York: Warner, 1978).
49. See Catharine A. MacKinnon, *Sexual Harassment of Working Women* (New Haven: Yale University Press, 1979).
50. EEOC, *Guidelines on Discrimination Because of Sex*, 29 C.F.R. Sec. 1604.11(a) (1985).
51. *Vinson v. Taylor*, 23 F.E.P. Cases 37, 42 (D.D.C. 1980).
52. *Vinson v. Taylor*, 753 F. 2d 141 (D.C. Circ. 1984).
53. *Meritor Savings Bank v. Vinson*, 91 L. Ed. 2d 49, 55, 60, 66 (1986). The citation is to *EEOC Guidelines*, see note 50 above.
54. 29 U.S.C. 701 Secs. 792, 794. Emphasis added.
55. *Griggs v. Duke Power Company*, 401 U.S. 424, 431 (1971).
56. *Meadows v. Ford Motor Company*, 5 F.E.P. Cases 665 (W.D. Ky. 1973).
57. *Albemarle Paper v. Moody*, 422 U.S. 405 (1975).
58. "Height Standards in Police Employment and the Question of Sex Discrimination," *Southern California Law Review* 47 (February 1974): 585; *Dothard v. Rawlinson*, 433 U.S. 321 (1977).
59. *Pond v. Braniff Airways*, 500 F. 2d 161 (5th Circ. 1974).
60. "Height Standards in Police Employment," note 58 above.
61. *Boyd v. Ozark Air Lines*, 568 F. 2d 50 (8th Circ. 1977).
62. *Rawlinson*, note 58 above.
63. Philip Goldberg, "Are Women Prejudiced Against Women?" *Transaction* 5 (April 1968): 28–30; *Discrimination Against Women*, Hearings of the Special Subcommittee on Education, House of Representatives, 91st Cong., 2nd Sess. (Washington, D.C.: U.S. Government Printing Office, 1970), Parts 1 and 2; Michelle Paludi and Lisa Strayer, "What's In an Author's Name? Differential Evaluations of Performance As a Function of Author's Name," *Sex Roles* 12 (1985): 353–61; Lynn Hecht Schafran, "Eve, Mary, Superwoman: How Stereotypes about Women Influence Judges," *Judges' Journal* 24 (1985): 12–17, 48–53; Susan A. Basow and Nancy T. Silberberg, "Student Evaluations of College Professors: Are Males Prejudiced Against Women Professors?" (Eastern Psychological Association, Boston, March 1985).
64. This system does not work perfectly. Authors and reviewers can often guess one another's identity, especially if the author is an established scholar. But the presumption in favor of anonymity makes it more difficult to act on bias than it otherwise would be. Furthermore, blind review does protect young scholars whose work is not known and who need to secure their professional careers by publishing their research.

65. *McDonnell-Douglas v. Green,* 411 U.S. 792, 802 (1973).
66. Respectively, the Civil Rights Act of 1968; *Jones v. Alfred H. Mayer Corp.,* 392 U.S. 409 (1968).
67. Respectively, *U.S. v. County of Fairfax,* 629 F. 2d 932 (4th Circ. 1980); *Hudson v. IBM,* 620 F.2d 351 (2d Circ. 1980), *cert. denied* 449 U.S. 1066 (1981).
68. *EEOC v. Sears, Roebuck,* 628 F. Supp. 1265, 1276, 1288–1328 (N.D. Ill., E.D., 1986). Samuel G. Freedman, "Of History and Politics: Bitter Feminist Debate," *New York Times,* June 6, 1986, pp. B1, B4.
69. Respectively, *Jepsen v. Florida Board of Regents,* 610 F. 2d 1359 (5th Circ. 1980); *Lynn v. University of California Regents,* 656 F. 2d 1337 (9th Circ. 1981).
70. *Namenwirth v. University of Wisconsin,* 769 F. 2d 1235, 1243 (7th Circ. 1985). In fairness, I should point out that Judge Luther Swygert dissented. It may also matter that the third judge, Richard Posner, is a former university professor.
71. See Robert Pear, "The Courts Try to Sort Out Challenges to Affirmative Action," *New York Times,* April 14, 1985, IV, p. 4; *Local 28 of Sheet Metal Workers v. EEOC,* 106 S. Ct. 3019 (1986); *Local Number 93 v. City of Cleveland,* 106 S. Ct. 3063 (1986); *U.S. v. Paradise,* 107 S. Ct. 1053 (1987).
72. See also *Green v. School Board of New Kent County,* 391 U.S. 430 (1968); *Swann v. Charlotte-Mecklenburg Board of Education,* 402 U.S. 1 (1971); *Keyes v. School District No. 1, Denver, Colorado,* 413 U.S. 189 (1973).
73. *University of California v. Bakke,* 438 U.S. 265, 281–315, 320 (1978).
74. Most forcefully in *Steelworkers v. Weber,* 443 U.S. 193, 219–255 (1979).
75. But not all such plans have been upheld. See, for example, *Wygant v. Jackson Board of Education,* 106 S. Ct. 1842 (1986); Kathleen M. Sullivan, "Sins of Discrimination: Last Term's Affirmative Action Cases," *Harvard Law Review* 100 (November 1986): 78–98.
76. *Fullilove v. Klutznick,* 448 U.S. 448 (1980).
77. *United Steelworkers v. Weber,* 434 U.S. 193, 219–20 and 231–35; 202, 208 (1979). The language quoted from Brennan's opinion is a citation of *United States v. Public Utilities Commission,* 345 U.S. 295, 315 (1953). The Court has invalidated plans which required white workers to be laid off before blacks with less seniority, in *Wygant* (see note 75), or which allowed white workers to be punished for infractions for which blacks went unpunished, see *McDonald v. Santa Fe Trail Transportation Co.,* 427 U.S. 273 (1976).
78. *Johnson v. Transportation Agency of Santa Clara County, California,* 107 S. Ct. 1442, 1446–48 (1987).
79. The reader is invited to test this assertion. Choose a few fellow students who are all in at least two of your classes, listen to your next class lecture in both of them, score each, and then compare the scores.
80. Appendix to Petition for *Certiorari,* p. 12a; cited, 107 S. Ct. 1442,

1475 n. 5 (opinion of Justice Scalia). The district court opinion was not published, but the appeals court decision identifies the judge as William J. Ingram. *Johnson v. Transportation Agency,* 748 F. 2d 1308 (9th Circ. 1984).

81. *Johnson v. Transportation Agency,* 107 S. Ct. 1442, 1448–49 (1987).

82. Ibid., pp. 1442, 1452, 1455, 1457.

83. Ibid., pp. 1458–59, 1460–65, 1465–67, 1475, 1476.

84. *Johnson v. Transportation Agency,* Brief for American Society of Personnel Administration as *Amicus Curiae,* p. 9, cited, 107 S. Ct. 1442, 1457 n. 17 (opinion of Justice Brennan).

85. Ibid., p. 1467.

86. *Green v. School Board,* note 72 above, p. 438.

87. *Richmond v. Croson,* 109 S. Ct. 706 (1989); *Wards Cove v. Atonio,* 109 S. Ct. 2115 (1989); *Griggs,* note 55 above; *Martin v. Wilks,* 109 S. Ct. 2180 (1989); *Patterson v. McLean Credit Union,* 109 S. Ct. 2363 (1989).

88. *Muller v. Oregon,* 208 U.S. 412, 421–22 (1908).

89. Judith A. Baer, *The Chains of Protection: The Judicial Response to Women's Labor Legislation* (Westport, Conn.: Greenwood Press, 1978), p. 90.

90. *Cleveland Board of Education v. LaFleur,* 414 U.S. 632, 634–39, 640–44, n. 9 (1974).

91. For workplace hazards generally, see Carolyn Bell, "Implementing Safety and Health Regulations for Women in the Workplace," *Feminist Studies* 5 (1979): 286–301; Wendy Chavkin, ed., *Double Exposure: Women's Health Hazards on the Job and at Home* (New York: Monthly Review Press, 1984); Jeanne Stellman, *Women's Work, Women's Health* (New York: Pantheon, 1977); Jeanne Stellman and Susan Daum, *Work Is Dangerous to Your Health* (New York: Vintage, 1973). On reproductive hazards, Ronald Bayer, "Women, Work, and Reproductive Hazards," *Hastings Center Report* 12 (1982): 14–19; Rosalind Petchesky, *Abortion and Woman's Choice* (New York: Longman, 1984), and "Workers, Reproductive Hazards, and the Politics of Protection," *Feminist Studies* 5 (1979): 233–45; Michael J. Wright, "Reproductive Hazards and 'Protective' Discrimination," same issue, 302–09. See also, Judith A. Baer, "Equality and Protection in the Twentieth Century," prepared for delivery at the annual meeting of the Midwest Political Science Association, 1984; Louise A. Williams, "Toxic Exposure in the Workplace," in Ellen Boneparth and Emily Stoper, eds., *Women, Power and Policy,* 2d ed. (New York: Pergamon Press, 1988), pp. 113–30.

92. See Wendy Chavkin, "Occupational Hazards to Reproduction," *Feminist Studies* 5 (1979): 310–25; Wendy W. Williams, "Firing the Woman to Protect the Fetus," *Georgetown Law Journal* 69 (1981): 641–704.

93. Bayer, "Reproductive Hazards," p. 18; Donna K. Randall and James F. Short, Jr., "Women in Toxic Work Environments," *Social Problems* 30 (1983): 410–24, 417; Baer, "Equality and Protection," pp. 18–19.

94. 886 F. 2d 871 (7th Circ. 1989). See *Secretary of Labor v. American Cyanamid*, OSHRC Docket No. 79-5762, p. 10; *New York Times*, January 16, 1980, p. 16, September 8, 1980, p. A14, October 3, 1989, p. 10.

95. See Harriet G. Rosenberg, "The Home Is the Workplace: Hazards, Stress, and Pollutants in the Household," in Chavkin, ed., *Double Exposure*, pp. 196–245.

96. Petchesky, *Abortion*, p. 352. For an excellent analysis of the fetal protection issue, see Barbara Katz Rothman, *Recreating Motherhood* (New York: W.W. Norton, 1989), Part II.

97. *Geduldig v. Aiello*, 417 U.S. 484, 496–97 (1974).

98. *General Electric v. Gilbert*, 97 S. Ct. 401, 406–09 (1976).

99. *Gilbert*, pp. 415–16. See also Baer, "Sexual Equality and the Burger Court," *Western Political Quarterly* 31 (December 1978): 470–91.

100. In *Newport News Shipbuilding v. EEOC*, 462 U.S. 669 (1983), the Court ruled that this law also applied to the spouses of male workers.

101. The literature on mother-infant bonding is extensive. See Boston Women's Health Collective, *The New Our Bodies, Ourselves* (New York: Simon & Schuster, 1984), chap. 20; T. Berry Brazelton, *Working and Caring* (Reading, Mass.: Addison-Wesley, 1985).

102. *California Federal Savings and Loan Association v. Guerra*, 107 S. Ct. 683, 687–88; Amy Wilentz, "Garland's Bouquet: A Landmark Supreme Court Ruling Supports Pregnancy Leave," *Time*, January 26, 1987, pp. 14–15.

103. *California Federal*, note 102, Brief for the American Civil Liberties Union as *Amicus Curiae*.

104. Wilentz, "Garland's Bouquet," p. 15; Lynn Arditi, "The Working Parents' Bill," *Ms*, June 1986, p. 26.

105. For a defense of policies accommodating women's domestic role, see Sylvia Ann Hewlett, *A Lesser Life: The Myth of Women's Liberation in America* (New York: William Morrow, 1986). Among the many critical reviews of this book was Sylvia A. Law, *New York Times Book Review*, March 30, 1986, p. 10.

106. See Baer, *Chains of Protection*, chaps. 1 & 2.

107. *Guerra*, note 102 above, pp. 694 (quoting 123 *Cong. Rec.* 29658), 698–702.

108. S1885. For a defense of ABC, see Nancy Folbre and Heidi Hartmann, "Better Child Care: A New Politics of Entitlement," *The Nation*, October 3, 1988, pp. 263–66; in opposition, Robert Samuelson, "The Debate Over Day Care," *Newsweek*, June 27, 1988, p. 45.

109. Two excellent reminders of conditions early in this century are found in Quentin Bell, *Virginia Woolf: A Biography* (New York: Harcourt Brace Jovanovich, 1972), vol. 2, chap. 2; Robert A. Caro, *The Years of Lyndon Johnson: The Path to Power* (New York: Alfred A. Knopf, 1982), chap. 27.

110. See, for example, Shelley J. Lundberg, "Equality and Efficiency: Anti-Discrimination Policies in the Labor Market," prepared for

presentation at the Constitutional Bicentennial Conference, Nelson A. Rockefeller Center, Dartmouth College, Hanover, N.H., January 27, 1987; June O'Neill, "The Trend in the Male-Female Wage Gap in the United States," *Journal of Labor Economics* 3 (January 1985): S91–S116.

Chapter 4. *Women and the Private Sphere: Beyond the Patriarchal Family*

1. Aristotle, *Politics,* esp. Book I; John Locke, *Two Treatises on Government* (1690). See also Jean Bethke Elshtain, *Public Man, Private Woman* (Princeton, N.J.: Princeton University Press, 1981), chaps. 1 and 3; Susan Moller Okin, *Women in Political Thought* (Princeton, N.J.: Princeton University Press, 1981).

2. See, for example, Elshtain, *Public Man,* chap. 5; Betty Friedan, *The Second Stage* (New York: Summit Books, 1981); Christopher Lasch, *Haven in a Heartless World* (New York: Basic Books, 1977); Alice Rossi, "A Biosocial Perspective on Parenting," *Daedalus* 106 (1977): 1.

3. One modern feminist who presented a cogent argument against the family was Shulamith Firestone, *The Dialectic of Sex* (New York: William Morrow, 1970). The preeminent ideological attack on the family was not feminist, but Marxist: see Friedrich Engels, *Origin of the Family, Private Property, and the State,* 4th ed. (New York: International Publishers, 1942).

4. See Michelle Zimbalist Rosaldo and Louise Lamphere, eds., *Women, Culture, and Society* (Stanford, Calif.: Stanford University Press, 1974).

5. United States Department of Commerce, Bureau of the Census, *Statistical Abstract of the United States,* 1987, Tables 42, 62.

6. Isabel Wilkerson, "Marriage Lets 8 Couples Reclaim Their Lives," *New York Times,* November 14, 1988, pp. A1, A11; Emily Stoper, "Raising the Next Generation: Who Shall Pay?" in Ellen Boneparth and Emily Stoper, eds., *Women, Power and Policy,* 2d ed. (New York: Pergamon Press, 1988), pp. 190–219.

7. *Griswold v. Connecticut,* 381 U.S. 479 (1965); *Eisenstadt v. Baird,* 405 U.S. 438 (1972).

8. *Bowers v. Hardwick,* 106 S. Ct. 2841, 2844.

9. *New York Times,* July 7, 1989, pp. A1, A12.

10. *Why Can't Sharon Kowalski Come Home?* (San Francisco: Spinsters/Aunt Lute, 1988).

11. See Judith A. Baer, *Equality Under the Constitution: Reclaiming the Fourteenth Amendment* (Ithaca, N.Y.: Cornell University Press, 1983), chap. 9.

12. *Village of Belle Terre v. Boraas,* 416 U.S. 1, 9 (1974).

13. 117 *Congressional Record,* December 10, pp. S21129–30.

14. See, for example, John J. Bonsignore et al., *Before the Law,* 3d ed. (Boston: Houghton Mifflin, 1984), pp. 12–27; Leo Kanowitz,

Women and the Law: The Unfinished Revolution, 2d ed. (Albuquerque, N.M.: University of New Mexico Press, 1969), chap. 3.

15. On a married woman's surname, see *People ex rel. Rago v. Lipsky,* 63 N.E.2d 642 (Ill. App. Ct. 1945); on domicile, *Carlson v. Carlson,* 256 P.2d 249 (Az. Sup. Ct. 1953) and *Clarke v. Redeker,* 259 F. Supp. 117 (D.C. Iowa 1966); on marital sexual relations, *State v. Haines,* 25 So. 372 (La. Sup. Ct. 1899); *State v. Lankford,* 102 A. 63 (Del. Ct. Gen. Sess. 1917); *Reed v. State,* 59 S.W. 2d 122 (Tex. Ct. Crim. App. 1933); Susan Brownmiller, *Against Our Will: Men, Women, and Rape* (New York: Simon & Schuster, 1975), pp. 240–41, 427–29; general sources include Kanowitz, *Women and the Law,* chap. 3, and *Sex Roles in Law and Society* (Albuquerque: University of New Mexico Press, 1973), chaps. 2, 4; Karen DeCrow, *Sexist Justice* (New York: Random House, 1974), chap. 8.

16. *Youngberg v. Holstron,* 252 Iowa 815, 108 N.W. 2d 498 (1961).

17. *United States v. Dege,* 364 U.S. 51 (1960).

18. *United States v. Yazell,* 382 U.S. 341 (1966).

19. Kanowitz, *Women and the Law;* Blanche Crozier, "Marital Support," *Boston University Law Review* 15 (1935): 28; Monroe Paulsen, "Support Rights and Duties Between Husband and Wife," *Vanderbilt Law Review* 9 (1956): 709; *McGuire v. McGuire,* 59 N.W. 2d 336 (Sup. Ct. Nebraska 1953).

20. *Reed v. Reed,* 404 U.S. 71 (1971).

21. *Stanton v. Stanton,* 421 U.S. 7, 10, 14 (1975).

22. *Orr v. Orr,* 440 U.S. 268, 279–80 (1979).

23. *Kirchberg v. Feenstra,* 450 U.S. 455 (1981).

24. *Stanton v. Stanton,* 517 P. 2d 1012 (1974).

25. *Stanton v. Stanton,* 421 U.S. 7, 14 (1975).

26. See above, note 23, pp. 459–60 (1981).

27. The Supreme Court did let stand a lower court decision requiring a name change in *Forbush v. Wallace,* 405 U.S. 970 (1972), and *Whitlow v. Hodges,* 97 S. Ct. 654 (1976), but these occurred long before *Feenstra.*

28. See, for example, Arlie Hochschild with Anne Machung, *The Second Shift: Working Parents and the Revolution at Home* (New York: Viking, 1989); *The 1985 Virginia Slims American Women's Opinion Poll,* The Roper Center, Storrs, Conn., p. 93, Table 6.8; J. A. Ericksen et al., "The Division of Family Roles," *Journal of Marriage and the Family* 41 (1979): 301; Philip Blumstein and Pepper Schwartz, *American Couples* (New York: William Morrow, 1983), pp. 144–46; Ruth Sidel, *Women and Children Last: The Plight of Poor Women in Affluent America* (New York: Viking, 1986).

29. Caroline Bird, *Born Female: The High Cost of Keeping Women Down,* rev. ed. (New York: David McKay, 1971), p. 72; Blumstein and Schwartz, *Couples,* pp. 53–59, 139–44.

30. Nan D. Hunter, "Women and Child Support," in Irene Diamond, ed., *Families, Politics, and Public Policy* (New York: Longman, 1983), pp. 203–19, 204; Aristotle, *Politics,* Book VII, chap. xvi; Jessie Bernard, *The Future of Marriage* (New York: World Publishing, 1972), chaps. 7, 8.

31. Department of Commerce, Bureau of the Census, *Statistical Abstract of the U.S.*, 1988, Table 81, p. 59.

32. Kanowitz, *Women*, pp. 93–99.

33. Margaret Mead and Frances Balgley Kaplan, eds., *American Women* (New York: Scribner's, 1965), Table 11.

34. See, for example, William Goode, *Women and Divorce* (New York: Free Press, 1965); Phyllis Chesler, *Mothers on Trial: The Battle for Children and Custody* (New York: McGraw-Hill, 1986); Lenore Weitzman, *The Divorce Revolution* (New York: Free Press, 1986), chap. 3.

35. DeCrow, *Sexist Justice*, chap. 8; Mead and Kaplan, *American Women*, Section 1.

36. See, for example, Morton M. Hunt, *The World of the Formerly Married* (New York: McGraw-Hill, 1966), chap. 7.

37. Hunter, "Child Support," pp. 203–04.

38. James Schouler, *A Treatise on the Law of Marriage, Divorce, Separation and Domestic Relations* (Albany, N.Y.: Matthew Bender, 1921).

39. Goode, *Women and Divorce*, p. 222.

40. Kanowitz, *Women*, pp. 93–95.

41. *Statistical Abstract*, Table 81.

42. Herma Hill Kay, "A Family Court: The California Proposal," in Paul Bohannon, ed., *Divorce and After* (New York: Doubleday, 1970), p. 248.

43. See *Morgan v. Morgan*, 366 N.Y.S. 2d 977 (Sup. Ct. 1975), and *O'Brien v. O'Brien*, 66 N.Y. 2d 576 (1985); *Moss v. Moss*, 80 Mich. App. 693 (1978); *In re Horstman*, 263 N.W. 2d 885 (Iowa 1978); *In re Marriage of Fleege*, 91 Wash. 2d 324 (1979); *Todd v. Todd*, 78 Cal. Rptr. 131 (1969); Weitzman, *Divorce Revolution*, Table C-5.

44. See Renee Cherow-O'Leary, *The State-by-State Guide to Women's Legal Rights* (New York: McGraw-Hill, 1987).

45. The definitive study is Lenore Weitzman, *Revolution*, pp. xii, xv. Her findings are supported by such writers as Judith Cassety, *Child Support and Public Policy* (Lexington, Mass.: Lexington Books, 1978); Judith Wallerstein and Joan Kelly, *Surviving the Breakup: How Children and Parents Cope After Divorce* (New York: Basic Books, 1980); Lucy Marsh Yee, "What Really Happens in Child Support Cases," *Denver Law Journal* 57 (1980): 21; Terry Arendell, *Mothers and Divorce* (Berkeley: University of California Press, 1986); and Emily Stoper and Ellen Boneparth, "Divorce and the Transition to the Single-Parent Family," in Boneparth and Stoper, *Women*, pp. 206–18. The poverty statistics are found in Bureau of the Census, *Characteristics of the Population Below the Poverty Level*, 1983, Series P-60, No. 147, Table 21, p. 91.

46. See Weitzman, *Revolution*, Introduction and chap. 11; Marianne Takas, *Child Custody: A Complete Guide for Concerned Mothers* (New York: Harper & Row, 1987), p. 8 (emphasis in original).

47. Bureau of the Census, *Child Support and Alimony* (1983), Special Studies, Series P-23, Tables 1, 3; Cherow-O'Leary, *Guide*, p. 23;

Weitzman, *Revolution*, chaps. 6, 9; *New York Times*, November 25, 1988, p. A8.

48. Lois Greenwood-Audant, "The Internalization of Powerlessness: A Case Study of the Displaced Homemaker," in Jo Freeman, ed., *Women: A Feminist Perspective*, 3d ed. (Palo Alto, Calif.: Mayfield, 1984), pp. 264–81.

49. It is impossible to determine the facts with any exactitude. The Census Bureau has collected these data only since the late 1970s, and only from a sample of the population. Data collected by scholars also come from samples. Some, like the studies conducted by William Goode and Lenore Weitzman, are representative samples drawn from all the divorces in a locality within a particular time period. Others, like Phyllis Chesler's study, are drawn from self-selected participants, and are therefore less representative. Essentially, all we can do is compare studies: what Goode found in Detroit in 1948, say, to what Weitzman found in California in 1977. All the studies, taken together, indicate that support is not awarded less often, nor is it less generous, nor is compliance less frequent, than was the case before divorce reform.

50. *Statistical Abstract*, Table 81.

51. Anthony Astrachan, *How Men Feel* (New York: Doubleday, 1986), pp. 233–34.

52. 88 Stat. (Statutes at Large) 2351–58.

53. 98 Stat. 1305.

54. Public Law 100-485, 102 Stat. 2343. See Tamar Lewin, "New Law Compels Sweeping Changes in Child Support," *New York Times*, November 25, 1988, pp. A1, A8.

55. 118 *Cong. Rec.* 8291 (1972); *New York Times*, July 18, 1975, p. 30.

56. Lewin, "New Law," p. 8.

57. *New York Times*, July 2, 1982, p. 11; August 5, 1982, p. 1; December 30, 1983, I, p. 11; Richard Cohen, "The War on the Poor," *Manchester Guardian Weekly*, February 27, 1983, pp. 15, 18.

58. Respectively, 94 Stat. 2071; 96 Stat. 730; 97 Stat. 2549; 98 Stat. 1426. The decision was *McCarty v. McCarty*, 453 U.S. 210 (1981). See Kathleen Shortridge, "Poverty Is a Woman's Problem," in Freeman, *Women*, pp. 492–501.

59. *Commonwealth v. Briggs*, 33 Mass. 203 (1834); Nancy D. Polikoff, "Gender and Child-Custody Determinations," in Diamond, *Families*, pp. 183–202.

60. *Bunim v. Bunim*, 76 N.Y.S. 2d 456 (1948), 298 N.Y. 391 (1949); Chesler, *Mothers on Trial*, p. 37.

61. See Henry H. Foster and Doris Jonas Freed, "Divorce in the Fifty States: An Overview," *Family Law Quarterly* 14 (1981): 229; Nancy Polikoff, "Why Mothers Are Losing: A Brief Analysis of Criteria Used in Child Custody Determinations," *Women's Rights Law Reporter* 7 (1982): 235.

62. Among the books were Charles Metz, *Divorce and Custody for Men* (Garden City, N.Y.: Doubleday, 1968), Daniel Amneus, *Back to*

Patriarchy (New York: Arlington House, 1979), and Louis Keifer, *How to Win Custody* (New York: Cornerstone, 1982). Fathers' Rights of America and the National Congress of Men are among the many groups which make up the fathers' rights movement.

63. See James A. Levine, "Fathering Books—A New Generation," *Psychology Today* 12 (1978): 152, 157.
64. Takas, *Child Custody*, p. 3.
65. See, e.g., Linley Stafford, *One Man's Family: A Single Father and His Children* (New York: Random House, 1978).
66. See Chesler, *Mothers*, pp. 425–32.
67. See Georgia Dullea, "Child Custody: Jurists Weigh Film vs. Life," *New York Times*, December 21, 1979, p. B6.
68. Takas, *Child Custody*, pp. 4–5.
69. Weitzman, *Revolution*, p. 233 (63 percent); Lenore Weitzman and Ruth Dixon, "Child Custody Awards: Legal Standards and Empirical Patterns for Child Custody, Support, and Visitation After Divorce," *University of California, Davis, Law Review* 12 (1979): 472 (from 35 percent in 1968 to 37 percent in 1972); Chesler, *Mothers* (70 percent); Polikoff, "Gender," pp. 184–85.
70. *Jarrett v. Jarrett*, 400 N.E. 2d 421 (Ill. Sup. Ct. 1979), *cert. den.* 449 U.S. 927 (1980).
71. *In re Marriage of Olson*, 98 Ill. App. 316 (1981).
72. David L. Chambers, "Rethinking the Substantive Rules for Custody Disputes in Divorce," *Michigan Law Review* 83 (1984): 480, 540–41.
73. *Salk v. Salk*, 393 N.Y. 2d 841 (1975).
74. Chesler, *Mothers*, Part I; Polikoff, "Losing"; Rena Uviller, "Fathers' Rights and Feminism: The Maternal Presumption Revisited," *Harvard Women's Law Journal* 1 (1978); Weitzman, *Revolution*, pp. 235–43.
75. Chesler, *Mothers*, p. 489.
76. *Dailey v. Dailey*, 635 S.W. 2d 391 (Tenn. Ct. App. 1981).
77. *Jacobson v. Jacobson*, 314 N.Y. 2d 78 (N.Y. Sup. Ct. 1981).
78. *Schuster v. Schuster* and *Isaacson v. Isaacson*, 582 P.2d 130 (Wash. Sup. Ct. 1978). See also Takas, *Custody*, pp. 94–98; Nan D. Hunter and Nancy Polikoff, "Custody Rights of Lesbian Mothers: Legal Theory and Litigation Strategy," *Buffalo Law Review* 25 (1976).
79. *M.P. v. S.P.*, 404 A. 2d 1256 (1979). See also Judith A. Baer, "Sexuality and the Law," in *Encyclopedia of the American Judicial System*, vol. 3 (New York: Scribner's, 1987), pp. 1252–70. Divorced fathers who are gay are also at risk from judicial homophobia. One judge ordered a noncustodial father with weekend visitation rights not to take his son to the gay church he attended, arguably violating at least two of the man's constitutional rights. *J.L.P. v. D.J.P.*, 643 S.W. 2d 865 (Mo. 1982). But male homosexuals are so small a percentage of the number of fathers seeking custody that there are not enough cases to permit any verifiable generalizations about their fate.

80. Chesler, *Mothers*, chap. 4; Polikoff, "Losing"; Takas, *Custody*, p. 152.
81. See John Bowlby, *Attachment and Loss*, 3 vols. (New York: Basic Books, 1969, 1973, 1980); Joseph Goldstein, Anna Freud, and Albert Solnit, *Beyond the Best Interests of the Child* (New York: The Free Press, 1984). For a review of the scholarship in this area, see Chambers, "Rethinking," pp. 504–41.
82. See Bowlby, *Attachment*, vol. 3; Chambers, "Rethinking," pp. 541–44.
83. Weitzman, *Revolution*, pp. 224, 310–18.
84. Robert H. Mnookin and Lewis Kornhauser, "Bargaining in the Shadow of the Law: The Case of Divorce," *Yale Law Journal* 88 (1979): 950, 964.
85. Richard Neely, *Why Courts Don't Work* (New York: McGraw-Hill, 1982), pp. 121–22; *Garska v. McCoy*, 278 S.E.2d 357 (W.Va. Sup. Ct. 1981); *Commonwealth ex rel. Jordan v. Jordan*, 448 A. 2d 1113 (Pa. 1982); Polikoff, "Losing," pp. 240–44. Chambers, "Rethinking," proposes that legislatures adopt such a rule.
86. A retired widow or widower who had paid Social Security tax is, of course, eligible for retirement benefits based on his or her own earnings. A widow (and, since 1977, a widower) whose survivors' pension would amount to more than his or her own benefits, because the spouse earned and contributed more money, is entitled to the higher amount.
87. *Weinberger v. Wiesenfeld*, 420 U.S. 636, 645 (1975); *Califano v. Goldfarb*, 430 U.S. 199 (1977). Congress amended the law in 1977 to require that all spousal benefits be "offset" by the amount of the applicants' own pensions, except for widows and dependent widowers who had anticipated the benefits to which they had been entitled before *Goldfarb*. The Supreme Court upheld this exception, *Heckler v. Mathews*, 465 U.S. 728 (1984).
88. Bureau of the Census, *Statistical Abstract*, Tables 39, 105.
89. Bureau of the Census, *Characteristics of Population Below the Poverty Level*, Table 21.
90. Weitzman, *Revolution*, chap. 5.
91. Cherow-O'Leary, *Guide*, Part 2; Shana Alexander, *State-by-State Guide to Women's Legal Rights* (Los Angeles: Wollstonecraft, 1975), chap. 7. Most lawyers advise clients who want to disinherit a spouse or child not to omit the person but to leave him or her a small sum such as one dollar. Such a move evinces intent rather than inadvertence, thus making it harder to contest the will.
92. DeCrow, *Justice*, pp. 146–47.
93. *Divorced Women's Handbook* (Boca Raton, Fla.: Globe Communications Corporation, 1987), pp. 27, 18–25.

Chapter 5. *Women and Reproduction*

1. The basic works are: John Locke, *Two Treatises on Government*

(1690), John Stuart Mill, *On Liberty* (1859), and, among others, Henry David Thoreau, *Civil Disobedience* (1847) and *Walden* (1854); David Riesman et al., *The Lonely Crowd* (New Haven: Yale University Press, 1950). Recent critiques of individualism include Philip Slater, *The Pursuit of Loneliness* (Boston: Beacon Press, 1970); *Earthwalk* (New York: Doubleday, 1974); Robert Bellah et al., *Habits of the Heart* (Berkeley: University of California Press, 1985).

2. Tamar Lewin, "Drug Use During Pregnancy: New Issue Before the Courts," *New York Times*, February 5, 1990, pp. A1, A12.

3. Elizabeth Rosenthal, "When a Pregnant Woman Drinks," *New York Times Magazine*, February 4, 1990, pp. 30ff, 49.

4. Michael Dorris, *The Broken Cord* (New York: Harper & Row), p. xvii.

5. See Lewin, "Drug Use," pp. A1, A12.

6. Kristin Luker, *Abortion and the Politics of Motherhood* (Berkeley: University of California Press, 1984), p. 97.

7. Margaret Sanger, *An Autobiography* (New York: W.W. Norton, 1938), pp. 90–91.

8. *Women's Suffrage and Woman's Profession* (Hartford: Brown & Gross, 1871), pp. 121–33; Calista Hall to Pliny Hall, in Carl Degler, *At Odds: Women and the Family in America from the Revolution to the Present* (New York: Oxford University Press, 1980), p. 211; correspondence between Harriet and Willis Williams, in Anne Firor Scott, *The Southern Lady: From Pedestal to Politics, 1830–1930* (Chicago: University of Chicago Press, 1970), p. 39; Elizabeth Longford, *Queen Victoria: Born to Succeed* (New York: Harper & Row, 1965).

9. See Peter Fryer, *The Birth Controllers* (New York: Stein & Day, 1966), Part 1.

10. Lucinda Cisler, "Unfinished Business: Birth Control and Women's Liberation," in Robin Morgan, ed., *Sisterhood Is Powerful* (New York: Vintage Books, 1970), p. 248. Emphasis in original.

11. Boston Women's Health Collective, *Our Bodies, Ourselves*, rev. ed. (New York: Simon & Schuster, 1976), pp. 211–12; *The New Our Bodies, Ourselves* (New York: Simon & Schuster, 1984), pp. 256–57. Sterilization is available to any adult male who requests it, without qualification.

12. See, for example, Eva Rubin, *Abortion, Politics, and the Courts* (Westport, Conn.: Greenwood Press, 1982), chap. 1.

13. Boston Collective, *New Our Bodies*, p. 309. See also Nancy Howell Lee, *The Search for an Abortionist* (Chicago: University of Chicago Press, 1969); Diane Schulder and Florynce Kennedy, *Abortion Rap* (New York: McGraw-Hill, 1971).

14. *Carey v. Population Services*, 432 U.S. 678 (1977).

15. *State v. Schweiker*, 557 F. Supp. 354 (1983).

16. *Buck v. Bell*, 274 U.S. 200, 207 (1927). Interpolations added.

17. Sandra G. Boardman and Glenn Frankel, "Over 7,500 Sterilized in Virginia," *Washington Post*, February 23, 1980, pp. A1, A20. The

quotation is from Leslie Friedman Goldstein, ed., *The Constitutional Rights of Women* (New York: Longman, 1979), p. 244. See also Judith A. Baer, *Equality under the Constitution: Reclaiming the Fourteenth Amendment* (Ithaca, N.Y.: Cornell University Press, 1983), pp. 196–98, and "The Burger Court and the Rights of the Handicapped: The Case for Starting All Over Again," *Western Political Quarterly* 35 (1982): 339; Walter Berns, "*Buck v. Bell:* Due Process of Law?" *Western Political Quarterly* 6 (1953): 762; Robert L. Burgdorf and Marcia Pearce Burgdorf, "The Wicked Witch Is Almost Dead: *Buck v. Bell* and the Sterilization of Handicapped Persons," *Temple Law Quarterly* 50 (1977): 955.

18. *Skinner v. Oklahoma*, 316 U.S. 535, 541 (1942).

19. Ibid., p. 544 (opinion of Chief Justice Harlan F. Stone).

20. *Stump v. Sparkman*, 436 U.S. 349 (1978).

21. Kay Mills, *A Place in the Sun: From the Women's Pages to the Front Page* (New York: Dodd, Mead, 1988), p. 236.

22. John D'Emilio and Estelle B. Freedman, *Intimate Matters: A History of Sexuality in America* (New York: Harper & Row, 1988), p. 255.

23. Boston, *New Our Bodies*, pp. 256–57; Cisler, "Unfinished Business," pp. 245–88.

24. *Hodgson v. Minnesota*, No. 89-1125 (1990).

25. Boston, *New Our Bodies*, p. 312.

26. CARASA (Committee for Abortion Rights and Against Sterilization Abuse), *Women Under Attack: Victories, Backlash and the Fight for Reproductive Freedom* (Boston: South End Press, 1988), p. 67.

27. D'Emilio and Freedman, *Intimate Matters*, p. 253. On the coercion suffered by disabled pregnant women, see Anne Finger, "Claiming All of Our Bodies," in Susan E. Browne et al., eds., *With the Power of Each Breath: A Disabled Women's Anthology* (Pittsburgh: Cleis Press, 1985), p. 305. Generally, see Boston, *New Our Bodies*, pp. 256–57.

28. See Sue Halpern, "Infertility: Playing the Odds," *Ms.*, January–February 1989, pp. 146–56. The figures cited are from the Congressional Office of Technology Assessment (OTA). For higher estimates (up to 10 million) and a discussion of the rise in infertility, see Boston, *New Our Bodies*, chap. 21.

29. See, for example, Barbara Eck Menning, *Infertility: A Guide for the Childless Couple* (Englewood Cliffs, N.J.: Prentice-Hall, 1977), pp. 147–51.

30. *New York Times*, September 22, 1989, p. A13.

31. Mary Beth Whitehead with Loretta Schwartz-Nobel, *A Mother's Story* (New York: St. Martin's Press, 1989). See, for example, Phyllis Chesler, *Sacred Bond: The Legacy of Baby M* (New York: Times Books, 1986); Elizabeth Kane, *Birth Mother* (New York: Harcourt Brace Jovanovich, 1988).

32. Robert Hanley, "Father of Baby M Granted Custody: Contract Upheld," *New York Times*, April 1, 1987, pp. A1, B2, B3.

33. Barbara Katz Rothman, *Recreating Motherhood* (New York: W.W. Norton, 1989), p. 130.
34. See Ellen Goodman, "Baby M—M for Money," *Washington Post*, February 17, 1987, p. A17; Charles Krauthammer, "A Triumph of Feminist Ideology," *Washington Post*, April 3, 1987, p. A27; Richard Cohen, ". . . Or Was It the Devil?", *Washington Post*, same date and page.
35. Robert Hanley, "Surrogate Deals for Mothers Held Illegal in Jersey," *New York Times*, February 4, 1988, pp. A1, B6.
36. Ellen Goodman, "In the Swirl of Surrogacy," *Washington Post*, February 6, 1988, p. A23.
37. See Irene Diamond, "Medical Science and the Transformation of Motherhood," in Ellen Boneparth and Emily Stoper, eds., *Women, Power, and Policy*, 2d ed. (New York: Pergamon Press, 1988), pp. 155–67.
38. *Poe v. Ullman*, 367 U.S. 497 (1961). See also Alexander M. Bickel, *The Least Dangerous Branch: The Supreme Court at the Bar of Politics* (Indianapolis: Bobbs-Merrill, 1962), pp. 143–56.
39. *Griswold v. Connecticut*, 381 U.S. 479, 484, 486 (1965).
40. *Eisenstadt v. Baird*, 405 U.S. 438, 453 (1972). Emphasis in original.
41. "Jane Roe" was the pseudonym of Norma McCorvey, a Texas woman who has emerged from anonymity to become a prominent pro-choice activist. Unable to get a legal abortion, she gave birth to a daughter whom she gave up for adoption.
42. *Roe v. Wade*, 410 U.S. 113, 153 (1973).
43. Ibid., pp. 148–52.
44. Ibid., pp. 159, 163–64.
45. Ibid., pp. 157–59.
46. Ibid., pp. 164–65.
47. Ibid., p. 164. Emphasis added.
48. Ibid., p. 153.
49. John Hart Ely, "The Wages of Crying Wolf: A Comment on *Roe v. Wade*," *Yale Law Journal* 82 (1973): 920, 923.
50. A noted example of this phenomenon is Louis Lusky, *By What Right? A Commentary on the Supreme Court's Power to Revise the Constitution* (Charlottesville, Va.: Michie, 1975). Lusky was, in fact, one of the founders of post-1937 judicial activism; as Justice Stone's law clerk, he drafted footnote 4 of *Carolene Products*. See Chapter 2.
51. The closest to such a defense is Leslie F. Goldstein, "Examining Abortion Funding Policy Arguments: An Attempt to Recast the Debate," *Women and Politics* 5 (1985): 41–64.
52. Luker, *Abortion and the Politics of Motherhood*.
53. See ibid.; Rosalind Petchesky, *Abortion and Woman's Choice* (New York: Longman, 1984), chap. 9.
54. See Ursula K. LeGuin, *The Left Hand of Darkness* (New York: Ace Books, 1989).
55. An infant girl is born with over 2 million follicles stored in her

ovaries. Most of these die. At puberty, about 500,000 remain. Four or five hundred of these follicles will mature into ova, leave the ovaries (usually one at a time), and arrive in the uterus, there either to be fertilized by spermatozoa or expelled during menstruation. Obviously, women have far more potential ova than will ever mature. See Robert H. Glass and Nathan G. Kase, *Woman's Choice: A Guide to Contraception, Fertility, Abortion, and Menopause* (New York: Basic Books, 1970), chap. 1. The reader versed in physiology might prefer to consult E. S. E. Hafetz, ed., *Human Reproduction: Conception and Contraception* (New York: Harper & Row, 1980), chap. 6.

56. Feminists who see motherhood as a value-neutral choice include Simone de Beauvoir, *The Second Sex*, trans. H. M. Parshley (New York: Alfred A. Knopf, 1952); Robin Morgan, *Going Too Far* (New York: Random House, 1977); Gloria Steinem, *Outrageous Acts and Everyday Rebellions* (New York: Holt, Rinehart & Winston, 1983). Feminists unwilling to accept this position include Sylvia Ann Hewlett, *A Lesser Life: The Myth of Women's Liberation in America* (New York: William Morrow, 1986); the women writers cited in Chapter 4, note 2; and Germaine Greer, *Sex and Destiny* (New York: Harper & Row, 1984).

57. *Roe v. Wade*, 410 U.S. 113, 153 (1973). Emphasis added.

58. See Boston, *New Our Bodies*, chap. 13.

59. See Judith A. Baer, "What We Know as Women: A New Look at *Roe v. Wade*," *NWSA Journal* 2, No. 4 (Fall 1990): 558–82.

60. *Planned Parenthood of Central Missouri v. Danforth*, 428 U.S. 52, 70–71 (1976).

61. See Baer, *Equality*, chap. 7; *New Jersey v. T.L.O.*, 469 U.S. 325 (1985); *Hazelwood School District v. Kuhlmeier*, 98 L. Ed. 2d 592 (1988).

62. *Akron v. Akron Center for Reproductive Health*, 462 U.S. 416, 440 (1983). Emphasis in original.

63. *Planned Parenthood v. Danforth*, pp. 74–75.

64. Ibid., pp. 102–03.

65. *H. L. v. Matheson*, 450 U.S. 398 (1981).

66. *Michael M. v. Superior Court of Sonoma County*, 450 U.S. 464, 481–82 (1981). The quotations are from the plurality opinion, p. 470.

67. *Bellotti v. Baird*, 443 U.S. 622 (1979); *Planned Parenthood v. Ashcroft*, 462 U.S. 476 (1983).

68. See note 61 above.

69. *Danforth*, p. 79.

70. *Akron*, p. 416; *Planned Parenthood v. Ashcroft*, 462 U.S. 476; *Simopoulos v. Virginia*, 462 U.S. 506, all 1983.

71. *Thornburgh v. American College of Obstetrics and Gynecology*, 106 S. Ct. 2169, 2178 (1986).

72. *Akron*, 462 U.S. 416, 456–58. Emphasis in original.

73. *Doe v. Bolton* (companion case), 410 U.S. 179, 222 (1973).

74. *New York Times*, October 13, 1977, p. 15; November 4, 1977, pp.

A1, A13; June 2, 1981, p. 1; Jane O'Reilly, *The Girl I Left Behind* (New York: Macmillan, 1980), pp. 83–86.

75. *Beal v. Doe*, 432 U.S. 438; *Maher v. Roe*, 432 U.S. 464; *Poelker v. Doe*, 432 U.S. 519.

76. *Maher*, pp. 472–74.

77. Ibid., p. 483.

78. *Griffin v. Illinois*, 351 U.S. 12 (1958); *Gideon v. Wainwright*, 372 U.S. 335 (1963).

79. *Harris v. McRae*, 448 U.S. 297, 316 (1980).

80. Ibid., pp. 343, 346–47. The citations are from the majority opinion, p. 325, and Justice Blackmun's dissent in *Beal*, p. 463.

81. Jane E. Brody, "Abortion Curbs Found to Have Limited Impact," *New York Times*, September 4, 1981, pp. A1, A8.

82. Boston, *New Our Bodies*, pp. 311–12.

83. *Webster v. Reproductive Health Services*, 109 S. Ct. 3040 (1989); *Hodgson v. Minnesota*, No. 89-1125 (1990). See note 87, Chapter 3.

84. *Webster v. Reproductive Health Services*, 109 S. Ct. 3040, 3053–58 (Rehnquist); 3058–65 (O'Connor); 3067 (Scalia).

85. Michel Foucault, *The History of Sexuality*, vol. 1, trans. Robert Hurley (New York: Pantheon Books, 1978), p. 103.

Chapter 6. *Gateways and Barriers: Education and Participation*

1. See Eleanor Flexner, *Century of Struggle*, rev. ed. (New York: Atheneum, 1971), chaps. 2, 8.

2. John K. Folger and Charles B. Nam, *Education of the American Population*, 1960 Census Monograph (Washington, D.C.: U.S. Department of Commerce, Bureau of the Census, 1967), Table V-5, p. 143.

3. Mary Frank Fox, "Women and Higher Education: Sex Differentials in the Status of Students and Scholars," in Jo Freeman, ed., *Women: A Feminist Perspective*, 3d ed. (Palo Alto, Calif.: Mayfield, 1984), pp. 238–55, Figure 1.

4. Susan Dworkin, *Miss America 1945* (New York: Newmarket, 1988).

5. Mary Lou Randour, Georgia L. Strasbourg, and Jean Lipmen-Blumen, "Women in Higher Education: Trends in Enrollment and Degrees Earned," *Harvard Educational Review* 52 (1982): 191; National Center for Educational Statistics, U.S. Department of Education, *Digest of Educational Statistics*, 1985–86, p. 132.

6. Fox, "Women and Higher Education," Figure 1.

7. Debra Renee Kaufman, "Professional Women: How Real Are the Recent Gains?" in Freeman, ed., *Women*, p. 355; *Statistical Abstract of the United States*, 1988, Table 627, p. 376.

8. See Alice de Rivera, "On De-Segregating Stuyvesant High," in Robin Morgan, ed., *Sisterhood Is Powerful* (New York: Random House, 1970), pp. 366–71.

9. *Brown v. Board of Education*, 347 U.S. 483, 495.
10. Robert Nisbet, "Review of Thomas Sowell, *Knowledge and Decision*," *Commentary*, July 1980, p. 70.
11. *Vorchheimer v. School District of Philadelphia*, 400 F. Supp. 326, 342, 329–32 (E.D. Pa. 1975).
12. Sec. 401, Title 22, Code of South Carolina; *Williams v. McNair*, 316 F. Supp. 134, 136, n. 3 (D. S.C. 1970).
13. *Heaton v. Bristol*, 317 S.W. 2d 86, 100 (1958).
14. *Allred v. Heaton*, 336 S.W. 2d 251 (Tex. Civ. App. 1960).
15. *Kirstein v. Rector and Visitors of the University of Virginia*, 309 F. Supp. 184, 187 (E.D. Va. 1970).
16. *Sweatt v. Painter*, 339 U.S. 629, 634 (1951).
17. *Williams*, pp. 138–39.
18. *Bray v. Lee*, 337 F. Supp. 934, 939 (D. Mass. 1972).
19. *Vorchheimer v. Philadelphia*, 400 F. Supp. 326, 329 (1975).
20. *Vorchheimer v. School District of Philadelphia*, 532 F. 2d 880, 887 (3d Circ. 1976).
21. *Vorchheimer v. Philadelphia*, pp. 329–32.
22. Ibid., p. 342.
23. *Vorchheimer v. School District*, pp. 880, 888.
24. Ibid., p. 889.
25. See Charles L. Black, Jr., "The Lawfulness of the Segregation Decisions," *Yale Law Journal* 69 (1960): 421, 425.
26. 118 *Congressional Record*, February 28, 1972, pp. 5803–15, 5805, 5814–15. See *New York Times*, March 1, 1972, pp. 1, 18; March 2, 1972, pp. 1, 45; March 9, 1972, p. 1; March 11, 1972, p. 15; H. Rep. 92–1335.
27. 118 *Congressional Record*, pp. 5805–09 (February 28, 1972); *Statistical Abstract of the United States*, 1988, Table No. 627, p. 376.
28. Bryan *Eagle*, January 8, 1971, p. 5; January 13, p. 3; January 17, p. 1; January 24, pp. 1, 6.
29. Kenneth Bastian, "Thank Title IX," *Washington Post*, August 5, 1984, C7, col. 1.
30. 20 U.S.C. Sec. 1681(a) Sec. 901(a); emphasis added by Justice White.
31. *Grove City College v. Bell*, 465 U.S. 555, 572 (1984).
32. Ibid., pp. 582–86.
33. Ibid., pp. 579–81.
34. Bastian, "Thank Title IX"; 134 *Congressional Record* p. H572 (March 2, 1988, remarks of Representative James Jeffords).
35. *New York Times*, March 17, 1988, pp. A1, A14, A36; 134 *Congressional Record* p. S205–56.
36. *New York Times*, March 3, 1988, pp. A1, A20.
37. 134 *Congressional Record*, p. S221 (January 28, 1988) (remarks of Senator Howard Metzenbaum).
38. *Civil Rights Cases*, 109 U.S. 3 (1883); *Shelley v. Kraemer*, 334 U.S. 1 (1948). The Court upheld the public accommodations section (Title II) of the Civil Rights Act in *Heart of Atlanta Motel v. United*

States, 379 U.S. 421 (1964). *Jones v. Alfred H. Mayer Company,* 392 U.S. 409 (1968), interpreted provisions of the Civil Rights Act of *1*866 to bar discrimination in the sale of real estate, but the effect of this case as precedent was muted by the passage of the 1968 law.

39. *Buck v. Bell,* 274 U.S. 200, 208 (1927).
40. *Seidenberg v. McSorleys' Old Ale House, Inc.,* 317 F. Supp. 593, 594 (S.D.N.Y. 1970).
41. 42 U.S.C. Sec. 1983.
42. *Seidenberg,* pp. 593, 599. Emphasis in original.
43. Ibid., pp. 605–06.
44. Ibid., p. 604, n. 20.
45. *Moose Lodge No. 107 v. Irvis,* 407 U.S. 163, 183 (1972) (Justice William O. Douglas, dissenting).
46. Ibid., pp. 176–77.
47. 18 Stat. 335.
48. *Roberts v. U.S. Jaycees,* 468 U.S. 609, 621, 626 (1984); *New York Times,* July 4, 1984, pp. A1, B5; August 17, 1984, p. A8.
49. *Rotary International v. Rotary Club of Duarte,* 107 S. Ct. 1940, 1946 (1987); *New York Times,* May 5, 1987, pp. A1, B5.
50. Bob Woodward and Scott Armstrong, *The Brethren* (New York: Simon & Schuster, 1979), p. 15.
51. *New York State Club Association v. City of New York,* 108 S. Ct. 2225 (1988); *New York Times,* June 21, 1988, pp. A1, A18.

Chapter 7. *Practitioners, Actors, Subjects: Women in the Legal System*

1. See Stuart A. Scheingold, *The Politics of Law and Order* (New York: Longman, 1984), chap. 2.
2. Susan Brownmiller, *Against Our Will: Men, Women, and Rape* (New York: Simon & Schuster, 1975).
3. Chief Justice Matthew Hale (1847), in Brownmiller, *Against Our Will,* p. 427.
4. In both categories of rape, penetration (not ejaculation) constitutes unlawful intercourse. The prosecutor in the *Michael M.* case, discussed in Chapter 2, who asked Sharon, "He did put his penis into your vagina?" was not being crude. It was necessary to ask that question to establish that the crime had occurred.
5. See Baer, "Sexuality and the Law," in *Encyclopedia of the American Judicial System,* vol. 3 (New York: Scribner's, 1987), pp. 1264–68.
6. See, for example, Lynn Mather, *Plea Bargaining or Trial?* (Lexington, Mass.: Lexington Books, 1979); Arthur Rosett and Donald G. Cressey, *Justice by Consent* (Philadelphia: J. B. Lippincott, 1976), chaps. 7, 8.
7. *New York Times,* October 7, 1989, p. 6; Bryan-College Station *Eagle,* October 6, 1989, p. 1.

8. Allan Griswold Johnson, "On the Prevalence of Rape in the United States," *Signs* 6 (1980): 136–46, 145. Emphasis in original. See also Baer, "Sexuality and the Law."

9. Brownmiller, *Will*, chap. 7; Baer, "Sexuality"; Hubert S. Feild and Leigh Bienen, *Jurors and Rape: A Study in Psychology and Law* (Lexington, Mass.: Lexington Books, 1980); Jennifer Wriggins, "Rape, Racism, and the Law," *Harvard Women's Law Journal* 6 (1983).

10. Brownmiller, *Will*, pp. 5, 448–49. Emphasis in original.

11. *Coker v. Georgia*, 433 U.S. 584 (1977).

12. See Robin Warshaw, *I Never Called It Rape* (New York: Harper & Row, 1988).

13. Mimi Schwartz, "A Legacy of Evil," *Texas Monthly*, September 1988, p. 158.

14. *Michael M. v. Superior Court of Sonoma County*, 450 U.S. 464, 483–85 and n.

15. James I. Inciardi, *Criminal Justice*, 2d ed. (New York: Harcourt Brace Jovanovich, 1987), p. 73.

16. See, for example, *Ingraham v. Wright*, 430 U.S. 651 (1977).

17. John J. Bonsignore et al., *Before the Law*, 3d ed. (Boston: Houghton Mifflin, 1984), pp. 18, 23, 15–17, 19–22 (emphasis in original). See also, for example, Roger Langley and Richard C. Levy, *Wife Beating: The Silent Crisis* (New York: E.P. Dutton, 1977), chaps. 3, 10.

18. Quotation from Langley and Levy, *Wife Beating*, p. 55. See also Charlotte Fedders and Laura Elliott, *Shattered Dreams: The Story of Charlotte Fedders* (New York: Harper & Row, 1987); *New York Times*, June 3, 1975, p. 36.

19. Richard J. Gelles and Murray A. Straus, *Intimate Violence* (New York: Simon & Schuster, 1988), p. 21.

20. Some husbands are abused. A study by Suzanne K. Steinmetz, published in 1978, found that most wives who injure their husbands do so in self-defense. But not 100 percent. Unfortunately, Steinmetz's study, widely publicized in the mass media, was misinterpreted as claiming that men were more often victimized than women. The resulting controversy was so bitter that researchers have avoided the topic since. Therefore, no reliable recent data on husband abuse exist. Gelles and Straus, *Intimate Violence*, pp. 104–06; Steinmetz, "The Battered Husband Syndrome," *Victimology* 2 (1978): 499–509.

21. Langley and Levy, *Wife Beating*, chap. 10.

22. *New York Times*, June 26, 1985, p. 6.

23. However, there are enough cases of forty-year-old lawyers being beaten by their boyfriends to suggest that financial dependency is not the only contributing factor to victimization. These explanations are not offered in an attempt to "blame the victim." As I suggested earlier, the fact that some women endure violence does not justify it. But we need to learn more about the societal forces

which contribute to victimization in order to determine what social changes are necessary to end it.

24. The state can charge a person who forcibly rapes a child—and it is difficult to conceive how intercourse with a prepubescent child can be anything else—for rape or sexual assault. However, for reasons to be discussed, convictions are often difficult to obtain, and such a defendant may end up being punished for a lesser crime.

25. See, for example, Louise Armstrong, *Kiss Daddy Goodnight* (New York: Hawthorne, 1978); Florence Rush, *The Best Kept Secret* (New York: McGraw-Hill, 1980); Diana E. H. Russell, *The Secret Trauma: Incest in the Lives of Girls and Women* (New York: Basic Books, 1986), especially Tables 4, 5, p. 72. The Freud controversy is covered in Janet Malcolm, *In the Freud Archives* (New York: Alfred A. Knopf, 1984); Jeffrey Moussaief Masson, *The Assault on Truth* (New York: Farrar, Straus & Giroux, 1984). The "friend sick" quote is from Frederick Storaska, *How to Say No to a Rapist* (New York: Warner, 1966), p. 199. The estimates of the incidence of this kind of abuse may seem incredible to many readers of this book; all mentioned here are the results of sample surveys, and are reliable indicators of national trends to the same extent that survey data in general are reliable.

26. *New York Times*, September 6, 1984, p. A16, and January 24, 1990, pp. A1, A12.

27. See Russell, *Secret Trauma*, p. 72; U.S. Department of Justice, Bureau of Justice Statistics, *Report to the Nation on Crime and Justice*, 2d ed. (Washington, D.C.: Government Printing Office, 1988), p. 25.

28. See Rush, *Secret*, chaps. 1, 9, 13; Kathleen Barry, *Female Sexual Slavery* (New York: New York University Press, 1984).

29. Sue Miller, *The Good Mother* (New York: Harper & Row, 1986).

30. *Roth v. United States*, 354 U.S. 476 (1957); *Miller v. California*, 413 U.S. 15, 24 (1973); *Paris Adult Theater I v. Slaton*, 413 U.S. 49 (1973).

31. *Miller v. California*, pp. 15, 21.

32. Catharine A. MacKinnon, "On Collaboration," in *Feminism Unmodified* (Cambridge, Mass.: Harvard University Press, 1987), p. 198.

33. Indianapolis Code Sec. 16-3, 16–17 (1984). See Donald Downs, *The New Politics of Pornography* (Chicago: University of Chicago Press, 1989).

34. *American Booksellers v. Hudnut*, 598 F. Supp. 1316 (S.D. Indiana 1984, emphasis in original). See also *Hudnut v. American Booksellers' Association*, 771 F.2d 323 (7th Circ. 1985); 106 S.Ct. 1172 (1986); Judith A. Baer, "The Limits of Constitutional Doctrine in Women's Rights," *Western Political Quarterly*, Spring 1992, forthcoming.

35. George F. Cole, *The American System of Criminal Justice*, 4th ed. (Monterey, Calif.: Brooks, Cole, 1986), chap. 2; Meda Chesney-

Lind, "Female Offenders: Paternalism Reexamined," in Laura L. Crites and Winifred L. Hepperle, eds., *Women, the Courts, and Equality* (Newbury Park, Calif.: Sage Publications, 1987), pp. 114–40. The data cited here come from *Uniform Crime Reports* (UCR), the FBI's annually published national statistical record of crimes reported to local police. UCR data are imperfect, both because of reporting errors and because many crimes are never reported to the police. Scholars supplement them with data from the National Crime Surveys, which are sample surveys conducted annually by the Bureau of Justice Statistics. For arrests and incarceration, however—indeed, for any data about criminals rather than victims or crime itself—the UCR is the most reliable source.

36. Freda Adler, *Sisters in Crime* (New York: McGraw-Hill, 1975), quoted in Cole, *American System*, p. 49; Rita Simon, "Women and Crime Revisited," *Social Science Quarterly* 56 (1976): 58.

37. Chesney-Lind, "Female Offenders"; Darrell J. Steffensmeier, "Sex Differences in Patterns of Adult Crime, 1965–1977: A Review and Assessment," *Social Forces* 58 (1980): 1080–1109.

38. Cole, *System*, pp. 50–51; Adler, *Sisters in Crime*, pp. 6–7.

39. Celestine Bohlen, "Number of Women in Jail Surges with Drug Sales," *New York Times*, April 17, 1989, pp. 1, 13.

40. For two opposite explanations, compare Richard Quinney, *Class, State, and Crime* (New York: David McKay, 1979), with James Q. Wilson and Richard Herrnstein, *Crime and Human Nature* (New York: Simon & Schuster, 1985). For an insider's view of this phenomenon, see Jean Harris, *They Always Call Us Ladies* (New York: Macmillan, 1988).

41. Rush, *Best Kept Secret*, p. 159.

42. Chesney-Lind, "Offenders," p. 117; Susan K. Datesman and Frank R. Scarpitti, eds., *Women, Crime, and Justice* (New York: Oxford University Press, 1980), Part I.

43. Rush, *Secret*, chap. 11.

44. Boston Women's Health Collective, *Our Bodies, Ourselves*, rev. ed. (New York: Simon & Schuster, 1976), p. 103.

45. Rosett and Cressey, *Justice by Consent*, p. 157.

46. *U.S. ex rel. Robinson v. York*, 281 F. Supp. 8, 16 (D.C. Conn. 1968); *Commonwealth v. Daniels*, 243 A. 2d 400 (Pa. Sup. Ct. 1968).

47. Chesney-Lind, "Offenders," contains an excellent review of recent studies on gender differences in sentencing.

48. Cole, *System*, pp. 548–55; Estelle B. Freedman, *Their Sisters' Keepers* (Ann Arbor: University of Michigan Press, 1981); Rose Giallombardo, *Society of Women: A Study of a Women's Prison* (New York: John Wiley, 1966); Harris, *Ladies;* Esther Heffernan, *Making It in Prison* (New York: John Wiley, 1972); James A. Inciardi, *Criminal Justice*, pp. 545–47, 574–76; John Irwin, *The Felon* (Englewood Cliffs, N.J.: Prentice-Hall, 1970).

49. *Bradwell v. Illinois*, 83 U.S. 130, 140–142 (1872).

50. See Eleanor Flexner, *Century of Struggle*, rev. ed. (New York:

Atheneum, 1971), chap. 8; Cynthia Fuchs Epstein, *Women in Law* (New York: Basic Books, 1981).

51. Lynn Hecht Schafran, "Practicing Law in a Sexist Society," in Crites and Hepperle, eds., *Women*, p. 192.

52. For the statistics in the last two paragraphs, see Schafran, "Practicing," pp. 191–94; Beverly Blair Cook, "Women Judges in the Opportunity Structure," p. 143, both in Crites and Hepperle, *Women*.

53. Schafran, "Practicing," pp. 193, 194, 195, 204, 199, 200–02; New Jersey Supreme Court Task Force (1984), "Report of the First Year," *Women's Rights Law Reporter* 9 (1986): 129; New York Task Force on Women in the Courts (1986), "Report," *Fordham Urban Law Journal* 15 (1987): 1; Epstein, *Women in Law*.

54. *Hishon v. King & Spaulding*, 467 U.S. 69 (1984); Epstein, *Women*, chaps. 3–5.

55. See, for example, Epstein, *Women*, Part VI; Margaret Hennig and Anne Jardim, *The Managerial Woman* (Garden City, N.Y.: Doubleday, 1977).

56. Tamar Lewin, "Family or Career? Choose, Women Told," *New York Times*, March 8, 1989, pp. 17, 24.

57. Lenore Weitzman, *The Divorce Revolution* (New York: Free Press, 1986), chap. 3.

Chapter 8. *Conclusion: From Patriarchy toward Equality*

1. Adrienne Rich, *Of Woman Born: Motherhood as Experience and Institution* (New York: W.W. Norton, 1976), p. 41.

2. See note 28, Chapter 4.

3. See Jack Ladinsky, "The Impact of Social Backgrounds on Law Practice and the Law," *Journal of Legal Education* 16/2 (1963): 127–38; Herbert Jacob, *Law and Politics in the United States* (Boston: Little, Brown, 1986), chap. 6.

4. See the references cited in note 105, Chapter 3; note 2, Chapter 4; note 56, Chapter 5.

5. Feminist jurisprudence, a growing subspecialty in legal scholarship, adopts the premise that law, written, interpreted, and practiced almost exclusively by males until recently, has an inherent male bias. The sexist application of no-fault divorce law has come as no surprise to these scholars. This topic is too complex to cover adequately in this book. However, feminist jurisprudence is a good subject for student research; its import is by no means limited to family law. See, for example, the writings of Catharine MacKinnon cited in the references for Chapters 1 and 3; and the articles by Lucinda Finley, Martha Minow, Ann Scales, Suzanna Sherry, and Robin West, listed in the references for this chapter.

6. Betty Friedan, *The Feminine Mystique* (New York: W.W. Norton, 1963), p. 89.

7. See Carol Hanisch, "What Can Be Learned: A Critique of the Miss America Protest," in Leslie B. Tanner, ed., *Voices from Women's Liberation* (New York: Signet Books, 1970), pp. 132–36.

8. Marge Piercy, *Woman on the Edge of Time* (New York: Fawcett Crest, 1976).

9. Margaret Atwood, *The Handmaid's Tale* (New York: Fawcett Crest, 1985); Genesis 30:1–3.

10. Piercy, *Woman*, p. 105.

11. For one relatively recent defense of extrauterine reproduction, see Shulamith Firestone, *The Dialectic of Sex* (New York: William Morrow, 1970), chap. 10.

12. This is not even a universal theme of feminist utopian fiction. However, some rearrangement of reproduction *is* fairly common in this sort of novel. See, for example, Charlotte Perkins Gilman, *Herland* (New York: Pantheon Books, 1979); Ursula K. LeGuin, *The Left Hand of Darkness* (New York: Ace Books, 1969); Joanna Russ, *The Female Man* (Boston: Beacon Press, 1975). A subgenre of feminist dystopian science fiction also exists. See Suzette Haden Elgin, *Native Tongue* (New York: Daw Books, 1984) and *The Judas Rose* (same publisher, 1987).

13. See, for instance, the works in political philosophy cited in note 1, Chapter 4.

14. See, for example, the works by Simone de Beauvoir, Robin Morgan, and Gloria Steinem, cited in note 56, Chapter 5 and the works by Nancy Chodorow and Dorothy Dinnerstein cited in this chapter's references.

15. See, for example, the works by Sylvia Ann Hewlett and Germaine Greer, cited in note 56, Chapter 5; and those by Jean Bethke Elshtain, Carol Gilligan, and Sara Ruddick, cited in the references for this chapter.

16. Friedan, *Mystique*, chap. 1.

17. *Plessy v. Ferguson*, 163 U.S. 537, 552 (1896).

18. See note 28, Chapter 4.

General Index

Names of parties in court cases are listed only
when the person's name does not appear in
the case citation. See the Index of Cases for
cases listed in the cross-references.

Index of Cases